Prisoners and the Law

Simon Creighton BA (Hons)
Solicitor, Prisoners' Advice Service

Vicky King BA (Hons)
Caseworker, Prisoners' Advice Service

Consultant
Ben Emmerson
Barrister

Butterworths
London, Dublin, Edinburgh
1996

United Kingdom	Butterworths a Division of Reed Elsevier (UK) Ltd, Halsbury House, 35 Chancery Lane, LONDON WC2A 1EL and 4 Hill Street, EDINBURGH EH2 3JZ
Australia	Butterworths, SYDNEY, MELBOURNE, BRISBANE, ADELAIDE, PERTH, CANBERRA and HOBART
Canada	Butterworths Canada Ltd, TORONTO and VANCOUVER
Ireland	Butterworth (Ireland) Ltd, DUBLIN
Malaysia	Malayan Law Journal Sdn Bhd, KUALA LUMPUR
New Zealand	Butterworths of New Zealand Ltd, WELLINGTON and AUCKLAND
Singapore	Reed Elsevier (Singapore) Pte Ltd, SINGAPORE
South Africa	Butterworths Publishers (Pty) Ltd, DURBAN
USA	Michie, Charlottesville, VIRGINIA

All rights reserved. No part of this publication may be reproduced in any material form (including photocopying or storing it in any medium by electronic means and whether or not transiently or incidentally to some other use of this publication) without the written permission of the copyright owner except in accordance with the provisions of the Copyright, Designs and Patents Act 1988 or under the terms of a licence issued by the Copyright Licensing Agency Ltd, 90 Tottenham Court Road, London, England W1P 9HE. Applications for the copyright owner's written permission to reproduce any part of this publication should be addressed to the publisher.

Warning: The doing of an unauthorised act in relation to a copyright work may result in both a civil claim for damages and criminal prosecution.

Any Crown copyright material is reproduced with the permission of the Controller of Her Majesty's Stationery Office.

© Reed Elsevier 1996

A CIP Catalogue record for this book is available from the British Library.

ISBN 0 406 02514 2

Printed by Clays Ltd, St Ives PLC

Prisoners and the Law

FOREWORD

During the past two decades, the treatment of prisoners has been increasingly opened up to the scrutiny of the outside world, and subjected to the rule of law. Unfairnesses in the prison system that were previously taken for granted have been increasingly questioned and reformed, and the closed, secretive system of prison administration inherited from the Victorians has been replaced by one in which the rules governing most aspects of prison life have at least become *accessible*, and enforceable; and prisoners now have to be given an explanation of the reasons for adverse decisions affecting such important aspects of their life in prison as parole, discipline, segregation and categorisation. In the process the domestic and the European Courts have played a crucial part by adopting a new and more generous approach to the justiciability of prison decisions, and by setting new standards of openness and fairness in the successive decisions of *St Germaine, Silver, Raymond, Leech, Doody, Thynne* and *Singh*.

But the most important development of all has been the increased availability to prisoners and their lawyers of information about the statutes, rules, circular instructions and policy statements that govern all aspects of prison life. Armed with this information, prisoners are in a better position to stand up for their own rights and pursue their own remedies; and the non-specialist lawyer is able to give them swift advice on their best course for immediate resolution of their problems. Effective and well-informed representations at an early stage often achieve real results – and so avoid both the delays and the uncertain outcome of full-scale litigation.

This book, therefore, is to be welcomed as a great contribution to the increasing process of enlightenment as to how the prison system works. It will be invaluable to prisoners and to their lawyers and other professionals involved in advising prisoners on their rights and remedies. It is a reliable, comprehensive, detailed and user-friendly guide to the labyrinth of statutes, rules, circular instructions and policy statements which govern the fate of prisoners in every important area of the law. In writing it, Vicky King and Simon Creighton draw on their unique years of experience giving prisoners daily advice on all manner of legal problems – from the esoteric to the mundane – and in bringing test cases to the domestic and European courts. Their great knowledge and sympathetic approach to the lot of the prisoner is everywhere in evidence.

This book is distinctive in its practical orientation. It places important emphasis on such neglected areas as how the allocation and classification system works, how the complaints system works, and how to make effective representations for parole. It also is the first book to deal with such recent developments as the privatisation system, the new privilege system, and the new restrictive system for granting home-leave. But it also contains a comprehensive review of recent case-law in the better-documented areas of the censorship of correspondence, parole and the disciplinary system. Finally, the authors have sympathetically addressed the special problems of certain minority groups – such as imprisoned mothers with babies, young offenders, prisoners who have been repatriated or extradited to this country, and prisoners with special medical needs such as those who are HIV positive.

Whilst the emphasis throughout is primarily practical rather than theoretical, the book includes a welcome critique of certain recent developments – such as the introduction of the new 'privilege' system, and a helpful forecast of likely future developments in such fields as the rights of HMP detainees.

Edward Fitzgerald QC

PREFACE

As long ago as 1910, Winston Churchill commented that:

'The mood and temper of the public in regard to the treatment of crime and criminals is one of the most unfailing tests of civilization of any country. A calm and dispassionate recognition of the rights of the accused against the State and even of convicted criminals against the state . . . [are the] mark and measure of the stored up strength of a nation, and are the sign and proof of the living virtue in it.'

It is difficult, in the present climate, to reconcile such views with the prevailing public perception of those in prison and the rights that should accrue to convicted prisoners. However, against the climate of public opinion, professionals who have a direct involvement in the criminal justice system have begun to accept the fundamental correctness of this approach. In September 1995, the Prison Governors' Association issued a 'Manifesto for Change' which harked back to the sentiments of Churchill and set out a profound disagreement with current penal policies:

'There is no evidence to support [the] assertion that "prison works" . . . Imprisonment is there to protect the public from dangerous offenders. It should also contribute to a reduction in crime by offering a facility that, in conjunction with other parts of the system, may be deemed to be appropriate as the best way of reducing that individual's offending. It must be used sparingly...' (pages 2-3 of the Manifesto)

This view is one which seems to be increasingly shared by the judiciary who have engaged in a number of public disagreements with the Home Secretary as to the use of executive powers in the criminal justice system. The level of judicial intervention in prison life and the increased use of the European Convention on Human Rights, both as a mechanism in its own right and as a source of acceptable rights in domestic litigation, has lead to a recognition that the use of custody touches on innumerable fundamental rights. These range from matters of liberty of the individual through to the right to a private and family life and the necessity for fair and transparent procedures to be adopted in the administrative decision making process.

It is, perhaps, this divergence of views that has lead to an increased awareness of the rights of those in prison and has made this book possible. The tension that exists between the concept of those who have forfeited their liberty to the state retaining residual rights and freedoms is one that is not easily resolved. Consequently, the courts have been required to extend their jurisdiction further and further into prison life. The process has not been one of straightforward progression, but is characterised by a series of hard fought battles which occasionally result in further rights being afforded to prisoners. Prisoners themselves have been at the forefront of this process and have, on many occasions, established important legal principles by taking litigation on their own account. Mark Leech deserves particular mention, not only for presenting his own cases before the highest courts, but also in continuing to promote the rights of prisoners since his release from custody.

During the years we have worked at the Prisoners' Advice Service we have been particularly fortunate in enjoying the confidence of such a large number of prisoners. The expertise of many prisoners is unmatched by their own lawyers and we would like to thank everyone who has contacted us and shared their first hand experience of the workings of the prison system.

We would also like to thank the staff and Management Committee of the Prisoners' Advice Service, especially Lisa Elford and Emily Evans for providing the administrative support that has made it possible to complete this book. Ed Fitzgerald QC, John Wadham, the Director of Liberty, and Kate Akester who now works for Justice, have pioneered litigation on prison law and have made enormous contributions to our work.

Ben Emmerson of Doughty Street Chambers deserves particular mention for his invaluable support and encouragement in editing the book. Tim Owen, also of Doughty Street Chambers, has worked closely with us for many years and was one of the first barristers to become a specialist in prisoners' rights. We would like to thank him for sharing his expertise with us.

Simon Creighton & Vicky King
6 February 1996

CONTENTS

Contents

SECTION II

Chapter 4 The Various Types of Prison 35

Chapter 5 Categorisation, Allocation and Sentence Calculation 46

Contents

Chapter 11   Parole and Release   166

Chapter 12   The Learmont and Woodcock Inquiries   183

TABLE OF STATUTES

References in this table to *Statutes* are to Halsbury's Statutes of England (Fourth Edition) showing the volume and page at which the annotated text of the Act will be found. Paragraph references printed in **bold** type indicate where the Act is set out in part or in full. Page numbers in *italic* type refer to page numbers to the appendices at the end of this book.

TABLE OF STATUTORY INSTRUMENTS

Paragraph references printed in **bold** type indicate where the Rule is set out in part or in full. Page numbers in *italic* type refer to page numbers to the appendices.

TABLE OF CASES

SECTION I

CHAPTER 1
INTRODUCTION

1.1 There is little published material on the legal workings of the prison system and the rights of prisoners. This can be attributed to the manner in which prison law has developed, with very little legislation and an historical reluctance on the part of the courts to become involved in this area of law. In recent years, the situation has begun to change as the High Court has extended its jurisdiction into all aspects of prison life and has required the Prison Service to adopt more open practices in the decision-making process. The present situation is that prisoners are more likely than ever to resort to the law, whereas there are still relatively few lawyers who are familiar with this topic.

1.2 The major piece of prison legislation was passed in 1952 and although it has been subject to amendments, the Prison Act has not substantially changed since that time. The reason why the statutory framework appears to be so static is that it is primarily enabling legislation. The power to make rules for the running of prisons is devolved upon the Home Secretary who exercises this power by way of statutory instrument. These rules provide for further devolution of a wide range of discretionary decisions to civil servants and prison governors. The policies and decisions that result are subject to the authority of common law and judicial interpretation.

1.3 The apparent hotchpotch of rules and regulations that results from the interplay between statute, statutory instrument, policy documents and court judgments can appear to be impenetrable. In practice, the rights and remedies which arise will be familiar to lawyers.

1.4 Prisoners will generally resort to the law in two situations, when seeking to enforce public law rights by way of judicial review and when pursuing private law remedies for damages. The distinction between public and private law in this context is relatively straightforward. From the time that a person is sentenced to imprisonment until the date of release, a series of administrative decisions will be made about prisoners. These will encompass issues ranging from the length of time to be served in custody and in which prisons the sentence will be served, through to the procedures and policies that are adopted for release. The decision maker derives the power to decide upon these matters from public law sources rather than from an agreement or action between private parties (for a full discussion of the distinction between public and private law, see *O'Reilly v Mackman* [1982] 3 All ER

3

1124 and *Council of Civil Service Unions v Minister for the Civil Service* [1985] AC 374). As such, all of these decisions will be within the realm of public law.

1.5   It is possible to further divide public law decisions into two separate areas. Firstly, there are rights which accrue to people in custody over which there is no discretion by the decision maker. These include, for example, the minimum number of visits a prisoner can receive (Prison Rules 1964 , rr 33, 34: see section II, chapter 8) or the right to be considered for parole at a certain stage of one's sentence (Criminal Justice Act 1991, ss 32–40: see section II, chapter 11). Secondly, there are a wide ranging number of situations where a decision maker is obliged to make a decision, but retains an element of discretion. These may include substantive parole decisions (eg *R v Secretary of State for the Home Department and the Parole Board, ex p Evans* (2 November 1994, unreported) and *R v Secretary of State for the Home Department, ex p Follen* (20 October 1995, unreported): see section II, chapter 11), security categorisation (*R v Secretary of State for the Home Department, ex p Duggan* [1994] 3 All ER 277: see section II, chapter 5) or the exercise of disciplinary and quasi-disciplinary powers (Prison Rules 1964, rr 43–56; *Campbell and Fell v United Kingdom* [1984] 7 EHRR 165 and *Leech v Deputy Governor of Parkhurst Prison* [1988] AC 533 on the exercise of formal disciplinary powers; and *ex p Ross* (1994) Times, 9 June on the use of the informal disciplinary system). A full discussion of the range of decisions that are amenable to judicial review follows in section I, chapter 3.

1.6   The private law remedies that are relevant to prisoners largely concern the circumstances in which the right to financial compensation will arise. This may be in respect of injuries suffered at work or through dangerous premises (*Ferguson v Home Office* (1977) Times, 8 October), negligent medical treatment (*Knight v Home Office* [1990] 3 All ER 237), assaults by other prisoners or members of staff (there is a range of cases on this topic, see eg, *H v Home Office* (1992) Independent, 6 May, *D'Arcy v Prison Comrs* [1956] Crim LR 56 and *Egerton v Home Office* [1978] Crim LR 494), loss of, and damage to property and intolerable conditions of detention (*R v Deputy Governor of Parkhurst, ex p Hague* [1992] 1 AC 58). The tortious principles that apply are discussed in detail in section I, chapter 3 and will be largely familiar to practitioners of civil law.

1.7   The main problem that arises when advising prisoners on matters of both public and private law, is to identify the provisions and regulations that guide decision makers and establish the duty of care that is owed to a prisoner. Section II of this book sets out these standards and the sources from which they are derived.

1.8   One of the key difficulties with the manner in which the law is applied to prisoners is that it is susceptible to change at very short notice and with no public explanation of these changes. For example, in 1994 various newspapers began to voice concern at prisoners' entitlement to home leave. As a result, Michael Howard made a policy statement that he intended to tighten these provisions and, in April 1995, a new policy was officially put in place by way of an Instruction to Prison Governors issued by the Prison

Service. The new rules were challenged in the High Court and in July 1995, the challenge was dismissed (*R v Secretary of State for the Home Department, ex p Briggs, Green and Hargreaves* (25 July 1995, unreported). In the space of a few months, the entire basis on which temporary release from prison is authorised had been changed by the Home Secretary and ratified by the High Court.

1.9   Any book on the law can only be as current as the latest court decision or change to statute, and nowhere is this more apparent than with prison law. Due to the vast extent of discretionary decision-making powers that exist, the interplay between politics and the law is at its most transparent and speeches made to political party conferences can be implemented as policy within a matter of weeks. Lawyers will therefore need to keep abreast of current developments in this field to ensure that they remain up to date. Aside from the usual legal periodicals that cover developments in the law, the various prison reform agencies, such as the Prison Reform Trust and the Howard League, publish quarterly magazines that provide updates on changes in the law and policy in our prisons.

CHAPTER 2

LEGISLATION

STATUTE AND PRISONS

2.1 There is very little primary legislation that is directly concerned with prisons and imprisonment. Although various Acts of Parliament do, from time to time, contain important provisions for prisoners (eg the Criminal Justice Acts 1967 and 1991), the only piece of legislation that deals solely with the prison estate is the Prison Act 1952. Thus there is no primary source that contains an exhaustive explanation of the rights to which those in custody are entitled and the facilities and privileges which they can expect.

2.2 Much of the Prison Act 1952 is concerned with establishing very basic principles, such as who has legal responsibility for managing prisons and implementing appropriate rules rather than with the actual rules and regulations themselves. More detail is supplied in the Prison Rules 1964 (as amended) which are issued pursuant to the Act but once again, this does not complete the full picture. In many instances, the Rules will make reference to discretionary powers which are to be exercised either by a prison governor or the Secretary of State. It is these discretionary powers that often get to the root of prison life and will in many cases be the matters on which prisoners will need advice and representation. The manner in which these powers are to be exercised and the details of how the Rules are to be implemented are contained in a series of policy documents issued by Prison Service Headquarters. These will be in the form of Standing Orders or Advice and Instructions to Governors.

2.3 The development of prison law has also been greatly affected by common law decision-making and in particular through the jurisdiction of the Divisional Court. One of the reasons why this has been such a fertile area for judicial review is precisely because there is little statutory material.

2.4 In order to gain an understanding of prison law and to be able to provide effective advice to prisoners, it is necessary to refer to the three different levels of source materials. The starting point is necessarily the Prison Act 1952 as, whilst it does not actually contain detailed information on the day-to-day life of prisoners, it is the primary source of decision-making power and sets the context for the management of our prison estate. There follows a discussion of the Prison Rules 1964, the relevance of changes introduced by the Criminal Justice Acts and then the status of policy documents. Finally, the legal status of 'contracted out' prisons is explored.

THE PRISON ACT 1952

2.5   The main purpose of the Act is not to make detailed provision for the running and management of prisons but to vest authority in those who do hold this power. The corollary of this is that the Act actually says very little about prisoners' rights and the obligations of the state to those in their custody.

2.6   The Home Secretary is charged with the duty of 'general superintendence' over prisons and is empowered to 'make contracts and do acts necessary for the maintenance of prisons and the maintenance of prisoners' (s 4(1)). Section 4(2) goes on to require the Home Secretary to ensure compliance with the Act and the Prison Rules. There is no explanation as to the manner in which compliance should be guaranteed. The section does, however, establish that the Home Secretary is the person ultimately responsible for the manner in which prisons are run and for ensuring that the duties and obligations of the state towards those in custody are properly fulfilled.

2.7   Section 4(2) is important in that it places a clear onus of responsibility on the Secretary of State and it is the Secretary of State who may be brought to task for any failure to properly comply with this duty. Conversely, this power was often invoked when defending actions brought by prisoners against prison governors' administrative and disciplinary decisions. The argument put forward was that s 4 amounted to an ouster clause whereby the power to ensure compliance with Prison Act and Rules was vested solely in the Secretary of State and it was only if he failed to fulfil this obligation that judicial review could be sought. It was not until 1988 that this view was finally laid to rest following the decision of the House of Lords in *Leech v Deputy Governor of Parkhurst Prison* ([1988] AC 533, Lord Bridge perceived this argument as an attempt to undermine the jurisdiction of the court in a manner which was incompatible with the principles of administrative law).

The Chief Inspector and Boards of Visitors

2.8   The Act goes on to make provision for two 'watchdog' bodies being the Chief Inspector of Prisons (s 5A) and the Board of Visitors (ss 6–9). The Chief Inspector is under a duty to inspect prisons with particular regard to conditions and the treatment of prisoners, to report to the Home Secretary and to submit an annual report that must be laid before Parliament. The Chief Inspector's powers are limited to reporting and it is not possible for binding recommendations to be made. The Chief Inspector will prepare reports on individual prisons throughout each year and will provide a general commentary on prison conditions in the Annual Report. The individual inspections are often highly critical and despite the fact that they have no formal legal status, they can provide important evidence of particular conditions and policies that are being pursued in a prison at a particular time.

2.9   The Home Secretary is also required to appoint a Board of Visitors for each prison and to allow these Boards to visit the prison and to hear complaints. The right of free access to any part of the prison at any time, and to see any prisoner at any time are protected by the Act (s 6(3)). Originally, the Board also had a disciplinary function in that they acted as adjudicators for disciplinary charges that were considered too serious to be heard by the governor. This power was abolished in 1992 following the Woolf Report when it was considered that their watchdog role was incompatible with that of upholding prison discipline. The confidence of prisoners in the Boards to hear and act upon their complaints was seriously undermined by the fact that they would also be hearing charges against them and awarding punishments of forfeiture of remission. There was a general assumption amongst prisoners that the Board was too willing to accept the authority of prison staff without question and that it was not possible to have a fair hearing at adjudications. This situation was exacerbated by the fact that the Board would be hearing the more serious charges and awarding significant punishments.

2.10   Following the removal of this power, all adjudications are now carried out by individual prison governors. There is a certain irony in this solution. Having removed the potential for a conflict of interests from one body, an even greater potential for conflict has been created. It is difficult to see how the dual roles of managing staff, implementing regulations for the running of the prison and acting as an impartial arbiter at disciplinary hearings can be properly reconciled (see chapter 7).

2.11   The Boards do still have a role to play in the maintenance of discipline in prisons. When a governor authorises the segregation of a prisoner, this can only be done for a period of up to three days in the first instance. Following that three-day period, any decisions to continue segregation must be authorised by the Board of Visitors (Prison Rules, r 43). The fact that there is a direct supervisory body for decisions of this nature is important in principle, but in practice there will be very few occasions when the Board will not sanction the governor's decision in such cases.

Prison staff

2.12   Prisons are required to have a governor, a chaplain, a medical officer and such other officers as 'may be necessary' (s 7). The statutory obligation for prisons to have a governor is of importance in assessing the nature of the governor's duties. These powers are distinguishable from those exercised by the Home Secretary and are defined in detail in the Prison Rules. Whilst it is true that the extent of the governor's powers is decided by the Home Secretary, the fact remains that it is the governor who is obliged to carry them out. The governor is empowered, with leave of the Secretary of State, to delegate the powers conferred directly on him/her to another officer at the prison (Prison Rules, r 98).

2.13   It was this point that was considered fundamental in the case of *Leech* ([1988] AC 533) when Lord Bridge held that governors' powers were amenable to judicial review in their own right. The court observed that whilst the Prison Rules established the offences against discipline and the punitive powers available, there was no provision for the Home Secretary to direct the governor on how to adjudicate a particular charge, or as to what punishment should be awarded (at 563D).

Location and accommodation

2.14 Section 12(1) states that prisoners may lawfully be confined in any prison, whether on remand or convicted and s 12(2) states that prisoners may be transferred from one prison to another. This power is expressed to rest with the Home Secretary but can (and in practice, is) delegated to the governor.

2.15 For practical purposes, the importance of s 12(1) is that it establishes that a prisoner has no right to be held in any particular prison. It is a common misunderstanding of prisoners and their families that there is a duty for them to be located in a prison convenient for visits. No such right exists and whilst a whole range of factors are to be taken into account when determining location, any challenges to the allocation decisions can only be made within the confines of administrative law (see section II, chapter 5).

2.16 Whilst in custody, the governor has responsibility (and liability) to each prisoner in his/her prison. This stems from the fact that the governor of the prison is deemed to be the legal custodian (s 13).

2.17 The accommodation available must be certified as being fit for its purpose by the Home Secretary (s 14). The certificate requires inspection of size, heating, lighting, ventilation and fittings. Certification is carried out by officers appointed by the Secretary of State and there is no independent system of certification. The requirements and standards that are to be met are not specified and consequently may be changed depending upon prevailing conditions and the changing requirements of each prison. The Chief Inspector of Prisons will frequently express opinions as to the living conditions in particular prisons and if standards were to fall below a certain level, the conditions of detention may give rise to a cause of action in domestic law or under the European Convention on Human Rights. In general, however, the section is only important in terms of litigation if a prisoner is detained in accommodation that has not been certified.

Disciplinary and miscellaneous provisions

2.18 The Act contains a number of further provisions that are of some importance to prisoners, although the powers created are expanded in far greater detail in the Prison Rules and policy documents. These sections are as follows:

(i) Section 16A provides the basis for mandatory drugs testing and gives all prison officers the power, on the authority of the governor, to require prisoners to provide a sample of urine (or other non-intimate sample) for the purposes of testing for the presence of controlled drugs.

(ii) Section 25 creates the power to authorise the early release of prisoners. The actual schemes that are put into place for remission of sentence are made under the powers created by s 47 (see below).

(iii) Section 28 creates the power to discharge prisoners temporarily on the grounds of ill health (a power that is vested to the governor under the Prison Rules, r 6).

(iv) Section 30 allows for discharge payments to be made to prisoners.

(v) Sections 39–42 create offences of assisting prisoners to escape from a prison, bringing alcohol, tobacco or other unauthorised articles into a prison and for notices to be displayed outside of prisons recording these provisions.

(vi) Section 49 states that any time spent unlawfully at large during the currency of a sentence does not count towards that sentence.

The power to make prison rules

2.19   Perhaps the most important section of the Act is s 47 which allows the Secretary of State, 'to make rules and regulations for the management of prisons, remand centres, detention centres and youth custody centres, and for the classification, treatment, employment, discipline and control of persons required to be detained therein.' These rules must be made by statutory instrument. At s 47(2), there is an important safeguard to any rules that are made:

> 'Rules made under this section shall make provision for ensuring that a person who is charged with any offence under the rules shall be given a proper opportunity of presenting his case.'

This section emphasises the duty that exists in common law and under the European Convention of Human Rights to ensure that the rules must follow the principles of natural justice in administering prison discipline.

THE PRISON RULES

The legal status

2.20   The Prison Rules were last fully drafted in 1964 although they are subject to regular amendment. They contain a mixture of provisions and refer to both general policies, such as the purpose of imprisonment (r 1), and to more specific obligations and duties that are imposed upon the Prison Service. A large number of the Rules confer discretionary powers which are supplemented by documents issued explaining how discretion should be exercised. The remaining rules of importance to prisoners are concerned with the formal disciplinary system that must be adopted.

2.21   The varying nature of the Rules and the fact that they contain a mixture of policy statements, obligations to prisoners and discretionary powers leads to much confusion as to their status. Broadly speaking, the Rules will set out general powers and duties which are to be implemented in the running of prisons. In order to ensure consistency and fairness throughout the system, a series of documents are issued described as Standing Orders and Advice and Instructions to Governors (formerly Circular Instructions). These documents are designed to actually fill in the details of the everyday management of prisons and will deal with everything from the fees to be paid to visiting dentists to the facilities that are to be allowed to prisoners, and to the arrangements for mandatory drugs testing.

2.22   The Prison Rules are not, in themselves, justiciable in private law and were not intended to be so. In 1972, Lord Denning commented that:

> 'If the courts were to entertain actions by disgruntled prisoners, the governor's life would be made intolerable. The discipline of the prison would be undermined. The Prison Rules are regulatory directions only. Even if they are not observed, they do not give rise to a cause of action.' (*Becker v Home Office* [1972] 2 QB 407)

2.23   Lord Wilberforce clarified the situation slightly ten years later when he stated that prisoners retain all civil rights that are not taken away, either expressly or by the fact of their imprisonment. However, he went on to say that as there is no contractual relationship between prisoners and the prison authorities there must be reliance on the normal laws of tort in order for an action to be brought (*Raymond v Honey* [1983] 1 AC 1).

2.24   It was not for another ten years that the present day position was fully established by the courts. In *R v Deputy Governor of Parkhurst Prison, ex p Hague, Weldon v Home Office* ([1992] 1 AC 58), the House of Lords looked at the public and private law rights of prisoners. Although the decision contains dissenting opinion, it was agreed that the Prison Rules do not give rise to any specific private law rights. As a result, prisoners retain the right to bring ordinary private law actions in cases of negligence, but there is no right to bring an action for breach of statutory duty in respect of the Prison Rules.

2.25   Thus, the manner in which the Rules are implemented is amenable to judicial review and breaches of them may be evidence in support of negligence actions, but the Rules do not confer any additional private law claim. However, practitioners do need to be familiar with the Rules in their context as the source of authority from which more detailed regulations are made.

The key provisions

2.26   The Rules are reproduced in the appendices and each Rule is discussed in the following individual chapters in context (a full and detailed examination of each individual rule and its European equivalent may be found in Loucks and Plotnikoff *Prison Rules – A Working Guide*, Prison Reform Trust 1993). Broadly, they are divided in the following manner:

Part I

2.27   The Rules have been described as falling into five distinct categories. These are comprised of general policy objectives, rules of a discretionary nature (normally concerned with privileges that may be afforded), rules concerning administration and rules of specific individual protection (see Livingstone and Owen *Prison Law* (1993) Clarendon Press, pp 18–19 for a full discussion). Whilst those concerned with discretionary rights such as temporary release (r 6), or correspondence (r 34) are of importance, the classes of prisoners who are allowed to benefit from these privileges and the manner in which that discretion should be exercised are set out in the policy documents issued by Prison Service Headquarters. Many of the Rules therefore do little other than to give a general power or create a general right that is then subject to policy and interpretation as to how it should be implemented.

2.28   The key Rules are those that are concerned with the formal and informal disciplinary system (ie those of 'specific individual protection'). In effect this means rr 43–56 which are concerned with maintaining good order and discipline and the formal disciplinary code that is applied to prisoners. These provide a list of the offences against prison discipline (r 47), the procedure to be followed when laying a charge (rr 48–49) and the punishments that can be awarded to prisoners once a charge has been proven (rr 50–55). Where new offences are to be created or the powers of punishment are to be extended, these must be incorporated into the Rules by statutory instrument.

2.29   There have been many calls for a revision of the Rules and for a national set of minimum standards to be approved and incorporated. In the Woolf Report, it was suggested that a set of accredited standards should be prepared and that prisons should be certified once they had reached these standards. Once they had been achieved, Lord Woolf suggested that:

'at that stage they would be incorporated in the Prison Rules and so would be legally enforceable by judicial review.' (Cmnd 1456, para 1.187)

Despite support for a minimum set of standards from many diverse bodies and individuals, the official approach to the Rules remains one of minor revision when considered necessary rather than a complete overhaul.

THE CRIMINAL JUSTICE ACTS

2.30 The only other legislation which is of direct relevance to prison issues are the various Criminal Justice Acts issued since 1967. These often contain major legislative provisions for parole, early and compassionate release, recall of prisoners on licence and computation of sentences (CJA 1991, ss 34–48). The Criminal Justice Act 1991 implemented perhaps the most radical overhaul of release and licence provisions since 1967, yet key sections from the older Acts remain in force (eg CJA 1967, s 67 concerning the computation of sentences).

2.31 The Criminal Justice Acts are primarily concerned with issues that affect the day-to-day running of prisons rather than the statutory authority for implementing rules and regulations. The various sections that are of relevance to particular prison issues are not discussed in this chapter but are dealt with in section II. Those parts of the Acts that deal with contracted out prisons are examined below.

STANDING ORDERS AND ADVICE AND INSTRUCTIONS TO GOVERNORS

2.32 The mechanics of the everyday running of prisons are largely determined by the guidance documents issued by the Prison Service referred to as Standing Orders and Advice and Instructions to Governors. Standing Orders are an amalgamation of policy and the exercise of discretion in a particular area. Hence, they are issued to cover topics such as reception to prison, discharge, temporary release, communications and calculation of sentences. Advice and Instructions to Governors are issued on an ad hoc basis and amend or update information in the Standing Orders. They are also the mechanism by which changes to policy, such as the revisions to home leave criteria, or new Prison Rules, such as those relating to mandatory drugs testing, are communicated to prison governors.

2.33 These directives, although often made under powers contained in the Prison Rules, do not have any statutory authority. An example of the relationship between statute, statutory instrument and these directives may be found by examining the changes made to Standing Order 5B which deals with prisoners' correspondence.

2.34 Standing Order 5B has been subject to a number of challenges both domestically and in international law. In *Raymond v Honey* ([1983] 1 AC 1), it was found that prisoners were being denied the right to have unfettered access to a court as letters being sent by a prisoner were being stopped in accordance with Standing Order 5B. Standing Order 5B had been issued, inter alia, to provide a code of working practice that complied with r 37 of the Prison Rules which allowed privileged communications to be sent to certain classes of people in certain circumstances. It was held that neither the Prison Act 1952 nor the Prison Rules 1964 contained any provisions that would allow correspondence of this nature to be impeded. Lord Bridge took the view that:

> 'Standing Orders set out an elaborate procedure designed to discourage a prisoner from instituting proceedings in person and impliedly assume that he requires leave of the Secretary of State to do so, which the Secretary of State has an absolute discretion to withhold. The only statutory provision relied on . . . is the power in s 47 of the Prison Act 1952 to make rules for the "discipline and control" of prisoners. This rule making power is manifestly insufficient for such a purpose and it follows that the rules, to the extent that would fetter a prisoner's right of access to the courts . . . are ultra vires.' ([1983] 1 AC 15C)

The result was that the Standing Order had to be amended to ensure that this right was protected.

2.35 More recently, in *Campbell v United Kindom* ((1992) 15 EHRR 137, Series A no 48), the European Court of Human Rights held that the right afforded to prisoners to privileged correspondence with lawyers was insufficient to comply with the Convention. As a result, r 37 of the Prison Rules was amended to allow privileged correspondence in a far wider variety of cases and an Instruction to Governors was issued to remedy the defect. The Instruction to Governors declared the new policy and procedures that were to be adopted and these will ultimately be incorporated into Standing Order 5B.

2.36 Whilst it is established that these documents are amenable to judicial review when they lead to unlawful administration, it is also arguable that they can establish explicit rights for, and obligations to, those in custody. This arises because they set out particular obligations that the Prison Service undertakes to fulfil vis-à-vis prisoners. Therefore, if the Prison Service decides to adopt a particular procedure or policy in one of these documents and subsequently fails to follow its own procedures, these actions may be reviewable (see eg *R v Deputy Governor of Parkhurst Prison, ex p Hague, Weldon v Home Office* [1992] 1 AC 58).

2.37 It has been argued that these additional rights arise as a legitimate expectation that prisoners can expect a particular type of treatment has been created (see Livingstone and Owen, *Prison Law* (1993) pp 20–21). The concept of legitimate expectation for prisoners has not always been well received by the courts and it would appear that legitimate expectations can be altered during the currency of a prison sentence providing that the correct procedures are followed. The cases where it has been successfully argued that prisoners are entitled to receive certain rights arising from Instructions to Governors tend to involve procedural requirements, such as the giving of reasons when a decision has been made (see *Ex p Hague*, above). Cases that have argued that a legitimate expectation can arise when a change has been made to a substantive policy decision, such as the criteria for parole or home leave, have been conspicuously less successful.

2.38 Since the decision of the House of Lords in *R v Secretary of State for the Home Department, ex p Doody* ([1994] 1 AC 531, HL), it may be easier to describe this process as the Prison Service being forced to adopt good administrative practice. Certainly, in recent attempts to challenge changes in the policy to home leave on the basis of legitimate expectation, the application was dismissed by Kennedy LJ with the following comments:

> 'So, Mr Beloff [for the Home Secretary] submits, that upon analysis, all that the applicants could legitimately expect was to have their application for home leave decided by reference to the criteria current at the time of the application. We think this is right.' (*R v Secretary of State for the Home Department, ex p Briggs, Green and Hargreaves* (25 July 1995, unreported, DC)).

2.39 The compromise of these two positions appears to be that 'rights' which do not appear in statute or the Prison Rules can be afforded to a prisoner by the Home Secretary voluntarily adopting a particular policy or procedure. If these rights concern the adoption of good administrative practice, then they acquire an independent status which makes it more difficult for them to be subsequently removed. However, if they are concerned with expectations as to discretionary decisions or privileges, it is possible for them to be changed providing that the proper procedures are followed and primary legislation is not infringed.

CONTRACTED OUT PRISONS

The statutory basis

2.40 One of the more contentious statutory changes that has been made in recent years has been to introduce contracted out prisons. These are effectively privatised prisons that operate within the framework of the rest of the Prison Service. The first provision for contracted out prisons was made in the Criminal Justice Act 1991, ss 84–88. These were accompanied by provisions to allow private escorts to be introduced (ss 80–83).

2.41 The Act allowed the Secretary of State to introduce contracted out prisons for remand prisoners immediately and for sentenced prisoners by future statutory instrument. The appropriate instruments were subsequently passed in 1992 (eg CJA 1991 (Contracted Out Prisons) Order 1992) and were fully incorporated into the statutory framework by the Criminal Justice and Public Order Act 1994. This Act effectively permitted all prisons, whether newly built or part of the existing prison estate, to be contracted out (CJPOA 1994, s 96). The CJPOA 1994 also extended the provisions to Scotland and made minor amendments to the general contracting out provisions.

The provisions in detail

2.42   The Prison Act 1952 continues to apply to all contracted out prisons except that a different set of officers are put in place to run the prisons (CJA 1991 s 84(1)). In place of governors, directors are appointed to run the prison. Directors have the same powers as governors save that they are not allowed to conduct adjudications or to segregate prisoners, apply restraints or to order confinement in a special cell, except in cases of extreme emergency. Controllers are appointed by the Secretary of State, effectively to oversee the running of the prison by the director. The disciplinary powers that are removed from the director are vested in the controller who is also charged with the responsibility for reviewing the running of the prison and reporting to the Secretary of State (s 85). In an attempt to promote uniformity in the system, area managers are now the direct line managers for such prisons as they are for state prisons (AG 21/95). Therefore appeals against operational and disciplinary decisions should be directed to the area manager.

2.43   The officers employed to run the prison are known as 'prison custody officers'. The duties of these officers are stated to be to prevent escapes from custody, to detect and prevent the commission of unlawful acts, to ensure good order and discipline and to attend to the well-being of prisoners. Reasonable force may be used in pursuance of these duties (s 86(3), (4)). These officers have the power to search inmates in accordance with the Prison Rules and to conduct searches of visitors. Searches of visitors do not extend to full body searches and only outer layers of clothing may be removed (s 86(1)). Provision has also been made for such staff to work in directly managed prisons, those which are not contracted out and vice versa (CJPOA 1994, s 97). The purpose of these provisions is to enable services at directly managed prisons to be contracted out if so desired.

2.44   The Secretary of State is empowered to intervene in the running of the prison in cases where the controller appears to have lost control or where it is necessary to preserve the safety of any person or to prevent serious damage to property (s 88). In such cases, a Crown servant can be appointed to act as governor of the prison and this person then assumes the powers of both the director and the controller.

Private escorts

2.45   The contracting out of prisons was accompanied by a contracting out of the prisoner escort system. This covers the delivery of prisoners to court, to and from police stations and other prisons and for the custody of prisoners outside of prison for temporary purposes (CJA 1991, s 80). The persons who provide escorts are described as prison custody officers and have similar duties and responsibilities to those of prison custody officers in contracted out prisons. Disciplinary breaches by prisoners under such escort are to be treated as if they had been committed in the custody of the governor or controller of the prison (s 83). The charge may be laid by the prison custody officer (CJPOA 1994, s 95).

The contract document

2.46   The standards to be utilised in the running of the prison will be set out in the contract between the contractor and the Secretary of State. The actual contracts are not public documents, although the absurdity of this secrecy was highlighted when the Prison Reform Trust managed to obtain such a contract from the United States as the parent company was obliged to make it public in that jurisdiction (*Prison Report*, Issue 28, Autumn 1994). The tender documents make it clear that the Prison Rules 1964 will apply but that policy documents such as Standing Orders may not. The Secretary of State can oblige the contractor to comply with any policy and procedural decisions that are deemed necessary.

2.47   The contract sets out the regime standards that are to be applied in the prison including such matters as time out of cells, association, medical care and suicide prevention. Although it was widely anticipated from tender documents that the contracted out regimes would be designed to produce more positive regimes, the reality may prove to be somewhat different in the long run. In the contract for Doncaster, for example, the certified population was to be 771 but provision was made for up to 1,169 prisoners to be held (*Prison Report*, Issue 28, Autumn 1994). The numerous problems that have been experienced in the running of these prisons, in terms of contract compliance, assaults on staff, poor medical care, escapes from custody and suicides are documented by the Prison Reform Trust in their quarterly publication, *Prison Report*.

The legal implications

2.48   The privatisation of prisons and escort services has taken place fairly rapidly. By 1995, five contracted out prisons had been established, with plans for at least two more new prisons to be built. The majority of escort services have also been either contracted out or are due to be placed for tender. Perhaps surprisingly, the legal status of prisoners in such custody is no different from that of prisoners in state prisons. To all intents and purposes, the contracted out prisons are required to adopt the same procedures as state prisons in terms of operational and disciplinary measures.

2.49   Prisoners seeking a remedy for unlawful acts committed in a contracted out prison will continue to have the same actions available as in state prisons. The power of the Secretary of State to contract out the running of prisons does not allow the abrogation of responsibility for the running of such prisons, merely the delegation of duties to a new set of properly appointed officers.

CHAPTER 3

BASIC LEGAL REMEDIES

THE INTERNAL MECHANISMS

3.1   There exists within the prison system, a series of structured, internal mechanisms for prisoners to ventilate complaints and make requests. However, prior to utilising the formal structures, prisoners are advised to make use of the informal system that is in operation.

3.2   The informal system is really no more than a suggestion that prisoners should first discuss their problem with a wing officer and make use of wing applications. These are simply one-sheet forms allowing a prisoner the opportunity to write a brief description of the problem. This is known as a 'governor's application' but in practice it will often be replied to by a senior or principal officer. There is no code of practice that requires this to be answered within a specified period of time and although replies are supplied fairly quickly, they do tend to be brief.

3.3   There is no requirement to make use of this process before engaging in the formal request/complaints system. The main use of this informal method is where the matter is relatively simple and straightforward, and the prisoner feels that it can be resolved without difficulty. It can also be useful for prisoners who have a good relationship with officers on their wing and who do not wish to be perceived as 'troublemakers'.

The formal system

3.4   It is a requirement of the Prison Rules 1964 that a mechanism for dealing with prisoners' requests and complaints is in operation. This duty is firstly placed upon the governor (Prison Rules, r 8) and secondly on the Board of Visitors (Prison Rules) rr 8 and 95 (SI 1964/388). Rule 8 states that:

> '8 (1)   A request or complaint to the governor or Board of Visitors relating to a prisoner's imprisonment shall be made orally or in writing by the prisoner.
> (2)   On every day the governor shall hear any requests and complaints that are made to him under paragraph (1) above.
> (3) A written request or complaint under paragraph (1) above may be made in confidence.'

3.5   The present scheme was established in 1990 and was designed to replace an ad hoc and inefficient system that did not in effect provide any real independent avenue of complaint for prisoners. One of the most frequently voiced criticisms was the lack of any timescale for dealing with enquiries. The actual system that is in operation at the present time bears little resemblance to the outline contained in r 8. For example, the requirement to hear requests and complaints each day may be delegated to another officer of the prison. As such, there is no right for prisoners to see the governor in charge of the prison and in practice, this rarely occurs. However, the consistent and formalised structure that has been implemented does work reasonably well within the obvious constraints of a system that investigates itself.

3.6   The 'Staff Manual on the Requests/Complaints Procedure' issued by the Prison Service envisages that the new system will benefit both prisoners and staff by:

'*   preserving and building on the arrangements for resolving requests and complaints informally or by oral applications;
*   enabling more decisions to be taken and explained locally;
*   inspiring greater confidence in prisoners that their needs and welfare are being looked after;
*   reducing tension and anxiety;
*   promoting better relationships between prisoners and staff.' (page 1)

3.7   The Manual suggests that prisoners should seek to resolve problems wherever possible through the informal channels but this is not a requirement before the formal procedures can be utilised. The formal process is effectively split into three, being complaints to be dealt with in the prison, requests for the review of decisions and complaints to be dealt with by Prison Service Headquarters. One of the stated aims of the system is to try and devolve greater decision-making responsibility to the prison. In the first instance, request/complaint forms will be dealt with at the prison itself. The reply is to be given within seven days and may be dealt with by the governor or referred on to another member of staff.

3.8   Certain subjects cannot be dealt with internally, such as enquiries about parole or matters concerning category A prisoners. These are referred to as 'reserved subjects' and must be forwarded onto the appropriate department at Headquarters (for a full discussion of the operation of the request/ complaints system and a list of reserved subjects, see section II, chapter 6) Answers to replies sent to Headquarters are required to be dealt with within six weeks of receipt. If a reply cannot be made in that time, then an interim reply should be sent explaining the reasons for the delay and when a full reply can be expected.

3.9   If a prisoner is unhappy with any decision made by the governor, either in response to a request/complaint form or a disciplinary decision such as an adjudication, the system allows for forms to be sent to the area manager for the prison to be reviewed. Again, the time limit for receiving a reply to such enquiries is set at six weeks. There is no right of appeal or review within the

Prison Service against decisions made by the area manager or other departments at Headquarters.

Confidential access

3.10 Rule 8(3) of the Prison Rules allows for written complaints to be made confidentially to the governor or the area manager. This is kept within the same overall request/complaint system on the same forms. In such cases the Manual provides that prisoners should be given an envelope with the form provided to them. It advises that the prisoner writes the reasons why the matter is confidential on the envelope to assist in ensuring that it is passed to the person best placed to deal with the enquiry. Confidential matters for the area manager's attention are supposed to be sent out of the prison unopened (para 3.4.22).

3.11 In practice, the confidential access is not always effective, particularly on matters raised inside the prison. Staff can often be suspicious and obstruct the issue of such forms. There is no guarantee that the envelope will be opened by the most appropriate person and once opened, a decision is made unilaterally as to whether confidential access was appropriate and as to whether the allegations/complaints should be passed on to the person against whom they are made. The prisoner has no input into this process. Similarly, the area manager can decide that confidential access is inappropriate and return the complaint to be dealt with by the prison without giving prior notification to the prisoner that this course of action has been taken. For a full discussion of the requests/complaints system, see section II, chapter 6.

Complaints to the Board of Visitors

3.12 Rule 8 authorises the Board of Visitors to hear oral or written complaints from prisoners and this is supplemented by r 95 which directs Boards and their members to, 'hear any complaint or request which a prisoner wishes to make to him or them.' This is not a daily requirement but does impose a duty upon the Board to hear these problems when they are in the prison. Arrangements for visits by the Board will vary from prison to prison but as a general rule, visits will take place at least twice a week.

3.13 Complaints to the Board have no formal role to play in the request/complaints procedure and the Board have no statutory powers to resolve or uphold the complaints that they receive. There is no requirement on prisoners to utilise this procedure before entering the formal disciplinary system and indeed, the Prison Service in fact envisaged that the Boards would become involved once the more formal system has been utilised. In the Staff Manual the advice that staff are recommended to give to prisoners is:

> 'You may also ask to speak to a member of the Board of Visitors. . . . The Board will also consider your written request or complaint if you ask them. But the Board will normally expect you to have already tried to solve the problem by oral application and written request and complaint to the governor.' (p 4, para 8)

3.14   The extent of the Board's powers, or lack of them, is emphasised in the same document which goes on to explain what might be expected in response to such an enquiry:

> 'If you have already made a written request or complaint, the Board will look at the reply you were given and any other relevant information. If there is likely to be a delay, you will be told what is happening. The Board will let you know what it has decided to do about your request or complaint. It could, for example, ask the governor to think again about the decision which has been reached, or it could bring it to the attention of the area manager or even the Home Secretary.' (p 4, para 8)

The right to petition

3.15   The right to petition was not removed following the introduction of the present system. Every British citizen has the constitutional right to petition the reigning monarch and this right is extended to citizens of other countries as a matter of courtesy. The right to petition the Secretary of State is extended to all inmates. Standing Order 5C explains that this process enables prisoners to raise matters with Prison Service Headquarters that cannot be dealt with in the prison (para 1).

3.16   Broadly speaking, the purpose of petitioning is now redundant as the request/complaints system provides a formal mechanism for problems to be ventilated. This is illustrated by the range of subjects on which it is envisaged that prisoners will present petitions such as parole, adjudications, appeals against conviction, the prerogative of mercy and production at court. In practical terms, all of these matters can now be dealt with by formal procedures and applications that are far more satisfactory. The petitioning procedure therefore has little practical import and is largely an anachronism.

The Prisons Ombudsman

3.17   The Woolf Report was strongly in favour of the appointment of a 'Complaints Adjudicator' to ensure that the then new grievance procedure had an independent element. It was envisaged that this adjudicator would have the power to act as a final arbiter in disciplinary decisions and to assess replies made to request/complaints on both the merits of the individual case and the procedures that were followed. Despite some initial objections, the White Paper, 'Custody, Care and Justice' broadly accepted the worth of these proposals (Cmnd 1647, p 93).

3.18   These proposals were finally realised when the Prisons Ombudsman (presently Sir Peter Woodhead, a former Admiral) was appointed and his office opened in October 1994. The position was slightly different from that envisaged by Woolf in that no primary legislation was put in place for the creation of this office and as such, the Ombudsman's powers are limited to making recommendations and are not binding on the Prison Service or the Secretary of State. The appointment was, however, a great improvement on the previous situation whereby the only Ombudsman with any power to oversee the Prison Service was the Parliamentary Commissioner for Administration. The Commissioner's powers are limited to reviewing administrative errors and delays rather than the merits of decisions, and complaints to the Commissioner must be made through a member of Parliament. These limitations severely curtailed the extent to which prisoners could make use of the Commissioner.

3.19 The Prisons Ombudsman has a fairly broad remit and can receive complaints on most aspects of the prison system from matters as minor as the quality of food to more serious matters such as categorisation and adjudications. Complaints can also be made about the actions of prison staff, including those employed at contracted out prisons, probation officers or members of the Board of Visitors. The matters which are outside of his remit are:

(i)   miscarriages of justice and appeals against conviction and sentence;
(ii) decisions concerning release (eg the merits of parole decisions or the release of lifers);
(iii) the actions of outside agencies such as the police or the Immigration Department;
(iv) medical decisions taken by prison doctors. (This limitation is presently under review and it is likely that this power will be extended to the Ombudsman in the near future. It appears that it will have to be exercised in conjunction with the Health Services Ombudsman);
(v)   the Ombudsman cannot receive complaints that are already subject to litigation or legal proceedings.

3.20 In order to make a complaint to the Ombudsman, a prisoner must first utilise the formal request/complaints system. This includes appealing any decisions to the area manager where this right exists. In general, complaints must be made by the prisoner in person and they must be received within one month of the decision which forms the basis of the complaint. The Ombudsman has the power to investigate both the merits of the case and the adequacy of the procedures. It is aimed for all complaints to be investigated and a report prepared with the findings of the investigation within 8–12 weeks of receipt.

3.21 If a complaint is upheld, the report is sent to the Director General with a recommendation as to what can be done to rectify the problem. The Director General aims to reply within one month but is not required to do so. If recommendations are not upheld, the prisoner can use the report as the basis for an action for judicial review or to support a claim for negligence but there is no form of redress within the system. In cases where the complaint is rejected, there is no right of appeal although the Ombudsman has proved amenable to criticism and is not inflexible in reconsidering decisions.

3.22 As with Boards of Visitors, the Ombudsman does not form part of any formal system of complaint. Prisoners cannot be required to make use of this avenue before commencing legal action (ie it is not one of the remedies that have to be exhausted when applying for judicial review). One of the major values of the Ombudsman lies in the fact that for the first time, an independent body exists which has the power to investigate complaints rather than merely to review decisions made by, or on behalf of, the executive. The fact that the merits of decisions are under scrutiny also provides an outlet for problems which are not suitable for judicial review, but where the exercise of discretion may have been unduly harsh or simply unfair.

3.23 In September 1995, the Ombudsman published a review of the first six months of operation (Prisons Ombudsman, '6 Month Review': 11 September 1995). In this period, 870 complaints were received of which 71% proved to be ineligible. By far the majority (64%) had failed to complete request/complaints procedure. Of the 253 that were eligible for investigation, 51% of complaints were upheld. The recommendations made were fully accepted in 82% of cases, partially accepted in 3% and rejected in 15%. The conclusions to the report cite categorisation, adjudications, prisoners' property and temporary release as the main areas of concern. Criticism was directed at the application by the Prison Service of confusing and inconsistent criteria and information on these areas.

3.24 The number of recommendations that have been rejected is an indication of some resistance to the work of the Ombudsman. In such cases, the report can form valuable information in support of legal action, whether it is an application for compensation for lost property or for judicial review. Litigation has been commenced by a small number of prisoners in cases where the recommendations have been rejected with the report forming part of the body of evidence but at the time of writing, none of these cases have yet been decided.

JUDICIAL REVIEW

3.25 As such a large part of prison life is concerned with the making of operational and administrative decisions, the most relevant area of litigation for prisoners is that of judicial review. This is unfortunate for prisoners on two counts. Firstly, the nature of judicial review is such that it is not a remedy that can easily be pursued as a litigant in person. Secondly, solicitors can be reluctant to take on such cases as the actual administrative procedures and guidelines that are in question will often be unfamiliar. When these factors are combined with the traditional reluctance of the courts to interfere with the running of prisons, it can appear that a formidable barrier is in place.

3.26 The reality of the situation is somewhat less bleak. Public law remedies are nowadays better utilised than they were in the past and the courts have shown an increasing willingness to intervene in prisoners' cases. The reluctance to disturb security arrangements is still apparent, but in other areas the Divisional Court has pursued a far more interventionist approach. In particular, the mandatory life sentence system has been the subject of repeated attack and the court has taken it upon itself to provide strict regulation of a sentence that has attracted strong criticism from all levels of the judiciary. The comments of Lord Justice Steyn in the case of *R v Secretary of State for the Home Department, ex p Pegg* ((1994) Times, 11 August, DC) are indicative of this attitude:

> 'Given the essential unfairness of the system in relation to prisoners serving mandatory life sentences the courts have to bear in mind that fundamental rights are at stake. But courts can do no more than to be extra vigilant in the exercise of their powers of judicial review.'

The contrast between the current interventionist approach and the more conservative views of the Court of Appeal in *Payne v Lord Harris of Greenwich* ([1981] 1 WLR 754, where mandatory lifers were refused the right to know of the reasons for the refusal to recommend release) could not be more apparent.

The decisions that can be reviewed

3.27   The problem of whether decisions fall within the ambit of public law and are therefore potentially amenable to judicial review is now fairly clear cut in prisoners' cases. In general, all decisions made in respect of prisoners, be they operational, managerial or disciplinary will fall within the sphere of public law (see *O'Reilly v Mackman* [1983] 2 AC 237).

3.28   The decisions that prisoners seek to review will fall into two broad categories: policy matters, such as the contents of the Prison Rules, and decisions made in respect of individuals. The review of policy decisions has never posed a problem on procedural grounds as the decisions fall within the realm of public law. It is a basic principle of administrative law that such decisions are justiciable. As far as decisions made in respect of individuals are concerned, it has long been established that disciplinary decisions made in the prison of a quasi-judicial nature are susceptible to judicial review (*R v Board of Visitors of Hull Prison, ex p St Germain* [1979] QB 425). At the time, this was confined to the powers exercised by the Boards of Visitors but was formally extended to the powers exercised by governors in 1988 following the case of *Leech v Deputy Governor of Parkhurst Prison* ([1988] AC 533). The court had also decided that it had the power to exercise jurisdiction over decisions to transfer prisoners *(R v Secretary of State for the Home Department, ex p McAvoy* [1984] 1 WLR 1408). More recently, the decision to categorise prisoners was scrutinised by the Divisional Court and found to be amenable to judicial review (*R v Secretary of State for the Home Department, ex p Duggan* [1994] 3 All ER 277). Attempts by the Secretary of State to argue that the Prison Act 1952, s 4(2) conferred a unique duty to ensure observance of the rules on the minister in person and that this ousted the jurisdiction of the court, were rejected by Lord Bridge in the *Leech* case ([1988] AC 533).

3.29   The ambit and jurisdiction of the court was fully debated by the House of Lords in 1992 in the case of *R v Deputy Governor of Parkhurst Prison, ex p Hague, Weldon v Home Office* ([1992] 1 AC 58). The House of Lords took the view that operational and managerial decisions affecting prisoners' segregation and transfer were susceptible to judicial review. This effectively removed the last remaining barriers and extended the jurisdiction of the court to all aspects of imprisonment.

3.30 This judgment did not, as the Home Office feared, lead to a flood of applications for judicial review. The House of Lords put many practical barriers in the way by accepting that governors have a wide discretion in their decision-making, particularly when dealing with disciplinary matters. In proceedings under RSC Order 53, the Divisional Court will not become involved in deciding factual disputes and in any event, it is likely that without powerful evidence to the contrary such disputes would be resolved in favour of the Prison Service. The wide degree of discretion and the court's reluctance to decide upon issues of fact means that challenges as to the reasonableness of a decision alone can be notoriously difficult to win. Some evidence of deficiencies in the procedural elements of a decision is usually required in order to provide sufficient base for an application for judicial review.

The judgment in *Doody*

3.31 The duty that is imposed on the Prison Service in relation to their administrative duties to prisoners was significantly clarified and advanced by the House of Lords in the case of *R v Secretary of State for the Home Department, ex p Doody* ([1994] 1 AC 531). This case involved the right of mandatory lifers to know of the level at which their tariff had been set and to make effective representations to the Secretary of State about this decision. Although the right to make representations had always existed, mandatory lifers had no right to be officially told the length of their tariff or the views of the trial judge and Lord Chief Justice that had informed the Secretary of State's decision.

3.32 Lord Mustill took the view that a prisoner was unable to make any effective representations without this information:

> 'To mount an effective attack on the decision given no more material than the facts of the case and the length of the penal element, the prisoner has virtually no means of ascertaining whether this is an instance where the decision-making process has gone astray.'

The relevance of this view lies in the fact that a requirement to make full disclosure is effectively imposed on the Prison Service when making decisions that will affect the length of an individual's detention. As the majority of decisions made about prisoners will have either a direct or indirect impact of the length of time spent in custody, the judgment reaches into all aspects of prison discipline and administration.

3.33 Although Lord Mustill accepted the argument of the Secretary of State that there is no freestanding duty to give reasons for administrative decisions, he identified six principles for openness in the decision-making process. The three most important of these are:

(i) there is a presumption that administrative powers will be exercised fairly;
(ii) where a person may be adversely affected by a decision, fairness dictates that the person should have the opportunity to make representations either

before it is taken to procure a favourable result or after it is made to have it modified, or both;
(iii) fairness will often dictate that the person is informed of the gist of the case that is to be answered otherwise it is not possible to make effective representations.

3.34 It is arguable that this judgment has significantly increased the onus on the Prison Service to be accountable to prisoners in reaching decisions, particularly those which will have a direct bearing on their prospects of release. The range of decisions that are affected is potentially vast and can include categorisation, disciplinary transfers, segregation and temporary release amongst others. The impact of the decision was apparent in the next case to come before the Divisional Court which concerned categorisation (*R v Secretary of State for the Home Department, ex p Duggan* [1994] 3 All ER 277). The court, newly freed from previous authority, was able to conclude that category A prisoners have the right to regular reviews of their categorisation with a review process that includes disclosure of the gist of reports prepared upon them, the right to make representations and the right to be informed of the gist of the reasons for the subsequent decision.

3.35 The cumulative effect of these judgments is to firmly exert the court's authority over all decisions made in respect of prisoners. The courts have always been especially keen to exert authority in areas which have a direct bearing on the liberty of the subject, such as release on licence, and it is arguable that the majority of decisions made in respect of prisoners have a direct bearing on the conditions of their detention and release prospects. For example, a decision not to authorise temporary release may appear to be a freestanding decision with no detriment to the prisoner other than the loss of the benefit of temporary release on a particular occasion. The reality is that it will have far deeper consequences and may affect future applications to be placed in a lower security category or for release on parole licence. The realisation of the impact of seemingly routine decisions combined with the more stringent duty to observe the principles of administrative fairness have effectively brought all such decisions within the ambit of judicial review.

3.36 Whilst prisoners face very few inhibitions to the principle of making such an application, the manner in which the courts will receive them will vary depending on the nature of the application. Consequently, the exercise of quasi-judicial powers such as adjudications and decisions as to release will come under very strict scrutiny. Conversely, decisions made in the pursuance of maintaining good order and discipline will attract a weaker level of scrutiny and providing proper procedures are followed, the courts are very reluctant to interfere with a governor's judgment. Thus, in *Ex p Ross* ((1994) Times, 9 June, CA), the Court of Appeal decided that a prison governor is best placed to decide upon whether a prisoner is being disruptive.

PRIVATE LAW CLAIMS

Actions in negligence

3.37   The view of Lord Wilberforce in *Raymond v Honey* ([1983] 1 AC 1) that prisoners retain all civil rights, save for those expressly or impliedly taken away by the fact of their imprisonment, confirms the right of prisoners to commence actions in private law. Whilst the administration of the prison system falls within the realm of public law, there will still be many situations in which a prisoner is seeking to enforce private law rights to compensation arising from the negligence of the prison authorities. In order to plead negligence, it is necessary to establish that there has been a failure to exercise the care which the circumstances demand and, that the resulting loss was a reasonable foreseeable result of those actions. These principles will be familiar to civil practitioners, although the context in which such claims arise for prisoners will be less familiar.

Property claims

3.38   Property belonging to prisoners will fall into two categories, that held in their own possession ('in-possession property') and that which is held as stored property by the prison. The Prison Service take the view that any damage or loss to stored property may be their responsibility, depending upon the circumstances of the loss. However, in-possession property is officially treated as being held at the risk of the individual prisoner and the policy is for no liability to be accepted for any loss or damage.

3.39   This policy is legally unsustainable as there are many circumstances in which a prisoner can no longer exert any control over the property and that any resultant loss or damage must fall within the responsibility of the prison. Examples of this will include when a cell is searched, or when a prisoner is moved to segregation and the cell is supposed to be sealed by staff. The ordinary tortious principles will apply in such cases and providing the loss or damage can be identified to have occurred at a time when the responsibility or control must have reverted to prison officers, then liability will arise (*Winson v The Home Office* (18 March 1994, unreported, Central London County Court): a full discussion on how to conduct such claims appears in section III, chapter 14).

Negligent medical treatment

3.40   Whilst a person is serving a sentence of imprisonment, responsibility for medical care rests with the medical officer of the prison in which s/he is located. Medical staff owe a duty of care to prisoners to ensure that they receive adequate treatment whilst in custody. The duty owed by medical staff interplays with the duty owed by the prison authorities to provide access to treatment both in the prison and at outside hospitals (eg, by providing escorts). The duty of care that is owed in a custodial context can differ from that which is provided to those at liberty due to the difference in the function of prison hospitals and the constraints that exist when providing medical care (*Knight v Home Office* [1990] 3 All ER 237, a case which was concerned with the standard of care owed to a mentally ill prisoner detained in a prison hospital).

Dangerous premises and working conditions

3.41   Prison governors are required to ensure compliance with the main statutes that deal with health and safety at work. These include, inter alia, the Factories Act 1961, the Health and Safety at Work etc Act 1974, the Food Act 1984 and the Offices, Shops and Railway Premises Act 1963 (see Standing Order 14). Prisoners will therefore retain rights provided for in common law and statute in relation to the provision of safe premises and a safe working environment. These duties are limited only to the extent that there is no contractual relationship between a prisoner and the prison authorities and so any rights arising from the existence of a contract (eg employment rights) are inapplicable.

3.42   There are a range of claims that have been brought by prisoners where it has been alleged that the relevant standard of care has not been complied with. These include claims for injuries resulting from defective premises (*Cristofi v Home Office* (1975) Times, 31 July where a prisoner fell on a broken step); from being required to work with dangerous equipment; or from working in conditions injurious to health (*Ferguson v Home Office* (1977) Times, 8 October and *Pullen v Prison Comrs* [1957] 1 WLR 1186).

Negligent supervision

3.43   The nature of the prison environment is such that assaults on inmates by other prisoners is an inevitable fact of life. Claims will lie directly against the assailant for the torts of assault and battery but in the majority of cases, the proposed defendant will not have the funds to meet any damages awarded rendering such an action futile. In such cases, the main possibility for legal action will be against the Home Office for failing to properly fulfil the duty of care owed to people in their custody.

3.44   The general tortious principle that no person can hold a duty to control another person in order to prevent damage being done to a third party (*Smith v Leurs* (1945) 70 CLR 256) is modified in the custodial context. The speech delivered by Lord Diplock in *Home Office v Dorset Yacht Co Ltd* ([1970] 2 All ER 294) sets out the circumstances in which this duty of care would arise. The factors that he considered relevant are:

(i)   that the assailant is in the legal custody of the Home Office;
(ii) that the Home Office has the legal right to control the proximity of the victim to the assailant;
(iii) that reasonable care in the exercise of the right of custody could have prevented the tortious act; and

(iv) that the Home Office could reasonably foresee that the victim was likely to suffer injury if reasonable care is not taken.

These principles have long been accepted in the context of a custodial setting (see eg *Darcy v Prison Comrs* [1956] Crim LR 56 or *Ellis v Home Office* [1953] 2 QB 135).

3.45 The difficulty in bringing claims in such circumstances is in establishing facts that are strong enough to satisfy the court that the prison should have been aware that a particular prisoner was in danger of being assaulted and that sufficient steps were not taken to safeguard that person. Each case will have to be considered on its particular merits when assessing whether a claim will be successful. Prisoners that are most likely to be assaulted are those classed as 'vulnerable', either by virtue of their offences or from an inability to cope with prison life. Damages have been awarded where the negligent disclosure of past convictions for sex offences lead to an assault by other prisoners (*H v Home Office* (1992) Independent, 6 May) and where a prisoner was escorted by an officer from a vulnerable prisoners' unit through a normal wing despite his fears of assault and was duly assaulted by other prisoners (*Burt v Home Office* 27 June 1995, unreported, Norwich County Court. In contrast, the Home Office was not considered to be negligent when a prisoner was assaulted when returning to normal location after a period in segregation, despite the fact that the escorting officers had not been informed that he had been attacked prior to his segregation. The court accepted the argument that an experienced officer could not have foreseen the actual attack that took place (*Egerton v Home Office* [1978] Crim LR 494).

3.46 Prisoners who are not considered 'vulnerable' at the time of an assault will face even more difficulties in satisfying the court that the prison should have been aware of the danger to them and failed to take all reasonable steps to ensure their safety. In one case a prisoner was stabbed by another prisoner who was considered to be highly dangerous but nevertheless, had been allowed to work in a tailor's workshop with access to scissors. Although it was accepted that he was highly dangerous, Lord Justice Neill took the view that it was not possible to keep a prisoner permanently segregated, except in very extreme cases and it was also desirable to provide work where possible. In balancing these considerations, the governor had not been negligent (*Palmer v Home Office* (1988) Guardian, 31 March, CA). In a similar vein, a prisoner who had been attacked previously and had informed prison staff was attacked two weeks later in the television room. The court accepted the governor's view that he did not consider the prisoner to be at serious risk and that he had discharged his duty by instructing staff to keep a closer eye on him (*Porterfield v Home Office* (1988) Independent, 9 March).

3.47 The case law highlights the difficulty in assessing how extensive the duty of care is in such cases. In order for the duty of care to arise in the first place, the prison staff will have to be aware either that a particular prisoner is a serious danger to other inmates or that an individual is in danger of being assaulted. The steps taken to ensure safety have to be balanced against the operational needs of the prison as a whole and the duty of the governor to allow reasonable facilities to inmates.

The decision in *Hague*

3.48   Two cases brought by prisoners concerning their alleged mistreatment by the prison authorities were heard together by the House of Lords (*R v Deputy Governor of Parkhurst Prison, ex p Hague, Weldon v Home Office* [1992] 1 AC 58). The decision established important principles which define and limit the extent of tortious claims that may be brought by prisoners. Hague sought judicial review of a decision to segregate and transfer him and damages for false imprisonment. Weldon commenced a private law claim for assault and false imprisonment following an assault by prison staff and his detention in a strip cell. In their judgment, the House outlined the various private law remedies available to prisoners. A discussion of these follows.

Breach of statutory duty

3.49   The House of Lords rejected the idea that claims could be brought by prisoners solely for breach of statutory duty, a decision reached with particular consideration of the provisions of r 43 of the Prison Rules which provides the authority for segregation. Lord Jauncey considered that the mere fact that the statutory provision was designed to protect prisoners did not in itself confer a private law right of action. In order for this right to arise, it was necessary for the statute to contain enabling regulations providing for enforcement. Lord Bridge took the view that as the Prison Rules were concerned with the management and administration of prisons and prisoners, rather than solely being designed to protect prisoners from personal injury, it gave no right to a private law claim for breach of the Rules in isolation.

False imprisonment

3.50   The House of Lords also rejected the possibility of prisoners bringing claims for false imprisonment. Previous decisions had indicated that a right to commence claims in such circumstances did not arise (eg *Williams v Home Office (No 2)* [1981] 1 All ER 1211). In *Hague*, the House of Lords also rejected the concept that prisoners retain an element of residual liberty that can be denied by their detention in more onerous conditions. Lord Bridge took the view that false imprisonment required freedom of movement to be denied and that if a prisoner was lawfully detained in the first place, the complaint was merely that another form of restraint had been applied rather than his freedom being infringed ([1992] 1 AC 130 at 139D). Lord Jauncey commented in a similar vein that:

> 'a prisoner at any time has no liberty to be in any place other than where the regime permits. . . . An alteration of his conditions therefore deprives him of no liberty because he has none already.' (ibid at 177E)

It should be noted that this claim in some circumstances can still be brought against prisoners who hold another prisoner hostage. The legal foundation that prevents the claim being pursued against prison staff, namely that the prisoner is already lawfully detained, does not apply to the actions of another prisoner who has no such authority.

3.51 Whilst this decision places limitations on the types of claims that prisoners are entitled to bring, it does provide clear guidance as to the private law claims that are possible. In addition to general claims in negligence as detailed above, prisoners may look to commence actions for assault and battery resulting from the actions of prison staff, and in exceptional circumstances, for misfeasance in public office. Public law remedies will, however, continue to be the main method of seeking to challenge the conditions of detention.

Assault and battery

3.52 The right of prisoners to bring claims for assault and battery is an important safeguard over the actions of the authorities, particularly as claims for false imprisonment are unavailable. These torts have been long established with an assault defined as an action which causes a person to fear the unlawful infliction of force (*Stephens v Myers* (1830) 4 C & P 349) and a battery involves the actual application of force during an assault (*Cole v Turner* (1704) 6 Mod Rep 149 where Holt CJ commented that, 'the least touching of another in anger is a battery').

3.53 In a prison context, prison officers will routinely be required to apply force in a lawful context. The question that will normally arise therefore, is whether it was necessary for force to be applied and whether the extent and duration of the force were reasonable. The most likely scenarios in which such a claim will arise are:

(i) a deliberate attack by a prison officer (also, see misfeasance in public office below);
(ii) when a restraint continues to be imposed after a prisoner has ceased to be a danger, either to others or to him/herself *(Rodrigues v Home Office* [1989] LAG Bulletin, February, p 14);
(iii) where excessive force is used to carry out a lawful order;
(iv) where force is used to execute an unlawful order.

3.54 In order to make an assessment as to whether the actions of prison staff constitute an assault, it necessary to look at the scope of their powers in a particular situation. Therefore, if a prisoner is placed in a mechanical restraint or placed in a strip cell without the proper procedures being followed and the proper authority sought from an office of suitable rank, this can constitute an assault. In cases where officers are alleged to have acted outside, or in excess of their powers, it is also necessary to look at the tort of misfeasance in public office.

Misfeasance in public office

3.55 In *Hague*, the House of Lords made express reference to the tort of misfeasance in public office as an appropriate remedy where it is alleged that prison officers have deliberately abused their powers. The elements of the tort are onerous and aside from establishing that damage to the person has been caused, it must be established that the tortfeasor is the holder of a public office, that the damage was caused to a foreseeable plaintiff and that the actions were malicious or taken with the knowledge that they were outside of lawful powers (*Jones v Swansea City Council* [1990] 1 WLR 54). The evidential problems in establishing malice or actions undertaken deliberately outside of lawful powers are formidable.

3.56   In the prison context, the prevailing view had been that if a prison officer acted outside of his/her powers, then the Home Office could not be vicariously liable for these actions. In *Hague*, Lord Bridge commented that:

> '. . . if the officer deliberately acts outside the scope of his authority, he cannot render the governor or the Home Office vicariously liable for his tortious conduct.' ([1992] 1 AC 58 at 164D)

3.57   In the case of *Racz v Home Office* ([1994] 2 AC 45), the House of Lords had the opportunity to consider the issues of vicarious liability that arise from this tort. The Court of Appeal had accepted the Home Office argument that misfeasance, by its nature, was a cause of action to which vicarious liability could not attach. This was because it is an element of the tort that the perpetrator was acting in a deliberate abuse of authority. This was rejected by the House of Lords which held that the issue of vicarious liability for misfeasance in public office must be determined by the individual facts of each case.

SECTION II

CHAPTER 4

THE VARIOUS TYPES OF PRISON

MEN'S PRISONS

Local prisons

4.1 Local prisons are so called because they tend to be located in towns or cities. They are where prisoners are held on remand and when first convicted. Local prisons are almost always old buildings, some still do not have integral sanitation, and due to the general state of the buildings they are more likely to be infested with vermin and cockroaches than the other newer prisons (see eg the Annual Report of Wandsworth Board of Visitors 1993–94).

4.2 Prisoners are generally held on remand in the local prison nearest to the court where their case will eventually be heard, and there is a constant turnover of prisoners.

4.3 Regimes at local prisons are the most deprived in the system and prisoners often complain that they are locked up for 23 hours a day.

4.4 The Chief Inspector of Prisons' report on a Full Inspection of HMP Wandsworth (published 26.5.95) found that association facilities for 268 remand prisoners held on A Wing consisted of a television, a table tennis table, and a 'small library facility'. Prisoners were unlocked for association three or four times a week. Some physical education was available as was participation in educational classes, although the allocation of places 'seemed haphazard'. In addition, NACRO was in the process of setting up two activity areas for unconvicted prisoners. However, at the weekend unconvicted prisoners had no association, no visits on Sundays, and no access to the gym. Thus it is likely that prisoners would be locked up for 23 hours a day over the weekend.

4.5 A report published by the Chief Inspector following a Full Inspection of HMP Leeds (15 February 1995) described conditions there as 'deeply unsatisfactory'. The prison was 'bereft' of any constructive employment for prisoners, there were insufficient activities for the prisoners held there. The report detailed the daily routine for prisoners as containing nothing other than the statutory one hour's exercise a day, and being unlocked to collect meals or use the cardphone. Only one of the wings for unconvicted prisoners had evening association.

4.6   After conviction prisoners are categorised and allocated to other types of establishment. The exceptions to this are where someone is serving such a short sentence that there is not enough time to allocate them elsewhere, or where they elect to stay behind as 'retained' labour at the local prison.

Dispersal prisons

4.7   Until the early 1960s there were no especially secure prisons in the English prison estate. However, following highly publicised escapes of prisoners considered to be particularly dangerous, Lord Mountbatten was asked to conduct an inquiry into security within the prison system. Broadly speaking, Mountbatten recommended that prisoners should be categorised according to the level of security needed in order to prevent their escape; that prisoners who were afforded the highest level of security categorisation, A, should be held together in a maximum security prison on the Isle of Wight, and that within high security prisons the regime should be made more constructive and liberal in order that the desire to escape would be reduced and that good order within the prisons would be more likely to be attained.

4.8   The Home Secretary accepted Mountbatten's recommendations with regard to categorisation, however the Advisory Council on the Penal System were asked to give further consideration as to the regimes in which long-term prisoners should be held. The subsequent report 'The Regime for Long-Term Prisoners in Conditions of Maximum Security' did not agree with Mountbatten that all category A prisoners should be held together in one prison, and recommended that they should be 'dispersed' amongst category B prisoners in several prisons whose physical security would be upgraded in preparation.

4.9   This heralded the start of the dispersal prison system, which is still in use today. At the present time, there are five dispersal prisons – Full Sutton, Frankland, Long Lartin, Whitemoor and Wakefield. All of the dispersals take standard risk category A prisoners, but only Frankland, Full Sutton and Whitemoor are considered secure enough to provide suitable accommodation for high risk category A prisoners. Exceptional risk category A prisoners are held in special security units (see below). Each dispersal prison will only take a specific quota of category A prisoners, and the rest of their populations are largely made up of category B prisoners and the occasional category C or D prisoner who the prison have not been able to transfer to conditions of lesser security (eg because the prisoner requires full-time medical treatment).

4.10   Prisoners held in dispersal conditions are generally those serving the longest sentences. In a short inspection of HMP Full Sutton published on 3 June 1994, the Chief Inspector of Prisons found that of the 528 prisoners held there, 28 were serving between four months and three years, 28 were serving three to four years, 226 were serving four to ten years, 116 were serving determinate sentences of more than ten years and 130 were serving life. The Board of Visitors told the Chief Inspector that the prisoners serving shorter sentences had an unsettling effect on other prisoners.

4.11   Because of the length of time that the majority of prisoners in dispersal conditions are serving, they are likely to receive a much better regime than that offered in other prisons. There are more educational facilities and there should be work for every prisoner. The Chief Inspector's report following a short inspection of HMP Whitemoor (5 August 1993) showed that there were 498 jobs available for prisoners and a total of 484 prisoners. Employment ranged from wing cleaning, kitchen work, and work in the tailors' workshop to full-time education.

4.12   Dispersal prisons often have facilities for prisoners to purchase and cook their own food. It is also increasingly common practice for dispersal prisoners to be able to wear their own clothing and to have the facilities to wash and dry their clothes.

4.13   The list of items that dispersal prisoners are allowed to keep in their possession is extensive and covers far more items than those allowed for prisoners in other parts of the system. However, one of the recommendations in the report of the Woodcock Inquiry was that dispersal prisoners' property allowances should be severely restricted as excessive amounts of property hinder effective searching. In view of this it is likely that the Prison Service will revise the list of possessions allowed (see chapter 12).

Special security units

4.14   Special security units (SSUs) were conceived in the 1960s as a result of the recognition that there were a group of prisoners for whom escape should be made impossible. Initially, special security wings were established at HMPs Durham and Leicester. However, it was considered that these did not provide secure enough accommodation as they were housed in local prisons. Furthermore, their regimes were limited and oppressive. By the late 1970s the Prison Service had decided to build SSUs at dispersal prisons.

4.15   Special security units are effectively prisons within a prison. They are fully self-contained and facilities include an exercise yard (which is completely enclosed), a gym, facilities for association including television, hobbies room etc, and their own visits room and segregation cells.

4.16   Special security units have their own perimeter security overlooked by closed circuit television cameras. The perimeter security of the dispersal prison where the SSU is housed surrounds both the prison itself and the walls of the SSU. Until 1994 when six prisoners escaped from Whitemoor SSU, it was thought that escape from an SSU would be impossible.

4.17   There are currently three SSUs at Parkhurst, Whitemoor and Full Sutton prisons. They hold exceptional risk category A prisoners. Prior to the escape from Whitemoor conditions within SSUs were deliberately designed to give prisoners as much comfort as possible in order to offset the effects of being held in extremely claustrophobic conditions with a small group of other men. In response to a letter from an MP criticising the Whitemoor SSU for its 'hotel style conditions', a briefing note dated 11 March 1994 from the former Director General of the Prison Service, Derek Lewis, to the Home Secretary stated:

> 'Some prisoners live in SSUs for many years. They have no access to staff or prisoners outside the unit, workshops, education, and training facilities, the library or the prison shop. In these circumstances, the regime is limited to catering, gardening, hobbies and PE. From my own inspection I know it is extremely claustrophobic. The decision to make the surroundings marginally more comfortable was taken when the prison was built, in order to provide a modest counterbalance to some of the more draconian aspects of the environment and regime.'

4.18 The regime of the Whitemoor SSU was criticised in the Report of the Woodcock Inquiry (Cm 2741), and the recommendations made in the Report will have far-reaching consequences for the management of prisoners in SSUs if they are implemented.

4.19 On 21 September 1995 the Prison Service published AG 46/95 which announces the establishment of 'a project to examine the feasibility of one or two maximum security facilities' as a response to the escapes from Whitemoor and Parkhurst. If finally implemented this would represent acceptance of the recommendations made by Mountbatten almost 30 years ago.

Special units

4.20 From 1969 to 1983 there were ten major disturbances and riots in the prison estate. In response to this a Home Office working party was established to 'review the maintenance of control in the prison system including the implications for physical security, with particular reference to the dispersal system, and to make recommendations'. This working party became known as the Control Review Committee (CRC), and published its report 'Managing the Long-Term Prison System' in 1984.

4.21 In considering how prisoners who presented particular control problems should be dealt with, the CRC said that the existing facilities of transfers in the interest of good order and discipline and segregation were not long-term solutions. They recommended that

> 'a number of small units should be established for prisoners in this group (ie prisoners presenting control problems which cannot be dealt with in normal prison conditions)'.

This provides the basis of the special unit system.

4.22 Detailed guidance on allocation to Special Units is laid out in chapter 7.

4.23 At the present time there are three special units for disruptive prisoners, and these are housed on C Wing at Parkhurst, A Wing at Hull, and the

Keynes Unit at Woodhill. The Hull and Woodhill Units cater for category A and B long-term prisoners who will typically have displayed violence towards staff or other prisoners, or will have been found guilty of numerous disciplinary offences whilst they have been in prison.

4.24 The Parkhurst special unit mainly contains prisoners who have a history of mental health problems. Many are diagnosed as having suffered schizophrenia, psychosis or depression and have a history of drug dependency and self-mutilation. Prisoners in the Parkhurst special unit may be transferred into the special hospital system, although as many are labelled as 'untreatable' the psychiatrist at Parkhurst has encountered difficulty in finding places.

4.25 The special units take very limited numbers of prisoners and have a high staff to inmate ratio. The aim is to work with them intensively by providing psychological help, a structured regime with opportunities for work and education. Prisoners who respond well to the special unit regimes at Whitemoor and Woodhill would expect to be returned to normal location at other prison establishments, and the Prison Service would hope that they would not continue to pose control problems once out of the unit. The Special Unit Selection Committee do not view the role of the units in terms of 'successes' and 'failures', and thus no statistics to this effect are available.

4.26 Ironically, many prisoners appear to be transferred out of special units on the basis that their presence there undermines good order and discipline (IG 28/95). Such prisoners will generally be held in the segregation blocks of local prisons until they are reallocated permanently, either to another special unit or to a dispersal prison.

Category B training prisons

4.27 There are ten category B training prisons at Albany, Blundeston, Dartmoor, Garth, Gartree, Grendon, Kingston, Maidstone, Nottingham and Swaleside.

4.28 Category B training prisons tend to have a secure perimeter and relatively high levels of staffing. However, they offer a more relaxed regime than in dispersal prisons and there is less internal security. Opportunities for work and education should be available.

4.29 Each category B training prison has different criteria that operate in its allocations criteria, and this inevitably affects the type of regime offered and the type of prisoners received. All of these prisons take life sentence prisoners – Gartree is a main lifer centre taking prisoners who are in the first three years of their sentence, and Kingston only takes life sentence prisoners. Maidstone and Albany run sex offender treatment programmes and assessments for the programme.

4.30 Levels of physical security at category B prisons differ dramatically. Swaleside's security is not dissimilar to a dispersal prison and it is generally considered to be the highest security category B training prison. Conversely,

Maidstone is considered to be low security and will not take prisoners who have recently been on the escape list. Albany, Parkhurst and Gartree are former dispersal prisons who have changed their role in recent years.

4.31   Category B, C and D prisoners may be held in category B training prisons, although those of lower security categories will almost certainly be applying for transfers elsewhere.

Category C prisons

4.32   Category C prisons make up one of the largest parts of the prison estate, and there are 35 such establishments. Like category B trainers, they vary enormously from prison to prison.

4.33   In general, category C prisons have lower levels of staff supervision and less perimeter security. Until recent years they tended to have a younger population serving shorter sentences. However, following disturbances at HMP Wymott in the summer of 1994, the Prison Service reviewed the population of category C prisoners and identified prisoners aged under 25 at conviction, those sentenced to less than four years, and those serving sentences for robbery or burglary as the most likely to pose control problems. Quotas were set on the numbers of such prisoners that each category C prison should take (see chapter 5).

4.34   Many category C prisons have dormitory accommodation rather than, or as well as, cellular accommodation, and long-term prisoners may find this difficult to cope with. Because there is less staff supervision, there will often be more rules in operation. Prisoners found to be in breach of the rules will be more likely to be charged with breaches of r 47 of the Prison Rules than they would be in conditions of higher security. In general prisoners are expected to be more accountable for their actions and to take more responsibility for their behaviour.

4.35   Category C and D prisoners are held in these prisons.

Open prisons

4.36   There is very little security in category D prisons, and prisoners tend not to be locked up, and often retain their own keys to their rooms. Perimeter security tends to consist of little more than a fence, and some governors at open prisons have remarked that this serves more to keep the media out than the prisoners in.

4.37   Prisoners are only transferred to open conditions if the Prison Service is satisfied that they can be trusted not to abscond. Because of the ease with which prisoners could abscond many open prisons will not take prisoners convicted of sexual offences, although Leyhill is the main exception to this.

4.38   Prisoners may be engaged in work at the prison or alternatively be released from prison every day to do community work (often with the elderly or at schools for children with special needs).

4.39 Prisoners in open conditions are likely to be released from prison frequently in order to work, take town visits and temporary releases on resettlement licence. Open prisons do not have full-time medical staff, and so prisoners will be released to attend local hospitals, dentists and opticians rather than being treated by Prison Health Care staff. Prisoners with serious medical problems which require constant attention or monitoring will often not be allocated to open conditions and will remain in prisons where there is full-time medical care.

4.40 At the present time a review of the use of open prisons is being conducted. Its terms of reference are:

'to consider the role of open prisons in relation to the purpose of the Prison Service and to make recommendations about the future use of open prisons (with particular reference to PRES and Resettlement) and consequent capacity requirements together with optimum geographical locations.' (AG 39/95)

Resettlement prisons

4.41 The first resettlement prison to open was at HMP Latchmere House in 1991. Since then several smaller units have opened at local and category C prisons.

4.42 The concept is similar to that of a pre-release employment scheme hostel in that long-term prisoners are transferred there towards the end of their sentences in order that they might re-establish their links with their families and the wider community and obtain paid employment. It is hoped that this will significantly diminish rates of recidivism.

4.43 Because much of prisoners' time will be spent outside the prison, the facilities at resettlement prisons will be poorer than at other prisons. Prisoners found guilty of breaches of prison discipline are often transferred out to higher security establishments as are those who are suspected of being involved in any subversive behaviour. Such prisoners will usually not be given the full substance of any information received about them, and this is often a cause of great concern amongst prisoners and their families.

Pre-release employment scheme hostels

4.44 There are pre-release employment scheme (PRES) hostels at Maidstone, Wormwood Scrubs and Wakefield prisons. Life sentence prisoners of working age are almost always required to complete a satisfactory period of six to nine months in a hostel before they are released on life licence. Whilst in a hostel they will be expected to find paid employment and re-establish their links in the community. In general prisoners will be allowed to spend weekends and daytimes away from the hostel, but there are curfew times in the evenings.

Prison staff work in the hostels and keep a check on prisoners' behaviour to ensure that no areas of concern arise.

4.45 A few determinate sentenced prisoners will also spend the latter months of their sentences in PRES hostels.

Vulnerable prisoners' units

4.46 Historically, prisoners convicted of sexual offences and others who would not be acceptable to the mainstream prison population, have asked to be segregated for their own protection under the provisions of r 43 of the Prison Rules. Whilst this removed the immediate threat of violence from other prisoners, it meant that the most vulnerable prisoners in the system were often held in the very worst conditions in the prison system.

4.47 In response to an increase in the number of prisoners held on r 43 for their own protection, the Prison Service set up a number of vulnerable prisoners' units (VPUs) which were intended for

> ' . . . a relatively small number of medium and long sentence prisoners – mainly sex offenders and child abusers – who will fail all attempts to survive on normal location and who will need to remain in a protected environment until their discharge, whilst having the benefit of the facilities available to other medium and long term prisoners.' (Report of the Prison Department Working Group on the Management of Vulnerable Prisoners (1989))

4.48 The Programmes Department in DSP 2 at Prison Service Headquarters has carried out a review of VPUs, and found that the numbers of prisoners held separately has significantly increased. They considered that the population of VPUs tended to rise in proportion to the number of available spaces, and that many of these prisoners should be able to survive on normal location. Governors were asked not to create new VPUs without permission from Headquarters and to be more flexible about accepting prisoners for normal location despite them having been held in a VPU or on r 43 in the past. Routine transfers of vulnerable prisoners are to be seen as an opportunity to integrate prisoners on to normal location (IG 82/95).

4.49 Further instructions on the management of vulnerable prisoners are due to be issued in late 1995.

WOMEN'S PRISONS

4.50 There are 13 prisons in the female prison estate and on 30 June 1995 2,002 women were in prison in England and Wales – the highest number ever recorded. Unlike men's prisons, women's prisons are simply categorised as either open or closed. Female young offenders are held in prisons with adult prisoners which will have certain areas designated as young offender institutions (see chapter 5).

4.51 Five prisons operate as remand centres (Low Newton, Risley, Holloway, New Hall and Pucklechurch) and women will be held in one of these prisons whilst they are on remand, until they are allocated to another establishment after conviction and where they are serving short sentences. Female category A remand prisoners are normally held at Holloway prison, as are women who are in need of psychiatric care.

4.52 The closed women's prisons are Styal, Durham, Cookham Wood and Bullwood Hall, and Winchester. These operate similar regimes as category B and C prisons in the men's prison estate. Holloway and New Hall also keep some long-term prisoners for significant parts of their sentences, although they also operate as remand prisons. Convicted category A women are held in H Wing of Durham (whose other function is a local prison for male prisoners). This is the highest security prison in the women's prison estate.

4.53 There are three open women's prisons – Askham Grange, Drake Hall, and East Sutton Park. Askham Grange also has a pre-release employment scheme hostel.

4.54 Mother and baby units are found at Styal, Holloway, New Hall and Askham Grange prisons. These aim to:

> 'create as many opportunities as possible for the mother to exercise and develop her parental responsibilities, duties and skills, and to maximise the potential for the child's proper development.' (Mother and Baby Unit Regimes, HM Prison Service 1992, p 2)

4.55 Holloway has facilities for women to keep their babies with them up until they are nine months old, and the other units will allow mothers to keep their babies until they are 18 months old. In considering women's applications to go to a mother and baby unit, the factors taken into account are:

> '– the age of the child
> – the expectation that the child will be cared for by the mother after her release from prison
> – whether the mother's ability to care for the child is seriously impaired by physical or mental disorder
> – the views of social services or the courts regarding custody of the child
> – the suitability of alternative arrangements for the child
> – the mother's custodial behaviour
> – whether the mother will be willing to care for her child within the context of the regime offered
> – whether the mother consents to the child being searched by prison staff
> – the mother's awareness that units are drug free, and if she tests positive for drugs, she may be removed from the unit
> – whether placement in a mother and baby unit is in the best interests of the child.' ('Prison Mother and Baby Units', Howard League for Penal Reform, October 1995)

MALE YOUNG OFFENDER INSTITUTIONS

4.56   Prisoners between the ages of 15 and 21 are held in young offender institutions (YOIs). Those who turn 21 during their sentence are generally transferred into the adult prison system at that stage, although if they are due for release shortly afterwards, they may remain in a YOI.

4.57   The male YOI estate is similar to the women's prison system in that the only distinctions between prisons is whether they are open or closed. At the present time there are 20 closed YOIs (Aylesbury, Castington, Deerbolt, Dover, Feltham, Guys Marsh, Hindley, Hollesley Bay Colony, Huntercombe/ Finnamore Wood, Lancaster Farms, Low Newton, Northallerton, Onley, Portland, Reading, Stoke Heath, Swinfen Hall, Werrington and Wetherby), and two open YOIs (Hatfield and Thorn Cross). Young offenders may also be held on remand in a wing of a male local prison.

4.58   Young offender institutions are governed by the Young Offender Institution Rules 1988 rather than the Prison Rules 1964, although they are very similar in effect.

4.59   The main difference between the regimes at YOIs and those at adult prisons is that prisoners under the compulsory school leaving age should be provided with at least 15 hours of education. In their report 'Banged Up, Beaten Up, Cutting Up' (1995), the Howard League for Penal Reform found that school age children in prison are not offered the national curriculum, and that although 'most establishments try to encourage all young people to attend classes . . . the quality of facilities is often more of a deterrent than an incentive' (p 25).

4.60   The physical conditions in YOIs can be very impoverished. The Howard League found that teenage prisoners were often accommodated in cellular accommodation on wings of up to 60 people, that integral sanitation was not available throughout the YOI estate, and that overcrowding was 'endemic' in virtually all of the establishments they visited. The newer YOIs gave the impression of being maximum security prisons, whereas young offenders held in male local prisons had 'no proper communal eating or recreation space' and the cells were 'cramped and bare' (ibid p 25). Following a visit to the young offender's wing at Hull prison, one of the Howard League's Commissioners wrote

> 'I find it hard to describe exactly how awful I found it. The building lacks natural light almost completely. Landings are narrow, separated by flights of stairs and suicide nets. . . . The building is quiet but sounds echo. Furniture and furnishings are of poor standard, and often piled into inappropriate rooms. The atmosphere is of "making the most of it", while facilities are poor and damaged. To me, the young people looked confused and aimless.'

4.61   In terms of regimes, the YOI estate tends to mirror that of the adult prison system with sentenced prisoners being offered better facilities and having more opportunity for constructive employment, and remand prisoners merely being contained until their cases are dealt with by the courts.

4.62 The main differences in the way that young offenders are treated in relation to adult prisoners are highlighted throughout the text of this book.

CHAPTER 5

CATEGORISATION, ALLOCATION AND SENTENCE CALCULATION

THE DEFINITION OF CATEGORIES

The authority to categorise

5.1   The Prison Rules 1964, r 3, requires the Secretary of State to classify prisoners. The power is expressed broadly to take account of:

'age, temperament and record and with a view to maintaining good order and facilitating training and, in the case of convicted prisoners of furthering the purpose of their training and treatment . . .' (r 3(1))

The arrangements for the separation of inmates should not 'unduly deprive a prisoner of the society of other persons'.

5.2   Rule 3 goes on to state that unconvicted prisoners should be kept out of contact with convicted prisoners to the extent that the governor considers that this can reasonably be done. An unconvicted prisoner may never be required to share a cell with a convicted prisoner. This relaxes the previous provisions that forbade mixing in living areas under any circumstances. One of the reasons why remand and serving prisoners were previously kept apart is due to the fact that unconvicted prisoners are unclassified unless a decision has been made to allocate them as category A. Remand prisoners are generally held in local jails with security commensurate to that in place for category B prisoners. It would appear that these changes are designed to ease the pressures caused by overcrowding in the system.

5.3   Women prisoners and young offenders are not assigned to formal categories, other than those who are deemed to be category A (see below). These prisoners are therefore only assigned to either closed or open conditions. Broadly speaking, if a woman prisoner or young offender would normally meet the equivalent criteria for category D, they can expect to be located in an open prison.

The Mountbatten criteria

5.4   The broad power that is created once again leaves a great deal of detail to be filled in by the policy documents issued by the Home Office.

The present categories were first established following a report of the Inquiry into Prison Escapes and Security by Earl Mountbatten in 1976. This established four security categories ranging from A, reserved for the most dangerous prisoners, to D, the lowest category. These criteria were most recently affirmed in the Security Manual, a document which holds the same status as Standing Orders and Advice and Instructions to Governors. The Manual is continually updated and the guidelines on categorisation were reissued in 1993. It contains some materials that are considered to be highly sensitive and is not generally available outside of the Prison Service. The provisions on categorisation do not fall into this area and are widely available.

5.5   All prisoners can be made category A, whether unconvicted, female or juveniles. A full discussion of the procedures and implication for category A prisoners appears below. The remaining three categories of B, C and D are reserved for convicted, adult male prisoners. The Security Manual sets the following criteria for categorisation:

> '*Category A*: Prisoners whose escape would be highly dangerous to the public, the police or the security of the state, no matter how unlikely that escape might be; and for whom the aim must be to make escape impossible.
>
> *Category B*: Prisoners for whom the very highest conditions of security are not necessary but for whom escape must be made very difficult.
>
> *Category C*: Prisoners who cannot be trusted in open conditions but who do not have the resources or will to make a determined escape attempt.
>
> *Category D*: Prisoners who can be reasonably trusted in open conditions.'
> (para 31.2)

Escape list prisoners

5.6   It is possible for a prisoner to be identified as an 'escape risk'. This is not a security category as such, but a security decision relevant to the matter of category. The decision to place a prisoner on the escape list rests with the governor of that prison. The guidelines indicate that this may be necessary when there has been a recent escape attempt from closed conditions or an escort or, where there is 'recent and reliable security intelligence that an escape is being contemplated' (Security Manual, para 45.2).

5.7   If a prisoner is to be placed on the escape list, the governor must ensure that s/he is re-categorised to B and if located in a lower security prison, that an immediate transfer to a prison of the appropriate security is effected. The prisoner must be notified orally and in writing of the reasons for the decision, although the reasons will be drafted to ensure that security is not compromised. Monthly reviews of the decision will be made.

5.8   Escape list prisoners are subject to stringent security measures that require them to be located in the most secure cells available with a low-wattage night light for observation at night. Hourly checks must be carried out whilst in cells and cells must be changed at least once a month, without prior notice. In addition, jackets and trousers with distinctive yellow markings, known as 'patches' must be worn at all times.

The initial categorisation decision

5.9   The decision to allocate a prisoner to a security category, save for category A prisoners, rests with the governor of the prison. Circular Instruction 7/88 provides guidance on the exercise of this power to ensure there is consistency throughout the system. Perhaps the most important part of this Instruction is that the decision must only be made with reference to the likelihood that a prisoner will try to escape and the risk to society if the escape succeeds. The considerations of control, good order and discipline, the ability to mix with other prisoners and educational or medical needs are relevant to location and not categorisation. The Instruction further makes provision that all prisoners should be in the lowest category possible that is appropriate to the risk posed at each stage of their sentence (para 4).

5.10   These guidelines are of extreme importance to prisoners as security category will determine the type of prison to which one is allocated and the entitlement to privileges such as temporary release on licence. Parole decisions are also greatly affected by the security category of the applicant.

5.11   Prison Service Headquarters issue a flow chart under cover of CI 7/88 to assist in the initial categorisation decision. Briefly this provides the following guidance:

Category B: prisoners who have a current or previous sentence of over 10 years. Also, if one or more of the following apply, category B is appropriate: the present offence is of a serious nature (eg violence, importing drugs, sexual or arson), the prisoner has escaped from a closed prison or an escort in the past or has served a previous sentence of over seven years.

Category C: If only one of the above applies or if a prisoner has a previous conviction for arson or for drugs offences or has absconded, breached bail or had a home leave failure in the past five years, category C is appropriate. If a prisoner's present offence is for violence *and* is over 12 months *or* there has been a previous sentence of over 12 months, he will also be made category C.

Category D: this is appropriate for all other prisoners.

Subsequent decisions and challenges

5.12   In light of the importance of security categorisation, it is perhaps unsurprising that the interpretation of these guidelines is often a major bone of contention between prisoners and prison governors. Most governors now delegate their duties to 'categorisation boards' which sit in the prison. These boards will consider the prisoners' behaviour in custody, the nature of their convictions and whether there have been any previous abuses of trust, either in this sentence or in the past. If an application is unsuccessful, the board will often recommend that no further applications are made for a period of time, in some cases as long as 12 months.

5.13 The problem that arises for prisoners in this context is two-fold. Firstly, it is difficult to ensure that considerations which are not strictly relevant to category do not inform the decision. For example, a prisoner who is considered to be 'difficult' or a 'trouble maker' may not in fact present an escape risk or a danger to the public. A refusal to de-categorise will often be made based on the perceived difficulties with custodial behaviour despite the provisions of CI 7/88. The extent to which this can be challenged will depend on the precise reasons that are given for the decision. It is in the nature of administrative decisions such as these that if carefully worded reasons are given for a decision, a challenge can be extremely difficult to mount.

5.14 The second problem lies with the timing of the reviews of category. There is no guidance as to how frequent such reviews should be and CI 7/88 merely states that each prisoner should in the lowest category possible at each stage of their sentence. Various possibilities are given as triggers for reconsideration such as a successful application for temporary release or a parole decision (even if unsuccessful). The problem remains that without a formal structure for considering the timing of reviews, many governors will instruct prisoners whose applications are unsuccessful to reapply in 6–12 months as a matter of course. In such circumstances, there is nothing to prevent a prisoner making an earlier application for reconsideration if it is felt that there has been a material change or even if the passing of time warrants fresh consideration. A refusal to reconsider an application in these circumstances may be vulnerable to challenge on the basis that each prisoner is required to be in the lowest category possible at each stage of their sentence.

Category A status

5.15 This is the only category that can apply to all prisoners, whether male, female, juvenile or remand. The decision to so classify a prisoner is made by the Category A Committee which is comprised of various senior Prison Service officials. The Committee can order that remand prisoners are 'provisionally' category A until the time of their trial and if convicted, categorisation is reviewed at that time. The reality for a 'provisional' category A prisoner is that s/he will be subject to the same security restrictions as a convicted category A prisoner.

5.16 There are further subdivisions within category A, relating to the escape risk of an individual. The definition of this category is to make escape impossible for prisoners, 'no matter how unlikely such an escape may be'. The corollary of this definition is that a wide range of prisoners will fall within this definition despite the fact that it is accepted that many will never have the potential or resources to mount a serious escape attempt. Therefore, such prisoners can be made an exceptional, high or standard escape risk. For those with a high or exceptional escape risk, even more restrictions will be placed upon them whilst in custody.

5.17 The implications for a prisoner classified as category A are far reaching. Only a small number of prisons are designated to hold prisoners of this category on a permanent basis, by and large the dispersal prisons and

HMP Belmarsh. However, even within the dispersal system, some prisons are not deemed secure enough to hold high or exceptional escape risk prisoners. Parkhurst was forced to decant all such inmates whilst security was tightened following the escapes in December 1994 and Long Lartin is only deemed sufficiently secure for standard escape risk category A prisoners.

5.18 The restrictions that are faced by such prisoners fall into two levels. Firstly, there are the straightforward restrictions on contact with people outside of prison. Visits can only be received from official visitors (eg solicitors, probation officers) or friends and family members who have been approved by the Home Office. The procedure for obtaining approval is for a list of the proposed visitors to be given to the category A section who will then arrange for the police to visit and compile a report on suitability. At the time of writing, all exceptional risk category A prisoners have been placed on closed visits, even for visits to legal advisors. Leave has been granted in two judicial review applications for the removal of these restrictions for legal visits on the basis that the right to confidential legal advice has been breached. There is no indication that the Prison Service intends to settle the action before a full hearing.

5.19 The second level of restrictions relate to the regimes which are in operation within the prison itself. It is not possible to provide a comprehensive list of the restrictions in force as these will vary from week to week and from prison to prison. In 1977, Cantley J described a number of disadvantages that were faced at the time (*Payne v Home Office* (2 May 1977, unreported)) which is still broadly relevant today. These included lack of access to educational classes, frequent cell searches and moves within the prison system and ineligibility for parole. The situation has changed very little in the intervening 20 years.

5.20 Category A prisoners are liable to be moved more often that other prisoners, both from cell to cell within a prison and between prisons. No notification is given before moves are made to ensure that security is not compromised. This makes it extremely difficult to maintain effective communications with family members and places an additional stress on visitors. It is not uncommon for visitors to complain that the person they were seeking to visit had been moved and that no notification was given before they arrived at the prison. In view of the often inaccessible locations of the dispersal prisons, this is a source of particular concern and conflict. The only manner in which such moves can be challenged in domestic law is if a decision to move is taken unreasonably. The courts are extremely reluctant to interfere in what they see as the disciplinary and security functions of prison governors when reaching such decisions and challenges can be very difficult to sustain. In the case of *Ex p Ross* ((1994) Times, 9 June, CA) Lord Justice Waite considered that the governor of a prison was best placed to decide whether a category A prisoner posed a threat to discipline and providing general reasons were given, the court would not interfere.

5.21 Attempts to challenge the apparently random movement of high security prisoners through the European Convention on Human Rights would also appear to be difficult following the finding of the Commission in *Roelofs v*

Netherlands (1.7.92, No 1943592: see [1993] LAG Bulletin, January, p 16). This Dutch prisoner had been held in isolation and moved continually following allegations from an informer that he was to escape from custody. The Commission found the case to be inadmissible on the grounds that administrative decisions such as these were imposed for security reasons and not as a sanction and could not therefore be regarded as a determination of the person's rights.

5.22   The facilities available to category A prisoners, both educational and rehabilitative will depend very much on the resources of the particular prison in which they are located. In the period following the Woolf Report, the emphasis slowly moved towards rehabilitation but in recent months, the Woodcock Report prepared following the escapes from Whitemoor prison in September 1994 has begun to shift the focus of the prison system and dispersal prisons in particular towards security. In general, the courses designed to address offending behaviour that are available to category A prisoners are very limited and there is little uniformity between the facilities and courses available in the various dispersal prisons. In his report on Full Sutton (which held 94 category A prisoners at the time) published in June 1994, the Chief Inspector of Prisons commented that whilst progress at Full Sutton was encouraging, it was not helped by the differences in privileges at different dispersal prisons. He recommended to the Director General that these privileges should be applied uniformly and that local differences should be stopped (Appendix 1).

The judgment in *Duggan*

5.23   The enormous impact of category A status was finally recognised by the Divisional Court in December 1993 in the case of *R v Secretary of State for the Home Department, ex p Duggan* ([1994] 3 All ER 277). Historically, the position had been that category A prisoners were not entitled to know of the reasons for their categorisation following the case of *Payne v Home Office* (2 May 1977, unreported). Cantley J took the view that the provision of sufficient information to allow prisoners to fully understand the reasons for their categorisation could seriously hamper and frustrate the proper management of prisoners!

5.24   The antiquity of such views was exposed by the House of Lords in *R v Secretary of State for the Home Department, ex p Doody* ([1994] 1 AC 531). The Woolf Report had already recommended that reasons be given for decisions as a matter of good administration and management. In *Doody*, Lord Mustill set out six principles of good administrative practice that included the right to know of the reasons why decision have been made:

> 'Fairness will very often require that a person who may be adversely affected by a decision will have the opportunity to make representations on his own behalf either before the decision is taken with a view to expressly procuring a favourable result, or after it is taken, with a view to procuring its modification: or both.'

5.25   Lord Justice Rose was freed from earlier constraints by this judgment and in *Duggan*, he was able to approve his own comments from the earlier case of *R v Secretary of State for the Home Department, ex p Creamer and Scholey* ((1992) Independent, 27 October) where he had still been bound by the case of *Payne*. His view was that:

> 'A prisoner's right to make representations is largely valueless unless he knows the case against him and secret, unchallengeable reports which may contain damaging inaccuracies and which result in the loss of liberty are, or should be, anathema in a civilised, democratic society.'

5.26   It was accepted by the court that the criteria for placing a prisoner on category A meant that release became an impossibility and that the Home Secretary would never sanction the release of such a prisoner even if so recommended by the Parole Board. As the decision has a direct impact on the liberty of the subject, it was held that prisoners are entitled to know of the gist of the reports that have been prepared, to make representations and to be informed of the gist of any reasons to maintain them as category A. This was subject to any exemptions that may arise from public interest immunity.

The implementation of the judgment in *Duggan*

5.27   Following an inevitable delay, the new procedures for the review of all category A prisoners are now in force. Reports are distilled into a gist which is disclosed to the prisoner. This gist tends to be very limited and will often amount to no more that 50–100 words, comprising of a recital of the convictions and sentence, recent custodial behaviour and work that has been undertaken into offending behaviour. The recommendations in the gist are often contradictory with some reporters recommending downgrading whereas others will express reservations, often based on the nature of the original offences.

5.28   After this has been disclosed, representations can be made by the prisoner and the case will be referred to the Committee. Decisions are notified some two to three months after the Committee sits. The whole process can take up to six months and this leads to problems in keeping the gist up to date, particularly when a prisoner has been moved, and in disclosing all of the information that has been considered by the Committee. Decision letters tend to be as cursory as the gist and will on occasion make reference to material that has never been seen by the prisoner.

5.29   Applications for leave to challenge the extent of disclosure were issued by two prisoners in July 1995 (*R v Secretary of State for the Home Department, ex p Parry and O'Rourke* (18 July 1995, unreported)). It was argued that compliance with the judgment in *Duggan* required disclosure of each and every matter of fact and opinion relevant to the determination of category and that a general conclusion of dangerousness must be supported by a proper explanation of the material submitted that allows the conclusion to be drawn. At the application for leave, the Home Office agreed that disclosure had been inadequate in many cases and that new gists would be prepared to take account of these criticisms. On that basis, Owen J adjourned the applications pending the preparation of new gists that would reflect the Home Office's position on the extent of the disclosure that must be made. It remains to be seen whether this will resolve the situation or whether further litigation will be necessary to determine the duties of the Category A Committee in this regard.

Remand prisoners and category A

5.30 The judgment in *Duggan* did not extend to remand prisoners. The court was specifically concerned with the bearing that categorisation has on release and accepted the need for speedy categorisation decisions to be made in the public interest. As a consequence, the initial decision was not subject to the review procedures, but only the formal annual review. Following this decision, the Prison Service took a stringent line and refused to extend the requirements imposed upon them to remand prisoners.

5.31 The view of the Prison Service remains that it is not bound to give reasons for decisions made to make remand prisoners category A. The slightly absurd position whereby unconvicted prisoners are deemed to have less rights in respect of the conditions of their detention is likely to be less well received by the courts at the present time. Perhaps in recognition of this likelihood, the Prison Service will, in most cases, provide written reasons for such decisions on request. Any refusal to do so should be made the subject of judicial review. On a practical level, however, once the reasons have been disclosed the possibility of a successful challenge to the decision is likely to be limited. The Prison Service will undoubtedly have reached the decision on the basis of information supplied by the police. Unless compelling evidence can be put forward to counter the allegations, a court is unlikely to be persuaded that it is wrong to rely on this information.

THE BASIS OF ALLOCATION

Adult male prisoners

5.32 In the minds of prisoners security categorisation and allocation are often inextricably linked. However, Circular Instruction 7/1988 warns that the two procedures are 'distinct' and that staff responsible for categorisation and allocation should not let a decision on one influence the other.

5.33 Whilst security categorisation takes account of the risk that a prisoner might escape and the risk that would be posed should this occur, the allocation of a prisoner to a particular prison establishment is influenced by the following factors:

(i) the needs of security;
(ii) the needs of control;

(iii) the need to make the best use of establishments, ie ensure that all training prisons are kept full at all times; and
(iv) the needs of the individual prisoner (CI 7/1988).

5.34   Staff who work in observation, classification and allocation units (OCA), are advised that the most important determining factor in considering where a prisoner should be transferred to after conviction, is the security category. However, officers should also assess whether a prisoner may pose a control problem in a particular establishment, whether he is suitable to be held in particular types of accommodation (taking into account 'age, sexual tendencies, drug use or ability to mix with other prisoners'), any relevant medical or psychiatric needs, the distance that visitors will have to travel, any educational or training needs, and whether any agreement has been made with a local authority to restrict allocation.

5.35   Thus, whilst a prisoner should be given the lowest possible security categorisation at all stages in his sentence, other factors may come into play and cause a prisoner to be allocated to a prison which is of a higher security category than his categorisation would appear to merit. This may be because of the type of offence that he has been found guilty of – open prisons may have an agreement with the local authority that sex offenders will not be allocated there – or it could be because the only places available in an open prison are in a dormitory and a particular prisoner may be considered too much of a 'loner' to be able to cope there.

5.36   Where a prisoner is allocated to a prison of a higher security category than he is, this should be confirmed by a senior officer and detailed records and reasons should be kept. A prisoner who has been allocated to a prison of a higher security category may seek the reasons for that decision through the requests/complaints procedure, and make representations against them. Depending on the reasons given for the initial decision and any subsequent affirmation of it, an application for judicial review may be appropriate.

5.37   Where a prisoner is serving a very short sentence, it will often not be possible to categorise and allocate them because of the constraint on time. Such prisoners will serve their sentences in a category B local prison.

Reallocation

5.38   Many prisoners will serve their sentences in a number of different prisons. For example, a prisoner serving more than ten years could be initially allocated to a category B dispersal prison, and then 'progress' through to a category B training prison, category C conditions and finally an open prison.

5.39   Reallocation most commonly occurs when a prisoner has applied for a reduction in his security category and this has been granted. At that stage the prison will make arrangements with a prison of a lower security category for the prisoner's transfer there.

5.40 However, reallocation may also occur if a governor decides that a prisoner is causing problems at the prison and that it would be in the interests of good order and discipline to remove him (see chapter 7).

5.41 Life sentence prisoners are allocated by the Lifer Management Unit at Prison Service Headquarters rather than being considered under the above criteria. See chapter 10 for details.

5.42 Category A prisoners are allocated by the Category A Section at Prison Service Headquarters. For the most part they will be held in dispersal prisons unless they are 'exceptional' or 'high' risk in which case they will be held in Special Secure Units (see chapter 4).

Particular considerations for allocation to category C prisons

5.43 In September 1994, new instructions came into effect changing the allocation criteria to category C prisons (IG 55/94). Following serious disturbances at HMP Wymott, research was conducted into the 'effects of population make up on the risk to good order in category C prisons'.

5.44 The research drew three main conclusions:

(i) that those prisoners who were under 25 years old when convicted, serving sentences of less than four years, and convicted of burglary and robbery offences were more likely to be guilty of disciplinary offences, and that where a high proportion of them are held together there is a greater risk of riots taking place;
(ii) that the design of a prison was an important factor in maintaining good order. In particular, secure buildings with cellular accommodation, good sight lines and secure internal gates were considered aids to the maintenance of control;
(iii) that where there was a rising number of new receptions to the prison, and a rising number of disciplinary hearings against prisoners, there would be an increasing potential for disturbances.

5.45 In view of the research findings, category C prisons were divided into the following four groups depending upon whether their control capability is deemed 'very good', 'good', 'medium' and 'poor'. The aim was to regulate the number of prisoners meeting the high risk criteria outlined above by awarding one point for being under 25 at the date of conviction, one point for serving less than four years, and one point for serving a sentence for burglary or robbery. A category C prisoner who meets all three of the above is defined as a 'Score 3' inmate. Each group of prisons is allowed to take a certain percentage of score 3 prisoners. Where control is deemed to be 'very good' the population may comprise 18% score 3 inmates, where control is 'poor' a maximum of 8% of the population may be score 3.

Allocation of male young offenders

5.46   Male young offenders are allocated to either open or closed conditions, and the decision is taken primarily on the basis of risk. Subordinate to this is the need to place the prisoner as near as possible to his home. There is a general provision that young male offenders should be held in young offender institutions (Criminal Justice Act 1988, s 123(4)), although the Secretary of State retains the discretion to direct that a young offender over the age of 17 may serve his sentence in an adult prison (s 123(4)).

5.47   Information relevant to the allocation decision is collated before the decision is made. This includes the prisoner's

(i)   age;
(ii)   home area;
(iii)   current offence and sentence;
(iv)   time spend in the care of a local authority;
(v)   medical requirements;
(vi)   nature of any outstanding charges;
(vii)   whether the prisoner is appealing against conviction or sentence;
(viii) social enquiry reports;
(ix)   previous prison reports (CI 37/1988).

5.48   Staff working in the observation, classification and allocation unit use a standard assessment form in determining whether someone is suitable for open or closed conditions. The assessment is largely based upon a risk assessment involving the prisoner's current and past offences. Prisoners serving over three years or prisoners who have been convicted of murder, manslaughter, wounding, GBH, robbery, aggravated burglary, rape, buggery, sexual offences attracting sentences of over 12 months, arson, and importation or dealing in drugs will be allocated to closed conditions initially.

5.49   Prisoners whose current offence is for death by dangerous driving, possession of an offensive weapon, affray, ABH, assault on the police, malicious or wilful damage, threatening behaviour, other minor violence, unlawful sexual intercourse, incest, indecency between males, and minor sex offences will be allocated to closed conditions if as well as the current conviction they have a previous conviction for one of the offences outlined above.

5.50   Prisoners who do not fall into any of the above categories will be allocated to open conditions unless they can fall into two or more of the following three groups: a current conviction for motor theft, three or more previous convictions for motor thefts, have absconded from local authority care – if so they will go to closed conditions. These last criteria were set after research was conducted into the characteristics of young male prisoners who had absconded from open conditions (CI 37/1988).

Allocation of female adult prisoners

5.51 The allocation of women prisoners is considerably less complex than the allocation of men. Women are allocated to Durham H block or Holloway if they are category A prisoners, and otherwise they are simply allocated to 'open' or 'closed' conditions.

5.52 In deciding whether a woman is suitable to be allocated to open or closed conditions, a risk assessment is conducted and this takes into account the need for security and control. The following factors are relevant to the allocation decision:

(i)   age;
(ii)   home area;
(iii)   current offence and sentence;
(iv)   previous custodial sentences;
(v)   whether time has been spent in local authority care;
(vi)   the nature of any outstanding charges;
(vii)   any medical requirements;
(viii) time left to serve;
(ix)   any outstanding appeal against sentence or conviction;
(x)   whether there is information indicating that the prisoner is an escape or an abscond risk;
(xi)   if the prisoner is liable to be detained under the Immigration Act 1971 (CI 2/1991).

5.53 Prisoners who are serving sentences of over three years, or who are serving sentences for offences of attempted murder, manslaughter, causing death by dangerous driving in the course of committing a crime, wounding, grievous bodily harm, aggravated burglary, sexual offences, arson, drug smuggling, drug trafficking, or who are liable to be detained under the Immigration Act should be initially allocated to closed conditions. Staff are advised that a decision to deviate from this policy should be 'capable of justification as truly exceptional and a decision to allocate such an offender to open conditions should be confirmed by a more senior officer' (CI 2/1991, para 10).

5.54 Aside from the above, some other factors may be relevant to a woman's allocation, and these are whether she is a young offender, is in need of full-time medical care, is due to be released within 14 days, has a further court appearance within 14 days, is pregnant and likely to have her baby during her period of imprisonment, or has a baby and has applied to be allocated to a mother and baby unit.

5.55 There are only 13 prisons in the women's prison estate. Low Newton, Risley, New Hall and Pucklechurch serve as allocation centres where women are held on remand and immediately after conviction until they are allocated elsewhere. Holloway has the above functions and also operates as a closed female establishment for convicted prisoners. Styal, Durham, Cookham Wood, Winchester and Bullwood Hall are closed prisons for convicted prisoners, and Askham Grange, East Sutton Park, and Drake Hall are open prisons for convicted prisoners. Holloway, Askham Grange, and Styal have mother and baby units.

5.56   Once a woman has been deemed to be suitable for either open or closed conditions she should be allocated to the nearest prison establishment of that status to her home.

The allocation of female young offenders

5.57   There is no female equivalent to a young offenders institution which holds only people over 21. Thus young women are allocated to 'partly designated young offender institutions', ie an adult women's prison with spaces made available for young offenders. Young women will be allocated to open or closed conditions on the principles outlined above. In each 'partly designated young offenders institution' particular areas will be deemed to be YOIs and other areas will be deemed to be an adult prison. The application of the Prison or Young Offender Rules will depend on which area in the prison a woman sleeps rather than upon her age.

5.58   Whilst it is possible to locate an adult woman in a young offender institution designated area (Prison Act 1952, s 43(2)(a) as substituted by Criminal Justice Act 1982, s 11(2)), and a young woman aged 17 or more in a prison (Criminal Justice Act 1982, s 12(5)) there are guidelines which state when this might not be appropriate. Adult women who are to be 'mixed' with young women should be selected on the basis that they are a 'good influence', they should not have been convicted of offences against children, serious violent offences or drugs offences (unless they have given up drugs and are thought likely to be influential in dissuading young women from involvement with drugs) (CI 31/1988).

5.59   Young women aged under 17 cannot be permanently allocated to the part of an establishment designated as a prison, and thus governors are warned to be particularly vigilant in ensuring that the allocation of a young woman to prison designated accommodation is legal.

5.60   At the present time there is young offender institution designated accommodation for convicted prisoners in Bullwood Hall, Drake Hall, East Sutton Park, New Hall and Styal prisons.

TRANSFERS BETWEEN JURISDICTIONS

Transfers between prisons in England and those in Scotland and Northern Ireland

5.61   In a Parliamentary answer on 23 November 1992 the then Prisons Minister, Peter Lloyd, outlined arrangements for the transfer of convicted prisoners between UK jurisdictions. Prisoners who are convicted of offences in England and Wales may be transferred to Scotland or Northern Ireland provided that:

(i) they have at least six months left to serve at the time of application; and

(ii) they were ordinarily resident in the receiving jurisdiction prior to their imprisonment; or

(iii) they have close family there and there are reasonable grounds for believing that they:
  (a) intend to reside there upon release from prison; or
  (b) would receive visits there; and

(iv) both jurisdictions are satisfied that the prisoner will not disrupt or attempt to disrupt a prison, or pose an unacceptable risk to security if transferred.

5.62 Applications for transfer which fall outside these criteria may be granted if there are other strong compassionate or compelling grounds. However, if the effect of transfer is that a prisoner convicted of a very serious crime would serve a substantially lower sentence, an application may fall to be refused.

5.63 Prisoners held in England and Wales should apply for permanent or temporary transfer through the request/complaint procedure. The governor will collate all relevant documents and forward them to Prison Service Headquarters for consideration. This process will include consultation with the Home Department of the other jurisdiction.

5.64 Prisoners who are temporarily transferred to another jurisdiction may be returned to England or Wales if they do not comply with the regime in the receiving prison system.

The Repatriation of Prisoners Act 1984

5.65 The Repatriation of Prisoners Act 1984 came into effect on 15 April 1985, and facilitated ratification of the Council of Europe Convention on the Transfer of Sentenced Persons.

5.66 The Convention enables foreign nationals convicted and sentenced to terms of imprisonment to be transferred back to the country of which they are a national and serve their sentence there (so long as the crime of which they are convicted also constitutes a criminal offence in their country of origin). Sentenced prisoners from countries which are signatories to the Convention are eligible to apply for repatriation so long as they have at least six months of their sentence left to serve until their earliest date of release and are not appealing against their sentence or conviction.

5.67 The Convention requires the government to inform all foreign prisoners who may be eligible for transfer of the substance of its provisions, and thus all prisoners whose country of citizenship has signed the convention should be aware that they may ask to be repatriated. Each time a country ratifies the Convention, Prison Service Headquarters sends a notice to all prison governors and a list of the names of the prisoners who should be informed of their eligibility to apply for repatriation.

5.68   A prisoner who wishes to be considered for repatriation should make his or her application to the governor of the prison where s/he is held. This is done through the requests/complaints procedure, and the prisoner should give details including their full name, date of birth, address in their home country, passport number and the place and date of issue (IG 101/95).

5.69   When the governor has received the prisoner's request, this should be forwarded to the Directorate of Security and Programmes at Prison Service Headquarters, and the following documents should be attached by the prison:

(i)   copies of indictment, warrants and court orders relating to the period of imprisonment;
(ii)   notice of recommendation for deportation (if relevant);
(iii)   an assessment of the security and control risks which the prisoner is thought to pose;
(iv)   the prisoner's disciplinary record;
(v)   an assessment of the prisoner's medical condition including any recommendations for future treatment;
(vi)   copies of social inquiry reports and probation reports;
(vii)   details of previous convictions;
(viii) two recent photographs of the prisoner;
(ix)   police and/or customs and excise reports on the offence (IG 101/95, annex C).

5.70   After receipt of the application, Prison Service Headquarters consults with the Secretary of State and the government of the country of which the prisoner is a national to decide whether repatriation is considered appropriate by all parties. The main bone of contention at this stage is the length of sentence which the prisoner will have to serve if s/he is repatriated.

5.71   The 1984 Act specifies two separate procedures under which sentences to be served after repatriation may be calculated – the continued enforcement procedure, and the conversion of sentence procedure.

5.72   The continued enforcement procedure essentially means that the maximum sentence which the prisoner would serve if s/he were repatriated would remain the same as it would be were s/he to serve the sentence in this country. The period of time which has been served here prior to repatriation is taken into account, and the prisoner takes with them any remission earned in this country. If the sentence given in this country is longer than a sentence which could be imposed for the same offence in their home country, it can be changed to the nearest equivalent sentence lawfully imposed in that country, although this could not be longer than the original sentence (IG 101/95, annex B). If this method of calculation is used, the prisoner is informed of the exact length of sentence that has to be served prior to transfer and is given an opportunity to accept or reject this.

5.73   If the conversion of sentence procedure is used, then a prisoner will not know exactly how long they will have to serve after repatriation until that event has occurred. This is because after transfer a court in the prisoner's home country will convert the sentence into one which would have been given if the offence had been committed in that country. Thus when the application for transfer is being considered the prisoner can only be given rough details of how long a sentence such an offence would be likely to attract. Again, the sentence cannot be longer than the original sentence and will take into account the period of time that the prisoner has already spent in custody, and the prisoner will be asked to consent to repatriation in view of the information given by the government of their home country (IG 101/ 95, annex B).

5.74 The main problem that prisoners experience in applying for repatriation appears to be where the sentence that they would have to serve in their home country is significantly shorter than the sentence that they are serving in this country. In these circumstances the British Government is likely to refuse to repatriate on the basis that for the sentence to be so reduced would undermine the British criminal justice system and reduce the deterrent effect to other foreign nationals.

5.75 If a prisoner is repatriated, his/her sentence will be enforced according to the law of the country in which they are then serving their sentence. However, if the prisoner subsequently decides to appeal against sentence or conviction, they would have to do so through the courts in this country and their home country would have no jurisdiction.

5.76 A prisoner who is accepted for repatriation may be required to pay his/her own fare home at the discretion of the other country concerned.

5.77 At 19 October 1995, the following countries had repatriation agreements with the UK:

Austria, Bahamas, Belgium, Bulgaria, Canada, Croatia, Cyprus, Czech Republic, Denmark, Finland, France, Germany, Greece, Hungary, Italy, Iceland, Ireland, Luxembourg, Malta, Netherlands, Norway, Nigeria, Malawi, Poland, Portugal, Slovakia, Slovina, Spain, Sweden, Switzerland, Thailand, Trinidad and Tobago, Turkey, United States of America, Zimbabwe.

SENTENCE CALCULATION

5.78 Following conviction, all prisoners will be notified of their relevant release dates. These are calculated in the prison by the Discipline Department under the guidance contained in Standing Order 3C (and various amending Instructions to Governors). The Prison Service accepts that to a prisoner this is the most important information necessary to allow him/her to prepare for their sentence. The dates that will be calculated will depend on the length of sentence that is received:

(i) Prisoners serving under four years will be informed of the automatic release date that applies, being one half of the sentence.
(ii) Prisoners serving four years or more will be notified of their parole eligibility date (PED) and non-parole release date (NPRD). The PED is at one-half of the sentence and the NPRD at two-thirds.

61

(iii) Existing prisoners who were sentenced before 1 October 1992 continue to be treated under the terms of their original sentence and will keep a PED of one-third and release at two-thirds (see chapter 11 on parole and release from prison).

5.79   In calculating these dates, attention must be paid to all relevant time that has been spent in custody and whether the prisoner is serving more than one sentence, be they consecutive or concurrent. There are three principles that must be borne in mind when making these calculations:

(i)   any time that is spent in custody, either at a police station or on remand will count towards sentence (CJA 1967, s 67);
(ii) prisoners serving more than one sentence will have this calculated into a 'single term' whereby their dates are calculated as if they are serving just one sentence (CJA 1991, s 51(2) and Sch 12, para 8);
(iii) any days spent unlawfully at large during the currency of a sentence do not count towards sentence (Prison Act 1952, s 49(2)).

Remand time

5.80   The general principle is that remand time and time in police custody counts towards the length of a sentence. On a simple calculation, if a prisoner spent exactly six months on remand and then received a sentence of 18 months, there would be a balance of three months still to be served. This period of time also falls to reduce the dates on which a prisoner is eligible for parole. Time spent in police custody on matters relating to the offence for which the prisoner was convicted will also count as remand time. Any part of a day in such custody, however brief, falls to reduce the length of a sentence.

5.81   When assessing whether remand time is relevant to reducing sentence, two principles apply. Firstly, the offence must have been committed before the date of the first remand into custody and secondly, the proceedings out of which the sentence arises must have been before the court on or before the date of the first sentence (SO 3C, para 4.2). These two provisions are linked and both must be satisfied.

5.82   It follows that if an offence is committed after the first date of remand (eg the prisoner is remanded then bailed then commits a new offence and is remanded back into custody), the subsequent sentence will only be reduced by periods of remand which occur after the offence was committed. If a second offence is committed in custody, remand time will only reduce any sentence imposed for the offence from the date that the prisoner first appears in court on the charge. In order to understand the full implications of these provisions, they must be considered with the calculation of the single term.

5.83   One-day appearances at court to answer to bail and the time spent at court attending a trial, where bail has been granted, do not count as days in custody. If the judge or magistrate orders that the person be confined to the court cells during any recesses, this will normally count as relevant remand time.

5.84 Juveniles will often be remanded into the care of the local authority prior to conviction. Remands to secure accommodation which is certified as being provided for the purpose of restricting liberty will always count to reduce sentences. It is also possible for time spent in non-secure accommodation to be counted if the following criteria are met:

(i)   the accommodation was a children's home;
(ii) s/he was not permitted to live at home with parents;
(iii) s/he was not permitted to leave;
(iv) education was provided on the premises (IG 51/95).

The single term

5.85 All sentences that prisoners receive are to be calculated into a single term (CJA 1967, s 104(2) and CJA 1991, s 51(2)). This means that where a prisoner receives a sentence and is later sentenced to a further term of imprisonment, whether concurrent or consecutive, the two sentences are effectively added together to make one sentence of imprisonment. The sentence is then calculated in accordance with the provisions that were in force at the time the first sentence was passed. Therefore, if a prisoner is sentenced to 10 years in 1990 and in 1994 received a further consecutive sentence of two years, the single term would be calculated by adding the sentences together into a term of 12 years. The prisoner would then be subject the release schemes that operated at the time of the first sentence as an 'existing prisoner'. Therefore, instead of serving two-thirds of the ten-year sentence and one-half of the two-year sentence, the prisoner would be required to serve two-thirds of a twelve-year sentence with a PED at one-third (ie four years).

5.86 The calculation of consecutive sentences is relatively straightforward. The second sentence is simply added to the first one that has been imposed. The appropriate release scheme is then calculated on the basis of the resulting single term. If a prisoner is serving a sentence of three years and then receives a second, consecutive sentence of two years, the relevant release scheme is based on the single term of five years. Thus the prisoner would be eligible for parole after serving one-half of the sentence and would be automatically released after serving two-thirds. It is *not* the case that one-half of each sentence will be served. Prisoners in this situation will therefore be significantly disadvantaged and ideally, the sentencing court should be made aware of the effect of imposing a consecutive sentence that extends the total term of imprisonment beyond four years. In cases where remand time has been served on any of the consecutive sentences, it will reduce the total time to be served.

5.87 The calculation of concurrent sentences is slightly more complex. A concurrent sentence takes effect from the day on which it is imposed and so the only method of calculating the single term is to make two separate calculations as to the length of time to be served. Remand time should be excluded at this stage. When the two sentences have been calculated, the latest sentence expiry date must be taken. If this date is the one which applies from the first sentence to be imposed, then the second, concurrent sentence has no effect on the release date of the prisoner. The remand time served on the first sentence can then be taken from the length of time to be served.

5.88   If the latest sentence expiry date is that which applies to the second sentence that was imposed, the proper release scheme must be calculated. This is done by adding the total number of days from the date of the first sentence to the end of the second sentence. This then becomes the single term that is to be served. Once the relevant release scheme has been identified, the remand time which is relevant to the latest sentence can be used to reduce the length of time to be served. Remand time that was served solely on the original sentence will not be counted in this calculation unless the prisoner was remanded on both charges but the sentences were passed on different occasions.

Time spent unlawfully at large

5.89   Any time that a prisoner spends unlawfully at large (UAL) does not count towards the length of the sentence to be served (Prisons Act 1952, s 49(2)). The effect for prisoners who spend time UAL is that their release dates are simply delayed by the relevant period of time by adding this period to the sentence. Whilst this seems straightforward, problems arose with prisoners who went UAL, then committed further offences and received concurrent and overlapping sentences.

5.90   The manner in which such sentences were calculated was to start the calculation from the date of the first sentence, then to count the number of days to the end of the second sentence. This calculation included the time spent UAL. The UAL period was then added on to the total length of time to be served. The effect of this calculation was that prisoners were effectively having the period UAL added into their sentence twice, firstly in the overall length and then by delaying the final release date. As a result of the prejudicial effect on the prisoners involved, the policy was amended so that the number of days in the length of sentence was calculated ignoring the period UAL and this is then added onto the end (AG 19/95). The practical effect has been substantial and has lead to sentences for some prisoners being reduced by several months.

Time spent awaiting extradition

5.91   Time spent in a foreign jurisdiction awaiting extradition does not automatically count to reduce sentence (CJA 1991, s 47). Case law on the subject indicates that this time should be considered by the sentencing judge when passing sentence and it should be stated whether any allowance is being made for this time. Relevant considerations will include the general conduct of the prisoner and whether extradition was resisted (see eg *R v Scalise and Rachel* (1985) 7 Cr App Rep (S) 395, *R v Stone* (1988) 10 Cr App R (S) 322). A failure by the sentencing judge to take account of such time or to take enough account of this time, can be subject to appeal.

Default and civil sentences

5.92   Sentences imposed under civil powers or confiscation orders imposed to run consecutively to the criminal penalty must not be calculated into the single term. Civil sentences that attract early release will be treated as follows:

(i)   Sentences of 12 months or less will have an automatic release date set at one-half of the sentence.

(ii)   Sentences of 12 months and over will have an automatic release date set at two-thirds of the sentence (CJA 1991, s 45).

(iii) Sentences of imprisonment to be served in default and consecutive to a criminal sentence will be treated separately. The sentence will be calculated to run from the time that the criminal sentence has expired. Such prisoners will still be eligible for parole and if parole is granted, the default sentence takes effect from that date.

5.93   The following civil sentences are subject to early release provisions:

(i)   Contempt of court, unless the court has fixed the date for release on the warrant of committal.

(ii)   Persons committed under the Magistrates' Courts Act 1980, s 63(3) for the non-compliance of an order of the court, other than for the payment of a sum of money.

(iii) A parent or guardian committed in default of payment of a fine or damages to be paid in respect of a young person under the provisions of the Criminal Justice Act 1982, s 26 (but *not* sums due under CJA 1991, s 58(3)).

(iv) Persons committed in default of entering into a recognizance with or without a surety.

CHAPTER 6

THE REQUESTS/COMPLAINTS PROCEDURE

AN OVERVIEW OF THE PROCEDURE

6.1   The prisoners' requests/complaints procedure was established in 1990 with the aim of improving the management and control of prisons by 'inspiring greater confidence in prisoners that their needs and welfare are being looked after; promoting better relations between inmates and staff; and reducing tensions and anxieties' (Prisoners' Requests/Complaints Procedures Staff Manual, para 1.1).

6.2   The system was designed to enable prisoners to make complaints about their treatment within the prison system, and for the first time provision was made for a complaint to be kept confidential from staff at the prison where the prisoner is held. Responses to written applications were to be made in writing, and a right of appeal to more senior prison officials was built into the system.

6.3   The importance of giving reasoned replies to the prisoner is highlighted, and staff with responsibility for providing written replies were told that they have a particular responsibility to ensure that they bear the principles of the requests/complaints procedure in mind when doing so.

6.4   The principles of the system are stated to:
- '• protect the prisoner's rights to make requests or complaints
- provide – in line with the European Prison Rule 42 (3) – confidential access to an authority outside the establishment
- ensure that requests and complaints are fully and fairly considered – both from the inmates' and staff's viewpoints – and that well-founded complaints can be remedied
- allow appeals to higher management levels
- produce timely and reasoned replies' (para 1.3).

6.5   In practice, most prisons appear to adhere to the principles of the procedure reasonably well, although at some establishments reasons given in rejecting a complaint can be sparse, and replies may take longer than the specified period. In addition, prisoners who submit numerous written requests/complaints may find that staff consider that they are a management problem in terms of the amount of staff time that is occupied in dealing with their complaints and providing written answers. Further, a very few prisoners who have been transferred in the interests of good order and discipline have attributed this to the fact that as well as submitting their own requests/ complaints they encouraged other inmates to make written complaints about their treatment or made many complaints on behalf of others.

6.6 The Staff Manual lays down the stages of the requests/complaints procedure as follows:

'• Daily oral applications to wing staff
- Oral applications to designated members of the establishment's senior management team
- The first step – the establishment stage – of the formal procedure where a prisoner's written request or complaint receives a written reasoned reply
- The second stage – the Headquarters stage – of the formal procedure where a prisoner's written appeal against a decision by the establishment receives a written reasoned reply. Headquarters also deals with requests or complaints on reserved subjects.

As a safeguard
- Confidential access, where a prisoner may write using a sealed envelope to the:
  – Governor of the establishment
  – The Chair of the Board of Visitors
  – The Area Manager at Prison Service Headquarters
- Oral or written applications to the Board of Visitors' (para 2.2)

6.7 Where the problem is not resolved after following these stages, further avenues of complaint are suggested by the Manual. These include MPs, MEPs, the police, petitioning the Queen or Parliament, the Commission for Racial Equality, the Criminal Injuries Compensation Authority, the European Commission for Human Rights, legal advisers and organisations in the voluntary sector.

6.8 Since 1994, the Prisons Ombudsman has been investigating prisoners' complaints, and although he is only able to make recommendations to the Prison Service, his thorough investigations often provide a more effective remedy than many of the above.

HOW THE PROCEDURE WORKS WITHIN PRISON ESTABLISHMENTS

6.9 The Prisoners' Requests/Complaints Procedures Staff Manual does not lay down in detail how the system should operate within each prison and this responsibility is delegated to governors. However, all governors are asked to ensure that they provide clear guidance on who has responsibility for considering complaints and should seek to ensure that as a complaint progresses it is considered by progressively more senior staff (para 2.4–5).

Oral applications

6.10 Oral applications are the first stage in the requests/complaints procedure. A prisoner may raise such an application informally with a personal officer, or formally by making a wing or landing application. Wing and landing applications should be heard every day in a private office and out of the hearing of other prisoners. The member of staff dealing with the application should consider the query given by the prisoner and advise as to how it may be resolved.

6.11 Governors' applications should be heard every day except Sundays and bank holidays. Thus if the problem is not resolved by wing or landing staff, the prisoner may make an application to see a governor. Prisoners do not have any right to see the governing governor (often known as the number 1 governor), who is able to delegate the duty to hear oral applications (Prison Rules, r 98).

6.12 Brief records of all oral applications should be kept in an applications book which is held at the prison.

Formal requests/complaints

6.13 Formal requests and complaints are submitted on a request/complaint form (known by prisoners as a 'CARP form') which is available by oral application or from a member of staff. Request/complaint forms are A4 size and prisoners complete them by providing the names of the members of staff that they have raised the matter with previously and giving full details of the problem. Guidance given on the form tells prisoners that they should confine themselves to raising only one problem on each form that they submit.

6.14 For the most part the request/complaint will be dealt with by designated staff within the prison. However, there are two scenarios where this will not occur. Firstly, if the complaint is about a 'reserved subject' it will be sent to the relevant department at Prison Service Headquarters. Reserved subjects are those where the governor at the establishment has no power to make a decision. The reserved subjects include appeals against adjudications, allegations against the governing governor, early release to take up employment, litigation against the Prison Service, lifer issues (change of name, temporary release from prison, release on licence, transfer and allocation), category A prisoner issues (approved visitors, categorisation, change of name, marriage, 'supergrass casework', transfer and allocation), artificial insemination, repatriation, transfer to Scotland or Northern Ireland, mother and baby units, allocation of s 53 young offenders, and parole for determinate sentenced prisoners. Although the response is made by staff at Headquarters, the views of staff at the prison will often be sought before any decision is made. Thus, if a life sentence prisoner submits a request to be temporarily released, staff dealing with lifers at that prison will be asked to give their views as to whether the lifer will comply with licence conditions, the reason for the temporary release etc. Therefore although the final decision rests with Headquarters' staff, prison staff will have a large input into the decision-making process.

6.15 Secondly, if the prisoner has asked for a complaint to be submitted to either the governor, chair of the Board of Visitors or the area manager, then the form should be handed in in a sealed envelope marked 'confidential access' and delivered to the relevant person unopened. Confidential access does not mean that the contents of the form will be kept confidential, it merely aims to provide an 'unfettered channel of communication between the prisoner, and the governor, area manager or chair of the Board of Visitors'. Once the form has been delivered, its recipient may decide that they are not the most appropriate person to deal with the complaint and refer it elsewhere for a reply to be made or involve other staff in investigating issues raised in the form. It is therefore important that prisoners who use the confidential access scheme should make out their reasons for doing so on the form and specify why the matter should be kept confidential. Although this will not ensure secrecy, it is hoped that the person in receipt of the form will respect the prisoner's reasons and act with discretion.

6.16   Where the request/complaint form is to be dealt with inside the prison itself, staff are reminded that prisoners may ultimately take judicial review of any adverse decision. Thus replies should be reasoned and 'decisions should not be taken arbitrarily or give the impression that they were taken arbitrarily' (para 3.2.5). If a prisoner's request/complaint is governed by clear rules and regulations, staff are advised that it is good practice to explain these so that the decision is more likely to be respected by the prisoner. It is not enough for a governor simply to say that a previous decision is correct, and an explanation of why this is the case should be provided.

6.17   If, however, an adverse decision is taken as a result of an exercise of discretion, replies to queries should 'avoid being abrupt or adversarial' (para 3.2.11). Instead, staff should focus upon the factors that were taken into account in reaching the decision and why that particular decision was reached.

6.18   Prisoners should generally receive a substantive response to their request/complaints within seven days of submission of a form which is answered at establishment level. If this is not possible because further investigation is needed, then an interim reply should be sent within seven days, and this should explain the reason for the delay.

Role of the Board of Visitors

6.19   Prisoners may apply to see a member of the Board of Visitors at any time, and staff should ensure that the application is referred to the Board without undue delay. Boards of Visitors have a statutory duty to satisfy themselves that prisoners are being treated properly and to hear any requests or complaints that they have.

6.20   The procedures followed by the Board of Visitors will vary from prison to prison. However, in general, a Board member will hear a prisoner's complaint and advise the prisoner as to the best avenue of redress. Some Board members will actively take up prisoners' complaints by pursuing them with a Governor. It is also relatively common for Board members to refer prisoners to outside organisations. Members of Boards of Visitors have no powers to overturn governors' decisions.

6.21   Requests/complaints may be sent to the chair of the Board of Visitors under 'confidential access'. However, although the Board of Visitors are independent of the prison authorities, the Chair may still pass the reply back to Prison Service staff for a response if s/he considers that this is appropriate.

6.22   Boards of Visitors are also given the responsibility of monitoring the operation of the requests/complaints system at their establishments. If they discover that there are problems or delays in providing responses, these should be drawn to the governor's attention.

THE CONSIDERATION OF REQUESTS AND COMPLAINTS AT PRISON SERVICE HEADQUARTERS

6.23   If prisoners are not happy with the answer to a request/complaint which was dealt with in the prison establishment, they have the right to appeal to Prison Service Headquarters. Such appeals are usually dealt with by the office of the area manager for the prison at which the complaint arose, regardless of where the prisoner is located or where the initial request/complaint was lodged. However, reserved subjects will be dealt with by the department with overall responsibility for the issue raised, and complaints which raise substantive policy issues will be dealt with by the department which deals with the relevant policy subject.

Appeals against the governor's decision

6.24   Appeals to the area manager's office are submitted on a blue request/complaint appeal form which is in exactly the same format as the first request/complaint form. The prison will append the original request/complaint form containing the decision being appealed against, and will also give any other information which was relevant to the decision-making process, including information which has not been disclosed to the prisoner.

6.25   In considering appeals, staff in the area manager's support team should familiarise themselves with all of the facts of the case, check the relevant rules and regulations, and consider whether the governor's decision was fair and reasonable, and whether adequate reasons for the decision were given to the prisoner. Consideration should also be given to whether the circumstances of the case would allow an exception to be made to any relevant rules.

6.26   The Staff Manual advises caseworkers that the point of the review is to 'consider whether in the light of all of the available information, there is any reason to think that the decision was other than fair and reasonable'(para 4.1.5). If fault is found with the decision made at the prison then caseworkers draft an reply to the prisoner, and a memo to the governor explaining the reasons for the decision to depart from the prison's decision and asking the governor to take any necessary action. The drafts are approved by the area manager personally before being sent out to the prison.

Reserved subjects

6.27   The following issues cannot be dealt with at establishment level, and any requests and complaints submitted by prisoners will be referred to the relevant department within Prison Service Headquarters or the Home Office.

6.28   Category A prisoners.   Requests/complaints submitted by category A prisoners can be dealt with by the prison unless the prisoner's category A status is relevant to the issues raised in the request/complaint. Queries about their security categorisation, Headquarters' decisions refusing to downgrade them and issues relating to their transfer, allocation and production at court will all need to be considered at Headquarters level rather than at the establishment.

6.29   Life sentence prisoners.   Lifers' requests/complaints will be reserved subjects if they relate to transfer and allocation, temporary release, life sentence reviews, the Parole Board's refusal to recommend their release on life licence, revocation of life licence, delays in their Parole Board reviews, or a request to change their names.

6.30   Parole.   There are two departments dealing with parole at Prison Service Headquarters, and between them they will answer all requests and complaints relating to any aspect of the parole process. There is no formal right of appeal against a Parole Board refusal, and although prisoners may submit requests/complaints this will not lead to their papers being put back in front of the Parole Board unless there have been major changes in the prisoner's circumstances which were not considered when the parole decision was made; there has been procedural impropriety. The Staff Manual states that if a complaint does not raise one of the above factors or is not about delay in the parole process, then the prisoner will simply receive a standard reply saying that there is no right of appeal against the decision.

6.31   Adjudications.   If a prisoner complains about a finding of guilt at adjudication, the area manager's office will conduct a full paper review. The transcript of the adjudication and any other documentation should be forwarded by the prison, and the adjudicator should also provide a memo containing their comments on the issues raised in the prisoner's complaint.

6.32   Deportation.   Prisoners liable to deportation are able to submit requests/complaints relating to this. However, these will be forwarded to the Immigration and Nationality Department rather than within the Prison Service. Prisoners who want to appeal against a decision to deport them or to make representations asking to be given further leave to remain in the UK should seek advice and representation from a solicitor or an organisation specialising in immigration issues such as the Joint Council for the Welfare of Immigrants, UKIAS or the Refugee Legal Council.

6.33   Release on compassionate grounds.   Requests/complaints asking for compassionate release should be dealt with by the Parole Unit at Prison

Service Headquarters. The prison will be asked to give detailed supporting evidence or obtain this from other agencies (eg hospitals, social workers etc). See chapter 12 for further details.

6.34   Meritorious acts.   Prisoners may apply for early release from prison on the basis that they have rendered 'some commendable service to the prison authorities or to the community at large that merits some tangible recognition' (Staff Manual, Annex M para 1). Such applications are made via the request/complaint system and the governor will need to provide supporting evidence. Applications are considered by the area manager's office initially, and a decision is taken as to whether early release should be effected by Royal Prerogative of Mercy or whether additional days awarded at adjudication could be restored with the effect of releasing the prisoner earlier than would otherwise have been the case. The minimum number of days remitted from a sentence is usually seven days.

6.35   Examples of conduct meriting early release from prison and the longest periods of time remitted from their sentences at the time of publication of the Staff Manual are:

(i)   assisting staff in danger of death or injury – eight months;
(ii) supplying information to the prison authorities – 56 days;
(iii) firefighting – 35 days;
(iv) assisting staff in a prison context (eg providing interpretation service, unblocking a sewer) – seven days;
(v) assisting a prisoner in danger of death or injury – 42 days;
(vi) assisting the public – 28 days.

6.36   Allocation of young offenders sentenced under the Children and Young Persons Act 1933.   Such young offenders are centrally managed at Prison Service Headquarters. Governors will be asked to give their views.

6.37   Mother and baby units.   Prisoners' complaints relating only to the refusal to admit them to a mother and baby unit, a decision to separate them from their child, or any aspect of their treatment whilst in a mother and baby unit are dealt with by staff at Prison Service Headquarters

6.38   Artificial insemination.   Applications for artificial insemination are dealt with at Prison Service Headquarters, and will only be granted where there 'are exceptionally strong reasons for doing so' (para 3.4.17). Applications are only considered if the couple are married, but aside from that no set criteria apply and each application is considered on its own merits. Although the Prison Service has refused applications in the past, as far as is known, they have always reversed their decisions where legal action has been initiated.

6.39   Wrongful conviction or sentence.   Requests/complaints about conviction and sentence are dealt with by C3 Division in the Home Office. Prison staff will append full details of conviction and sentence, and disclose whether the prisoner has appealed to the courts.

Confidential access to the area manager

6.40 Requests and complaints sent to the area manager's office under confidential access should not be opened before they leave the prison. When they are received at the area manager's office, they will be read and consideration will be given as to whether they should have been sent under confidential access or not. If the complaint should have been raised at the prison first, the area manager should consider the reasons given by the prisoner for using the confidential access system and decide whether to simply forward the request/complaint form to the prison for a response, or to write to the prisoner advising that the matter is raised in a fresh request/complaint to the governor. In making this decision, the area manager should have regard to the urgency and seriousness of the complaint and whether it would make sense for the matter to be referred directly to the governor (para 4.1.7).

6.41 Allegations against the governor or a senior member of staff at any prison should not be referred back to the establishment and should be dealt with by the area manager's office. Aside from that, most other requests and complaints sent to the area manager's office under confidential access are liable to be referred back to the prison unless they raise reserved subjects, in which case they will be referred to the appropriate department within Prison Service Headquarters.

6.42 Prisoners should receive a response to requests and complaints forms dealt with at Prison Service Headquarters within six weeks of the date of submission. If this is not possible, an interim reply should be sent detailing the reasons for the delay.

THE PRISONS OMBUDSMAN

6.43 The Woolf Report into the disturbances at Strangeways Prison in 1990 recommended that prisoners should be able to take their grievances to a complaints adjudicator who should be independent of the Prison Service. In response, the Home Secretary eventually appointed a Prisons Ombudsman with the remit to provide 'an independent point of appeal for prisoners and young offenders who have failed to obtain satisfaction from the internal requests and complaints system' (IG 69/94, para 2).

6.44 The Ombudsman has no power to investigate complaints which relate to decisions made outside the Prison Service (eg by the police, Immigration and Nationality Department, or by the Parole Board), decisions which are the subject of litigation through the civil courts or subject to criminal proceedings, the clinical judgment of prison doctors, or ministerial decisions about the review and release of life sentence prisoners. Complaints about the Prison Service's administrative role in any of these areas may be investigated by the Ombudsman (eg delay in referring applications to the Parole Board).

6.45 The Ombudsman's remit extends to cover complaints about prison staff who are not directly employed by the Prison Service, including prison

73

probation officers, staff in privately run prisons, prison teachers, and members of Boards of Visitors.

6.46   Before a complaint is eligible for consideration by the Ombudsman, prisoners must first follow the internal requests and complaints procedure by submitting forms to the governor and area manager or other relevant department at Prison Service Headquarters.

6.47   Complaints must be submitted to the Ombudsman's office within one month of the response from Headquarters. If a complaint to Headquarters remains unanswered after six weeks, then it will be eligible for consideration by the Ombudsman at that stage.

6.48   A complaint to the Ombudsman does not have to be made on any specific form, and may be submitted in the form of a letter. The Ombudsman will not consider complaints submitted by anyone other than a prisoner, and this means that solicitors and advisers asked to draft a complaint for a prisoner should do so by writing a letter and asking the prisoner to sign it. A straightforward letter from a solicitor raising a complaint on behalf of a prisoner would not be eligible for consideration.

6.49   Prisoners' letters to the Ombudsman may be sent under confidential access, and although this does not mean that the nature of the complaint will not be disclosed to prison staff (as the Ombudsman may need to discuss the complaint with prison officials in the course of investigating it), it does mean that the letter should not be opened by prison staff before being sent to the Ombudsman's office. Letters sent under confidential access may only be opened at the prison if there are reasonable grounds to suspect that it would be a criminal offence to send it (eg it contains indecent or obscene material) (IG 69/94). Letters to the Ombudsman are sent at public expense. Correspondence from the Ombudsman prisoners should be clearly identified as such on the envelope and marked as confidential. They should not be opened by prison staff unless there is reason to believe that they did not originate from the Ombudsman's office and in such a case, they should be passed to the governor who should check with the Ombudsman's office that an inquiry is ongoing. If there is any remaining doubt, a letter purporting to be from the Ombudsman should only be opened in the presence of the prisoner concerned (IG 69/94, para 13).

6.50   The Prisons Ombudsman has full access to all Prison Service documents, establishments, and individuals whilst conducting an investigation. This includes classified material. The consent of the prisoner is needed if medical records are to be perused by the Ombudsman, and the Ombudsman has agreed not to disclose information to the prisoner who has made a complaint if such disclosure would be 'sensitive'. Prison staff who are in the process of providing information to the Ombudsman must therefore identify matters which should not be disclosed on the grounds that it is 'against the interests of national security, likely to prejudice security measures, likely to put individuals at risk, likely to be detrimental on medical or psychiatric grounds to the mental or physical health of a prisoner, or of classified material or any other information which may be covered by public interest immunity' (IG 69/94, para 15).

6.51   Staff from the Prison Ombudsman's office may visit any prison establishment in the course of an investigation and may interview prison staff (who can take a colleague or trade union representative with them) or prisoners who consent to an interview. Visits with prisoners should be in the sight but out of the hearing of prison staff, and do not count against a prisoner's allowance of visiting orders.

6.52   The Ombudsman's office aims to complete investigations within eight weeks of receiving the complaint. A detailed report gives the facts of the complaint, and the investigation is prepared. If the prisoner's complaint is upheld then the Ombudsman will send a copy of his report to the Director General of the Prison Service or the Home Secretary making recommendations as to the remedy that should be offered to the prisoner. The Prison Service should reply within six weeks either accepting or refusing the recommendation.

6.53   The Ombudsman published a 'Six Month Review' of the complaints investigated between October 1994 and April 1995, and this showed that 253 complaints were accepted for investigation. Of the investigations completed before publication of the report, 51% upheld the prisoner's complaint, and 49% rejected it. The Prison Service accepted 82% of the recommendations, partially accepted a further 3% and rejected 15%.

6.54   If the Prison Service rejects a recommendation, then the Ombudsman's office may enter into further correspondence with the Prison Service. However, ultimately, the prisoner would be best advised to seek legal representation with a view to pursuing the matter through the courts.

CHAPTER 7

PRISON DISCIPLINE

THE FORMAL DISCIPLINARY SYSTEM

Offences against prison discipline

7.1　The power to discipline prisoners for misconduct whilst they are in prison is contained in the Prison Act 1952, s 47. This provides for rules to be made for the discipline and control of prisoners, and gives prisoners the right to have a proper opportunity to present their case if charged with an offence. An offence against prison discipline may be treated as having been committed in the prison at which the prisoner is held (Criminal Justice Act 1961, s 23(1)), and thus a prisoner who commits an offence at one establishment may be charged and adjudicated upon at another prison. Unless a contrary indication is made, all references in this section relate to paragraphs of the 1995 edition of the Discipline Manual.

7.2　The list of offences against prison discipline with which a prisoner may be charged are contained in r 47 of the Prison Rules 1964 (as amended), the full text of which follows:

'47.　A prisoner is guilty of an offence against discipline if he
(1)　commits any assault;
(2)　detains any person against his will;
(3)　denies access to any part of the prison to any officer or any person (other than a prisoner) who is in the prison for the purpose of working there;
(4)　fights with any person;
(5)　intentionally endangers the health or personal safety of others or, by his conduct is reckless whether such health or personal safety is endangered;
(6)　intentionally obstructs an officer in the execution of his duty, or any person (other than a prisoner)who is at the prison for the purpose of working there, in the performance of his work;
(7)　escapes or absconds from prison or from legal custody;
(8)　fails to comply with any condition upon which he is temporarily released under Rule 6 of these Rules;
(8A)　administers a controlled drug to himself or fails to prevent the administration of a controlled drug to him by another person (but subject to Rule 47A below);
(9)　has in his possession

(a) any unauthorised article, or
(b) a greater quantity of any article than he is authorised to have;
(10) sells or delivers to any person any unauthorised article;
(11) sells or, without permission, delivers to any person any article which he is allowed to have only for his own use;
(12) takes improperly any article belonging to another person or to a prison;
(13) intentionally or recklessly sets fire to any part of a prison or any other property, whether or not his own;
(14) destroys or damages any part of a prison or any other property, other than his own;
(15) absents himself from any place he is required to be or is present at any place where he is not authorised to be;
(16) is disrespectful to any officer, or any person (other than a prisoner) who is at the prison for the purpose of working there, or any person visiting a prison;
(17) uses threatening, abusive or insulting words or behaviour;
(18) intentionally fails to work properly or, being required to work, refuses to do so;
(19) disobeys any lawful order;
(20) disobeys or fails to comply with any rule or regulation applying to him;
(21) in any way offends against good order and discipline;
(22) (a) attempts to commit,
(b) incites another prisoner to commit, or
(c) assists another prisoner to commit or to attempt to commit, any of the forgoing offences.'

Charging

7.3 Prisoners are generally charged with a disciplinary offence by any officer who witnessed the breach of the Rules. Alternatively the charge can be laid by an officer who discovers that the offence has been committed. Rule 48 of the Prison Rules requires that a prisoner should be charged as soon as possible, and at the latest within 48 hours of the offence being discovered. If the charge is not laid within 48 hours then a finding of guilt at adjudication will be void unless there are 'exceptional circumstances'. A charge is laid when a form F1127 (Notice of Report) is handed to the prisoner. Form F127 contains details of the time, date and place of commission of the offence, the paragraph of r 47 under which the prisoner has been charged, details of the allegations made against the prisoner, and the time of the hearing. The charge must be laid out in sufficient detail for the prisoner to have a full understanding of the allegation made (para 2.11). Prisoners are advised that they may write out their defence to the charge on the back of the form, and state whether they wish to call any witnesses. At the same time as being handed the F1127, prisoners may also be given an information sheet, F1145 Explanation of Procedures at Disciplinary Charge Hearings which provides a brief explanation of the stages that the adjudication will follow. Prisoners should be allowed time to prepare their defence, and thus they must be charged at least two hours before the adjudication takes place.

7.4 A charge cannot be reduced during the adjudication, and therefore if it is not clear which of two charges a prisoner may be guilty of, staff are advised to lay two separate charges, one or both of which may be dropped at adjudication if it transpires that there is not enough evidence against the prisoner to support it (para 2.6).

7.5   Although prisoners can be charged with several separate offences which arise from the same incident (eg a prisoner who breaks a window whilst fighting with another prisoner could be charged under para (4) for fighting and under para (14) for damaging prison property), they cannot be charged twice for what is essentially the same offence. Thus a prisoner who breaks a window whilst fighting with another prisoner may be charged under r 47(4) for fighting, and r 47(14) for damaging prison property, but a prisoner who refuses to go to work cannot be charged under r 47(18) for refusing to work, and r 47(19) for disobeying an officer's order that he should go to work. Prisoners may not be charged with continuing offences, and therefore a prisoner who refuses an order to clean the toilets and is charged with that offence may not be charged again if he refuses the same order a couple of hours later (para 2.12).

7.6   If, in the course of an adjudication, the adjudicator considers that a prisoner is not guilty of the offence with which he has been charged, but may be guilty of a different offence, the original charge may be dropped and a new charge laid so long as this is still within 48 hours of the discovery of the alleged offence. In this case, the proceedings must be started afresh and a different governor should hear the newly laid charge (para 2.5).

7.7   Before the adjudication a prisoner should be examined by the medical officer who is asked to certify whether s/he is fit enough to attend the adjudication and to undergo cellular confinement, and to inform the adjudicator of anything in the prisoner's physical or mental health which may be relevant to the adjudication process. Such an examination is a requirement under the Prison Rules, r 53(2) and the adjudication should not go ahead unless the examination has taken place.

7.8   In order to adequately prepare their defence, prisoners are allowed to request copies of any statements that will be used in evidence against them, and they should not be charged any photocopying fees. Prisoners should also be afforded the facilities in which to interview any witnesses who may be able to give evidence at the hearing, although whether such interviews take place within or out of the hearing of prison staff is at the discretion of the governor. However, if witnesses are only to be interviewed in the presence of staff, the supervising officer should be someone who is unconnected with the hearing.

Legal representation

7.9   Prisoners who are charged with an offence against prison discipline should be allowed to consult a solicitor if they so wish. Adjudicators are advised to adjourn the proceedings if a prisoner has not had enough time to contact a solicitor between the charge being laid and the adjudication starting.

7.10 At the beginning of an adjudication, the adjudicator should ask the prisoner if s/he requires any assistance in putting forward a defence. This could be either a solicitor or a McKenzie friend. A McKenzie friend only has a limited role in the proceedings, and may attend the hearing, take notes, and offer advice and support to the prisoner (para 3.4). Prisoners may choose their own McKenzie friend, but the adjudicator can remove the McKenzie friend from the hearing if it is considered that s/he is interfering with the proceedings or participating without the adjudicator's permission.

7.11 The adjudicator has discretion as to whether to allow a solicitor to represent, or a McKenzie friend to attend the hearing. In considering whether to grant a request for assistance the adjudicator should comply with the judgment in *R v Secretary of State for the Home Department, ex p Tarrant* ([1984] 1 All ER 799). This held that there was no right for a prisoner to be legally represented at an adjudication, but that in deciding whether a request for representation should be granted, the adjudicator should have regard to the following factors:

(i)   the seriousness of the charge and the potential penalty;
(ii) whether any points of law are likely to arise;
(iii) the capacity of the prisoner to present his own case;
(iv) whether or not there are likely to be any procedural difficulties;
(v)   the need for reasonable speed in hearing the charge;
(vi) the need for fairness as between prisoners and between prisoners and prison staff.

7.12 If legal representation is granted then the hearing will be adjourned for the prisoner either to instruct a solicitor or find a McKenzie friend. If the request is denied, then the request will be noted on the record of the proceedings together with the reasons for refusal. The adjudication will then go ahead.

7.13 Where, in the course of explaining why they need legal representation, the prisoner incriminates himself by disclosing something which would make it impossible for the adjudicator to be unprejudiced in hearing the charge, the adjudication should be adjourned and heard by another adjudicator at a later date.

7.14 If legal representation is granted for the prisoner, then the Prison Service will also instruct solicitors to act for them. A solicitor acting for a prisoner may ask for access to the prison or to prison staff prior to the hearing in order to interview potential witnesses or to look at the place where the incident took place. Such requests should be dealt with by a member of prison staff who is not involved in the adjudication process.

7.15 Solicitors may advise prisoners about their adjudications under the Green Form scheme, and may claim for preparation. However, where a prisoner is in a contracted out prison, the Legal Aid Regulations allow their solicitors to claim for representation under the ABWOR scheme.

An in-depth look at the charges

7.16   The Prison Discipline Manual contains detailed guidance to adjudicators on the elements of each charge under r 47. In order to find a prisoner guilty of a charge, the governor must be satisfied beyond reasonable doubt that the prisoner is guilty, regardless of how the prisoner has pleaded (para 7.1).

7.17   (1) Commits any assault.   A prisoner is guilty of assault if s/he intentionally or recklessly applies unlawful force to another person, or causes another person to fear the immediate application of unlawful force (although adjudicators are advised that a charge under para 17 is preferable in this instance). In order to find a prisoner guilty of assault, the adjudicator must be satisfied that:

(i)   the prisoner applied force to another or committed an act which put the other person in fear of immediate application of force;
(ii)   the prisoner intended to do so or was reckless as to whether this would happen;
(iii) the force was unlawful, ie was not applied in self-defence or in order to prevent the commission of a serious crime (paras 6.3–6.5).

7.18   (2) Detains any person against his will.   This relates to situations where a prisoner takes a hostage. Adjudicators are advised to consider whether the hostage and the hostage taker were acting together, and if so to consider whether a charge may more appropriately be brought under para (3) (if staff have been denied access to part of the prison where the incident took place).

7.19   In order to find a prisoner guilty of this offence, the adjudicator must be satisfied that:

(i)   the hostage's freedom of movement was inhibited by force or by the threat of force;
(ii)   the hostage was detained against their will. If the accused can show that the victim collaborated, then this will be a complete defence, although the adjudicator should establish whether the incident started out as a joint venture, and then turned into a situation whereby the victim was prevented from withdrawing against their will. In such circumstances a prisoner may be found guilty;
(iii) the prisoner intended the victim to be detained against their will, or was reckless as to whether this would happen (paras 6.6–6.8).

7.20   (3) Denies access to any part of the prison to any officer or any person (other than a prisoner) who is at the prison for the purpose of working there.   Prisoners who erect barricades or deny access to a part of the prison are liable to be found guilty of this offence. In order to find a prisoner guilty, the adjudicator must be satisfied that the following elements of the charge are present:

(i)   someone working at the prison was denied access to any part of it;

(ii) the prisoner intended that this should be so, or was reckless as to whether it would happen (paras 6.9–6.11).

7.21   (4) Fights with any person.   In order to find a prisoner guilty under this paragraph, the adjudicator must be satisfied that:

(i)   the prisoner intentionally committed an assault by inflicting unlawful force on another prisoner in the context of a fight;
(ii) the fight must involve at least one other person and constitute more than one blow. It should have continued for 'a sufficient time to amount to a fight in the ordinary sense of the word'.
(iii) self defence is a complete defence, and so where two prisoners are charged with fighting each other, one may be found guilty of fighting and the other found not guilty on the basis of self defence (paras 6.12–6.13).

7.22   (5) Intentionally endangers the health or personal safety of others, or, by his conduct, is reckless as to whether such health or personal safety is endangered.   The elements of this charge are that:

(i)   there was a 'definite and serious' risk of harm to the safety of at least one person other than the prisoner;
(ii) this danger was caused by the prisoner's behaviour;
(iii) the prisoner intended to cause the danger, or was reckless as to whether it would occur.

7.23   (6) Intentionally obstructs an officer in the execution of his duty, or any person (other than a prisoner) who is at the prison for the purpose of working there, in the performance of his work.   This charge covers both physical obstruction of an officer and situations whereby a prisoner might provide false information to an officer. The elements of the charge are as follows:

(i)   there was some sort of obstruction;
(ii) the person who was obstructed was working at the prison, and was attempting to perform his or her work;
(iii) the prisoner intended that the person should be obstructed (paras 6.17– 6.19).

7.24   (7) Escapes or absconds from prison or from legal custody.   This charge is aimed at prisoners who actually get away from the prison and are not caught as they are attempting to escape or abscond. An adjudicator may only be satisfied to the guilt of a prisoner when the following elements of the charge are made out:

(i)   the prisoner was held in legal custody, including on escort to or from a prison or whilst working outside the prison;
(ii) the prisoner escaped or absconded;
(iii) the prisoner had no authority to do so;
(iv) the prisoner intended to escape or abscond (ie s/he knew that s/he was leaving lawful custody without authority);
(v)   it is a complete defence for the prisoner to plead that s/he believed that s/he had authority to leave (paras 6.20–6.22).

7.25 (8) Fails to comply with any condition upon which he is temporarily released under r 6 of these Rules. When a prisoner is temporarily released they will be issued with a licence which lists the conditions which should be complied with. An offence under this paragraph could range from failing to return to prison on time to drinking alcohol whilst temporarily released.

7.26 Many prisoners who fail to return to prison on time use the defence that they were too ill to travel and licences should include a statement which should be signed by a doctor if the prisoner is unfit to return. If this statement is signed by a doctor then the prisoner has a complete defence to the charge. If the prisoner produces any other medical evidence, the adjudicator should consider whether or not this amounts to certification that the prisoner was unable to travel back to the prison on time.

7.27 For a finding of guilt to be made, the adjudicator must be satisfied of the following:

(i) the prisoner was released on a temporary release licence containing clear conditions of which the prisoner was aware. The licence was signed by a governor with authority to do so;
(ii) the prisoner intentionally or recklessly did not comply with one or more of the conditions;
(iii) there was no justification for the prisoner's failure to comply with the condition(s).

7.28 A prisoner who did not return on time will have a defence to the charge if they can show that they were genuinely unable to get back to the prison because of circumstances beyond their control. Prisoners who are charged with a criminal offence committed on temporary release may be charged with an offence against prison discipline if they have also breached their licence conditions.

7.29 The Prisoners (Return to Custody) Act 1995 makes it a criminal offence to be unlawfully at large without reasonable excuse following a period of temporary release on licence, or whilst knowing or believing that an order has been made for their recall to prison and failing to take all necessary steps to comply with it as soon as is reasonably practicable without reasonable excuse. Prisoners convicted of this criminal offence may be sentenced by a magistrates' court to up to six months' imprisonment and/or a fine not exceeding level 5 on the standard scale (see chapter 8 for further details).

7.30 (8A) Administers a controlled drug to himself or fails to prevent the administration of a controlled drug to him by another person (but subject to r 47A/50A). This is a recent addition to the Prison Rules, and came into effect in 1995. Prisoners may be required to give a urine sample that will be tested to check for the presence of controlled drugs (Prison Act 1952, s 16A as amended by the Criminal Justice and Public Order Act 1994, s 151). Samples of sweat and non pubic hair may also be requested for this purpose, however samples of blood and semen may not.

7.31 All categories of prisoner are liable to be tested for drugs, and will be selected on a random basis, although if officers have a reasonable suspicion that a particular prisoner is involved in misusing drugs, that person may be tested more frequently than others ('The Introduction of a Mandatory Drug Testing Programme for Prisoners in England and Wales: a guide to the main issues', IG 15/95, paras 7–8).

7.32   Governors may make their own provisions for the collection of urine samples within their establishments, although the following provisions should be a common feature in establishments:

(i)   prisoners will not be given prior warning that they will be required to give a sample;
(ii) prisoners should be given precise instructions, asked to remove bulky outer clothing, and be searched thoroughly;
(iii) prisoners will be given 'as much privacy as is consistent with the need to prevent adulteration or substitution of false samples . . . a greater invasion of privacy may be necessary of those individual prisoners caught cheating'
(iv) samples will be divided, and one half will be kept in case of appeal. Samples will be sealed and the seals signed by the prisoner (IG 15/95, para 17).

7.33   Prisoners who refuse to provide a sample can be charged under r 47(19) of the Prison Rules for disobeying a lawful order, and where prisoners cannot provide a sample they may be segregated for up to five hours and provided with controlled amounts of water (r 46A(7)).

7.34   If the prisoner tests positive then so long as the sample was taken under the provision of r 46A, the prisoner may be charged with an offence under r 47(8A). Rule 47A provides statutory defences and these are:

(i)   that the controlled drug was lawfully in the prisoner's possession for their own use;
(ii) that the controlled drug was administered in the lawful supply of the drug by another person;
(iii) that there was no reason for the prisoner to know or suspect that the controlled drug was being administered;
(iv) that the drug was administered under duress or without consent in circumstances where it was unreasonable to resist.

7.35   **(9) Has in his possession (a) any unauthorised article, or (b) a greater quantity of any article than he is authorised to have.**   Paragraph (a) of this charge covers situations where the prisoner had something in possession which is unauthorised (eg drugs, firearms) or an article which is authorised in itself but is not authorised in this instance (eg because it was issued to another prisoner). Paragraph (b) aims to deal with prisoners who have more of an article in their possession than they are allowed to have (eg tobacco and telephone cards).

7.36   Before a prisoner can be found guilty under this paragraph, they should be satisfied that the following three elements of the charge have been made out:

(i)   Presence – that the article exists, that it is what it is alleged to be, and that it was found where alleged.
(ii) Knowledge – that the prisoner knows what the article is, and knew that it was present.
(iii) Control – that the accused had either sole or joint control over the article (para 6.32). (See also *R v Deputy Governor of Camphill Prison, ex p King* [1984] 3 All ER 897).

7.37   Thus, if two prisoners are sharing a cell and one has a tin containing cocaine, the other should not be convicted if he believed it was milk powder, or if he knew the substance was cocaine but exercised no control over it.

7.38   In respect of charges under both (a) and (b) above, the governor must be satisfied that the prisoner was aware that an article was unauthorised or was restricted in terms of quantity allowed in possession. A genuine belief that the article was allowed or that there were no restrictions on quantity will be a defence (para 6.33).

7.39   **(10) Sells or delivers to any person any unauthorised article.**   This charge covers articles which are unauthorised in themselves or are not authorised to a particular prisoner. Before finding a prisoner guilty the adjudicator must be satisfied that the following are established:

(i)   the article was sold or delivered by the accused to another person (who does not have to be a prisoner);
(ii) the article was not authorised;
(iii) the prisoner intended to sell or deliver the article or was reckless as to whether they were selling or delivering it. It would be a defence for the prisoner to plead that they believed they were authorised to pass on the article in that way.

7.40   **(11) Sells, or without permission, delivers to any person any article which he is allowed to have only for his own use.**   In finding a prisoner guilty, the adjudicator does not have to establish whether the article was sold or delivered, however the following elements of the charge must be made out:

(i)   the article was sold or delivered to someone;
(ii) it was authorised only for the prisoner's own use;
(iii) the prisoner did not have permission to pass the article to someone else.

7.41   **(12) Takes improperly any article belonging to another person or to a prison (or young offender institution).**   This is essentially theft, and in order for a prisoner to be found guilty at adjudication, the adjudicator must be satisfied of the presence of the following elements of the charge:

(i)   there was an article which belonged to another person or to a prison;
(ii) the prisoner took physical control of the article without permission;
(iii) the prisoner intended to take the article without permission, or was reckless as to whether s/he did so (6.43).

7.42   It is a defence for the prisoner to plead that they thought that they had permission to take the article or that they believed that it belonged to them (para 6.43(e)).

7.43 **(13) Intentionally or recklessly sets fire to any part of a prison (or young offender institution) or any other property whether or not his own.** In order to be satisfied of the guilt of a prisoner charged with this offence, the adjudicator should establish the following:

(i) the prisoner set fire to part of the prison or some other property of a tangible nature;
(ii) the prisoner acted with intent or was reckless as to whether they set fire to the property.

7.44 **(14) Destroys or damages any part of a prison (or young offender institution) or any other property, other than his own.** This is similar to the charge of criminal damage in criminal law. It is not sufficient to show merely that the prisoner was in possession of a damaged article, and before a finding of guilt can be made, the adjudicator must be satisfied that:

(i) part of a prison or some other property of a tangible nature was damaged;
(ii) the property belonged to someone other than the prisoner;
(iii) there was no lawful excuse for the damage to the property;
(iv) the prisoner intended that the property should be destroyed or damaged or was reckless as to whether this should occur.

7.45 It is a defence for the prisoner to plead that they thought that the property belonged to them.

7.46 **(15) Absents himself from any place where he is required to be or is present at any place where he is not authorised to be.** This charge can apply to situations which occur both inside or outside a prison. For example if a prisoner leaves an open prison to go and meet someone in the locality but has every intention of returning to the prison, then this would be appropriate rather than a charge of absconding. Likewise, if a prisoner in a closed prison leaves the workshop and decides to go to the gym, they could be charged under this paragraph.

7.47 For a finding of guilt to be made, the adjudicator must be satisfied that the following elements of the offence are made out:

(i) the prisoner was required to be in a particular place or did not have permission to be in the place that they were found;
(ii) the prisoner was in fact absent from the place where they were required to be or was in fact present at the place that they did not have permission to be in;
(iii) the prisoner was not able to justify their actions;
(iv) the prisoner intended to commit the offence or was reckless as to whether it was committed.

7.48 A prisoner who pleads a genuine belief that they had permission to be somewhere, or was not required to be in a particular place will have a defence (paras 6.49–6.51).

7.49 **(16) It is disrespectful to any officer, or any person (other than a**

prisoner) who is at the prison for the purpose of working there, or any other person visiting a prison. For the purposes of this charge, disrespect can be shown by both verbal and physical behaviour. To be satisfied that the prisoner is guilty of the offence the adjudicator should ensure that the following elements are present:

(i) there was an act which was directed towards a specific person or group of people;
(ii) the act was disrespectful in the ordinary meaning of the word and in the particular circumstances;
(iii) the person at which the act was aimed was either an officer, visitor to the prison, or a person working at the prison;
(iv) the prisoner intended to be disrespectful or was reckless as to whether they were being so.

7.50 If a prisoner pleads a genuine belief that they did not consider the act to be disrespectful, this would be a defence (paras 6.52–6.54).

7.51 (**17**) **Uses threatening, abusive or insulting words or behaviour.** An adjudicator hearing a charge under this paragraph should be satisfied that the following elements are present before finding a prisoner guilty:

(i) the prisoner did a specific act, adopted a general pattern of behaviour or said specific words;
(ii) the above conduct was either threatening, abusive or insulting (in the ordinary senses of these words) rather than annoying or rude;
(iii) the prisoner intended to be threatening abusive or insulting or was reckless as to whether s/he was so (paras 6.55–6.57).

7.52 (**18**) **Intentionally fails to work properly or, being required to work, refuses to do so.** In laying a charge under this paragraph, an officer must specify which of the two separate offences it is alleged that the prisoner has committed. Where a prisoner is charged with intentionally failing to work properly, a finding of guilt can only be made if the adjudicator is satisfied that:

(i) the prisoner was lawfully required to work at the time and in the circumstances specified;
(ii) the prisoner failed to work properly (this is measured against a standard of work expected);
(iii) the prisoner intended not to work properly or was reckless as to whether they were doing so.

7.53 Thus, to be found guilty a prisoner must know that his work was not or may not be up to the required standard. A prisoner who pleads that s/he thought that s/he was working hard enough would have a defence to the charge (paras 6.59–6.60).

7.54 Where a prisoner is charged with refusing to work, the adjudicator must establish that the following elements of the offence are made out before making a finding of guilt:

(i) the prisoner was lawfully required to work at the time and in the circumstances specified;

(ii) the prisoner refused to work, either by act or omission;

(iii) the prisoner intended to refuse to work or was reckless as to whether they were doing so.

7.55 In order to find a prisoner guilty the adjudicator must be satisfied that the prisoner knew that s/he was required to work or been aware that s/he may have been so required. If the prisoner genuinely believes that they did not have to work then they would have a defence. Prisoners charged with this offence often say that they were medically unfit to work, and in such circumstances the adjudicator should investigate the assertion and seek evidence as to the prisoner's state of health (paras 6.61–6.62).

7.54 (19) Disobeys any lawful order. A lawful order is defined as 'one which a member of staff has authority to give in the execution of his or her duties' (para 6.65). When hearing a charge under this paragraph the adjudicator must ensure that the following are established before finding the prisoner guilty:

(i) the action of the member of staff was an order. An order is 'a clear indication by word and/or action given in the course of his or her duties by a member of staff requiring a specific prisoner to do or refrain from doing something'(para 6.66(a));

(ii) the order was lawful;

(iii) the prisoner did not obey the order within a reasonable period of time;

(iv) the prisoner intended not to comply with the order or was reckless as to whether it was complied with.

7.57 In defence, a prisoner may plead that they did not understand what was being asked of them (paras 6.64–6.66).

7.58 (20) Disobeys or fails to comply with any rule or regulation applying to him. Many prisons have local rules which are not contained in the Prison Rules, and this charge aims to discipline prisoners who are alleged to have acted in breach of such rules.

7.59 Before a prisoner can be found guilty of this offence, the adjudicator must be satisfied that the following are established:

(i) the rule/regulation applied to the prisoner who must have been aware of its existence, or reasonable steps must have been taken to draw it to their attention;

(ii) the rule or regulation was lawful in respect of the particular prisoner concerned;

(iii) the prisoner did not obey the rule/regulation, either intentionally or recklessly (6.67–6.69).

7.60 (21) In any way offends against good order and discipline. This charge is designed to catch any perceived acts of indiscipline where they cannot be tried under any of the above paragraphs. It should not be used if any of the other charges are applicable, and adjudicators should not find a prisoner guilty of offending against good order and discipline if there is not enough evidence to find them guilty of another offence. When trying a prisoner under this paragraph the adjudicator must establish how the prisoner has offended against good order and discipline, and whether they did so intentionally or recklessly (para 6.71).

7.61   Despite this guidance, a recent report published by the Prison Reform Trust ('Anything Goes . . .' by Nancy Loucks) found that of 1,707 charges placed under r 47(21), 97.5% should have been laid under another paragraph of r 47.

7.62   **(22) (a) Attempts to commit, (b) incites other prisoners to commit, or (c) assists another prisoner to commit or attempt to commit any of the forgoing offences.**   This charge must specify whether (a), (b) or (c) above is relevant and must also specify the relevant paragraph of r 47.

7.63   Where a prisoner is charged with an attempt, the adjudicator should be satisfied of the following:
(i)   the prisoner did an act which was more than merely preparatory to the commission of the offence;
(ii) the prisoner intended to commit the full offence (paras 6.73–6.74).

7.64   Incitement is defined as 'seeking to persuade another prisoner to commit a disciplinary offence' (para 6.76(b)).   If the charge is one of inciting, the following elements should be made out before the prisoner is found guilty:
(i)   the prisoner's action was communicated to other prisoners who were near enough to be able to respond to the incitement;
(ii) the act was capable of inciting other prisoners to commit the full offence;
(iii) the full offence was the consequence or the subject of the incitement;
(iv) the prisoner intended or was reckless as to whether they incited other prisoners to commit the offence (paras 6.75–6.76).

7.65   If a prisoner is charged with assisting the commission of an offence, the adjudicator must make out the following elements:

(i)   another prisoner committed an offence (including an attempt);
(ii) the prisoner on the current charge actively assisted in the commission of the offence and intended to do so (para 6.78).

7.66   Being aware that the offence being committed is not sufficient for a finding of guilt. In *R v Board of Visitors of Highpoint Prison, ex p McConkey* ((1982) Times, 23 September) the Divisional Court held that a prisoner's presence whilst knowing that an offence was being committed by other prisoners is not an offence against prison discipline.

The conduct of adjudications

7.67   Section 10 of the Discipline Manual describes a model procedure for the conduct of an adjudication. The main points of this are as follows.

7.68   Proceedings must always start afresh without reference to any previous hearings of the same charge. This enables the adjudicator to determine the case only on the evidence presented at the hearing (para 10.1).

7.69   At the start of the hearing, the adjudicator should not have access to the prisoner's prison record or record of previous findings of guilt at adjudication (para 10.2).

7.70   The adjudicator should check:

(i)   that the charge has been laid properly;
(ii) that the preliminary parts of the Record of Hearing and Adjudication Form (F256) have been completed with the same information as that contained in the charge sheets;
(iii) that each charge is outlined in enough detail for the prisoner to know its 'precise nature';
(iv) that the Explanation of the Procedure at a hearing of a Disciplinary Charge by a Governor Form was given to the prisoner in sufficient time for him/her to read and understand it. This is normally deemed to be at least two hours before the hearing;
(v)   that the medical officer has certified that the prisoner is fit to appear on adjudication, and is fit to be subjected to the punishment of cellular confinement, and that any further report made by the medical officer is available to the adjudicator (para 10.4).

7.71   At the beginning of the adjudication, the adjudicator must:

(i)   identify the prisoner;
(ii)   check that the prisoner has received the charge sheet, the explanatory information, and that they understand the procedure;
(iii) read out the charge;
(vi)   check that the prisoner understands the charge;
(v)   ask the prisoner if they have had time to prepare their defence and whether they have made a written answer;
(vi)   ask the prisoner whether they wish to apply for legal representation;
(vii) ask the prisoner if they are pleading guilty or not guilty to the charge. If the prisoner pleads guilty the adjudicator should still hear evidence so as to be sure that the prisoner fully understands the charge against them. If the adjudicator believes that the prisoner is pleading guilty as a result of misunderstanding the charge, then the prisoner should be advised to change their plea to not guilty. Whether or not the prisoner consents to this, an adjudicator may proceed on the basis of a not guilty plea and dismiss the charge;
(viii) ask the prisoner if they want to call any witnesses (para 10.7).

7.72   If the adjudicator believes that the prisoner needs more time to prepare a defence, or to prepare a request for legal representation or needs more information about the charge or the procedure, then the adjudication should be adjourned (para 10.9).

7.73   In investigating the charge, the adjudicator should first hear the evidence of the reporting officer and then ask the prisoner if they wish to cross-examine the officer. The adjudicator may also ask further questions (para 10.12). The prisoner should be asked whether they have any defence to the charge, or if they want to give any explanation or evidence (para 10.14).

7.74   Where the prisoner wants to call witnesses, the adjudicator may ask what their evidence will show. Unless it is considered that their evidence is irrelevant, the witnesses named should be called. If the adjudicator refuses to allow the witnesses to be called, then s/he must note the reason for refusal on the written record of the adjudication. The prisoner must be told the reason and allowed to comment upon it. Where witnesses are produced, they should be invited to say all that they know of the incident. The adjudicator, prisoner and the reporting officer will be allowed to cross examine them (paras 10.15–10.20).

7.75   When all of the evidence has been heard, the adjudicator should ask the prisoner whether they wish to say anything further before considering the question of guilt. The adjudicator should only find the prisoner guilty if satisfied that all of the essential elements of the charge are present (see above) (para 10.22). The adjudicator may not reduce or change the charge during the hearing, and thus if it is thought that the prisoner is guilty of a lesser charge the current charge must be dismissed and a new one laid so long as it is still within 48 hours of the discovery of the alleged offence. Any new hearing should be before a different adjudicator (para 10.23).

7.76   The adjudicator must announce whether the prisoner has been found guilty or not guilty, and record the finding on the written record. A prisoner who is found guilty of a charge should be asked whether they want to put forward any mitigating evidence, and may also call witnesses in support of the mitigation (paras 10.24–10.25).

7.77   Before the adjudicator decides on an appropriate punishment, an officer will be called to give a report as to the prisoner's custodial behaviour, including previous findings of guilt at adjudication. The prisoner should be given an opportunity to question the officer on the information contained in the conduct report (paras 10.24–10.26). Unless the adjudicator decides to adjourn the hearing to consider the matter of the punishment to be awarded, the prisoner should be told what the punishment is to be, if the prisoner has been found guilty of more than one offence whether the punishments are to be consecutive or concurrent, and if a suspended punishment imposed at a previous hearing is to be activated the adjudicator must inform the prisoner of this and explain it (paras 10.27–10.29).

Punishments

7.78   An adjudicator may only award those punishments that are listed in the Prison Rules 1964, rr 50, 52, and 54 or the Young Offender Institution Rules 1988, r 53 and 60. Punishments should take into account the circumstances and seriousness of the offence; the previous custodial behaviour of the prisoner; the type of prison establishment in which the offence took place; the prisoner's circumstances; whether the commission of the offence had any effect upon the regime; order and discipline within the prison; and the need to have a deterrent effect on the offender and other prisoners (Discipline Manual, para 7.6).

7.79 The Prison Service does not provide any central guidance to adjudicators on the appropriate punishments for particular offences. However, punishments handed down within any establishment should be consistent and to achieve this governors may set up a local tariff system. Adjudicators should be able to consult a list of recent offences and punishments awarded so that the chance of significant variation is diminished (para 7.7).

7.80 An adjudicator can suspend punishments for up to six months (para 7.33) or impose them to run concurrently to other punishments imposed at the same time. Suspended punishments may be ignored, activated in full, activated in part (in which case the remainder will lapse), or change the suspension period by suspending the punishment for a further six months from the date of the current adjudication if the prisoner commits another breach of prison discipline within the original period of suspension (paras 7.33–7.34).

7.81 Otherwise, all punishments other than the award of additional days of imprisonment to be served will take effect immediately they are handed down (paras 7.11–7.12). Pregnant women should not normally be given punishments whereby they will be segregated, and if an adjudicator thinks that someone is unfit to be punished, then no punishment should be imposed (paras 7.10 and 7.13).

7.82 The punishments contained in the Prison and Young Offender Institution Rules are listed below together with a brief explanation of what they entail:

(i) Caution – a warning not to repeat the offending behaviour.
(ii) Forfeiture of facilities – the withdrawal of facilities listed in Standing Order 4 for up to 42 days for adult prisoners and up to 21 days for young offenders.
(iii) Exclusion from associated work or activities – this punishment is usually served on normal location in the prison and is for a maximum of 21 days for adult prisoners. The equivalent punishment for young offenders is that they may be excluded from any activity taking place in the YOI other than training courses, work, education or physical education.
(iv) Stoppage of earnings – all or part of a prisoner's pay may be stopped for up to the equivalent of 42 days full pay for adults or 21 days for young offenders. This punishment may be spread over 84 days and 42 days respectively.
(v) Cellular confinement – may be imposed for up to 14 days for adult prisoners and seven days for young offenders so long as the medical officer certifies that the prisoner is fit to undergo this punishment. Cells should be set aside in which prisoners serving a period of cellular confinement are located. These should contain a bed, bedding, table, chair and access to sanitary facilities. The bedding and mattress may be taken from the cell during the daytime for up to the first three days of the punishment if the adjudicator so specifies at adjudication. Otherwise, prisoners should be allowed all facilities other than those which are 'incompatible with cellular confinement' such as use of the canteen, use of private cash, and association with other prisoners (para 7.22). Prisoners who are serving periods in cellular confinement should be checked on

by an officer at least once every hour, and visited every day by the chaplain and the medical officer (para 7.24). Prisoners should be allowed to receive visits and have access to the telephone unless their 'behaviour and attitude made removal from cellular confinement impracticable or undesirable'(para 7.23). In practice it is rare for prisoners to be refused visits, and any visitor turned away from an establishment should make enquiries of the governor as to the reasons for the refusal and contact a legal adviser if they are worried.

(vi)   Additional days – adult prisoners may be awarded up to 42 additional days of imprisonment in respect of any one offence (or offences arising from a single incident) if they are serving a determinate sentence. Lifers cannot be given additional days as a punishment. Additional days affect the prisoner's sentence by pushing back the parole eligibility date of prisoners sentenced before 1 October 1992 and the non-parole release date of prisoners serving sentences of four years and over. Remand and unsentenced prisoners may be given the prospective punishment of additional days and this will only take effect if they are sentenced to a period of imprisonment.

(vii)   Extra work – is only available as a punishment for young offenders, who may be required to work for up to two extra hours a day for up to 21 days.

(viii) Removal from a wing or living unit – may only be used to punish young offenders for up to 21 days. Young offenders undergoing this punishment will be held in a cell or a room away from their normal wing but will otherwise be able to participate in the full regime of the YOI.

(ix)   Possessions of unconvicted or unsentenced prisoners – the right to have books, writing materials and 'other means of occupation' can be forfeited for any period. If found guilty of escaping or attempting to escape they may forfeit their right to wear their own clothing (paras 7.15–7.32).

Appealing against findings of guilt

7.83   Prisoners may 'appeal' against a finding of guilt at adjudication through the requests/complaints procedure by submitting a request/complaint appeal form to the area manager's office at Prison Service Headquarters. The prisoner may ask for a transcript of the adjudication in order to prepare their appeal, and they should not be charged any photocopying fees in connection with this (para 9.5).

7.84   The area manager's support team staff will conduct a paper review of the case and has the power to quash the finding of guilt and remit any punishments awarded. Specialist staff at Prison Service Headquarters are on hand to advise the area manager as to whether the finding of guilt is lawful, although it is clear from reviews conducted by the Prisons Ombudsman that the area manager does not always heed their advice.

7.85   Guidance in the Prisoners' Requests/Complaints Procedures Staff Manual states that where a solicitor writes to the area manager's office asking for a transcript of the adjudication, the adjudication should be reviewed and the transcript sent out only if the guilty verdict is not quashed (Annex N, para 3.3).

7.86 If, after considering representations from a solicitor or a request/complaint from the prisoner the area manager upholds the finding of guilt, the prisoner may ask the Prisons Ombudsman to review the decision within one month.

7.87 Applications for judicial review may be lodged either against the adjudicator's finding of guilt, the area manager's decision to uphold that finding, or the Prison Service's refusal to act upon a recommendation from the Ombudsman that the finding of guilt should be quashed.

7.88 The question of whether a governor's finding of guilt can be directly reviewed has been the subject of much litigation. However, in *Leech v Deputy Governor of Parkhurst Prison* ([1988] 1 All ER 485) the matter was finally settled. The House of Lords confirmed that although governors are servants of the Home Secretary in general terms, they are not acting as such when they are fulfilling their disciplinary roles. In those circumstances governors are exercising 'the independent power conferred . . . by the Rules' and thus the Home Secretary has no authority to direct the governor. Judicial review proceedings may be taken directly against a governor's decision.

Offences under r 47(8A) in particular

7.89 The Home Office has not yet set out any specific procedures for appealing against positive drug tests. In particular, who will review the results of disputed tests has not yet been established and this may prove to be a particular problem in terms of both the practicality of upholding findings of guilt and as to who will meet the costs involved. It is recognised that the samples can give misleading results and that legal substances can appear similar to banned substances in the testing procedure. As the burden of proof is 'beyond reasonable doubt' it is difficult to see how adjudicators can reach such a conclusion where the prisoner disputes the charge.

Applying for restoration of additional days

7.90 Rule 56(1) of the Prison Rules allows prisoners who have been awarded additional days of imprisonment at adjudication to apply to have them remitted. In order to be eligible to have an application considered, a prisoner must have been awarded no further additional days for a period of six months if an adult or four months if a young offender (para 8.5). The prisoner need not have been in prison custody throughout that period, and may have been in a special hospital, community home, in police custody, or temporarily released under r 6 of the Prison Rules (para 8.6).

7.91 The application process starts when a prisoner completes form F2129A and submits it for consideration. A prison officer will complete form F2129B which details the offences which lead to the award of additional days, and also gives information about the prisoner's behaviour since. Where the prisoner has been held in another prison for at least half of the qualifying period, staff there should also be asked to submit a report. Reports from prison staff should be accurate and unbiased and should not include unsubstantiated information (paras 8.9–8.12).

7.92 The application is considered by a governor within one month of being submitted by the prisoner. Prisoners are allowed to appear before the governor and give information about the application orally if they wish to do so. In such cases all reports considered by the governor should also be read to the prisoner so that s/he has an opportunity to comment on them. The report writers should also be present so that the prisoner may ask questions of him/her or give further information if necessary (para 8.13).

7.93 In making a decision as to whether to remit the additional days awarded, paragraph 8.15 advises that the governor should take the following factors into account:

(i) whether the prisoner has a constructive approach to their imprisonment, makes the most of opportunities to participate in the regime and respects any trust placed in them;
(ii) whether there has been any genuine change of attitude on the prisoner's part;
(iii) the nature of the original breach of prison discipline for which the additional days were awarded and whether it is appropriate to remit days in recognition of a constructive approach and a change of attitude.

7.94 If a governor decides to remit additional days that were awarded at a governor's adjudication, the number of days remitted should not normally amount to more than half of the days awarded for any one offence unless it is considered that the offence was not serious, there are exceptional circumstances, or the additional days date back to an adjudication conducted by the Board of Visitors (para 8.15(c)).

7.95 Prisoners are informed of the outcome of the application immediately and they should also give a written decision on form F2129C within seven days of consideration of the application. This form should give details of the reasons for the decision, when they may apply again for the restoration of additional days, and where appropriate any amendments to their sentence dates (para 8.17).

Referrals to the police

7.96 Where a serious criminal offence has been committed, this should be reported to the governor immediately regardless of whether or not the offender has been identified. The governor should decide whether the police need be informed and should give details of the incident to the Intelligence and Incident Support Unit at Prison Service Headquarters (para 11.1).

7.97 Any suspects should be charged with an offence against prison discipline within 48 hours of discovery of the offence, but if the matter is being investigated by the police an adjudication should be opened and then adjourned pending the outcome of their enquiries. If the police or Criminal Prosecution Service decide not to prosecute the governor should decide whether to pursue the internal charge at that stage.

7.98 Circular Instruction 3/92 gives guidance to governors on when offences should be referred to the police for investigation. Broadly, offences falling within the following categories should be referred:

(i)   Assault – alleged murder, manslaughter, non-consensual buggery and rape, attempts at the above, threats to kill if there appears to be intent, assaults with a weapon likely to cause serious injury, where serious violence has been used or serious injury caused, sexual assaults involving violence or where the victim was especially vulnerable, and hostage taking.

(ii) Escape – from closed establishments or secure escorts and alleged escape attempts provided that the attempt is more than preparation.

(iii) Possession of unauthorised articles – allegations that a prisoner was in possession of firearms or explosives, other offensive weapons if there is evidence that the weapon was to be used to commit a serious criminal offence, class A drugs, class B drugs if there appears to have been intention to supply.

(vi) Criminal damage, arson – where the cost of the damage exceeds £2,000, or there was a risk of the fire taking hold.

(v)   Robbery – with serious violence or the threat or use of a weapon.

(vi) Major disturbances – involving a number of prisoners where the governor appears to be in danger of losing control or has lost control over any part of the establishment, and mass disobedience involving the use or threat of violence or the commission of serious criminal offences.

7.99 If there is clear evidence of racial motivation in any of the offences described above, the case for referral to the police will be strengthened (Discipline Manual, Appendix 3, para 7). The governor should take into account the wishes of the victim and accede to the victim's request that an alleged criminal offence is referred to the police (Appendix 3, paragraph 6).

THE INFORMAL DISCIPLINARY SYSTEM

Rule 43 Good Order and Discipline (GOAD)

7.100 Rule 43 of the Prison Rules provides for the removal of prisoners from normal location to the segregation block of an establishment. This may be for the prisoner's own protection (most commonly for sex offenders, prisoners who are in debt to other prisoners, or informants), or as a solution to the problem of managing prisoners whose presence on the wing is thought to pose a threat to the good order and discipline of the wing.

7.101 Governors have a power to segregate prisoners in the interests of good order and discipline for up to three days (r 43(1)). Segregation for a longer period requires the approval of a member of the Board of Visitors or the Home Secretary. Circular Instruction 6/93 states that members of the Board of Visitors who authorise segregation should see the prisoner personally unless there are exceptional circumstances which prevent this (eg freak weather conditions which make the prison inaccessible). Governors who believe that it may be necessary to segregate a prisoner for longer than three days are advised that they should inform the Board of this within 36 hours of the initial decision to segregate being taken (Addendum to CI 6/93, para 5).

7.102   When segregation has been approved by a member of the Board of Visitors prisoners may be segregated for up to one month (r 43 (2)). However, although segregation may have been authorised for this period it should not necessarily follow that a prisoner has to be segregated throughout that whole time. In fact, the Addendum to CI 26/90 states that prisoners' cases should be kept 'under continuous review and, as soon as segregation is no longer necessary in the interests of good order and discipline the inmate must be returned to normal location'(para 6).

7.103   A doctor or the managing medical officer should visit a prisoner as soon as possible after they have been segregated, and at least once every three days throughout the period of segregation (CI 26/90, para 9). If at any time the medical officer recommends that the prisoner is unfit for segregation, then s/he must be returned to normal location (r 43(3)).

7.104   Although CI 26/90 states that,

'it is important . . . that feelings of isolation are eased as much as possible by regular face-to-face contact and out of cell activity' (para 7)

the reality for most prisoners is that they will be subjected to an impoverished regime held in a cell in the segregation block for 23 hours per day, with the other hour being spent on the statutory exercise period. Segregation blocks have their own exercise yards and these are usually extremely small and often have a cage like appearance. In some segregation block prisoners are required to exercise completely alone, in others more than one prisoner is allowed out at a time.

7.105   Circular Instruction 26/90 states that governors should not deliberately provide a restricted regime to prisoners held on r 43 (GOAD) by denying facilities which are available to other prisoners, although it concedes that restriction on regime activities will be inevitable because of 'the inmate's separate location, and limitations of accommodation, manpower and other resources' (para 20). However, prisoners should not be subjected to any restrictions which are not 'an unavoidable consequence of their separation from the rest of the prison population' (para 21). Thus education, and library facilities should be made available to them (para 22).

7.106   Historically, prisoners segregated in the interests of good order and discipline were allowed to have access to the privileges contained in Standing Order 4. However, in July 1995 IG 74/95 introduced a National Framework for Incentives and Earned Privileges for Prisoners which aims to ensure that prisoners earn privileges by their 'responsible behaviour and participation in hard work and other constructive activity'(para 1). All governors were asked to operate local incentive schemes and produce a list of key earnable privileges. Rule 4 of the Prison Rules was revised to reflect the changes in policy. As a consequence, prisoners held in segregation in the interests of good order and discipline may find themselves unable to earn certain privileges although this will vary from prison to prison.

7.107 A governor should visit each prisoner held on r 43 (GOAD) every day, and during the visit the governor should speak with the prisoner and assess whether there is any need for the period of segregation to continue (CI 26/90).

7.108 Recommendation 12 of the Woolf Report said that prisoners should be given written reasons for their segregation in the interests of good order and discipline, and this was implemented by CI 26/90, Annex C, which recommended that reasons were given. An addendum to the instruction dated 29 August 1991 went further and stated that:

> 'any inmate who is segregated must be advised in writing of the reasons as soon as far as is practicable, and as soon as possible. In general this should be done before, or at the time that, the inmate is placed in conditions of segregation. But an inmate does not have an absolute right to be informed of the reasons before the decision is taken or before or at the time that the inmate is placed in conditions of segregation, if the interests of good order and discipline dictate otherwise.' (para 14)

7.109 A period of segregation under r 43 (GOAD) can be extended at the end of each month for an indefinite period so long as the governor and the Board of Visitors authorise segregation, and the medical officer does not object.

7.110 Prisoners may query their segregation by submitting a request/ complaint to the governor asking for the reasons to be amplified and the decision to be reviewed. Many prisoners will also want to apply for a transfer to a different prison where they will be able to start afresh. Appeals against the governor's reply may be submitted to the area manager, and the Prisons Ombudsman may be asked to review area manager's decisions.

7.111 The litigation on the use of and conditions of segregation has produced disappointing results. In the conjoined appeals *R v Deputy Governor of Parkhurst Prison, ex p Hague and Weldon v Home Office* [1992] 1 AC 58, prisoners argued that their segregation under r 43 (GOAD) and detention in a strip cell constituted breach of statutory duty and false imprisonment by depriving them of their residual liberty. The House of Lords held that no prisoner could bring an action for breach of the Prison Rules as they were merely regulatory and not designed to protect a prisoner against loss, injury or damage. Furthermore, no right of action lay in false imprisonment as the prisoners were lawfully committed to prison and had no right to do what they wanted, when they wanted as their lives were governed by the prison regime. Detention could not become unlawful when the conditions became intolerable.

7.112   However, the House of Lords confirmed that a person who is held lawfully in prison and who is subjected to intolerable conditions does have remedies. These would be an action in negligence where the intolerable conditions caused the prisoner to suffer injury to his health, an action for assault where appropriate, an action for misfeasance in public office if malice could be established, and the termination of such conditions by judicial review.

Instruction to Governors 28/93

7.113   Introduction.   Instruction to Governors 28/93 provides a 'Management Strategy for Disruptive Inmates'. The instruction came into effect in November 1993 and replaced Circular Instruction 37/90. New instructions were thought necessary in view of the old instruction's failure to provide guidance on how to deal with prisoners who were thought too disruptive to be held in special units. In practice, the main difference between IG 28/93 and its predecessor is that IG 28/93 gives staff at Prison Service Headquarters the power to compel prison governors to accept 'disruptive' prisoners at their establishments, although governors do have the right to appeal against the allocation of a prisoner whom they do not want to accept.

7.114   The management strategy outlined in IG 28/93 has the following underlying principles:

(i)   local resolution of local problems;
(ii) central management of the strategy when wider ranging solutions are required;
(iii) progression of disruptive inmates through a five stage management programme (para 5).

7.115   All convicted prisoners held in category B prisons are liable to be dealt with under the strategy if they are deemed to pose '*serious* control problems'. The aim is to 'secure the return of a disruptive inmate to a settled pattern of behaviour on normal location'.

7.116   The instruction recognises that this might be achieved by the prisoner following anything from one of the stages to all five of them. In practice many of those who reach stage 5 will find themselves held in the segregation blocks of various prisons for lengthy periods of time, without any prospect of return to normal location.

7.117   Following the recommendations contained in the Woolf Report, Circular Instruction 37/90 was amended to offer more safeguards to prisoners who were being 'ghosted' (transferred in the interests of the good order and discipline of an establishment). These safeguards have been incorporated into IG 28/93:

(i)   no inmate should be transferred as a form of punishment;
(ii) the reasoned grounds for transfer must be recorded and noted on an inmate's record;
(iii) inmates must be advised in writing of the reasons for their transfer or segregation within 24 hours of such actions;

(iv) all appropriate security measures must be taken over the transfer of category A inmates, including the prior approval of the Population Management Section in the case of exceptional and high risk inmates;

(v) requests/complaints about a transfer must be replied to within seven days by the governor of the establishment where the transfer decision is taken;

(vi) intending visitors should be notified of an inmates transfer including, where appropriate, by the inmate himself;

(vii) decisions on segregating inmates under r 43 are matters for the governor, and subsequently the Board of Visitors, in the establishment in which the inmate is then being held.

7.118 The Five Stage Management Programme: Stage 1 – Internal action at the parent establishment.   In the first instance governors are advised that when a disruptive or subversive prisoner comes to their attention, they should consider whether there is cause to lay a disciplinary charge against that prisoner for breach of r 47, try to ascertain the reasons for disruptive behaviour, and try to persuade the prisoner to change that behaviour. Consideration should be given to moving the prisoner within the prison, either to another prison wing or to the segregation block under r 43 (GOAD). If this approach does not cause the prisoner to settle, or there are other 'exceptional' (undefined) circumstances, the prisoner will move on to stage 2.

7.119 Stage 2 – Temporary transfer from the parent establishment.   If the governor considers that the temporary transfer of a 'seriously disruptive inmate is unavoidable', then transfer to a local prison may be arranged. This transfer is arranged in consultation with the Population Management Section at Prison Service Headquarters who advise as to the availability of vacant cells, which are always in the segregation blocks of local prisons. The prisoner is then transferred for a period of up to one month, and at this time the expectation will be that the prisoner will return to the parent establishment when the month expires. Prisoners and prison staff refer to this period as a 'lay down' and the idea is that it will provide a suitable cooling off period for the prisoner who will then be prepared to settle.

7.120   If, however, the governor of the parent establishment does not want to take the prisoner back, then s/he may apply to the Population Management Section (PMS) or the Lifer Management Unit (LMU) explaining the reasons why a return to the establishment is thought to be unsuitable. PMS or LMU may accept the governor's representations and arrange for the prisoner to be allocated to another prison (stage 3), or they may reject the representations and order the governor to take the prisoner back.

7.121 Stage 3 – Centrally managed transfers to training and local establishments.   If it is decided that the prisoner will not return to the parent establishment then PMS or LMU arrange reallocation to either a dispersal prison, a local prison or a category B training prison. Governors are compelled to accept prisoners who are allocated to their establishments under stage 3, although they are able to 'appeal' to their area managers who liaise with PMS or LMU in an attempt to reach a solution.

7.122   Stage 4 – Transfer to a CRC special unit.   If a governor believes that a prisoner is particulary disruptive or aggressive, s/he may ask that the prisoner is considered for a transfer to one of the three special units (Woodhill, Hull and Parkhurst). Applications are considered every six weeks by the Special Unit Selection Committee (SUSC). Prisoners accepted into the special units are likely to have had a history of:

(i)   violence to staff or other prisoners;
(ii)   regular disciplinary reports;
(iii) causing serious damage to prison property;
(iv) dangerous behaviour such as rooftop protests or hostage taking;
(v)   failure to respond in stages 1–3 above;
(vi) mental abnormality (for transfer to Parkhurst unit only) (para 24).

7.123   As well as containing a special unit, Woodhill prison also has a special assessment unit where prisoners may be transferred pending consideration of their cases by SUSC. Such prisoners must meet at least one of the criteria outlined above, have had at least one transfer under stage 2 of the programme, have been on r 43 (GOAD) for at least one month, and have not been considered by SUSC for two years or located in a special unit for five years.

7.124   Stage 5 – Continuous assessment scheme.   Prisoners who are transferred to a special unit may be transferred out for a variety of reasons. Occasionally prisoners are released direct from units, are downgraded to category C and transferred to other locations, or are transferred back into the mainstream dispersal prison system if it is considered that their behaviour is no longer so disruptive as to merit the regime offered in the unit. More commonly, prisoners are transferred out of a special unit on the basis that they are too disruptive to be located there and that their presence undermines the smooth running of the unit.

7.125   Prisoners transferred on this basis move to stage 5 of the programme and SUSC are able to direct the governors of category B training, local and dispersal prisons to hold the prisoner. SUSC reviews the progress of all prisoners on the continuous assessment scheme at their six weekly meetings. Prisoners will often be transferred from prison to prison in order to 'relieve the pressure on the holding establishment'. Although IG 28/95 does not direct governors to segregate such prisoners, in practice all prisoners will initially be received into a segregation block. Prisoners may apply to the governor to go on to normal location within the prison, but in practice such prisoners will have built up a such a reputation from their previous disruptive behaviour that governors consider them to be a control problem and are reluctant to put them on a wing.

7.126   Decisions to move prisoners through the five stages are judicially reviewable, although a successful challenge is unlikely. Whilst prisoners are entitled to be informed in writing of the reasons for their transfer under IG 28/93, such reasons will often be vague. In *ex p Ross* (1994) Times, 9 June, a prisoner was transferred on the basis that he was a 'disruptive prisoner who is doing his best to destabilise the wing'. No specific incidents were alluded to, and when pressed the governor did not provide any evidence against the prisoner in question. In judicial review proceedings the Court of Appeal found that the governor was under no requirement to give 'chapter and verse' of the reasons why the prisoner was transferred, and said that a governor could make such a decision if he thought the prisoner's behaviour might in any way threaten the smooth running of the prison.

7.127 Representations against such decisions may be made to the relevant governor(s) and to SUSC, PMS or LMU depending on who has overall responsibility for the prisoner's management. Staff from SUSC are frequent visitors to the special units and may visit particular prisoners in other prisons to interview them for a unit or to discuss their placement on the continuous assessment scheme.

Prisoner informants

7.128 Governors will often run into problems in providing prisoners with the reasons for their segregation under r 43 (GOAD) or their transfer under IG 28/93 because of the need to protect the identity of other prisoners. It is relatively common for one prisoner to provide information about the activities of another by placing a 'note in the box'. Each prison wing has a box on it where prisoners post the correspondence that they wish to send out of the prison. Sometimes, a prisoner will also post an anonymous note informing the authorities of the activities of another prisoner, for example that an escape attempt is being planned, drugs are being sold, or someone is planning to take a hostage. The notes will be referred to the Security Department within the prison, and if the information is thought to be reliable, the suspected prisoner will be segregated or transferred.

7.129 There is also a more formal Inmate Informant System, the mechanics of which are laid out in the Prison Service's Security Manual.

7.130 The Inmate Informant System recognises that prisoners are one of the best sources of security intelligence, and that the best informants are 'prisoners who have the respect of other prisoners and who are regarded as above suspicion' (Security Manual, para 15.1). Prison governors do not have to adopt the Inmate Informant System, although they are advised that to do so will maximise security intelligence and ensure that staff dealing with informants behave properly.

7.131 Each prison which adopts the Inmate Informant System should appoint a manager who is responsible for staff dealing with informants, available to advise and brief staff, and who ensures that all information received is processed and assessed for reliability. The manager also identifies likely informers, records rewards given to them and maintains secure records of the names of informants.

7.132 Seven particular types of prisoner are identified as being most likely to be willing to provide information:

(i) those who are well settled in prison and unlikely to welcome disruption to their life styles from other prisoners;

(ii) those who relate easily to staff;
(iii) those anxious to change their life style and distance themselves from other more criminal prisoners;
(iv) those whose offences suggest that their criminality is not well established;
(v) those who are known to have provided information to prison or police authorities in the past;
(vi) those due for release in the near future (para 15.13).

7.133 Prisoners who pass information to the prison authorities can expect to be rewarded for their trouble. Rewards given are supposed to relate to the usefulness of the information that they have provided. The following rewards are suggested:

(i)   a commitment to report directly on the informant's work to third parties (including the Parole Board);
(ii) acknowledgement that a prisoner's approach to criminal behaviour has changed, justifying progress to better regimes or lower security categorisation;
(iii) the sympathetic consideration of transfer requests where security factors permit;
(iv) additional facilities, for example longer visits, favourable job allocations, and access to other discretionary facilities available within the establishment;
(v)   payments of incentive bonuses within the provisions of the prisoners' pay scheme;
(vi) in particularly worthy cases, a recommendation may be made that the use of the Royal Prerogative of Mercy be considered to remit part of a sentence as a reward for meritorious acts (para 15.14).

7.134 Staff dealing with informants are warned that they should only offer the above rewards; that they must only reward a prisoner when information has been delivered and after they have received any necessary authority; that rewards may be visible to other prisoners and this may place the informant at risk. The risk of informers using the system for their own means and providing fabricated information in order to receive a reward is recognised.

7.135 Staff who 'handle' informants may be selected for their skills in developing relationships, their post within the prison or their experience of working within prisons. In particular, staff who frequently deal with prisoners in privacy whilst they are conducting cell searches, acting in a personal officer role, or dealing with prisoners' applications are the best placed to extract good quality information without arousing the suspicion of other prisoners and thus putting the informant at risk.

CHAPTER 8

RIGHTS AND PRIVILEGES

INTRODUCTION

8.1   The perception of what is a 'right' for a prisoner and what is a 'privilege' can be confusing. This can be attributed in no small part to the fact that the rights protected by statute are relatively few, and as a result, the privileges that are commonly available throughout a sentence come to be perceived as rights. The crucial difference between rights and privileges is that prisoners' rights can only be altered following a change in primary or secondary legislation. Privileges, on the other hand, are subject to policy changes throughout a prisoners' sentence and can potentially be enhanced or withdrawn at the discretion of the Secretary of State. By way of illustration, the most recent example of such a decision where a change was made to prisoners' privileges relates to temporary release and home leave, the scope of which were radically reduced by the Secretary of State for both newly sentenced and existing prisoners. The Divisional Court upheld the right of the Secretary of State to make such policy changes in respect of privileges afforded to prisoners, providing proper consultation is undertaken before the new policy is implemented and the new scheme is not *Wednesbury* unreasonable (*R v Secretary of State for the Home Department, ex p Briggs, Green and Hargreaves* (25 July 1995, unreported, DC).

8.2   Rule 4 of the Prison Rules, which deals with the privileges to be afforded to prisoners was radically redrafted in the last amendment to the Prison Rules in June 1995. In its previous form, it simply allowed the Secretary of State discretion to operate a system of privileges (or facilities) for prisoners. The new form specifically allows the Secretary of State to make provision for a system of privileges to be enforced at all prisons which can be linked to prison behaviour and is cross-referenced to several other rules concerning matters such as correspondence and visits. The rule is therefore more explicit than its predecessor in establishing the manner in which privileges may be controlled and linked to the informal disciplinary system and in seeking to distinguish privileges from rights.

8.3   There is, of course, a 'grey area' where the concept of rights and privileges will overlap. This would cover areas where the right is accepted but the manner in which it is exercised is subject to debate. An example which has formed the basis of substantial litigation is the right of prisoners to privileged correspondence with legal advisors. Whilst this has always been protected to some degree, the precise extent has been subject to numerous actions both domestically and before the European Commission of Human Rights. It is therefore important to bear in mind that fundamental rights may be at stake and the policy or even statute may be vulnerable to legal challenge.

8.4   It is only possible to form an assessment as to whether a prisoner has been denied his/her legal rights, or has been subject to a unfavourable administrative decision by looking at the key areas in turn. A full discussion of the implications of the change to r 4 and the manner in which privileges will be linked to custodial behaviour is only then possible.

VISITS

Social visits

8.5   Rule 34(2) of the Prison Rules states that prisoners are entitled to receive, as of right, two visits in every four-week period, but this may be reduced to one visit in each four-week period if so directed by the Secretary of State. This allowance of visits is known as 'statutory visits'. The Rules do make allowance for the right to a visit to be deferred by the governor whilst a prisoner is subject to cellular confinement (r 34(5)).

8.6   In addition to statutory visits, the Rules make provision for 'privilege visits' to be allowed. These may be conferred by the governor (r 39(3)) or the Board of Visitors (r 39(4)). The Secretary of State also has the power to authorise additional visits for individual or particular classes of prisoners (r 39(7)). Governor's privilege visits are to be allowed where necessary for the welfare of the prisoners' family but there is no express guidance as to when the Board of Visitors should utilise its power to authorise extra visits or to allow a statutory visit to last for longer than normal.

8.7   Prisoners are also entitled to special visits from legal advisors and other people visiting in a professional capacity such as probation staff, priests and consular officials. Privilege and special visits do not count against the number of statutory visits to which a prisoner is entitled.

Remand prisoners

8.8   Unconvicted prisoners are entitled to receive as many visits as they wish, 'within such limits and subject to such conditions as the Secretary of State may direct, either generally or in a particular case' (r 34(1)). At the present time, the entitlement is to at least 90 minutes per week but it is up to the governor of each prison as to how these visits will be structured. In most prisons, it is arranged for remand prisoners to have a visit each day (except Sunday) of at least 15 minutes' duration. However, it is becoming more common for as few as three visits a week to be allowed, but each visit will last longer than 15 minutes. Visitors do not need a visiting order to enter the prison, although many prisons are now asking visitors to remand prisoners to telephone in advance to try and allow visiting arrangements to be better structured. Once on a visit, the same rules apply as for convicted inmates.

Standing Order 5A

8.9 The policy document which sets out how the visits system should be administered is Standing Order 5A. This document was issued several years ago and is in urgent need of updating, but it is still the only public source of policy on this topic. The main purpose of visits is to enable prisoners to maintain meaningful contact with the outside world during their time in custody. Consequently, the normal class of persons who are entitled to visit is defined as close relatives. These include, spouses (including 'common law' partners), parents, siblings (including half and step bothers and sisters), fiancées and people who have been in loco parentis for the prisoner or for whom the prisoner has been in loco parentis (para 30). Social visits are also allowed from other persons but are more vulnerable to be stopped by the governor if he feels that good order and discipline or security may be threatened.

8.10 All visitors must be in possession of a valid visiting order to enable admittance to the prison. Visiting orders are issued to the individual prisoner who then sends them out to the proposed visitor. They should be issued in sufficient time to enable the visit to take place as soon as it becomes due (paras 22–23). The conditions for social visits are loosely defined so as to take place in 'the most humane conditions possible' (para 24). They are to be taken in the sight of a prison officer and are liable to take place within hearing of an officer if it is deemed necessary in the interests of security (para 25). In general, up to three visitors are permitted at any one time and they should take place in a visiting room with a table. Prisoners and visitors should be allowed to embrace each other. No tape recordings or photographs may be taken and if such items are found, they will be confiscated. It will then be sealed and sent to Headquarters and the visitor will be informed of their right to request the return of the tape or film. Visits may be conducted in any language but there are provisions for visits not conducted in English to be monitored by a person who speaks the relevant language or for the visit to be tape recorded for later translation if this is considered necessary for the interests of prison security, national security or the prevention of crime.

8.11 Special allowances are made for prisoners to accumulate visits and to visit other prisoners. If a prisoner is located in a prison where s/he are unable to receive visits, it is possible to accumulate between three and 26 visiting orders. The prisoner can then apply for a temporary transfer to a prison where it is possible to receive these visits. Normally, such transfers are for one month and may be taken only once a year (paras 11–18). Visits are also allowed between two prisoners at different prisons who fit the definition of close relatives. Arrangements can be made, subject to security and the availability of transport and accommodation, for the prisoners to be transferred to a prison where they can have a visit with each other. This privilege is to be permitted once every three months and each prisoner must surrender one visiting order (paras 20–21).

Restrictions on social visits

8.12 Closed visits may be ordered whereby prisoners and their visitors will be afforded no, or limited contact (para 24). This is commonly used when prisoners are suspected of receiving unauthorised articles during visits or where behaviour in the visits room has breached standards of good order and discipline. There is no limitation on the time for which closed visits may be enforced although they are commonly used for periods of one to two months in the first instance. Closed visits do not form part of the punishment available following an adjudication and the decision must be made on its own merits. It therefore follows that this decision can be made even when there have been no formal disciplinary charge made against a prisoner.

8.13 Rule 33 of the Prison Rules contains a catch-all provision allowing restrictions to be placed upon visits in the interests of good order and discipline or the prevention of crime. The power to exclude visitors should only be used in exceptional circumstances for close relatives but is more widely available for other classes of persons. In general, it is more appropriate to consider the use of closed visits before a decision to exclude a visitor is made. The governor is also empowered to exclude visits to or from persons under 18 years of age where it is felt that this would not be in the best interests of the visitor or the inmate. If this power is to be used in relation to close relatives, authority must be obtained from Prison Service Headquarters (para 33).

8.14 Visits by journalists are subject to special provisions. The general guidance is that if these are made in a professional capacity, they should not be allowed. The governor has authority to exclude these without reference to any higher authority. If the visit is in a personal capacity, the governor can require that an undertaking is given by the prospective visitor that any material obtained will not be used for publication or other professional purposes (para 37). The legal effect of such an undertaking is debatable and it is unlikely that it would necessarily be a bar to publication.

Searching

8.15 Both prisoners and their visitors are liable to be searched. Governors have a general power to search prisoners in their custody as they deem necessary and it appears to be increasingly common for searches to take place both before and after visits. The power to search visitors must be exercised more circumspectly and it is arguable that a greater level of suspicion is required. In general, visitors to prisons will be subject to perfunctory 'pat down' searches on arrival and will be screened by the use of metal detecting equipment. The visitor cannot be required to submit to such a search, but access to the prison may be denied in that situation. More stringent searches can only be carried out with the consent of the visitor or by calling the police to carry out such procedures in accordance with the PACE Act 1984 (see chapter 9 for a detailed discussion of searching provisions). Visits may be terminated if an officer believes it is necessary to prevent violence, where an unauthorised article has been passed, where it is suspected that the rules concerning correspondence are being contravened (eg by passing out a letter) or where a conversation is overheard that indicates an escape attempt, or a plan to commit criminal offences (para 25).

Visits to category A prisoners

8.16 Category A prisoners are subject to special provisions. All visitors to prisoners in this category must be authorised by Prison Service Headquarters. The procedure is for category A prisoners to submit details of their proposed visitors to Headquarters who then make arrangements foror them to be vetted by the police. It is only once this approval has been obtained that the visitor is authorised to visit the establishment. Visitors to category A prisoners are more likely to be asked to submit to a search and the Woodcock Report has lead to more frequent strip searches of these prisoners before and after visits. Recent Instructions to Governors, issued following the Woodcock Report have required all exceptional risk category A prisoners at Belmarsh and Whitemoor special security units to take all visits as closed visits. It seems likely that this will be extended throughout this section of the prison population.

Visits by legal advisors

8.17 Rule 37(1) of the Prison Rules requires facilities to be made available to legal advisors who are acting for prisoners in connection with legal proceedings to which the prisoner is a party. These facilities should allow the prisoner to be interviewed in sight of, but out of the hearing of a prison officer. Rule 37(2) authorises this facility to be extended for the purposes of any other legal business but makes the authority subject to any further directions that the Secretary of State may issue.

8.18 The phrasing of this rule has been designed to take account of numerous problems that had arisen over the construction of being party to legal proceedings. Many applications had been made, both to the domestic and European Courts (see eg *Guilfoyle v Home Office* [1981] QB 309 and *R v Secretary of State for the Home Department, ex p Anderson* [1984] QB 778) in which the precise meaning of these words was debated. The Rules had previously not extended access to legal advisors for 'other legal business' and the new phrasing is clearly designed to circumvent such problems.

8.19 One potential problem that has arisen under the new Rules concerns the privacy that is afforded to legal advisers during such meetings. Various prisons have introduced new security arrangements for legal visits with high security category A prisoners, such as observation cameras mounted above the tables at Belmarsh and 'closed visits' at Whitemoor. The use of such security measures raises problems as to how confidential advice may be given and one solicitor describes having to get on to her knees to shout through a glass partition whilst at Whitemoor. At the time of writing, applications for leave to move for judicial review have been issued to challenge such security measures.

LETTERS

8.20   The provisions for correspondence are also contained in rr 33 and 34 of the Prison Rules and are closely linked to visits. Rule 34(2)(a) allows convicted prisoners to send one letter a week at public expense. Provisions are also made for prisoners to receive privilege and special letters and to exchange visiting orders for letters, at the discretion of the governor. It is necessary to look to the Standing Orders for a more detailed explanation of what is actually permitted in practice.

8.21   Standing Order 5B commences with the following statement of principle:

> 'The policy of the Prison Service is to encourage inmates to keep in touch with the outside world through regular letter writing, to respect the privacy of correspondence to and from inmates as far as possible and to ensure that it is transmitted as speedily as possible.' (para 1)

8.22   Standing Order 5B authorises prisoners to send as many privilege letters as they wish each week, save at establishments where routine reading is in force (see below). The cost of sending such letters is met from prisoners' own funds. Where routine reading is in force, the governor has a discretion to set the number of privilege letters that may be sent, subject to a minimum of one a week for adults and two a week for young offenders (para 6).

8.23   Special letters are issued according to need. The general guidance is that they should be issue in the following circumstances:

(i)   immediately after conviction to settle business affairs;
(ii)   when a prisoner is to be transferred to another prison (either before transfer or on reception). The number of special letters issued should correspond to the number of outstanding visiting orders which the prisoner has;
(iii)   when necessary for the welfare of the prisoner or his/her family;
(iv)   in connection with legal proceedings to which the prisoner is a party (but see legal correspondence below);
(v)   if necessary to enable a prisoner to write to a probation officer or to an agency arranging accommodation on release;
(vi)   at Christmas, subject to the discretion of the governor;
(vii)   to write to the Parliamentary Commissioner for Administration (or the Prisons Ombudsman) (para 7).

The cost of special letters will normally be met from prisoners' own funds, save in the case of transfers when they should be sent at public expense.

Restrictions on correspondence

8.24 Rule 33 of the Prison Rules contains a number of provisions that authorise restrictions on correspondence. These include the right to prevent correspondence in the interest of good order and discipline or preventing crime, to read and examine all letters save where forbidden by the Rules and to withdraw the right to communicate with any person where such communication is a privilege rather than a right. These provisions are implemented so as to provide for a number of restrictions on the manner in which prisoners can correspond with the outside world.

8.25 Letters must be in a particular format which includes the name of the sender and the address of the prison. Anonymous letters are forbidden and the address of the prison can only be omitted on request to the governor (para 18). On the same basis, letters sent to the prison must normally show the sender's name and address. In general, letters may be sent to any person although restrictions are placed on the following classes of people:

(i)   correspondence with minors may be stopped if the person having parental responsibility makes such a request;

(ii)   the governor may prevent correspondence between a minor in custody and any person whom it is thought it would not be in that minor's interests to communicate with. In reaching this decision, the views of the minor's parents or guardian should be sought;

(iii) convicted inmates may write to each other if they are close relatives, or if they were co-defendants and the correspondence relates to their conviction or sentence. In all other cases, the approval of both governors must be obtained;

(iv)   correspondence between ex-inmates is permitted unless the governor considers that this would impede the rehabilitation of either party or that there would be a threat to good order or security;

(v)   if a prisoner wishes to write to the victim of their offences, an application must be made to the governor who will consider whether it would cause undue distress. This provision does not apply to unconvicted prisoners, or where the victim is a close family member or has already written to the prisoner;

(vi)   correspondence with any person or organisation can be stopped if the governor has reason to believe that the correspondent is engaged in activities or planning which may present a serious threat to the security or good order of that prison or the prison estate;

(vii) prisoners are only able to advertise for penfriends with approval of the governor and after submitting the text of the advertisement.

8.26 Correspondence may also be prohibited on the grounds of its contents (para 34). The following is a list of the material which is prohibited:

(i)   threatening or indecent or grossly offensive or which is known to be false;

(ii)   plans or material which would tend to assist in the commission of a criminal or disciplinary offence;

(iii) escape plans or material which jeopardises the security of the prison;

(iv)   obscure or coded messages which are not decipherable;

(v) material which would jeopardise national security;

(vi) material which includes incitement to racial hatred;

(vii) material intended for publication or broadcast which is in return for payment, which is about the prisoner's own crime or criminal history (unless it forms part of serious representations about conviction, sentence or comment on the criminal justice system) or which identifies individual members of staff or other prisoners;

(viii) in the case of convicted prisoners, material about the conduct of business activity unless it relates to a power of attorney, the winding up of a business following conviction or the sale or transfer of personal funds.

8.27 In general, there is no restriction on the length of letters but the governor can set a limit of not less than four sides of A4 if routine reading is in force. Routine reading is the method by which these regulations are policed. Routine reading is reserved effectively for all prisoners in maximum security prisons, all prisoners who are normally in maximum security prisons but are temporarily in another prison, all category A prisoners and those being considered for such categorisation, whether convicted or unconvicted, all prisoners in category A units whatever their category and all prisoners on the escape list (para 32). This has recently been extended by IG 73/95 to cover all prisoners convicted of making or attempting to make obscene telephone calls or sending obscene letters. In such cases, routine reading should continue as long as the governor considers necessary.

8.28 Other prisoners may also be subject to routine reading in exceptional circumstances. These will normally include the prevention or detection of a criminal offence, a threat to good order or the security of the prison. It will also be used if there is reason to believe that a prisoner may seek to infringe any of the general restrictions on correspondence or if it is in the prisoner's own interest (eg in the case of severe depression).

8.29 Governors have the power to copy and disclose prisoners' letters in limited circumstances (IG 87/95). This power exists only if it is necessary to prevent an escape from prison, to prevent or reveal a miscarriage of justice, to help in the recovery of the proceeds of crime or where national security or public safety is affected. Controversially, this power can also be used to help prevent and detect crime or to convict an offender. The agencies to whom this may be disclosed include the police, the Immigration Department, Customs and Excise, MI5 and the Serious Fraud Office. The police or other investigating bodies can also make such requests to the governor but the governor must be sure that the information sought is specific and that s/he is not being asked to conduct a 'fishing expedition'. Legal correspondence is excluded from these provisions.

Unconvicted prisoners

8.30 Rule 34(1) of the Prison Rules allows unconvicted prisoners to send and receive as many letters as they wish, but within such limits and subject to such conditions as the Secretary of State may direct. It is unusual for any restrictions to be placed on the number of letters sent and received. Incoming mail will be examined for unauthorised articles but will not normally be read and outgoing letters will not generally be subject to routine reading. Category A remand prisoners will find that their letters are read and in exceptional circumstances, the governor may direct that ordinary remand prisoners' letters are read in order to prevent the planning of escapes.

Legal correspondence

8.31 A series of legal challenges to the extent of correspondence has been fought for many years. Cases such as *Silver v United Kingdom* ((1983) 5 EHRR 347, Series A no 61) and *R v Secretary of State for the Home Department, ex p Leech* ([1993] 4 All ER 539). A succession of such cases culminating in *Campbell v United Kingdom* ([1992] 15 EHRR 137, Series A No 233), in which the European Court decided that routine reading of a Scottish prisoner's correspondence with his lawyer breached Article 8, has lead to a comprehensive revision of r 37A which deals with this matter.

8.32 Rule 37A now provides that a prisoner may correspond with his/her legal advisor and the court (the definition of a court includes the European Commission and Court of Human Rights and the European Court of Justice). Prisoners must be provided with writing materials on request for the purpose of sending such correspondence. There is no restriction imposed on this right, such as being party to legal proceedings. The governor can only open, examine and read such correspondence if there is reasonable suspicion that it contains an illicit enclosure or that there is reasonable cause to believe that its contents may endanger prison security, the safety of others or are otherwise of a criminal nature. A prisoner whose legal correspondence is to be dealt with under these provisions has the right to be present when it is opened.

8.33 Despite the re-phrasing of this rule, the relevant Standing Order has not been amended and there is considerable confusion amongst prison officers as to the proper provisions. Many seek to apply the old regulations contained in Standing Order 5B, para 34(3) and consequently fail to deal with privileged correspondence properly. Although this situation should improve as the new provisions are more widely circulated, the rule is vulnerable to abuse. Whilst it would be difficult for a governor to justify opening a letter sent by a solicitor, there is no such safeguard for prisoners seeking to write to solicitors. If serious problems do arise, it may become necessary for further litigation to be taken to further define the responsibility and powers in this regard.

TELEPHONE CALLS

8.34 All prisons now have card phones installed and this has lead to a major changes in prisoners' use of telephones. Prison card phones will only accept cards issued by the Prison Service. These may be purchased from the prison canteen from wages or private cash. Governors are entitled to impose restrictions on the purchase of such cards and the possession of cards above a specified number can be grounds for a disciplinary charge (see CI 21/92). These regulations are designed to prevent 'racketeering' in the prison.

8.35 All card phones are monitored and can be recorded by prison staff. Calls can be stopped on the same grounds as are utilised for stopping correspondence. Prisoners are not permitted to consult a telephone directory but can be given access to STD codes. Calls to the operator and emergency services are barred. The procedures for recording conversations are subject to the Data Protection Act 1984 and access may be obtained to such records under the Act.

8.36 Category A prisoners and those on the escape list are not permitted to retain phone cards. Whilst such prisoners are entitled to purchase the same number of cards as other prisoners, they will be held and calls logged in the wing office. All calls made by such prisoners must be pre-booked and to certain pre-approved telephone numbers. These calls will be simultaneously monitored and recorded. The guidelines state that they must be conducted in English unless prior approval is obtained to use another language in which case the recording may be kept for translation.

8.37 Calls to legal advisers are liable to be monitored as part of the general surveillance system. Although confidentiality cannot be guaranteed, governors are advised to notify their staff to turn off monitoring equipment when they realise a genuine call of this nature is being made. Details of the conversation cannot be disclosed and if a tape recording had inadvertently been made, this should not be listened to or played back (CI 21/92, paras 40–43).

8.38 Telephone calls to the media are now expressly forbidden following an incident where one of the Parkhurst escapees telephoned and participated in a radio chat show. Any unauthorised call to the media is now to be treated as a disciplinary offence (IG 73/95). Prisoners can make applications to use official telephones, either for urgent family circumstances, to speak to legal advisers or to contact the media. However, governors are strongly discouraged from allowing such applications and are asked to recover the costs of such calls from prisoners. If lawyers urgently need to speak with their clients, one way round these provisions is to ask the governor to allow a telephone call to be made to the prison at a pre-arranged time to an official extension.

TEMPORARY RELEASE

8.39 Rule 6 of the Prison Rules which provides the authority for temporary release was substantially redrafted in 1995. The purpose of this redrafting was to enable the Secretary of State to introduce more stringent measures in respect of temporary release and to provide punitive sanctions for those who failed to comply with the terms of their licence. The move was in response to a series of press stories about prisoners who had re-offended whilst on release but has been severely criticised for impeding the rehabilitative programmes that are available to prisoners.

8.40 Rule 6 provides authority for prisoners to be released temporarily from prison for the following purposes:

(i) on compassionate grounds;
(ii) to engage in employment or voluntary work;
(iii) to receive instruction or training not generally available in prison;
(iv) to participate in proceedings before any court or tribunal;
(v) to consult with legal advisers where the consultation cannot take place in the prison;
(vi) to assist the police in their enquiries;
(vii) to facilitate a transfer between prisons;
(viii) to assist in the maintenance of family ties or the transition from prison life to freedom;
(ix) to visit the locality of the prison (r 6(3)).

8.41 The rule provides that before release can take place, the Secretary of State must be satisfied that the person will not present an unacceptable risk of committing further offences (r 6(4)), or that the length of sentence and the frequency of release will not undermine public confidence in the administration of justice (r 6(5)). This duty is expressed in even more severe terms for prisoners who have committed further offences whilst released on licence (r 6(6)). Prisoners may be recalled to prison at any time during a period of temporary release, whether or not their licence conditions have been broken (r 6(7)).

8.42 The manner in which the rule is operated is contained in IG 36/95. This establishes that the following classes of prisoners are not entitled to temporary release in any circumstances: category A and escape list prisoners, unconvicted and convicted unsentenced prisoners, those subject to extradition proceedings and prisoners who are remanded on further charges or whom are awaiting sentence following further convictions (para 2.3).

Risk assessment

8.43 There are three forms of temporary release being compassionate licence, facility licence and resettlement licence. Although eligibility differs for each form of release, in all cases a risk assessment must be completed before the release can be authorised. The main factors to be considered in completing this assessment are the risk that is posed to the public, whether the licence will be adhered to, the availability of suitable accommodation and whether the purpose of release is likely to be acceptable to reasonable public opinion.

8.44 The assessment is carried out in the prison but is subject to approval by the Lifer Management Unit for life sentenced prisoners and the Home Office Controller for contracted out prisons. Instruction to Governors 36/95 contains a 10 page appendix setting out the main areas to be investigated. These include some obvious areas for assessment, such as a prisoner's previous response to temporary release, custodial behaviour and home circumstances. However, other considerations are less easy to assess, such as the position and views of known victims or an offence analysis to see whether a prisoner may be prone to recidivism. It is difficult to see how prison staff will have either the information or resources to accurately assess this aspect of offending.

8.45   Prisoners serving less that 12 months are not subject to sentence planning and as such less information is available on them. As a minimum, the prison must obtain details of the offence, sentence and previous record, and probation reports (pre or post-sentence), any police post-sentence reports and records of any previous custodial sentences. The application will be considered by a Board at the prison who can either make a recommendation or defer a decision for further information. Any decision to authorise temporary release must be made by a governor above grade 4 and if such a governor is not available, the application must be referred to the area manager for a decision.

8.46   Prisoners serving 12 months or more have more stringent arrangements in place. Within 12 weeks of sentence, a preliminary assessment must be prepared based on the same documents as listed for prisoners serving less than a year and attached to sentence planning documents. Once an application for a temporary licence is made, a request is sent to the outside probation office for a home circumstances report. The papers will then be considered by a Board in the prison (unless it is less than six months since the last grant of temporary release and there has been no significant change in circumstances). This Board will contain a governor, a prison officer, a seconded probation officer and for lifers, the lifer liaison officer. The prisoner can be invited to attend but there is no requirement for this to take place.

8.47   The Board will obtain, in addition to the preliminary reports, a probation report dealing with previous offending, the present offence and whether any areas of concern arise such as child protection issues. A report from the wing detailing prison behaviour, an assessment of what has been done to address offending behaviour and other relevant information must also be prepared. The medical officer can be asked to provide a report if considered relevant. In borderline cases, enquiries can be made of the police and the probation services if information on the victim is deemed necessary. The police must be asked to provide factual information only and not an opinion as to the suitability of release on licence. A recommendation can then be made to the governor, and if it is thought necessary, additional licence conditions may be imposed.

Compassionate licence

8.48   This is reserved for prisoners with exceptional personal circumstances that may include visits to dying relatives or funerals, marriage or religious ceremonies, medical appointments or for primary carers to resolve problems with their children. The two most common applications are to see ill relatives/ attend funerals or to attend medical appointments. In the case of prisoners who have terminally ill relatives or who wish to attend funerals, this will usually only be authorised for 'close relatives'. Medical evidence or proof of the funeral is required to allow an application to proceed. Close relative does not normally include 'in-laws' but may be extended beyond immediate relatives in certain circumstances, usually on the advice of the chaplain or a minister of the prisoner's religion. Release is normally for a very short period of time, for example, to attend a funeral and a brief period of family mourning but not attendance at a wake.

8.49 Prisoners may be allowed licence to attend medical appointments only once the full risk assessment has been carried out. Given the cumbersome process, this will often mean that compassionate release is unavailable in these circumstances and is only appropriate for prisoners who have to attend a series of outside appointments. The governor will seek the advice of the medical officer on the nature of the treatment and whether the prisoner is fit enough to attend unaccompanied. Lifers must have spent a minimum of six months in open conditions and have the application approved by the Lifer Section to be eligible.

Facility licence

8.50 In addition to those prisoners not eligible for any form of temporary release, category B prisoners may not be considered for facility licence. The general principles of this licence are to enable prisoners to participate in regime related activities (such as work experience, community service projects, educational courses) and for official purposes such as attending civil court hearings. In order to be eligible, prisoners must have served at least one-quarter of their sentence, including any time spent on remand.

8.51 Facility licence cannot be granted for social or recreational purposes but must have a 'clear and substantive purpose which will allow reparation or help prisoners to lead law abiding and useful lives' (para 4.2). The duration of such a licence must not be for more than five consecutive days, although this can be granted each week and the governor must be satisfied that excessive grants of such a licence do not undermine the punitive element of a sentence.

8.52 Meetings with legal advisors do fall within the scope of facility licence, but only in exceptional circumstances. This usually means cases where the volume of paperwork is such that it cannot be brought to the prison or where the prisoner needs to attend a legal conference where parties other than his/her legal advisors are present. Attendance for the purpose of attending court hearings will normally be allowed if the risk assessment is positive and the court requires the prisoner's attendance or if attendance will further resettlement into the community. However, due to the possibility of adverse reactions if the outcome is unfavourable, governors are required to seek approval from the area manager for all category C prisoners who have more than six months to their release date.

Resettlement licence

8.53 Eligibility to apply for resettlement licence is determined by length of sentence:

(i) Adult prisoners serving less than 12 months are ineligible.

(ii) Young offenders serving less than 12 months may apply after three months from the date of sentence or four weeks before their release date, whichever is the earlier.

(iii) Prisoners serving four years or more who were sentenced after 1 October 1992, are eligible after one-half of the sentence has been served (ie at the time of parole eligibility). The parole decision must have been made and if it is unfavourable, the prisoner must wait for a period of six months from the date of the refusal or the parole eligibility date, whichever is the earlier. At subsequent parole reviews, the delay is two months from the refusal. If a prisoner in this group has served one-third of their sentence and has had previous home leaves, applications can be made within 12 months of the parole eligibility date.

(iv) Prisoners serving 12 months but less than four years may apply after having served one-third of the sentence or after four months, whichever is the longer period.

(v) Prisoners sentenced before 1 October 1992 to sentences of four years or more may apply after having served one-third of their sentence (ie the parole eligibility date). Adverse parole decisions defer the timing of the application as above.

Lifers

8.54 Life sentenced prisoners are entitled to apply for all forms of temporary release. In order to be eligible, such prisoners must either have been in custody for a period of four months after having been notified of a provisional release date, or have been in an open prison for six months for compassionate and facility licence or nine months for resettlement licence. All decisions to grant temporary release must be approved by Prison Service Headquarters.

8.55 The purpose of release on resettlement licence is expressed to be to enable prisoners to maintain family ties and links with the community and to make suitable arrangements for accommodation, work and training on release. Licences may be granted for between one and five days at a time. Unless the prisoner is at a PRES hostel or in a resettlement prison, there must be a gap of eight weeks between each grant of a licence. Prisoners must also be in custody for at least seven days before final release from prison. For prisoners at PRES hostels and resettlement prisons, more frequent grants of resettlement licence can be made providing they have worked outside of the prison for at least two weeks.

Breach of licence conditions

8.56 Governors are required to make spot checks on prisoners on temporary release to ensure, for example, that the prisoner is at the correct address or has not gone to the pub. The most common breaches of such licences are failing to return to prison on time, failing to return at all or the commission of further offences whilst on licence. In all cases, this constitutes an offence against prison discipline and on return to prison, charges should be laid against the prisoner immediately. If any criminal charges have also been brought or if the police are mounting their own investigation, the disciplinary proceedings will be adjourned pending their outcome. The governor must notify the local police force in any case where a prisoner has failed to return and inform the supervising probation officer. Where a licence has been breached, governors are instructed not to make any further grants of temporary licence, save for exceptional cases, until the prisoner is four weeks from release on parole or automatic release.

8.57 The Prisoners (Return to Custody) Act 1995 makes it a criminal offence for prisoners to be unlawfully at large. The offence is committed either:

(i) by failing to return from a period of temporary release from prison within the time specified on the licence, without reasonable excuse; or
(ii) by knowing or believing that an order has been made recalling him/her to prison and failing to take all necessary steps to comply with this, without reasonable excuse.

8.58 Prisoners who are convicted of the offence will be tried in a magistrates' court who may impose a sentence of up to six months' imprisonment, and/or a fine not exceeding level 5 on the standard scale.

General

8.59 In many cases where in the past release on licence would have been granted, prisoners will find that they are no longer eligible or that there is insufficient time to make a full risk assessment. The changes to these rules were upheld by the Divisional Court (see *R v Secretary of State for the Home Department, ex p Briggs, Green and Hargreaves* (25 July 1995, unreported, DC)) and as such, prisoners may find that they are more reliant on escorted absences from prison for such matters as medical appointments or attending funerals than was the case in the past. In such cases, even where the same prisoner has suffered a substantial change in his/her entitlements, challenges need to be made on the individual merits of each case now that the scheme as a whole has been upheld.

AUTHORISED POSSESSIONS

8.60 Standing Order 4 is the document that was issued to provide a framework for prisoners' possessions and other facilities under the version of Prison Rule that was in force prior to July 1995. Broadly speaking, facilities were divided into two categories, those which shall be made available to prisoners and those which are more discretionary and can be granted or withdrawn by the governor. One of the chief facilities that is dealt with is the retention, acquisition and use of personal possessions, including the circumstances in which prisoners can wear their own clothes.

RETAINING PERSONAL POSSESSIONS

8.61   The statement of principle is for prisoners to be allowed to retain sufficient property to enable them to live as normal and individual an existence as possible within the constraints of custody. Property held by a prisoner in possession is for the use of that prisoner alone. It is only possible to lend, sell or give property to another prisoner with the permission of the governor, a measure designed to prevent racketeering. It is advised that the number of possessions should not be such that would make cell searching difficult, a theme that was emphasised in the Woodcock Report and has lead to discussions as to the possibility of limiting possessions to those that can be held in three boxes.

8.62   Standing Order 4 lists those possessions that prisoners are entitled to retain as:

(i)   a minimum of six newspapers or periodicals;
(ii)   a minimum of three books;
(iii)   a combined music system, or a radio and either a record, cassette or compact disc player;
(iv)   records/cassettes/compact discs in an amount that is reasonable;
(v)   smoking material (convicted prisoners may have 80 cigarettes or 62.5 grams of tobacco, unconvicted prisoners 180 cigarettes or 137.5 grams of tobacco);
(vi)   writing and drawing materials;
(vii)   a watch;
(viii) a manual typewriter;
(ix)   a battery shaver;
(x)   batteries for personal possessions;
(xi)   personal toiletries;
(xii)   one plain ring;
(xiii) a medallion or locket;
(xiv)   a calendar;
(xv)   religious articles at the discretion of the governor;
(xvi)   photographs, pictures and greeting cards;
(xvii) a diary, an address book, postage stamps and phonecards (Standing Order 4, para 9).

Prisoners' money

8.63   The majority of purchases a prisoner can make are from the prison canteen. There are a number of items that can only be purchased from the canteen, including batteries, food, phonecards and tobacco. The Secretary of State sets annual limits as to the amount of money prisoners are allowed to spend in addition to prison wages earned by the individual prisoner. Money sent into the prison is credited to a private cash account alongside the record of wages that a prisoner has earned. The most recent annual limit that was set was £120, but there is discretion for governors to set higher local limits. Figures of around £300 per annum are not uncommon. In addition to this, the costs of phonecards and batteries is often not included in this limit.

8.64   Although prisoners' purchases are mainly confined to the canteen, it is possible to buy items by mail order. For category A and B prisoners, these must be purchased from companies belonging to the Mail Order Protection Scheme and must be sent to the prison direct. Newspapers and periodicals can be subscribed to directly from publishers, newsagents or booksellers, either on order from the prisoner or from outside of the prison (r 41(3)).

Forfeiture of personal possessions

8.65   The governor has the power to remove possessions and to arrange for them to be placed in stored property or handed out to relatives if it is felt that the volume of personal possessions may be such as to make effective searching unduly difficult or if there is a risk to health and safety or good order and discipline. Magazines, newspapers and books can also be withdrawn if it is felt that they constitute a threat to good order and discipline, national security or the interests of the prison. This power has been commonly invoked by governors to prevent access to political publications (eg the anarchist magazine *Class War* or gay publications, see r 41. At present, no legal action has been taken to challenge the lawfulness of this type of censorship.

8.66   In addition to these discretionary powers, the governor has the power to order the forfeiture of items on disciplinary grounds. Rule 50(1)(b) of the Prison Rules empowers governors to order the forfeiture of privileges as part of a punishment at an adjudication for a period of up to 42 days (21 days for young offenders). Forfeiture of educational notebooks, radios, writing materials and postage stamps should not normally be ordered.

INCENTIVES AND PRIVILEGES

The basis of the new scheme

8.67   The system of privileges and facilities that were afforded to prisoners has been the matter of some discussion within the Prison Service and in July 1995 a framework document was issued to try and establish regimes that will link these to custodial behaviour (IG 74/95). All prisons are now required to operate a local incentives scheme intended to motivate prisoners to good behaviour and performance. Although the scheme was piloted in a number of prisons, the precise legal framework was laid out in the amended Prison Rules issued in June 1995 and in particular r 4(3) which states that:

> 'Systems of privileges approved under paragraph (1) may include arrangements under which privileges may be granted to prisoners only in so far as they have met, and for so long as they continue to meet, specified standards in their behaviour and their performance in work or other activities.'

8.68   The six privileges that have been identified as the 'key earnable privileges' are:

(i)   access to private cash;
(ii) extra and improved visits;
(iii) eligibility to participate in enhanced earnings schemes;
(iv) community visits for category D prisoners, adult females and young offenders (subject to normal risk assessment procedures);
(v) the wearing of one's own clothes;
(vi) time out of cells for association.

There have been a number of other privileges that have been discussed such as enhanced canteen facilities, employment in the most desirable jobs, cooking facilities and extra mail order purchases.

8.69   The first point to note from this framework document is that it relates to privileges and not rights. Therefore, whilst the length and frequency of visits is included, there is no right to remove the basic entitlement that prisoners have to two 30 minute visits every four weeks. Similarly, time out of cell is linked to this scheme but it is not possible to undermine the right of prisoners to one hour's exercise each day.

8.70   The earned incentives are to be operated on a three tier system of basic, standard and enhanced regimes. This may be operated either by establishing differentiated wings or simply on individual prisoners. The crucial difference will be between basic and standard regimes whereas the enhanced regime may only be slightly more favourable than standard, depending on the nature of the prison and the facilities available. It is a matter for governors to decide whether prisoners should enter the system on the standard level or the basic level. If entry is to be on the basic level, it is suggested that the system affords the opportunity for a fast progression to the standard level where appropriate.

8.71   Examples of how regimes may be differentiated can be illustrated through access to private cash and visits. The minimum that can be provided is for no access to private cash and two 30 minute visits a month. The basic regime is envisaged to allow £2.50 per week in private cash and the two monthly visits, the standard regime £10 per week in private cash and three visits per month and the enhanced regime, £15 private cash and four or five one hour visits per month.

Unconvicted prisoners

8.72   Differentiated regimes will also be operated for unconvicted prisoners, although these will have to take account of the particular rights which they are afforded. This means that certain behavioural indicators such as work performance cannot be utilised as remand prisoners cannot be required to work. Private cash limits will commence at £15 per week, rising to £30 on the enhanced regimes and the right to wear one's own clothes exists on all regimes. Entry will be to the standard regime in the first instance.

The assessment of behaviour

8.73 The only guide as to how behaviour will be assessed appears in IG 74/95 at annex D. Staff are firstly required to look at 'institutional behaviour' which incorporates performance at work, formal disciplinary offences and more subjective assessments as to how a prisoner relates to other prisoners and staff. Secondly, attitude to sentence planning including the use made of the personal officer scheme, the approach to the sentence and the willingness to make effective use of time in custody. Finally, the attitude to those outside prison, including family members and victims must be assessed. Behavioural criteria may be loosely defined by a number of indicators. These will be the absence of violence, bullying and aggressive behaviour, respect for establishment rules, maintaining personal hygiene and health and having regard to the health and safety of others and effort in constructive and work activities.

8.74 Whilst many of these criteria are laudable, it is difficult to see how an effective, objective monitoring system can properly be established. There is also a danger that behavioural targets could be linked to work undertaken on offending behaviour thereby increasing the problems faced by prisoners who are engaged in the appeals process or who maintain their innocence.

A new disciplinary system?

8.75 The incentives scheme can effectively be seen as an attempt to introduce a new informal disciplinary system that sidesteps many of the safeguards inherent in the formal system. It is now envisaged that governors will be able to deal with misbehaviour through adjudications, discretionary powers (eg r 43) which cannot be punitive in intent, or through administrative decisions as to which regime prisoners will be allocated.

8.76 In order to allow for the quasi-disciplinary aspect of the incentives scheme, certain limited safeguards have been built into the guidance given to governors. When local schemes are introduced, clear and easy to administer criteria for assessing behaviour and performance must be issued and rules established for decision-making and appeals procedures. Written reasons must be given for adverse decisions together with the information as to how an appeal can be made (r 4(4)). Any existing sentence planning, personal officer and 'compact' schemes in operation should be incorporated into this procedure. Finally, the targets set must be capable of being effectively monitored.

8.77 Governors are reminded of the need to make decisions based on the provision of correct information and to ensure that prisoners have some method whereby their own representations and responses can be taken into account. When reasons are given for adverse decisions, these must be sufficiently detailed to enable prisoners to understand how they have failed to meet relevant criteria and on what information the decision was based.

8.78   At the time of writing, the proposals have not been put into widespread operation so it is not possible to anticipate how effective and fair the scheme will prove to be. The pilot attempts have met with considerable opposition from prisoners who allege that the basic regime effectively amounts to no more than segregation with none of the in-built procedural safeguards. A number of prisoners from Swaleside obtained leave to move for judicial review in July 1995 based on the pilot scheme in operation at that prison but it is possible that the changes in the Prison Rules and the introduction of the framework document will supersede any success that they might have.

PRODUCTION AT COURT IN CIVIL CASES

The right to be produced

8.79   Prisoners who are engaged in civil litigation, be it against the Secretary of State, the Home Office, the Prison Service or any of its employees, or simply in other civil matters unrelated to their imprisonment such as child care, will often face difficulties when their action reaches the stage where their attendance at court is necessary. There has been a great deal of resistance to production in those circumstances and where production is authorised, the prisoner has been asked to pay a contribution towards the costs of production. These contributions were often set at a level which is impossible for the prisoner to pay.

8.80   The principle that a prisoner may be taken to court for these purposes arises from the Criminal Justice Act 1961, s 29. This gives authority for the Secretary of State to authorise any person detained in the UK to attend any other place in the UK where it is desirable in the interests of justice or for the purposes of attending any public enquiry (s 29(1)). Any person who is produced under this section, remains in custody throughout the time they are outside of prison (s 29(2)).

8.81   This section does not actually create any rights, being merely an enabling section to permit attendance at court. The power granted to the Secretary of State is to decide whether it is 'desirable' in the interests of justice for a prisoner to be so produced. There is no explanation as to when this power should be exercised in either the Prison Act 1952, or in the Prison Rules 1964. Similarly, there is no explanation as to whom should be responsible for the costs of such a production.

8.82   The judiciary have never developed a consistent approach to this matter (for earlier discussions on this point see *Becker v Home Office* [1972] 2 QB 407 and *R v Governor of Brixton Prison, ex p Walsh* [1985] AC 154) although detailed guidance can be obtained from the case of *R v Secretary of State for the Home Department, ex p Wynne* ([1992] QB 406, CA). The Court of Appeal looked at these provisions in some detail on behalf of a category A prisoner who was seeking to attend a judicial review hearing which he was conducting in person. The application was actually dismissed because the prisoner had failed to make a formal application to the prison governor to be produced and prisoners must be made aware that this is an essential step to take when attendance at court is necessary. Nevertheless, the court looked at the provisions for production in some detail. The court consisted of Lord Donaldson, the Master of the Rolls, Lord Justice Staughton and Lord Justice McGowan. Whilst the judgments did not concur on the precise extent of a prisoner's rights to be produced, Lord Donaldson gave the most detailed ruling and it is submitted that his views should prevail. Certainly, the Prison Service have accepted these arguments in all applications for production and there have been no further applications for judicial review on this subject. The law in this section is therefore extrapolated from Lord Donaldson's views, but it may be the case that if applications made on this basis are refused in the future, further guidance from the court will be necessary.

8.83 Lord Donaldson was unable to think of any circumstances in which it would not be desirable for a prisoner to attend court when it was adjudicating on his rights. This was seen as a basic human right, consistent with Article 6 of the European Convention on Human Rights. The question of whether it would cause administrative difficulty was not strictly speaking relevant to the issue of whether production is desirable. The dissenting view was that where the Secretary of State considered a case to be hopeless, as there is still a discretion to be exercised, production may not be desirable in the interests of justice. It seems unthinkable that this view could now prevail, particularly when it involves the exercise of an essentially judicial power by the Secretary of State, rather than the exercise of executive discretion. It would be impossible for this power to be utilised in cases where the action was against the Prison Service, the minister or an employee as this would effectively amount to the Secretary of State being 'judge in his own cause'.

The costs of production

8.84 The second, and more difficult point addressed by the court was the question of what direction should be made as to the costs of production. Whilst it was accepted that it is not unlawful or unreasonable for a charge to be made to the prisoner, the court took the view that the Secretary of State was under a duty to ensure that this charge was reasonable in light of the ability of the prisoner to pay. As the Criminal Justice Act 1961, s 29 was concerned with the interests of justice, it cannot be the position that a prisoner who is able to afford the costs should be in a better position that one who cannot.

8.85 The basis for the calculation of the costs must be made on production from the prison nearest to the court. Prisoners have no right to be detained in a prison of their choice and if this were not provided for in the judgment, it would have been susceptible to abuse simply by transferring the applicant to a prison as far away from the court as possible. Prisoners may not be required to contribute to the costs of the escort as this would amount to them contributing to the cost of their own imprisonment.

8.86   The question of legal representation is a relevant one when determining decisions of this nature and the amount of costs to be requested. If a prisoner is in receipt of legal aid, then the costs can be set closer to their true level rather than at a level commensurate with the prisoner's own ability to pay as these costs can be properly claimed from the legal aid fund. A prisoner who refuses to apply for legal aid will be in a difficult position as the disadvantage would be seen to be self-inflicted and the state could not be construed to have prevented the right to justice. Lawyers should still argue for the costs in such cases to be set at the lowest possible level so as to discharge their duty to the Legal Aid Board.

Conclusion

8.87   The dissenting views on production, and the costs of production, appear to have been made with a view to the possibility that prisoners would commence unmeritorious litigation in the hope of obtaining a free day out of prison. In cases of doubt, the dissenting view was that the judge hearing the matter would have the power to direct the attendance of the prisoner if it felt it was necessary and to make an assessment as to what costs should be recovered. This view seems somewhat antiquated in the present climate and it is certainly the case that Lord Donaldson's opinions have been accepted in arguments for production. If the policy were to change it would almost certainly lead to a breach of Article 6 of the European Convention on Human Rights.

CHAPTER 9

GENERAL AREAS

SEARCHING

9.1 Rule 39 of the Prison Rules requires that every prisoner will be searched when first taken into prison custody, upon being received at any prison, and at any other time that the governor believes a search to be necessary. Searches should be conducted 'in as seemly a manner as is consistent with discovering anything concealed' (r 39(2)). Prisoners may not be strip searched in the sight of another prisoner, and strip searches must not be conducted in the sight and presence of an officer who is not of the same sex.

9.2 Comprehensive guidance on searching is given in the Prison Service's Security Manual. At paragraph 66, governors are asked to 'devise an effective searching strategy' for their establishments and reminded of the need that this should take into account the following core standards which must apply to all searches:

(i)   Searches must be conducted in as seemly and sensitive a manner as is consistent with discovering anything concealed;

(ii) no person should be stripped and searched in the sight of anyone who is not involved in the search (unless there are exceptional circumstances, envisaged to include where the prisoner is subjected to control and restraint techniques);

(iii) no person should be stripped and searched in the sight or presence of an officer of the opposite sex, except that children aged 10 or under must always be searched by a female officer;

(iv) no visitor or member of staff may be intimately searched by any prison staff, including health care staff (Security Manual, para 66.3).

9.3 Beyond this, governors may devise a programme of searching taking into account the needs of their own establishments. The Security Manual envisages that an effective searching programme will include searches of the hand luggage and personal property of staff and visitors, pat down searches, rub down searches, strip searches, and intimate searches.

9.4 If a prisoner refuses to co-operate when informed that they will be searched, they may be charged with the disciplinary offence of disobeying a lawful order (see chapter 7). Rule 44 of the Prison Rules gives prison officers authority to use force only when this is necessary, and thus where a prisoner has consistently refused to submit to the search, it is possible that force may be used (para 67.16). However, only such force as is deemed necessary should be exerted. Prisoners who are subjected to excessive or unreasonable force may find remedies in the civil law actions of assault or misfeasance in public office although this will depend upon the circumstances of each case. Where the requirement to submit to a search is unreasonable then judicial review would be an appropriate remedy.

Searches of prisoners' accommodation

9.5   The rules on cell searching changed in May 1995 to reflect the recommendations in the Woodcock Report (Report of the Inquiry into the Escape of Six Prisoners from the Special Security Unit at Whitemoor Prison, Cambridgeshire, on Friday 9 September 1994, Cm 2741). Instruction to Governors 53/95 introduced the changes, and amended the Security Manual by producing a step-by-step guide on the searches of prisoners' living accommodation (para 68(3)).

9.6   The revised procedure states that unless a prisoner is 'not available' they should be informed that their cell will be searched and that this procedure will include a strip search. The prisoner should be taken to their cell, strip searched and then be taken to another part of the prison from where they should not be able to see their cell being searched (as their presence may 'intimidate and distract the searching officer, (para 68.3(c)). Before the search starts, the prisoner should be asked if they have any unauthorised articles and given the opportunity to give these in. Although they may still be charged with possession of such articles, it is possible that any punishment received at adjudication would be lesser so as to take account of this.

9.7   Other prisoners should be cleared from the immediate area where the search is due to take place. The cell should then be thoroughly searched including 'ventilators, ceiling, floor, walls, door, windows (inside and, where possible, out), grilles, pipes and fixed furniture and fittings'(para 68.3(f)). The officers conducting the search have the discretion to remove items from the cell to another area of the prison and search them thoroughly. This provision is designed to cover situations where for example, it is thought necessary to take electrical equipment and x-ray or dismantle it to see whether there is something concealed inside. If any unauthorised articles are found during the cell search, and these could constitute the basis for disciplinary proceedings to be taken against the prisoner, then they must be bagged up, sealed, and labelled to be used as evidence in the adjudication or in any court hearing if there is the possibility of prosecution through the criminal courts.

9.8   When the search has been completed, the staff who have been involved (known by prisoners as 'burglars') must tell the prisoner whether any articles have been removed from their cell, and if so whether this is because they are thought to be unauthorised, or whether they were taken to another area to be searched in which case they should be returned. If any damage has been caused to any of the prisoner's property they should be advised of this and told of the procedures that they should follow in order to claim compensation.

9.9 The new cell searching procedures have caused great concern amongst prisoners and prison reformers, primarily on the basis that under the previous procedures it was advised that prisoners should be present during a cell search so as to ensure that no allegation that articles had been planted could take place. Also, it has been argued that damage to prisoners' possessions is less likely to occur if the prisoner is on hand to point out fragile items and that officers may exercise a greater degree of care when handling property if its owner is present.

9.10 If a prisoner charged with possession of an unauthorised item complains that the item was planted in their absence, then at adjudication they should plead this as a defence. If they are found guilty of the offence an 'appeal' may be made to the area manager and an application may be made to the Ombudsman if the finding of guilt is upheld. Judicial review proceedings may be commenced at any stage in the process (see chapter 7).

Strip searches and intimate searches

9.11 Strip searches of prisoners may only be conducted by officers of the same sex (r 39(3)), and unless there are exceptional circumstances (see above) only two officers should carry out a strip search (Security Manual, para 67.9). Strip searches should usually take place in the prisoner's own cell or in other 'suitable premises' either in the reception of the prison or elsewhere. All prisoners should be strip searched on their reception to a prison and before a cell search. Governors are advised that they must use their discretion to authorise searches, but that they must exercise this discretion reasonably. 'In practice this will mean that searches should be conducted only where the interests of security or of good order and discipline so require' (para 65.3).

9.12 The Security Manual stresses that a strip search is a visual search of the prisoner only, and that other than when checking the head, there should be no need to touch a prisoner at all (para 67.11). However, metal detectors and 'other forms of equipment' may be used.

9.13 A step-by-step guide for strip searching a male prisoner is produced in the Security Manual, and this advises that the procedure is conducted along the following lines:

(i) The prisoner should first take off his shoes and socks, which should be handed over and examined.
(ii) The soles of each foot must be lifted and examined in turn.
(iii) The prisoner should take off his trousers and underpants and hand them over to be examined.
(iv) He should stand with his legs apart, and be observed from the front and rear.
(v) If it is thought that the prisoner has something hidden in his anal or genital area then he may be asked to position himself in 'such a way as

to allow staff to confirm this visually'. Governor's have discretion as to whether this would involve a prisoner being asked to bend or squat. However, 'suitable standards of dignity and decency for the prisoner must be observed' (para 67.10(e)).

(vi)   The prisoner's trousers and underpants should be given back to him immediately and he should be allowed to put them on before the search continues further.

(vii) The prisoner should take off the clothing from the top part of his body and hand it over for examination.

(viii) He should be asked to hold up his arms and be observed from both the front and the rear.

(ix)   The rest of his clothing should be returned to him without delay (para 67.10(a)–(i)).

(x)   The prisoner should be asked to remove any headgear which will be handed over to be examined. An officer may run their fingers through the prisoner's hair or may ask the prisoner to do so.

(xi)   An officer should look around and inside the prisoner's ears, nostrils, and mouth (para 67.5(d)–(f)).

9.14   The strip search should be conducted as 'briskly as is consistent with the need to examine each article of clothing closely' (para 67.11), and the prisoner should not be completely naked at any stage unless the search is conducted as part of the reception procedure (which also requires showering) in which case he should be given a dressing gown or a large towel before the search commences (para 67.12).

9.15   The strip searching procedure for women prisoners is basically the same as above. However, the normal practice is to check the top half of the woman's body before the bottom half. When the top half of her body has been searched, a woman should be given a dressing gown to wear for the rest of the search and she will be asked to lift this so that officers may visually examine the bottom half of her body. Staff are advised to check the dressing gown after the search to ensure that nothing has been put in the pockets or sleeves.

9.16   An intimate search (of body orifices) should only be undertaken by a medical officer, and because of the professional duty of care that medical practitioners owe to their patients, such a search can only be conducted with the prisoner's consent. If the prisoner is incapable of giving consent a medical officer should only conduct an intimate search if in their clinical judgment this is necessary in order to prevent death or serious harm to the prisoner. In such circumstances, the Security Manual advises that medical officers should act only after consulting the governor, seek the opinion of another doctor, and have the examination witnessed (para 67.14).

Rub down searches

9.17   Circular Instruction 37/92 introduced a change to the Prison Rules which allowing searches other than strip searches to be carried out by officers who are not the same sex as the prisoner. However, Prison Service policy is that rub down searches of male prisoners may be conducted by either male or female officers, whereas female prisoners may only be searched in this way by officers of their own sex (Security Manual, para 67.2). However, male prisoners who have 'genuine religious objections' to being searched by a female officer should not be subjected to this (CI 49/92).

9.18   Rub down searches are generally carried out by one officer, and the procedure that they should follow for a male prisoner is laid down in paragraph 67.5 of the Security Manual. This states that the officer should stand facing the prisoner and ask the prisoner to empty his pockets. The contents of the pockets should be searched together with any items that the prisoner is carrying. Any headgear that the prisoner is wearing should be handed over by the prisoner to be searched and the officer should then run their fingers through the prisoner's hair or ask the prisoner to do so. The officer should then look around and inside the prisoner's ears, nostrils, and mouth and feel behind and around the prisoner's collar and across the top of his shoulders. The prisoner should then be asked to raise his arms so that they are level with his shoulders with his fingers apart and his palms facing downwards whilst the officer runs both of his hands along the prisoners arms. Following this, the officer should check in between the prisoner's fingers and look at his arms and the backs of his hands. The officer should then run his hands down the front of the prisoner's body from the neck to waist, down the sides of their body from armpits to waist, the front of the waistband, the prisoner's back from collar to waist, the rear of the waistband and then the seat of the trousers. The back and side of each leg should be checked separately from the prisoner's crotch to his ankle, and the prisoner should then be asked to lift up each foot so that the soles of his shoes can be checked. The prisoner should then be asked to remove his shoes and socks so that these can be scrutinised together with the soles of his feet. The front and sides of each leg should be checked as should the prisoner's abdomen. Finally, the officer should look around the room to ensure that the prisoner did not drop anything either before or during the search.

9.19   The procedure for conducting a rub down search of a female prisoner is essentially the same as for a male. However, staff are reminded that they must check around and under the breasts. Although it is recognised that it may be difficult to check around the top of a woman's legs if she is wearing a skirt, the searching officer should nevertheless run her hands over the woman's legs outside her skirt.

Searches of visitors

9.20   Rule 86 of the Prison Rules allows the stopping and searching of any person or vehicle who is entering or leaving a prison. With regard to searching visitors to prisoners, the Security Manual lays down core standards that professional visitors should be able to retain their hand luggage, although this can be searched before and after a visit; children aged 10 or under should be searched by a female officer and older children should be searched by an officer of the same sex; children under 16 or visitors who appear to have learning difficulties should only be searched after the purpose and procedure of the search has been explained to their parent or a responsible adult companion who should also be present during the search (unless the person being searched is an adult and does not want to be searched in their presence); visitors cannot be detained against their will unless they have been arrested and cautioned (unless the governor's power to require a strip search is exercisable, see below) (para 69.3). All references in this section are to the Security Manual unless otherwise stated.

9.21   The most common type of searching procedure that visitors will be subjected to are pat down or rub down searches, which may involve the use of a metal detector when searching the person and/or an x-ray machine when searching luggage (paras 69.5–69.6). It is increasingly common for visitors to be required to leave their hand luggage in lockers outside the visits area.

9.22   Where a visitor refuses to co-operate with a search, the governor may direct that the visit should take place in closed conditions or that they will not be permitted access to the prison.

9.23   If prison staff have a reasonable suspicion that a visitor is trying to smuggle in items which are legal outside prison (eg alcohol or tobacco) they may decide to allow the visit but maintain close supervision, conduct a rub down search, allow only a closed visit, or refuse the visit. If the visit is allowed then it is possible that the prisoner will be strip-searched afterwards (para 69.10).

9.24   If it is suspected that a visitor is attempting to smuggle explosives, any weapons other than firearms, or items for use in an escape attempt, the police should be informed and asked to come to the prison. Where the police are not able to attend, or cannot do so promptly, the visit may be refused or the visitor asked to consent to waiting for the arrival of the police. In some circumstances the prison officer's power of arrest may apply (see below) (para 69.12).

9.25   If a visitor is reasonably suspected of being in possession of a firearm, a firearm and ammunition, or a class A, B, or C controlled drug, the police will be contacted and should then come to the prison and deal with the matter. However, if it becomes clear that the police will not attend, the governor can require a strip search. Other forms of search should be conducted first and if the offending items are discovered at that stage, it is unlikely that further action would be taken. If nothing is found in a rub down search and a search of the visitor's hand luggage, they may be taken to a private room, informed that they are suspected of smuggling an article and of the general nature of that article. The visitor will be asked to sign a form consenting to the strip search, and if they agree to do so the strip search will be carried out in accordance with the procedures outlined above for strip searching prisoners. If the visitor does not consent to a strip search it is possible that reasonable force may be used to make them subject to this. However, this should be 'a last resort' (para 69.13–69.17).

9.26 In *Bayliss and Barton v Home Secretary and Governor of HM Prison, Frankland* ([1992] LAG Bulletin, February, p 16), HHJ Marshall Evans ruled that the power to strip search a visitor to a prisoner would be unlawfully exercised if more than reasonable force was used, if the decision to search was perverse, and/or if the search was not conducted in a reasonably seemly and decent manner. The plaintiffs were awarded compensation following the judge's ruling that they had been unlawfully induced to strip, and that they had not been searched in a reasonably seemly and decent manner.

9.27 Section 24(6) and (7) of the Police and Criminal Evidence Act 1984 (PACE) states that a prison officer may arrest a person if there are reasonable grounds to suspect that they are guilty of, or are about to commit an arrestable offence. The following offences are highlighted as being relevant to prisons in the Security Manual (para 69.19):

(i) possession of a controlled drug;
(ii) possession of a prohibited weapon;
(iii) possession of any firearm or ammunition with intent to endanger life;
(iv) possession in a public place of a loaded shotgun, loaded air weapon, or any other firearm together with ammunition suitable for use in it;
(v) conveying a thing into a prison with intent to facilitate the escape of a prisoner.

9.28 Furthermore, PACE, s 25 gives prison officers the power to arrest anyone where there are reasonable grounds for suspecting that they are committing, attempting to commit, or have committed or attempted to commit any offence including:

(i) bringing alcohol or tobacco into a prison contrary to regulations (Prison Act 1952, s 40);
(ii) conveying anything into or out of a prison contrary to prison regulations (Prison Act 1952, s 41).

To effect an arrest on this basis one of the general arrest conditions must be fulfilled (ie the name of the person is unknown and cannot be readily ascertained; there are reasonable grounds for doubting that the person has given his real name or a satisfactory address; there are reasonable grounds for believing that arrest is necessary to prevent physical injury or damage to property; there are reasonable grounds for believing that arrest is necessary to protect a child or other vulnerable person from the person who is to be arrested) (para 69.19).

9.29 A prison officer exercising the power of arrest should fulfil the requirements of PACE by telling the person that they are being arrested, the reasons why, and cautioning them. Until the police arrive, an arrested visitor should be supervised by a member of prison staff who will note anything that the visitor says voluntarily as prison staff should not question them. Reasonable force may be used to detain the person until the police arrive.

WORK AND PAY

9.30   Rule 28(1) of the Prison Rules requires adult convicted prisoners to do 'useful work' whilst they are in prison, but limits the requirement to a maximum of 10 hours per day. Unconvicted prisoners are not required to work, but if they wish to do so, they should be able to work as if they were convicted (r 28(5)). In practice, unconvicted prisoners often find that there is no work available for them to do in local prisons. If an unconvicted prisoner asks to work, but turns down a subsequent job offer for 'no valid reason', the governor does not have to offer further employment (SO 6A, para 22).

9.31   The Prison and Young Offender Institute Rules provide that prisoners who are practising Christians should not be required to do any 'unnecessary' work on Sunday, Christmas Day or Good Friday, and that prisoners of other religions should not be required to do unnecessary work on their days of religious observance (r 15 and r 32 respectively). Prison Service Headquarters advise governors of the relevant days each year.

9.32   In order to allocate prisoners to suitable types of employment, the governor and the medical officer have responsibility for classifying them as No 1 (heavy), No 2 (medium), and No 3 (light) labour, and they should not be required to do work of a heavier type than their labour grade (SO 6A, para 9). Prisoners who are ill may be completely excused from work by the medical officer (r 28(2)).

9.33   The Young Offender Institution Rules 1988 require that prisoners are engaged in education, training courses, work and physical education for up to eight hours per day (r 34). Where young offenders are under the age of 17, they should participate in education or training courses for at least 15 hours per week (r 35). All male YOI inmates, and women aged under 21 should receive an average of two hours' physical education per week (r 38), and this is included in the working week. Work provided in young offender institutions:

> 'shall so far as is practicable, be such as will foster personal responsibility and prisoners' interests and skills, and help them to prepare for the return to the community.' (r 37)

9.34   The Governor should ensure that safe systems of work are in operation, and delegates this responsibility to the members of staff who are in charge of each work area. Health and Safety Executive Inspectors may conduct inspections under the Health and Safety at Work etc Act 1974 (SO 6A, paras 14–15).

9.35   Standing Order 6 provides for ex-gratia payments to be made for prisoners who are injured at work and are subsequently incapacitated upon their release from prison. Such payments should be made 'at the same rate as disablement benefit under the Industrial Injuries Acts following examination by a Medical Board of the Department of Social Security' (SO 6A, para 16). Members of staff who witness any such injury should complete reports of the accident and detail whether there was any degree of negligence, and upon receipt of this information the governor should make enquiries and arrange for the prisoner to be examined by the medical officer if appropriate.

9.36 Rule 27(1) of the Prison Rules states that prisoners not engaged in outdoor work or in an open prison should have one hour's exercise per day if the weather permits. Detailed guidance on this provision is given in Standing Order 6A, para 24:

'(a) prisoners who are employed indoors and who have evening association should have half an hour of exercise; other prisoners employed indoors who do not have evening association should have one hour of exercise. This will apply from Monday to Friday. Prisoners employed out of doors need not be given other exercise as well. On Saturdays and Sundays prisoners should have at least one hour of exercise, but work on Saturday mornings should not be curtailed for the sake of this, and prisoners who are out of doors for recreational purposes on Saturday afternoons need not be given formal exercise as well. If bad weather prevents outside exercise, prisoners who would otherwise be given it should go to work instead if they have been able to take part in outside exercise on either of the two preceding days. If outdoor exercises are not possible for two consecutive days, half an hour of indoor exercise should be given on the third day and every day after that while outside exercise remains impracticable;

(b) if there is a shortage of work, the governor may arrange for an additional period of exercise or physical education for any prisoners who are affected'.

9.37 Rule 28(6) of the Prison Rules makes provision for adult prisoners to be paid for their work, and r 34(5) of the Young Offender Institution Rules provides for young offenders to be paid for their work or other participation in the regime related activities. Convicted prisoners for whom no work is available are paid at a basic rate (currently £2.50 per week), and prisoners who are unable to work are paid at the same rate. In addition, there is a retirement rate of pay (£3.50 per week) which is given to prisoners who choose to retire when they reach retirement age. Such prisoners may elect to continue working if they so choose so long as the medical officer passes them as fit to work. Prisoners who refuse to work will not be paid, and they will also be likely to be charged with an offence against prison discipline (ie if they refuse a lawful order that they should work).

9.38 The Prisoner' Pay Manual was introduced in November 1992, and recognised that the previous levels of prisoners' pay did not even amount to 'pocket money' and provided no incentive for prisoners to work. It aimed to implement Woolf's recommendation of an average weekly pay of £8.00 per week for prisoners who were working. The new pay scheme aimed to provide a framework within which prisoners could be rewarded for taking part in 'purposeful activity' (work, training and daytime education) and be encouraged to put 'sustained effort' into their work (para 2.1).

9.39 Governors set standard rates of pay for each job available in the prison (which cannot be less than the employed rate specified by Prison Service Headquarters), and prisoners who complete their task to an acceptable level of quality are paid at that level. Bonuses for productivity and for attaining qualifications can be paid in certain circumstances. If a prisoner's work is of a sub-standard level deductions from pay of up to £1.00 per week can be made, unless the prisoner is guilty of a 'major failure to match standard performance' in which case it is possible for the pay to be reduced to nothing and the prisoner charged with a disciplinary offence.

FOOD

9.40   Prison Rule 21 provides that:

> 'the food prepared shall be wholesome, nutritious, well prepared and served, reasonably varied and sufficient in quality' (r 21(4)).

9.41   Despite this, many prisoners consistently complain about the quality of the food given to them, and will also find it difficult to obtain meals which fit in with their religious or medical dietary requirements.

9.42   The Race Relations Manual (July 1992) contains a policy statement that:

> 'An adequate and suitable diet is clearly one of the most basic of human needs. In prisons, it is clear that inadequate provision for dietary needs can become a source of complaints and conflict; proper attention to dietary matters can reduce problems in this area'. (para 6.6)

Thus it is recommended that diet should take account of the religious requirements and cultural preferences of prisoners from different ethnic groups.

9.43   Vegetarian dishes should be available to any prisoner who expresses a personal preference, whereas vegan diets are only provided to prisoners who 'are able to demonstrate a commitment to the principles of veganism'. Likewise, in order to qualify for a special diet, members of some religions must be able to 'demonstrate an adherence' to the dietary laws of their religion (CI 37/91). Recognised religious leaders and organisations may be allowed to provide food for prisoners during religious festivals (Race Relations Manual, para 6.6).

9.44   The medical officer of the prison and the Board of Visitors are both under statutory duties to inspect the food before and after it is cooked, and must report upon their findings to the governor (rr 21(5) and 95(2)). Such inspections do not have to take place every day. It is common practice for governors to taste the food prepared at their establishments on a daily basis, although this is not a statutory requirement.

9.45   Standing Order 14 deals with issues of food hygiene and states that the catering facilities of each prison will be inspected by the regional catering managers and independent Home Office health and safety officers in accordance with the standards laid down in the Food Hygiene (General Regulations) 1970. Governors are required to act quickly in response to their recommendations. Medical officers are required to carry out hygiene inspections twice a year and report to Prison Service Headquarters on their findings. In addition, random checks will be made by environmental health officers from the Department of Health each year (paras 28–30). The Food Safety Act 1990 is binding in prison establishments.

9.46 One of the main problems affecting the provision of meals to prisoners is that of transportation from a central kitchen to the wings. In his Annual Report 1992–3, the Chief Inspector of Prisons found that:

> 'the food, which was acceptable when it left the kitchen in a container, can become a tepid stewed mush by the time a prisoner has collected it on the wing and taken it up the stairs to his cell, where he has to eat often without a chair or table but off his bed, in a cell shared by another inmate, a pot or a toilet'. (para 3.11)

9.47 Another major problem is that prisoners' meal times are planned around staffing hours and thus three meals tend to be crammed into eight or nine hours of the day, with breakfast being taken at around 8.15 am, lunch at 11.50 am, and dinner at 4.20 pm (see eg the Chief Inspector's Report of a Full Inspection at HMP Leeds published 15 February 1995, appendix 2).

9.48 Prisoners may complain about the food through the request/complaint procedure to the governor and area manager. The Prisons' Ombudsman has upheld prisoners' complaints concerning food, and made recommendations to the Prison Service for improvement.

THE USE OF SPECIAL ACCOMMODATION AND MECHANICAL RESTRAINTS

Violent and refractory prisoners

9.49 Rule 46 of the Prison Rules (and r 49 of the Young Offender Institutions Rules) allows prison governors to direct that prisoners over the age of 17 may be put under restraint 'where this is necessary to prevent the prisoner from injuring himself or others, damaging property or creating a disturbance'. Prisoners may not be kept under restraint for longer than necessary, and this must not exceed 24 hours unless written authorisation is given by a member of the Board of Visitors or an officer of the Secretary of State. Where authorisation is given this must give reasons for the restraint, and the time that it is to continue for. Standing Order 3E states that this period may only exceed a further 24 hours in very exceptional circumstances (para 16). Prisoners may not be restrained as a punishment.

9.50 Mechanical restraints used in prison include body belts (with iron cuffs for male prisoners and leather cuffs for women), standard handcuffs (for men), leather wrist straps (for women), and ankle straps (SO 3E, para 4). Such restraints may only be used in the circumstances outlined in the Prison/YOI Rules as outlined above, and when the use of a restraint is 'absolutely necessary to meet the required objective' (SO 3E, para 5 (1)(a)). Approval must be given by the governor in charge, or if unavailable an officer who is of the rank of principal officer unless no such officer is available, in which case the most senior officer on duty should make the decision (para 12(1)). The governor should see the prisoner before the mechanical restraint is applied, or as soon as possible afterwards (para 12(2)). The medical officer should be informed of the decision, and should make arrangements to conduct 'an early medical examination' following which they will inform the governor of their opinion as to whether the prisoner is fit to be so restrained.

9.51   Particular considerations apply in deciding which mechanical restraint to subject a prisoner to. The use of body belts are deemed to be 'an exceptional measure' in circumstances when 'the use of, for example, standard handcuffs or leather wrist straps would not achieve the necessary purpose'(SO 3E, para 6). Prisoners should have one hand released in order that they may take food or drink, and this should be their left hand if they are right handed or their right hand if they are left handed (para 6).

9.52   Handcuffs are applied so that male prisoners' hands are behind their bodies, but they will be moved to the front to facilitate eating and sleeping (if the governor considers it dangerous to release prisoners' hands for these purposes). Female prisoners' wrist straps are only to be applied so that their hands are at the front of their bodies (SO 3E, paras 7–8), and again their hands should be freed temporarily for eating, drinking and sleeping unless it is considered dangerous to release them (para 10).

9.53   Ankle straps are used to prevent prisoners from kicking when they are being moved from one part of the prison to another and they are considered necessary to prevent injury to the prisoner or others. They should be removed as soon as the prisoner has been moved (SO 3E, para 11).

9.54   Although ratchet handcuffs do not appear in the list of approved mechanical restraints in Standing Order 3E para 4, there is provision for their use in para 21 of the Standing Order. This states that they may be applied temporarily if a violent prisoner has to be moved from one part of the prison to another part which is some distance away, the route contains narrow stairs or doorways and consequently it may be difficult to maintain approved holds on the prisoner. Furthermore, they may also be used where the 'prisoner is particularly violent or powerful, and failure to restrain the prisoner is likely to result in injury to the prisoner, another prisoner or staff, or in an escalation of the incident'(para 21(1)(b)).

9.55   The Prison Rules also provide for violent or refractory prisoners to be kept in a 'special cell' temporarily until they have ceased to be violent or refractory (r 45). Prisoners may not be detained in such accommodation as a punishment. Authority must be given by the governor in charge of the prison, and the procedure for the granting of initial authority of up to 24 hours and subsequent authority for a longer period is the same as that outlined above in the use of mechanical restraints.

9.56 The special accommodation provided will be one of two types – strip cells which are unfurnished except for a raised platform which serves as a bed, and special cells which are somewhat like a cell within a cell, and are soundproofed with double doors, opaque windows and dim lighting, any furniture would be designed so that no injury could be caused to the prisoner.

9.57 Prisoners held in special accommodation and/or subjected to mechanical restraints should be not be so detained for any longer than necessary, and as soon as the initial outburst of violence has passed the effect of removing the restraint, or removing the prisoner from special accommodation must be tested. The governor in charge of the prison and a medical officer must visit prisoners under restraint and/or in special accommodation personally at least twice a day, and the officer in charge of the wing must observe the prisoner every 15 minutes (para 18).

9.58 Somewhat strangely, there is provision for prisoners who are held in special accommodation to be taken out to exercise 'as soon and often as is considered desirable or practicable' (para 18(6)). This would appear to be totally incompatible with the principles that they should be released from the special accommodation as soon as they are no longer in danger of causing injury to themselves or others or of causing damage to property.

9.59 Prison officers' power to use force upon prisoners is contained in r 44 of the Prison Rules which states that prison officers may only use force when necessary, and that where the use of force is necessary, no more force than necessary should be used. Prisoners who are held in special accommodation or subjected to the use of mechanical restraints will have a potential action for assault if officers exceed their powers to use force in restraining them. In theory, the use of restraints and special accommodation would be terminable by judicial review proceedings, however, in practice, it is highly unlikely that the prisoner would be able to inform anyone of their plight whilst so confined.

Escorts

9.60 Prisoners who are under escort to another prison or elsewhere outside the prison may be handcuffed. Standard handcuffs should normally be used on all male prisoners, (although there is provision for ratchet handcuffs to be used where a young offender's wrists are too thin to apply standard handcuffs), and ratchet handcuffs should be used on female prisoners (Security Manual, para 53.1).

9.61 The Security Manual makes it clear that prisoners under escort outside the prison should normally be handcuffed at all times (para 53.3). However, unless there are reasonable grounds for believing that prisoners are likely to pose security or control problems, they will not be handcuffed where they are being transferred to open prisons, or if they are non-category A female prisoners (where a closeting chain may be used instead) (para 53.4). Such prisoners may be handcuffed in the course of the escort if they become 'violent or unruly or try to escape' (para 53.7). Mentally disordered prisoners detained under the Mental Health Act 1983 should not be handcuffed without the prior consent of the medical officer, which should only be given if the prisoner is likely to pose a control problem (para 53.7).

9.62   Where a prisoner being transferred to another prison is acting in 'an extremely violent manner or poses a clear threat of extreme violence', the use of a body belt, leather wrist straps (for female prisoners), or ankle straps may be authorised. In all such cases the governor in charge of the prison must make the decision, and the medical officer must sanction it. In addition, the use of a 'loose canvas restraint jacket' may be authorised by the medical officer and confirmed by the governor in charge (paras 53.25–53.26).

9.63   Whilst under escort, prisoners who have been handcuffed may have the handcuffs removed in the following circumstances:

(i)   if they are being transported in a cellular vehicle and the doors have been locked (unless there is reason to believe that they have a hidden weapon) (para 53.8(1));
(ii)   if they are produced in court (unless the judge orders that the handcuffs should not be removed) (para 53.15);
(iii) if they need to use the toilet (in which case a closeting chain must be applied) (para 53.8(3));
(iv)   during a marriage ceremony (para 53.8(4));
(v)   when, in an outside hospital, the doctor asks that the handcuffs are removed during treatment (para 53.8(5)).

RACE RELATIONS

9.64   The Prison Service first published a Race Relations Manual in April 1991. The Manual aims to set out the Prison Service's policies and their implications in terms of prison life, to provide a means by which prisons could audit their application of the policies and improve this, and to explain the responsibilities of individual members of staff in implementing the policies.

9.65   The Prison Service's Race Relations Policy Statement is as follows:

'1   The Prison Department is committed absolutely to a policy of racial equality and to the elimination of discrimination in all aspects of the work of the Prison Service. It is opposed also to any display of racial prejudice, either by word or conduct by any member of the Service in his or her dealings with any other person.
2.   All prisoners should be treated with humanity and respect. All prisoners should be treated impartially and without discrimination on grounds of colour, race or religion. Insulting, abusive or derogatory language towards prisoners will not be tolerated.
3.   Race relations concern every member of the Prison Service. It is the responsibility of every member of staff to ensure that the Department's policy is carried out in relation to other members of staff as well as prisoners.

4. Members of minority religious groups have the same right to practice their faith as those of the majority faith. Wherever feasible in prison circumstances arrangements are made to give them the same practical opportunity to do so.
5. All inmates should have equal access to the facilities provided in the establishment including jobs. The distribution of inmates throughout the establishment and its facilities should as far as is practicable and sensible be broadly responsive to the ethnic mix of the establishment.
6. No particular racial group should be allowed to dominate any activity in the establishment to the unfair exclusion of others.' (Race Relations Manual, p 4)

9.66 The Manual goes on to state a further 14 detailed policies relating to ethnic monitoring in prison: access to facilities and services; allocation of living accommodation; access to work, education and training; religion; diet; libraries and information; disciplinary matters; segregation; racially derogatory language; complaints; establishing outside contacts; membership of Boards of Visitors and Prison Visitors; and local recruitment. Each policy is accompanied by an 'action plan' to focus governors' minds on how they should be able to achieve the stated aims. However, no mention is made of any sanction being imposed upon prisons and staff who act in breach of any policy.

9.67 The Race Relations Manual instructed all governors to set up a race relations management team, which should be chaired by the governor or an 'appropriate functional head' (p 108). The team should meet quarterly and is responsible for monitoring race relations in the prison, identifying and discussing race relations issues, promoting staff awareness and training in race relations, auditing the implementation of race relations policies, developing and implementing action plans with reference to the policies contained in the manual, supporting the work of the race relations liaison officer, and reporting on the work of the team to the governor (p 120).

9.68 In addition, each prison is required to appoint a race relations liaison officer, whose tasks are to act as a source of information for prisoners and staff, to discuss prisoners' complaints about racial discrimination with them, and to take the lead in seeking to resolve such complaints. The race relations liaison officer must report back to the race relations management team and/or the governor on any racist incidents which occur (p 123).

9.69 Despite the introduction of the Race Relations Manual, prisoners still complain of institutionalised racism within the prison system, and their complaints range from being at the receiving end of racist and abusive language from officers, to being given the worst labour allocations.

9.70 There is only one reported case of a prisoner taking a successful case under the Race Relations Act 1976, and this also established that prisoners have the right to bring proceedings under the Act as this had previously been disputed by the Home Office. In *Alexander v Home Office* ([1985] CLY 1669) a West Indian prisoner was compensated for having been refused jobs in prison on racist grounds.

9.71 Prisoners complaining about race relations issues should complain to the race relations liaison officer and may also complain through the requests/ complaints procedure to the governor and area manager. The Prisons Ombudsman will also consider complaints and make recommendations. Prisoners may also contact the Commission for Racial Equality and their local racial equality councils who should be able to advise them and liaise with the prisons concerned.

HEALTH CARE

9.72 Rules 17–19 of the Prison Rules make provisions for prisoners to receive medical attention whilst they are serving their sentences or on remand. These lay down a system whereby the prison medical officer has responsibility for the physical and mental health of all prisoners detained in that prison, and has discretion to arrange for other practitioners to be consulted. There are two situations where a prisoner may be allowed to be seen by another doctor: an unconvicted prisoner may apply to the governor to be attended upon by another doctor, but if this request is granted, the prisoner will be responsible for paying any charge incurred (r 17(4)); and a prisoner who is taking legal action may be given 'reasonable facilities' to see a doctor in connection with those proceedings. Such a consultation should take place within the sight but out of the hearing of prison officers (r 17(5)).

9.73 More detailed guidance upon health care for prisoners is found in Standing Order 13. This outlines the roles of all health care staff, and gives guidance upon how they should discharge their responsibilities.

9.74 Most importantly, each prison should appoint a managing medical officer who should arrange for a doctor to attend the prison every week day, and for a doctor to be on call at all other times. The following tasks must be routinely completed by prison doctors:

'(a) separately examine as soon as possible and no later than 24 hours after reception all prisoners received
   – for the first time from court
   – from court after conviction or sentence
   – on transfer from another prison or return from an outside hospital after in-patient treatment or observation
   – after any temporary release under police escort
   – after any other temporary absence unless in a category specified by the managing medical officer after consultation with the governor as one in respect of which an examination need not routinely be carried out;
(b) conduct surgeries for all prisoners who wish to see a medical officer (in this connection the managing medical officer will ensure that adequate facilities exist for prisoners to apply to see a member of the medical staff and for such applications to be recorded);
(c) visit prisoners undergoing in-patient treatment or observation or who are under special supervision in any location;
(d) visit at least twice daily any prisoner placed in special accommodation or under body restraint;

(e) visit as soon as possible after adjudication or removal from association, and thereafter as considered necessary any prisoner undergoing cellular confinement as a consequence of a disciplinary award or removal from association for the maintenance of good order and discipline;

(f) visit as soon as possible after removal from association and thereafter at least every seven days any prisoner removed from association in his own interests;

(g) examine prisoners for the purpose of such reports as are required for official purposes;

(h) if a pharmacist is not in attendance, supervise the preparation of medicinal products; and

(i) separately examine every prisoner to be discharged or transferred to another prison, and those to be temporarily released or discharged to court other than in prison custody, and make arrangements for continuity of medical care if appropriate' (SO 13, para 3).

9.75 Prisoners who wish to see the doctor for non-urgent problems should report sick in the morning 'sick parade' or put in an application to see the doctor. However, when they are taken to the prison health care centre, it is likely that they will first be seen by a member of the medical staff who may be a prison officer working as a 'hospital officer'. These officers do not have formally recognised medical qualifications, although they undergo a prison service run course in basic health care. Many prisoners complain that if the officer considers that there is nothing wrong that warrants further medical investigation, they are simply returned to the wing after being given aspirins.

9.76 Prisoners who are in urgent need of medical treatment or who are too ill to get to the health care centre should be seen immediately by a member of the medical staff who will decide whether to call the medical officer, if the prisoner can be safely moved to the health care centre, and whether it would be appropriate to send the prisoner to an outside hospital (SO 13, para 28).

9.77 Many prisons contain 'hospitals' where prisoners can be treated as in-patients, at a few prisons surgical operations may be conducted. Prisoners are able to accept or decline treatment, and must sign their consent for any invasive surgery unless their lives may be endangered, serious harm would be likely or there would be an irreversible deterioration in the prisoner's condition. Subject to the above, the consent of a parent or guardian should be obtained where a prisoner is under 18 years old, and must be obtained if the prisoner is under 16 years of age (SO 13, para 25).

9.78 When prisoners go on hunger strike, this must be reported to the medical officer, and it is standard practice for such prisoners to be admitted to the health care centre in order that their physical condition may be monitored. If the prisoner continues to refuse food and water and their weight drops significantly or it is considered that their health is in danger of being damaged as a result of the hunger strike, an outside consultant may be called in. Such a consultant would be asked to assess whether the prisoner is suffering from a mental or physical illness which impairs their rational judgment. If so, a decision may be made to feed the prisoner artificially, and this should be taken by the medical officer in consultation with the outside consultant. If the prisoner is not found to be irrational, the medical officer should advise him/her that there will be a deterioration in their health if the hunger strike continues, and that this will continue unless the prisoner specifically asks for medical intervention (SO 13, paras 39–41).

9.79   The Prison Services' policy on AIDS and HIV aims to prevent the spread of infection, protect the health of prisoners and staff and provide care and support for infected prisoners (CI 30/91, Annex A). Condoms are not available to prisoners for their use inside prisons, although in some prisons they are available for those leaving the prison for periods of temporary release. Tablets for disinfecting syringes have recently been issued to prisoners and should be freely available within prisons (IG 96/95). Education is considered to be the 'vital element in the prevention strategy' and to this end the Prison Service has produced an educational package 'AIDS Inside and Out', which explains ways of avoiding infection. The Terrence Higgins Trust also produces information for distribution to prisoners.

9.80   Prisoners may be tested for HIV/AIDS at their own request whilst they are in prison, and will not be tested unless they consent. Prisoners who are HIV positive, or who have AIDS should generally be located on normal location within prison, and should have access to the same regime facilities, including education and employment and recreation, as other prisoners held on the same wing (CI 30/91, Annex A, para 18). However, governors do have discretion to opt out of this policy, and in some prisons, prisoners have been placed under 'viral infectivity restrictions'. This entails removing them from normal location to a different part of the prison, and excluding them from employment which carries the risk of physical injury, for example working with sharp implements (CI 30/91, Annex A, para 19). However, the Prison Service has announced that as from 1 November 1995, prisoners should no longer be subjected to viral infectivity restrictions on the basis that the risk of infection in the course of ordinary day-to-day contact with infected prisoners is 'insignificant' (IG 98/95). The same instruction also makes it clear that only health care staff should be aware of prisoners' HIV positive status.

9.81   The Prison Service has a policy of aiming to 'provide for identified HIV infected inmates no less a quality of care than they could expect to receive outside' (CI 30/91, Annex A, para 23), and to this end a proactive clinical approach is recommended, involving regular physical and psychological monitoring. Although a hospital for prisoners with HIV related illnesses was purpose built in the late 1980s, this has never been used for its intended purpose. Current policy is to locate such prisoners as near to their homes as possible in a prison health care centre with a full time medical officer, night nursing cover, and links with NHS facilities. Where prisoners become too ill to be managed by prison health care centres, they may be transferred to an NHS hospital or a hospice (CI 30/91, Annex A, para 27).

9.82   Problems relating to health care issues can be extremely difficult to deal with, and letters from solicitors asking that their client is treated often appear to meet with hostile responses from medical officers.

9.83 Prisoners may submit requests/complaints about their treatment to the managing medical officer as well as to the governor and area manager, and can also complain to the Directorate of Prison Health Care at Prison Service Headquarters. At the present time, the Prisons Ombudsman's remit does not extend to examining the clinical decisions of prison health care staff. However, other decisions relating to health care issues will fall within the scope of the Ombudsman's investigatory powers. For example, if the managing medical officer says that a prisoner has not got a broken arm and is suffering from psychosomatic symptoms, this cannot be investigated by the Ombudsman. Conversely, if the managing medical officer suspects that a prisoner's arm may be fractured, and asks that he is conveyed to an outside hospital for an x-ray, the Ombudsman could investigate the governor's failure to ensure that the prisoner is taken to hospital.

9.84 Where the prison's failure to treat a prisoner causes damage to their health, the normal rules of medical negligence will apply.

UNCONVICTED PRISONERS

9.85 Rule 25 of the Prison Rules states that:

'The governor or Board of Visitors may, on application by an unconvicted prisoner, permit him on payment of a sum fixed by the Secretary of State—

(a) to occupy a room or cell specially fitted for such prisoners and provided with suitable bedding and other articles in addition to, or different from, those ordinarily provided, and to have at his own expense the use of private furniture and utensils approved by the governor; and
(b) to be relieved of the duty of cleaning his room or cell and similar duties.'

9.86 However, in practice, this would appear to be completely inoperational – we have never heard of an unconvicted prisoner either applying for or being granted such a room, and have never heard of a prison where such accommodation is available.

9.87 The main differences between the way that unconvicted and convicted prisoners are treated relate to work, private cash, visits, letters, and medical treatment. They are dealt with in the appropriate sections of this text. In addition, unconvicted prisoners generally have the right to wear their own clothing, so long as it is 'suitable, tidy and clean' and their visitors may bring clean clothes for them to change into (r 20(1)). However, if they so wish, unconvicted prisoners may elect to wear prison clothing. In this case, their uniform will be brown, rather than the blue worn by convicted prisoners. Instruction to Governors 78/95 introduced a change in r 20(1) which places important restrictions upon unconvicted prisoners' right to wear their own clothes. Governors may now require unconvicted prisoners who are provisionally category A or on the escape list to wear prison uniform unless they are produced in court.

CIVIL PRISONERS

9.88   Civil prisoners are those who are committed to prison for contempt of court, or 'for failing to do or abstain from anything required to be done or left undone' (SO 12, para 1)(eg defaulting on maintenance payments, civil debts, legal aid contributions etc).

9.89   Essentially, civil prisoners are treated in the same way as convicted prisoners, except with regard to sentence calculation (see chapter 5), arrangements for them to receive visits, and send letters (see chapter 8). In addition civil prisoners may wear their own clothing so long as they are not working outside the prison or associating with convicted prisoners (SO 12, para 4(2)). In these respects, civil prisoners are treated in the same way as remand prisoners.

9.90   If a civil prisoner is employed in their cell, the governor has the discretion to leave the door unlocked (SO 12, para 4(3)).

SUICIDE PREVENTION POLICY

9.91   The number of prisoners committing suicide in prison is steadily rising to an all time high of 61 prisoners in 1994. In the nine months since the highly publicised suicide of Frederick West on New Years Day in 1995, there have been a further 47 unnatural deaths in the English prison system.

9.92   In terms of their duty to care for prisoners, the Prison Service states that they aim to:

> 'identify, and provide special care for prisoners in distress and despair and so reduce the risk of suicide and self harm' (IG 1/94, Part 1, p 1).

9.93   The Prison Service's overall strategy in reducing incidents of suicide and self-harm is based upon four separate levels of care and support in prisons (IG 1/94, part 1, p 1).

9.94   Primary care is envisaged as applying to prisoners throughout the system. It is stated that if prisoners are held in a 'safe, humane, and positive environment', where they are able to form trusting relationships with staff who will help them with their problems, then the chances of becoming suicidal or self-mutilating will be lessened. Statistics show that approximately half of the prisoners committing suicide each year are held on remand in local prisons which usually have the poorest regimes and staff-inmate relationships. It is arguable that the policy, though well meaning, identifies the problem without actually working out how the resources might be provided to make staff available to fulfil the kind of 'counselling' role which is advocated.

9.95   The second strand of the policy aims to identify and support prisoners 'in crisis', and to treat them with dignity. As part of the reception procedure into prison, a member of the health care staff should always assess the likelihood that prisoners are suicidal or liable to inflict injuries upon themselves, and IG 1/94 stresses the importance of this screening procedure. However, on 6 September 1994, Commissioners from the Howard League for Penal Reform observed an induction interview at Hull prison:

'Q: Now, you seem a sensible lad, you're not going to cut up are you? You're not suicidal are you?
A: No.'

9.96 After this, the prisoner was asked to sign 'a couple of bits of paper including one to say you're not suicidal' ('Banged Up, Beaten Up, Cutting Up, The Howard League for Penal Reform (1995) p 46). The prisoner being interviewed, a 16 year old, was given no opportunity to voice any concerns, and his interview lasted a mere five minutes in total. This is clearly not the detailed 'health screening procedure' envisaged in IG 1/94 (Part 2, p 1).

9.97 Prisoners who are identified as suicidal or likely to self-mutilate should be seen by a doctor 'as soon as possible and in any event within 24 hours'(IG 1/94, Part 2, p 2) and it is then up to the doctor to decide whether they should be treated as an in-patient or allowed to remain on normal location within the prison. In general, 'at risk' prisoners should be located in a cell with another prisoner, although exceptions will be made if their behaviour is considered 'too disturbing to other prisoners'(IG 1/94, Part 2, p 2). Prisoners who continue to be held in single cells are generally subject to a '15 minute watch'.

9.98 Staff responsible for the care of an 'at risk' prisoner should always be informed at shift handovers and when prisoners are being transferred between establishments or to court. 'At risk' prisoners should have their situations regularly reviewed, and should be monitored on a daily basis until it appears that they are able to 'cope satisfactorily' (IG 1/94, Part 2, p 3).

9.99 The third and fourth strands of the Prison Service's strategy for aiming to reduce the number of suicides and incidents of self-harm in prison, address the wider effects upon the whole of the prison community. Aftercare should be provided for 'close family and friends' as well as prisoners and prison staff who are affected (IG1/94, Part 1, p 2). Details of the kinds of support which may be made available are not given, and in practice it would seem doubtful that prisoners are given any support following the death of a fellow prisoner. In terms of a 'community' response, the Prison Service has stated that the whole of the prison system shares 'a responsibility to be aware of and support those in distress'. Such responsibility is discharged by providing staff training and support, encouraging other prisoners to share responsibility for each other, working with prisoners' families and community organisations, and ensuring co-operation between all of those individuals and agencies working with prisoners (IG 1/94, Part 1, p 2).

9.100 Where someone commits suicide in custody, the prisoner's spouse or next of kin should be informed 'at once', as should any one else who 'the prisoner may reasonably have asked' to be told (r 19(1)). The governor should also tell the coroner, the Board of Visitors and the Secretary of State (r

19(2)). The detailed provisions for reporting deaths in custody are contained in CI 52/90. In essence, this states that governors must inform the Home Office Press Office and the Incident Management Support Unit of the death in discharging their duty under r 19(2).

9.101   The organisation INQUEST provides support to the families of those who have died in prison custody, and may help in obtaining legal representation for families in coroners' court hearings. Legal aid is not available for families to obtain representation at coroners' court hearings, and INQUEST is currently campaigning on this issue.

CHAPTER 10

LIFERS

MANDATORY LIFERS

10.1 When a person is convicted of murder, the court has no discretion as to the sentence that they will receive – all murderers will be sentenced to life imprisonment (Murder (Abolition of the Death Penalty) Act 1965). Thus a life sentence for murder imposed on a person over the age of 21 years is known as a mandatory life sentence. Life sentences imposed for any other offence (commonly manslaughter, arson, rape, and armed robbery), are known as discretionary life sentences as the court is under no obligation to impose a life sentence for those convicted of such offences.

PRISONERS CHARGED WITH MURDER

10.2 Prisoners charged with murder and remanded in custody are held in local category B prisons until the time of their trial, and will be treated in line with the criteria for unconvicted prisoners. However, Circular Instruction 30/90 contains detailed instructions about the medical assessment of prisoners who are charged with murder. This states that the medical officer should keep a written record of the physical and mental condition of the prisoner, and this may be done on a daily basis. In order that the medical officer may form an adequate assessment of the prisoner's mental condition, a copy of the depositions taken before the magistrates and coroner will be requested from the Crown Prosecution Service. The guidance states that these depositions 'are furnished only so that he may be in possession of important and true particulars of the prisoner's recent history insofar as it has a bearing upon his mental state' (para 10).

10.3 When a prisoner charged with murder is committed for trial, the governor is instructed to forward a report from the medical officer to Prison Service Headquarters. This report should give the medical officer's opinion of the case and whether it is considered that any further psychiatric examination should be carried out. If such an examination is suggested on the grounds that 'there is reason to believe that the prisoner is not mentally normal' (para 11), the services of a psychiatrist independent of the Directorate of Prison Health Care should be carried out.

10.4   The medical records of prisoners charged with murder should be kept in locked cabinets and access to them should be restricted to the medical officer and hospital officers of principal officer rank and above.

PRISONERS CONVICTED OF MURDER

10.5   Mandatory life sentences have three distinct elements. The first element is the part of the sentence which is set by the Home Secretary to reflect the minimum period of time that the lifer should serve in the interests of deterrence and retribution, and is commonly known as the 'tariff' or the 'penal' element. After completion of this period, lifers may still be held on the basis that they represent a risk to the public. Finally, and most controversially, according to recent policy changes lifers who have served their tariffs and are considered to be no risk may be held in custody in order to maintain the public's confidence in the criminal justice system.

The tariff

10.6   All lifers have to serve up to their tariff date, and there is no prospect of release before this period has expired (unless the very stringent criteria for compassionate release are met, see chapter 12).

10.7   The tariff is set by the Home Secretary who seeks recommendations from the trial judge and the Lord Chief Justice as to the appropriate term to be served in the circumstances of the offence. These recommendations are not binding on the Home Secretary, who has reserved the power to take into account other factors, including public policy considerations. There is no obligation to set the tariff in line with the judicial views and it is apparent that the tariff is often set at a considerably higher number of years than that sentencing judge has recommended. (In the recent case of *R v Secretary of State for the Home Department, ex p Pierson* (27 October 1995, unreported), Mr Justice Turner quashed a decision by the Secretary of State to uphold a tariff at the same level it had originally been set at, despite accepting new representations to the effect that the offence was not premeditated. Mr Justice Turner held that this in fact amounted to an increase in the original tariff, a decision which he found to be unfair. He stressed the need for the utmost standards of fairness to be applied when considering tariff. The Secretary of State has lodged an appeal against the judgment). It is also becoming apparent that there is a small number of prisoners who are likely to have to serve whole life tariffs.

10.8   In the past mandatory lifers did not have the right to know the basis upon which their tariffs were set, or whether the Home Secretary has set them at a higher level than that recommended by the judiciary. The tariff setting procedure was examined in the case of *R v Secretary of State for the Home Department, ex p Doody* ([1994] 1 AC 531, HL). The judgment in this case gave mandatory lifers the right to know the minimum period the judge thought that they should serve and the gist of the reasons why that recommendation was made; the right to make representations in respect of the tariff before it is set; and the right to be informed of the reasons for any departure from the judge's recommendation when the tariff is set. A Tariff Unit has been set up at Prison Service Headquarters to disclose this information to prisoners, and to receive representations to be submitted to the Home Secretary.

10.9　Lifers whose tariffs were set before the new arrangements came into effect have also benefited to some extent. Following the *Doody* judgment all mandatory lifers received a letter outlining the gist of the judicial recommendation as to tariff, the level at which the tariff was set, and any reasons given by the Home Secretary of the day for that decision. They have the opportunity to make representations to the Home Secretary so that their tariff periods can be reviewed.

10.10　However, the disclosure which took place under the new arrangements initially proved far from adequate and consisted of a brief letter setting out the judicial recommendations and ministerial decision in a few lines. In some cases tariffs had been increased by up to 10 years above the trial judge's recommendation with no substantive reason given by the Home Secretary.

10.11　The case of *R v Secretary of State for the Home Department, ex p Raja and Riaz* (16 December 1994, unreported, DC) questioned whether this level of disclosure complied with the principles established in *Doody*. In these cases, tariffs had been set at 20 and 25 years respectively, increases of 10 years above the trial judges' recommendations. The court criticised the disclosure of the judge's comments as 'woefully inadequate' and considered that 'the reasons of the Secretary of State for differing from the judges were inadequately disclosed'.

10.12　Since 1994 the level of disclosure has improved, and prisoners who have indicated that they wish to make representations are sent copies of information which will be placed before the Home Secretary when the tariff representations are considered. These should include letters and reports from the trial judge which relate to tariff setting considerations, and the verbatim comments of the Lord Chief Justice.

10.13　It would appear that in the past poor records have been kept of the actual information which was placed before the Home Secretary when the tariff was originally set, and the Tariff Unit are often able to do little more than speculate as to this. Furthermore, in some cases the Home Secretary of the day appeared not to have recorded reasons for deviation from the judicial recommendation. The Tariff Unit may seek to withhold information on the basis that although it was probably before the Home Secretary of the day when the tariff was originally set, it will not be placed before him when the matter is reviewed. In response to this, lifers and their representatives may argue that the principles of administrative fairness outlined in *Doody* entitle them to see all information placed before the Home Secretary when the original tariff decision was made.

10.14   It has become apparent that there are a few mandatory lifers who have not had a tariff set despite having been serving their sentences for many years. These tend to be prisoners who are convicted of two or more homicide offences, and at the time that their tariffs were considered the Home Secretary merely stated that they should have their first Parole Board review at 17 years. This was in line with the policy in operation up to 1994, when a review at the 17 year stage indicated that the tariff was set at 20 years or more, and there was no obligation on the Prison Service to inform lifers of the actual length at which the tariff had been set. Prisoners falling into this category are currently in the process of having their tariffs set for the first time in line with the principles in *Doody*.

10.15   The fact that the *Doody* judgment forced the Home Secretary to disclose the minimum number of years that a lifer would need to serve in the interests of deterrence and retribution, created a politically sensitive problem for the Home Secretary in terms of how serious offenders who had attracted a good deal of adverse publicity should be treated. A tariff would have to be disclosed, and the level at which it would be set was open to public and media scrutiny. To get around this problem the concept of the 'whole life tariff' was created (see AG 51/94). Effectively this means that the lifer's crimes are so abhorrent that they should never expect to be released from prison.

10.16   As well as lifers' right to have their tariffs reviewed by the Secretary of State after making representations to this effect, mandatory lifers' tariffs are automatically reviewed when they have been in custody for 10 years. This 10 year ministerial review is to consider whether there are any grounds for shortening the tariff period and thus bring forward the date of the first Parole Board review. The review only takes into account the factors upon which tariffs are set, and custodial behaviour is irrelevant.

10.17   The 10 year review is conducted in secrecy and lifers are not routinely informed that it is about to commence, they are not invited to make representations or given any decision. If the Home Secretary decides to shorten the tariff then the lifer would simply be informed that their first Parole Board review has been brought forward. Prisoners who are serving a whole life tariff have an additional review after 25 years. This is another ministerial review, and its purpose is solely to consider whether the whole life tariff should be converted to a tariff of a determinate number of years. Again, the only factors that will be taken into account are those of whether the requirements of deterrence and retribution would be met by a prisoner serving a lesser period than the rest of their life. If the whole life tariff decision is upheld at the 25 year review, then the Home Secretary has indicated that 'further ministerial decisions will normally take place at five yearly intervals thereafter' (AG 51/94).

10.18   Under these existing arrangements prisoners with whole life tariffs will never have their cases referred to the Parole Board, and the Home Secretary will be the only person conducting any kind of a review of their continued detention.

Progression through the life sentence system

10.19   Following conviction, the local prison where the lifer has been held will send an Initial Life Sentence Report to the Lifer Management Unit (LMU) at Prison Service Headquarters. This report contains details of the offence, whether the lifer is considering an appeal, and any previous convictions. Personal information and details of custodial behaviour whilst on remand are also asked for (IG 59/94). This form is used to assist the LMU in deciding where the prisoner should be allocated to.

10.20   Lifers are centrally managed at Prison Service Headquarters, and governors of prisons are only responsible for their day-to-day management. Permanent transfers are always arranged by the LMU, as are changes in security categorisation. Prison governors may transfer lifers in the interests of good order and discipline under IG 28/93 (see chapter 7), but they would then have to ask the LMU to arrange a permanent move.

10.21   The majority of male life sentence prisoners will initially be allocated to one of the three main lifer centres. These are Gartree, Wormwood Scrubs and Wakefield prisons. Women lifers will be allocated to closed conditions. Category A status overrides all other considerations and so male category A prisoners will go to one of the dispersal prisons, and women category A lifers will go to HMP Durham. Category B male lifers should be allocated to the main lifer centre which affords the easiest access to their visitors, so long as there is space available. If a male lifer has been convicted of a sexual offence in the past, or if it is considered that the murder that they committed was sexually motivated, then they would be most likely to be transferred to HMP Wakefield as this is a sex offender treatment assessment centre.

10.22   Most lifers remain at their initial allocation for at least three years as this is considered to give them a chance to settle down and come to terms with the offence and their sentence. During this period staff should carry out initial assessments of the needs of each lifer, the areas of concern in their behaviour and identify factors which may have lead them to commit the offence for which they have been convicted.

10.23   Comprehensive reports are made about lifers throughout their sentences. Every lifer should have an internal review board each year and these assess the progress that has been made and the outstanding areas of concern that need to be addressed. Lifers are generally allowed to sit in on the review and to comment on the views that have been gained about them at the prison. A summary of the review board is sent to the LMU who will consider its contents in making a decision to reallocate lifers. Brief summaries of these reports are also considered by the Parole Board when they eventually consider lifers' prospects for progression to open conditions or release.

10.24   In addition to the long term review board, F75 reports are completed on lifers every three years, and thus the first set will be completed as most lifers are nearing the end of their period in a main lifer centre. These are more detailed reports and make recommendations as to where lifers should be allocated to serve the next part of their sentence. The F75 reports are forwarded to the LMU, who will consider them and decide whether to act on the recommendations of the prison staff. Although there is not any obligation on the prison to disclose the reports to the prisoner, in general this will be done, and lifers will be able to make representations to the LMU if they so wish.

10.25   The progress of lifers will vary dramatically after the completion of their first F75 reports. Some may be transferred to category C conditions, others will be transferred to category B training prisons. These decisions will be made depending on behaviour in prison, the degree of risk thought to be posed by each lifer, whether they have come to terms with their offence and begun to address their offending behaviour and how long of their tariff there is left to serve. Category A lifers will remain in dispersal conditions until the Category A Review Committee has downgraded their security categorisation.

10.26   Life sentence prisoners continue to have their progress monitored by prison staff at long term review boards and by completion of F75 reports. This ensures that the question of allocation is kept under review and progressive transfers to lower security conditions may be made. Likewise, if a lifer's behaviour gives cause for concern, the LMU may arrange a transfer to higher security conditions.

10.27   Lifers cannot progress to open conditions without the Home Secretary's approval and this will only be considered after a favourable recommendation has been made by the Parole Board. In general lifers are required to progress through all of the different types of prison before the Parole Board is likely to recommend that they are ready to move to open conditions.

Parole board reviews and release from prison

10.28   Mandatory lifers may only be released from prison under a tripartite procedure which involves a recommendation for release by the Parole Board, the views of the Lord Chief Justice and the trial judge (if still available) being obtained and finally, if approved by the Secretary of State (Criminal Justice Act 1991, s 35(2)). Parole Board reviews of detention are therefore the first stage in this lengthy process. There is no statutory procedure for this review process but Prison Service policy in force since the early 1980s has dictated that lifers should have their cases reviewed by the Parole Board when they are three years away from reaching the expiry of their tariffs. Lifers' Parole Board reviews are essentially the same as those for determinate sentence prisoners.

10.29   Prison staff prepare detailed reports about each life sentence prisoner and submit these to the Life Sentence Review Section at Prison Service Headquarters. These form the bulk of the lifer's parole dossier. Other documents included in the dossier are a Home Office Summary of the offence, psychiatric reports produced at trial, a list of the prisons where the lifer has been held during their period of imprisonment and a summary of the reports that have been submitted about them during their sentence.

10.30 On 16 December 1992 Kenneth Clarke announced that mandatory lifers would be given access to their Parole Board dossiers and would be given reasons for decisions reached about their subsequent management following Parole Board reviews. This was aimed to bring mandatory lifers in line with determinate sentenced prisoners following the commencement of the Criminal Justice Act 1991, and also to give them some of the benefits which had been extended to discretionary life sentence prisoners following the case of *Thynne, Wilson and Gunnell v United Kingdom* ((1990) 13 EHRR 666, Series A, No 190). The arrangements for disclosure came into effect for all mandatory lifer reviews starting after 1 April 1993.

10.31 Lifer dossiers are disclosed to lifers by staff at the prison, and prisoners may arrange to have this photocopied at their own expense. Otherwise, lifers are entitled to have access to the dossier in order to be able to prepare their representations. Representations should normally be submitted within 14 days of the dossier being received at the prison, although extensions of time are allowed on request. Many lifers ask solicitors to prepare representations for them, and this can be done under the Green Form scheme.

10.32 Representations are submitted to the Life Sentence Review Section, who attach these to the parole dossier and arrange for a Parole Board member to travel to the prison and interview the lifer. The interview follows the same format as for determinate sentenced prisoners. Following the interview the Parole Board member's report is disclosed to the lifer, who may wish to submit further representations. The report and any further representations are added to the dossier which is then submitted to the Parole Board secretariat and sent to the Parole Board panel who will be considering the case.

10.33 The Home Secretary has given guidance to the Parole Board on how they should consider the cases of mandatory life sentence prisoners (letter from Life Sentence Review Section to governors of lifer establishments, dated 1 April 1993). The appended Directions to the Parole Board on the Release of Mandatory Life Sentence Prisoners state that in considering whether a prisoner may be released they should have regard to the 'degree of risk involved of the lifer committing further imprisonable offences after release' and in view of this 'whether it remains necessary for the protection of the public for the lifer to be confined' (para 2). The directions state:

'In making this decision, the Parole Board should consider whether:
(a) the lifer has shown by his performance in prison that he has made positive efforts to address his attitudes and behavioural problems and the extent to which progress has been made in doing so such that the risk that he will commit a further imprisonable offence after release is minimal;
(b) the lifer is likely to comply with the conditions of the life licence and the requirements of supervision'. (para 4)

10.34 In addressing their minds to the above, the Parole Board should have regard to the Home Secretary's Training Guidance on the Release of Mandatory Life Sentence Prisoners. This advises:

'The following factors should generally be taken into account when recommending release on life licence. The weight and relevance attached to each factor may vary according to the circumstances of the case:

(a) the offender's background, including any previous convictions and their pattern;

(b) the nature and circumstances of the original offence and the reasons for it;

(c) where available, the sentencing judge's comments and probation and medical reports prepared for the court;

(d) attitude and behaviour in custody, including offences against prison discipline;

(e) behaviour during any home leave or other outside activities undertaken while in open conditions;

(f) attitude to other inmates and staff and positive contributions to prison life;

(g) insight into attitudes and behavioural problems, attitude to the offence and degree of remorse and steps taken to achieve the treatment and training objectives set out in the life sentence plan;

(h) (i) realism of the release plan and resettlement prospects, including home circumstances and the likelihood of co-operation with supervision, relationship with the home probation officer, attitude of the local community,

(ii) extent to which the release plan continues rehabilitative work started in prison and the extent to which it lessens or removes the occurrence of circumstances which led to the original offence;

(i) any risk to other persons, including the victim's family and friends or possibility of retaliation by the victim's family or local community;

(j) possible need for special licence conditions to cover concerns which might otherwise militate against release;

(k) any medical, psychiatric or psychological considerations (particularly where there is a history of mental instability).'

10.35   Following consideration of the above factors, the Parole Board may decide to recommend a provisional release date for the lifer concerned. If this is done, the Parole Board are asked that this is 'sufficiently far ahead to enable the prisoner to complete six to nine months on the pre-release employment scheme (if the prisoner is of working age) preceded, if necessary, by a period in open conditions' (Note for the Parole Board – Consideration of Mandatory Life Sentence Cases).

10.36   If the Parole Board considers that a lifer is not suitable for release, then they should turn their minds to the question of whether the lifer should be transferred to less secure conditions, including open conditions. Consideration as to suitability for transfer to open conditions is given in accordance with the Directions to the Parole Board on the Transfer of Life Sentence Prisoners to Open Conditions. This states that a period in open conditions is essential for most lifers in that it allows them to be tested in conditions which are closer to those in the community. The importance of temporary releases for lifers and increased responsibility for their actions are highlighted.

10.37   The Parole Board are instructed to 'balance the risks against the benefits to be gained by such a move' and to take into account the following factors:

'(a) whether the lifer has made *sufficient* progress towards tackling offending behaviour to minimise the risk and gravity of re-offending and whether the benefits suggest that a transfer to open conditions is worthwhile at that stage; and
(b) whether the lifer is trustworthy enough not to abscond or to commit further offences (either inside or outside the prison)'. (para 3)

10.38 The Directions go on to say that in making a recommendation to transfer a lifer to open conditions the Parole Board should consider whether:

'(a) the extent to which the risk that the lifer will abscond or commit further offences while in an open prison is minimal;
(b) the lifer has shown by his performance in closed conditions that he has made positive efforts to address his attitudes and behavioural problems and extent to which significant progress has been made in doing so;
(c) the lifer is likely to derive benefit from being able to continue to address areas of concern in an open prison and to be tested in a more realistic environment.' (para 5)

10.39 The Directions are supported by Training Guidance on the Transfer of Life Sentence Prisoners to Open Conditions, and these are almost identical to those outlined above in the Training Guidance on the Release of Mandatory Life Sentence Prisoners apart from they ask the Parole Board to consider any outstanding areas of concern in the lifer's offending behaviour and the benefits to the lifer of a transfer to open conditions. Furthermore, the Parole Board is told that the emphasis should be on the 'risk' aspect of a move to open conditions, and the 'need to have made significant progress in changing attitudes and tackling offending behaviour' (para 3).

10.40 If the Parole Board does not find the lifer suitable for release or for transfer to open conditions, they may nevertheless recommend a progressive move, for example to a category C prison, and they should also outline any areas of concern or points that should be clarified before the next Parole Board review.

10.41 Whatever the Parole Board's recommendation, they are required to give reasons which will be disclosed to the lifer. If the Parole Board do not recommend release, then they will recommend when the next review should take place. Normally this will be in a minimum of two years' time (Directions to the Parole Board on the Release of Mandatory Life Sentence Prisoners), although lesser or greater periods can be recommended. If so, the Parole Board should give reasons for their recommendation.

10.42 Recommendations made by the Parole Board are merely advisory and are considered by the Home Secretary. In practice, this means that recommendations for progression to category C conditions will be considered by senior staff in the LMU, who will either accept the recommendation and make arrangements for the prisoner to be transferred to category C conditions, or reject the recommendation and decide whether the lifer should be transferred to another prison of the same security categorisation as that where the review started. If the Parole Board has recommended release or transfer to open conditions then this will be considered by the Prisons Minister and possibly the Home Secretary in person. If the Parole Board has not recommended release, then the Home Secretary has no power to release a lifer.

10.43   A decision to release a lifer at their first Parole Board review would be very unusual because at that time, the lifer would still have approximately three years to serve before expiry of the tariff and release dates are not normally set so far in advance. Thus a lifer who has progressed through their sentence well may find that the Parole Board recommend transfer to open conditions with a further review in two years, by which time they will be close to completion of the tariff. If the two years in open conditions goes smoothly and there are no outstanding areas of concern, the second Parole Board review may recommend release, which would be via a Pre-Release Employment Scheme Hostel if the lifer is of working age. In this way, it is possible that lifers may be released upon completion of tariff.

Detention on the basis of risk and the need to maintain public confidence in the criminal justice system

10.44   Lifers who have completed their tariffs may be held on the basis that they may pose a 'risk' to the community, or that their release may undermine the public's confidence in the criminal justice system. In theory this period may last indefinitely. Lifers held on either basis will continue to have long term review boards each year, F75 reports every three years, and Parole Board reviews at intervals set by the Home Secretary taking into account the recommendations that the Parole Board has made as to when the lifer should next be reviewed. However, no lifer will be released unless the Parole Board recommend that s/he should be, and the Home Secretary accepts that recommendation.

10.45   Various attempts have been made through the domestic and European courts to introduce an independent system of review which is binding upon the Home Secretary, the most recent being the case of *Wynne v United Kingdom* (18.7.94 Series A, Vol 294–A (1994) Times, 27 July). In that case, the European Commission of Human Rights upheld the distinction that has been drawn between mandatory and discretionary life sentences and confirmed that mandatory lifers have no right to review before a 'court-like body'. The rationale for the decision was despite the fact that the mandatory sentence contains a punitive and protective period, it is essentially a fixed by-law with no element of discretion. The Court accepted the UK's arguments and commented that:

> 'the fact remains that the mandatory life sentence belongs to a different category from the discretionary sentence in the sense that it is automatically imposed as the punishment for the offence of murder irrespective of considerations pertaining to the offender. That mandatory life prisoners do not actually spend the rest of their lives in prison and that a notional tariff period is also established in such cases . . . does not alter this essential distinction between the two types of sentence.'

10.46   It is the Home Secretary's discretion in such cases that is at the root of the concern over the mandatory life sentence. The decision as to whether to authorise release is primarily based upon whether the lifer continues to pose a risk to the public. However, Michael Howard has specifically reserved the power to take into account the distinctly political considerations of 'public acceptability'. In a Parliamentary answer of 27 July 1993, he stated that:

'I wish to state that a mandatory life sentence prisoner should not assume that once the minimum period fixed for retribution and deterrence has been satisfied he will necessarily be released if it is considered that he is no longer a risk. . . . Accordingly, before any such prisoner is released I will consider not only (a) whether the period served by the prisoner is adequate to satisfy the requirements of retribution and deterrence and (b) whether it is safe to release the prisoner, but also (c) the public acceptability of early release. This means that I will exercise my discretion to release only if I am satisfied that to do so will not threaten the maintenance of public confidence in the system of criminal justice.'

10.47   The fact that mandatory lifers now have a right to disclosure of their Parole Board dossiers has brought to light the degree of subjectivity in the process of release and the extent to which both the Parole Board and the Home Secretary can choose not to accept the recommendations of report writers. In the case of *R v Secretary of State for the Home Department and the Parole Board, ex p Evans* (2 November 1994, unreported, DC) a lifer sought to challenge the refusal of the Parole Board and the Home Secretary to authorise release from a closed prison despite the fact that the reports prepared took the view that he was suitable for release and no longer presented a risk to the public. Indeed, the report writers were so incensed by the decision that they took it upon themselves to write letters of complaint to the Home Office about the decision reached. Leave had been granted on the basis that the reasons given for the decision were inadequate and a detailed affidavit was filed to expand upon the reasoning applied. Lord Justice Simon Brown refused to quash the decision made but was very critical of the failure to give adequate reasons prior to the commencement of proceedings. He commented that:

'The Board's duty to give reasons is not in dispute . . . where the Board find themselves unable to follow what I have already described as the clear, emphatic and unanimous view of the LRC and those reporting to them, they should explain why in language sufficiently clear and terms sufficiently full to ensure that the LRC properly understand the basis of the difference between them'. (pp 16–17 of transcript)

10.48   It is clear that this duty applies equally to the Home Secretary as it does to the Board and his final comments. Lord Justice Simon Brown made the point that the case contained important lessons for both the Board and the Secretary of State.

10.49   In the case of *R v Secretary of State for the Home Department, ex p Pegg* ((1994) Times, 11 August, DC) a decision of the Secretary of State not to release a lifer was also under scrutiny. Lord Justice Steyn, in accepting the fact that the mandatory life sentence system is one which has evolved by executive decree expressed his disquiet at the fact that the present system, from a constitutional point of view, 'makes no sense.' However, as the power to correct this lies with Parliament and not the courts, he went on to say that:

> 'Given the essential unfairness of the system in relation to prisoners serving mandatory life sentences the courts have to bear in mind that fundamental rights are at stake. But courts can do no more that be extra vigilant in the exercise of their powers of judicial review.' (p 15 of transcript)

10.50 These comments are quite extraordinary in the context of the mandatory life sentence and the operation of executive power. It would appear that the ordinary administrative duty of decision-making bodies to give reasons has been expanded by this judgment. The fact that the Home Secretary is exercising powers which are judicial in their nature has prompted the court to require his decisions to accord with a higher degree of fairness and openness.

Recall

10.51 Once a mandatory lifer has been released from prison, s/he will remain subject to the terms and conditions of a life licence. This is the method by which the sentence is made truly indeterminate and provides for a mandatory lifer to be supervised for the remainder of his/her life. This means that such a person may be recalled to prison at any time for the remainder of their life.

10.52 The procedure for the recall of lifers is contained in the Criminal Justice Act 1991, s 39. The procedure for initial recall envisages that this may be done by the Secretary of State either acting on the recommendation of the Parole Board (s 39(1)) or, where it is expedient in the public interest, by the Secretary of State acting alone (s 39(2)). The most common reasons for a decision to recall a lifer are when new criminal charges have been made or on the advice of the supervising probation officer.

10.53 Once a lifer has been recalled, under either set of procedures, s/he is entitled to have fresh consideration of the decision by the Parole Board. In accordance with the policy of open reporting before the Parole Board and in order to accord with the rules of natural justice, recalled lifers are entitled to receive the reasons for their recall together with any reports or other material that will be placed before the Board when the recall is reconsidered. There is statutory provision for written representations to be made to the Board in such cases (s 39(3)). It is always advisable for a lifer to have legal advice concerning these representations as they will be crucial in determining the length of time that will be spent in custody.

10.54 The Board must be concerned with the level of dangerousness that a lifer poses when considering such cases rather than factors such as disobedience (*R v Secretary of State for the Home Department, ex p Cox* [1993] Administrative Law Review 17). In practice, it is not always a simple matter to persuade the Board to make such a distinction and it is important to bear in mind the circumstances of the original offence when addressing the Board on dangerousness in such cases. For example, if the original conviction was for a crime committed on the spur of the moment, a rational and thought-out decision or course of action, even if criminal, may not necessarily be linked to the 'dangerousness' apparent in the original offence. Alternatively, if the new behaviour is thought to be impulsive and irrational, then links could reasonably be drawn.

10.55   The Parole Board holds a unique power when considering the recall of mandatory lifers in that if they recommend immediate release, this is the only occasion on which the Secretary of State is bound by the decision (s 39(5)). If any other recommendation is made, this is purely advisory as with other life sentence reviews and the Secretary of State has the discretion not to accept the recommendation (*R v Secretary of State for the Home Department, ex p Gunnell* ([1984] Crim LR 170, DC)). The prisoner will then fall to be detained under the terms of the original sentence with reviews and release at the discretion of the Secretary of State.

10.56   The meaning of immediate release is of some importance to prisoners in this position as it has been held to be precisely that, namely that the prisoner can be released that day (per *Gunnell*). This has been the cause of some difficulty particularly where the prisoner is subject to further criminal charges which may not have been heard or has received a short custodial sentence. In such cases, if the Board recommends release at the end of the sentence this is not a binding recommendation for immediate release (*R v Secretary of State for the Home Department, ex p De Lara* (22 March 1995, unreported, DC)). Similarly, if the Board decides that they wish to defer their decision pending the outcome of further charges, the Secretary of State can treat this as a decision. The prisoner then falls to be reviewed under the terms of the original sentence and the Board loses its powers to make binding recommendations. In such cases, representations should be submitted to the Board with the addendum that if immediate release is the recommendation that they wish to make, they should formally adjourn the case without reaching a decision and then reconvene when the obstacle to immediate release has been removed. This is particularly important in cases where further charges are pending as the Board's decision may be completely dependent on whether a conviction is obtained.

10.57   There have been many criticisms of the recall procedure and the lack of any real judicial element to the procedures. These are compounded by the fact that in most cases, the Parole Board will be fulfilling a dual function of recommending the initial recall and then reviewing their own decision. Attempts to bring this procedure within the ambit of Article 5(4) of the European Convention on Human Rights which ensures that all persons have the right to have their detention reviewed speedily by a court-like body have so far been unsuccessful (see eg *Wynne v United Kingdom* Series A, volume 294–A (1994) Times 27 July). The European Court has thus far accepted the argument that the detention is actually made under the terms of the original life sentence and that all subsequent release and detention decisions may properly be considered a discretionary power of the Secretary of State. The requirements of Article 5(4) are thus safeguarded by the original trial. This is likely to be an area of law that will continue to develop with further exploration, both domestically and through the European Court of Human Rights (ECHR) of the arguments that the Parole Board is fulfilling a dual function of reviewing its own decisions and that the reasons for recall cannot always be linked to the original conviction and therefore the decision to detain is entirely fresh and not related to the original conviction.

PERSONS DETAINED AT HER MAJESTY'S PLEASURE

10.58   The sentence of detention at 'Her Majesty's Pleasure' (HMP) was originally conceived in an attempt to ensure that children did not face the death penalty for murder. The Children and Young Persons Act 1933, s 53(1) authorises the detention of people under the age of 18 who are convicted of murder to be detained at HMP. Section 8 of the Criminal Justice Act 1982 authorises the detention of persons between the ages of 18–21 who are convicted of murder to be detained for life. Prisoners who receive such sentences are treated as if they have received a mandatory life sentence.

10.59   At the present time, the law is such that there is really no difference between young offenders who receive such sentences and adult offenders. Although the initial reception to prison will differ in that they will be held in conditions deemed appropriate for their age (eg a young offender's institution rather than an adult prison), these children receive a tariff in the same manner as mandatory life sentenced adults and are subject to the same release procedures. As people serving these sentences will inevitably be transferred to an adult prison prior to the end of their sentence, there is, to all intents and purposes, no distinction between the two sentences.

10.60   It is likely that this position will change in the near future. Lord Justice Evans in the case of *R v Secretary of State for the Home Department, ex p Prem Singh* ((1993) Times, 27 April, DC) took the view that in reality, the sentence is closer in nature to the discretionary life sentence as it contains a fixed punitive element and on balance, that further detention could only be justified on the grounds of dangerousness. In December 1994, the European Commission of Human Rights made a finding in the cases of *Abed Hussain and Prem Singh v United Kingdom* (application numbers 21928/93, and 23389/94, 19 December 1994, unreported) in connection with children and young persons subject to these sentences. The Commission took the view that the sentence of HMP bears a greater resemblance to the discretionary life sentence in that it contains a fixed penal element. As such, they found that the right to review of continued detention by a court-like process (such as a discretionary lifer panel) does exist. The Government have failed to reach a friendly settlement in this matter and the application is to proceed to a full hearing before the European Court of Human Rights. If the Court accepts the findings of the Commission, it will represent a significant inroad into the concept of indeterminate sentencing and it is likely that this group of prisoners will become, in effect, discretionary lifers.

DISCRETIONARY LIFE SENTENCED PRISONERS

10.61 The discretionary life sentence may be imposed for a number of offences, commonly manslaughter, buggery, arson or rape. The rationale for the sentence is that offences have been committed which are grave enough to require a long sentence, that the person is of unstable character and is likely to commit such offences in the future and that the nature of these offences is such that the consequences will be particularly injurious to others (such as offences of a sexual nature).

10.62 There is a not inconsiderable overlap between the imposition of such a sentence and an order made under the Mental Health Act 1993. The court must be satisfied when passing such a sentence that there is some element of unpredictability and dangerousness that, whilst it may diminish with the passing of time, means that the person presents a serious danger to life and limb and that the person cannot be dealt with under the Mental Health Act. At the same time, the purpose of the sentence is only to detain the person so long as they may cause a danger to others (see eg *R v Wilkinson* (1983) 5 Cr App Rep (S) 105).

10.63 Historically, discretionary lifers were treated in precisely the same manner as mandatory lifers with the same tariff setting and release procedures. In recent years, the nature of the sentences have diverged quite considerably but treatment within the prison system itself is still fairly similar. In terms of what a discretionary life sentenced prisoner can expect from the prison system, there is virtually no difference to that for mandatory lifers and so the same reception and allocation decisions will be made. The differences that need to be explored have resulted from both domestic court decisions and from statutory changes imposed following a decision of the European Court of Human Rights. These relate to tariff setting and release procedures.

Tariffs

10.64 In 1987, the court considered the procedure for the setting of tariffs for discretionary lifers (*R v Secretary of State for the Home Department, ex p Handscomb* (1987) 86 Cr App Rep 59). It was held that the procedure whereby no tariff was set for the first three or four years of a sentence had the effect of delaying the potential release of a prisoner until some six or seven years had been served due to the lengthy reviews whereby release comes to be authorised. Consequently, this amounted to a minimum sentence for all discretionary lifers which was at variance with the concept that the prisoner was only to be detained until safe for release. This procedure made no allowance for the widely different sentence lengths that may be appropriate for such prisoners.

10.65 The result of this case was that the Home Secretary was to obtain the view of the trial judge on the length of tariff immediately after the trial and that the first Parole Board review would be set in accordance with the judicial view. Although this latter point was overruled by the Court of Appeal, it signified the first moves to remove the Secretary of State's discretion and to impose a judicial tariff for discretionary lifers.

10.66   The Criminal Justice Act 1991 formalised the tariff setting procedures for discretionary lifers. The Act made substantial changes to the entire discretionary life sentence system as a result of the European Court's decision in *Thynne, Wilson and Gunnell v United Kingdom* ((1990) 13 EHRR 666). In respect of tariff, s 34 authorises the sentencing judge to specify the relevant part of the sentence that must be served, taking into account the seriousness of the offence. The Lord Chief Justice has directed that it is only in very exceptional cases that the trial judge can decline to make such an order (*Practice Direction (Crime: Life Sentences)* [1993] 1 WLR 223).

10.67   Tariffs for discretionary lifers are now, therefore, almost identical to determinate sentences in the manner in which they are set. The Court of Appeal has decided that it has the authority to exercise control over the 'relevant period' to be served on the basis that it is an order within the meaning of the Criminal Appeal Act 1968, ss 9 and 50(1) and have recently reduced a tariff from 12 to 10 years (*R v Dalton* [1994] 41 LS Gaz R 40). The length of time that is to be considered the 'relevant period' for the purposes of sentence calculation is to be calculated on the same grounds as for determinate sentenced prisoners with remand time counting towards sentence (Criminal Justice and Public Order Act 1994, s 46 and Sch 9).

Discretionary lifer panels

10.68   The gradual acceptance of the domestic courts that discretionary and mandatory life sentences could be distinguished was formalised by the Criminal Justice Act 1991, introduced to comply with the requirements of the European Court (see *Thynne, Wilson and Gunnell v United Kingdom* (1990) 13 EHRR 666). The court accepted that as there was a distinct, fixed element to the sentence, prisoners were entitled to a proper review of their detention at the expiry of the tariff period by a court-like body in accordance with Article 5(4). Paper reviews by the Parole Board, even with full disclosure of documents do not meet this criteria and as such a mechanism for a proper oral hearing had to be established.

10.69   The result was the present system of discretionary lifer panels (DLPs) which replaced the reviews that still exist for mandatory lifers. Whilst discretionary lifers are still subject to internal lifer reviews held within the prison to assess their progress, they are no longer subject to a formal Parole Board review three years before the expiry of tariff.

10.70   The Criminal Justice Act 1991, s 34(5) contains the right for discretionary lifers to require the Secretary of State to refer their case to the Parole Board at any time after the relevant part of the sentence has been served, or if it is more than two years since the Board last considered a reference. In practice, such a reference is automatically made and there is no necessity for the prisoner to make such an application.

10.71 The actual timing of the reference has been the subject of some litigation as to precisely when this reference should take effect. The wording of the statute is for the reference to take place once the relevant period has expired. The actual administrative procedures for a review means that DLP hearings are fixed on six months' notice (see below). This means that detention will not actually be reviewed until at least six months after the tariff has expired and in most cases, around 12 months. In August 1995 the European Commission of Human Rights accepted that a complaint from a discretionary lifer that delays in setting the first DLP of more than one year following the expiry of a tariff was a prima facie breach of the Convention and was declared admissible. A decision on the individual merits of the application is pending (*Taylor v United Kingdom* [1995] No 20448/95, 2 August 1995, unreported). This was followed by the ruling of the High Court that the system whereby prisoners may be required to wait for up to a year over tariff before the DLP was constituted was unfair and unreasonable (*R v Secretary of State for the Home Department, ex p Norney* (1995) Independent, 28 September). The court commented that the present system may also be considered to be in breach of the European Convention. The effect of this judgment is likely to be that in future, references for DLP hearings will have to be fixed to take place in order to potentially allow release on the expiry of tariff.

Procedure at DLPs

10.72 The procedural rules for DLP hearings are set by the Secretary of State (CJA 1991, s 35(2)) and the Parole Board Rules 1992 were issued under this authority. DLPs are appointed by the Chair of the Parole Board and must be chaired by a judge, in the more serous cases a High Court judge and in others, a circuit judge. The second member will normally be a psychiatrist but can be a psychologist or probation officer if there is no serious area of psychiatric concern. The third member is a lay member of the Board.

10.73 The prisoner will be notified of the date of the hearing 26 weeks before it is due to take place. They are given five weeks to inform the Board as to whether they wish an oral hearing to take place and whether they wish to attend in person. In that time, the Board must also be notified as to whether a representative will appear on behalf of the prisoner. Representatives may not include serving prisoners, people who have been released from prison but are on licence, people with unspent criminal convictions or people who are liable to be detained under the Mental Health Act 1983 (r 6). Legal aid is available (Advice by Way of Representation) and in most cases, solicitors will be appointed as the representative.

10.74 Within eight weeks of the reference, the prisoner is entitled to receive the information that is prepared by the Secretary of State for the purposes of the hearing (r 5(1)). This will comprise of a dossier, not dissimilar to a mandatory lifer's dossier, containing details of the offence, behaviour in custody, previous DLP decisions and a series of current reports prepared by prison and probation staff together with psychiatric and psychologists' reports. This will also contain the Secretary of State's view as to the prisoner's future. It is often the case that these reports are not prepared by the deadline and all subsequent actions should only be undertaken once the dossier has been disclosed.

10.75 On receipt of the dossier, the prisoner has four weeks to notify the Board as to what witnesses will be called and a further three weeks to submit any written representations deemed to be necessary. The Chair of the Board will then decide what witnesses will be called to give oral evidence. It may be the case that expert witnesses will be required, particulary if psychiatric evidence in is dispute. Payment for the cost of the preparation of expert reports and attendance at the hearing is covered under the ABWOR certificate.

10.76 There is a discretion to withhold information from the prisoner if the Secretary of State considers that it would adversely affect the health and welfare of that prisoner or others (rr 5(2) and 9(1)(d)). In such cases it will be served on the Chair of the Board who will decide whether to uphold that decision. If the information is to be withheld, it will still be disclosed to the prisoner's representative. Any part of the hearing dealing with that information will be conducted in the absence of the prisoner.

10.77 The hearing itself is normally held in the prison where the prisoner is detained, although they can be constituted elsewhere, normally at another prison (r 12). The time and location of the hearing are given out three weeks in advance (r 11(2)). Details of the proceedings may not be made public. Part III of the Rules allow the hearing to be conducted in a manner which the panel considers appropriate for the just handling of the case and that formality should be avoided (r 13(2)). When reviewing the procedure at panel hearings, the Divisional Court criticised situations whereby a report writer who may be required to give evidence at a hearing can appear as a representative for the Secretary of State, and emphasised the incompatibility of the two roles. It further decided that the chair is under a duty to record in writing the reasons for any decisions reached with reference to the substantial points that have been raised and the established points of law on which they rely (*R v Parole Board, ex p Gittens* ((1994) Times, 3 February, DC)).

10.78 The decision of the DLP must be communicated to the prisoner in writing within seven days of the hearing (r 15). A decision to direct release is binding upon the Secretary of State but all other decisions are advisory only (CJA 1991, s 34(3)). If a decision other than release is made, the DLP can recommend that a hearing be held in less than the two-year period that applies by statute. Again, this recommendation is not, at the present time, binding.

10.79 The panel must be satisfied that the prisoner no longer needs to be confined for the protection of the public before release can be ordered. The manner in which this test has been applied has been the subject of a great deal of litigation (see eg *R v Parole Board, ex p Bradley* [1991] 1 WLR 134). The courts have consistently held that the Parole Board are making a subjective decision based on the material before them. The court will be very reluctant to quash decisions for being unreasonable providing proper reasons have been given for the conclusions reached. For example, a decision that a prisoner who had made great progress and had very positive reports should be transferred for further testing in open conditions was commended as being a responsible and well-thought out conclusion (*R v Parole Board, ex p Telling* ((1993) Times, 10 May, DC)). The burden of proof rests with the prisoner to establish that s/he does not represent a risk to the public and not with the Secretary of State. Leggatt LJ took the view that:

> 'the Board must be satisfied that it is not necessary that he should be kept in prison and not that there would be a substantial risk if he were released. In other words it must be shown that the risk is low enough to release him, not high enough to keep him in prison.' (*R v Parole Board, ex p Lodomez* ((1994) Times, 3 August, DC, p 18 of transcript).

10.80 In 1994, the Parole Board heard 121 discretionary lifer cases. Release was recommended in 33 of these and included prisoners who were detained in category B conditions (1), category C (4) and a local prison (1). The remainder were in open prisons or PRES hostels. The last year where full figures are available for the acceptance of recommendations other than for release is 1993, in which 76% were accepted (Annual Report of the Parole Board 1994, p 13). In contrast, of 52 recommendations for the release of mandatory lifers that were made and considered, some six were rejected. All of these released were from open conditions or PRES hostels. These figures underline the importance to the prisoner of an oral hearing and the extent to which the Parole Board's binding powers for discretionary lifers are substantially to their benefit.

Recall

10.81 A discretionary lifer may be recalled to prison in the same manner as a mandatory lifer (CJA 1991, s 39). In such cases, an oral hearing similar to a DLP must be constituted speedily to decide whether the prisoner's licence should be revoked. The key issue in such cases will continue to be whether the prisoner is a danger to the public.

CHAPTER 11

PAROLE AND RELEASE

THE OLD PAROLE SYSTEM

11.1   The concept of early release from a sentence of imprisonment or parole was first introduced by the Criminal Justice Act 1967. In order to understand the workings of the present system, it is helpful for the history of the system to be explained together with the policy reviews that lead to an overhaul of the system when the Criminal Justice Act 1991 was introduced.

11.2   The Criminal Justice Act 1967 provided for the Home Secretary to appoint a Parole Board to advise upon the suitability of prisoners for early release on licence, and the establishment of a local review committee (LRC) at each prison to give initial consideration to the early release of prisoners and report to the Home Secretary on their findings. The system was governed by s 59 and Sch 2 of the Criminal Justice Act 1967, the Local Review Committee Rules 1967, SI 1967/1462 and the Local Review Committee (Amendment) Rules 1973, SI 1973/4 and 1983, SI 1983/622.

11.3   The scheme recognised that prisoners who were not considered to be a risk to the public would benefit from being released into the community under supervision, with the threat of recall to prison if their behaviour gave cause for concern. It was considered that after serving a third of their sentences, a period of parole of up to another third may have a more rehabilitative effect than remaining in prison which could lead some offenders to 'go downhill' (The Adult Offender, White Paper 1965). This principle is still very much in evidence in the parole system today.

11.4   The parole system came into effect on 1 April 1968, when all prisoners serving determinate sentences became eligible to be considered for release after serving either one-third of their sentence or one year, whichever period was the longer. Section 33 of the Criminal Justice Act 1982 allowed the Home Secretary to reduce the one year period as this had lead to the anomalous situation that prisoners serving long sentences could be released earlier than their counterparts serving shorter sentences. From 1 June 1984 the one year period for parole was duly reduced to six months.

11.5   On 30 November 1983, Leon Brittan announced to Parliament that prisoners serving sentences of five years or more for offences involving drug trafficking, arson, sex or violence would only be granted parole when 'release under supervision for a few months at the end of a sentence is likely to reduce the long-term risk to the public, or in circumstances which are genuinely exceptional' (*Hansard* (1983) (6th Series), written answers, cols 505–8). Thus the vast majority of prisoners serving long sentences knew that they would not get parole until the last review before their release. However they did still continue to receive a nominal review every year between their parole eligibility date (PED) and their earliest date of release.

11.6   The task of the LRC was to consider prisoners' suitability for release on licence in the period approaching their PED, or the anniversary of their PED if previous applications had been unsuccessful. Members of the LRC were generally governors, probation officers, and members of the Board of Visitors. Panels usually consisted of five members.

11.7   Approximately four months before the PED a member of the LRC would interview the prisoner to enable him/her to make verbal representations. The interview was the only opportunity for the prisoner to be actively involved in the process of consideration for parole, as both the LRC and the Parole Board met in private. A summary of the interview was added to the prisoners' parole dossier which was comprised of:

'a selection of documents . . . compiled for other purposes (including classification and allocation reports, social enquiry reports, police reports, dock officers' reports, prison review board reports, notification of prisoners being subject to a restriction order) supplemented by regular progress reports. When prisoners are due to be considered for parole, an assessment of their progress and prospects will be made by the governor or other appropriate senior officer'. (Standing Order 10, para 14)

11.8   Therefore the dossier contained enough information for the LRC, the Parole Board, and the Home Secretary to make a decision as to suitability for release. However, both the LRC and the Parole Board were able to ask the governor to obtain any further information thought necessary.

11.9   Following consideration by the LRC, the prisoner's parole dossier together with the LRC's recommendation was sent to the Parole Unit at Prison Service Headquarters. They would review the case and apply a statistical test to produce a 'reconviction prediction score'. If the LRC's recommendation was negative, and the statistical indicator showed that there was a high risk of re-offending, then notification of refusal of parole would be issued at that time without reference to the Parole Board.

11.10   In cases where there was a LRC recommendation that a prisoner was suitable for release on licence and/or there was a low reconviction prediction score, the papers would be referred to the Parole Board for their consideration. A panel of the Parole Board considered such cases in line with the Home Secretary's policy directions and training guidance to the Parole Board. The current provisions are set out at paras 11.33 and 11.34 below. As well as making a recommendation as to suitability for release, the Parole Board could also recommend that additional conditions should be placed upon the licence (eg geographical restrictions, psychiatric supervision, drink/drugs counselling) and where parole was not recommended, an early review.

11.11   The Parole Board's recommendation was referred back to the Parole Unit for further consideration. If the Board recommended release on licence the final decision was taken by civil servants, a minister or the Home Secretary depending upon the length of sentence or the particular circumstances of a case. If parole was not recommended by the Board then notification of refusal of parole was issued. There was no right to be given reasons for refusal of parole, and although it was possible for prisoners to make representations regarding the refusal, in practice this did not provide any kind of effective remedy as they had no idea as to what had been said about them in reports, nor as to why they had been considered to be unsuitable.

11.12   In 1987 the Carlisle Committee was set up to examine the parole system in England and Wales, with particular emphasis upon the way that it related to remission, remand time, and suspended sentences, as all of these factors came together to create wide discrepancies in the length of sentence and the time that a prisoner actually served. Prisoners serving long sentences had been eligible to be considered for parole at the one-third point of their sentences despite the operation of the 'five year rule', which meant that there was no realistic prospect of release on licence. This had the effect of overloading the parole machinery with work considered to be 'entirely nugatory', and also raised unrealistic expectations for families, and put the prisoner under pressure.

11.13   Amongst the Carlisle Committee's recommendations were the following:

(i)   Parole should be available only to prisoners who were serving more than four years, and they should become eligible after serving one-half of their sentences. Poor custodial behaviour should delay the parole eligibility date and the date of release where parole is not granted. This date should fall at two-thirds of the sentence where no additional days of imprisonment have been awarded at adjudication.

(ii)   Prisoners serving more than four years should be supervised upon their release until they have reached the three-quarters point of their sentence.

(iii)   Prisoners sentenced to four years or less should serve half of their sentences in prison, and the other half in the community. Their release should be delayed if additional days have been awarded.

(iv)   Remission should be abolished.

(v)   Where prisoners who have been released are convicted of a further offence punishable by imprisonment before they have completed their sentence, the court should be able to order that they serve all or part of the outstanding sentence as well as any further sentence given.

(vi)   The criteria for parole should be laid down by statute and the process should be subject to open reporting, with prisoners to be allowed sight of their parole dossiers.

(vii)   Reasons should be given for the refusal of parole.

(viii)   The decision to grant or refuse parole should be taken by the Parole Board alone, without reference to the Home Secretary.

(ix)   Local Review Committees should be abolished.

11.14   In 1990 the White Paper, 'Crime, Justice, and Protecting the Public' accepted the majority of the recommendations of the Carlisle Committee. The exceptions were that the Home Secretary would retain responsibility for the decision to grant parole to prisoners serving seven years or more and that there should not be open reporting. At the time, the view was expressed that if prisoners were to have a right to see these reports, then staff may not report as fully as they would have otherwise and the Parole Board's task would be hindered by the resultant lack of information. However, the objection to open reporting was later removed and was established as a principle of the new parole system.

THE NEW PAROLE SYSTEM

11.15   The system for the early release of prisoners was radically overhauled by the Criminal Justice Act 1991 ('the Act'). The Act appears to have been designed to implement two main policy objectives, these being the need to ensure a more rapid throughput of prisoners in order to ease overcrowding whilst at the same time ensuring that those convicted of more serious crimes would be obliged to spend a greater part of their sentence in custody.

11.16   The Act divides prisoners into three categories and operates differing release schemes for each. The categories are:

(i)   Sentences of less than 12 months.
(ii) Sentences of less than four years but 12 months or more.
(iii) Sentences of four years or more.

Prisoners in groups (i) and (ii) are described by the Act as 'short term' prisoners and those in group (iii) as 'long-term prisoners' (s 33(5)).

11.17   The Act came into force on 1 October 1992. Prisoners who were serving sentences imposed before that date, but who remain in custody, are defined as 'existing prisoners'. Any existing prisoner who receives a further sentence after 1 October 1992, will have their total sentence calculated into a single term and will continue to be treated as an existing prisoner (see chapter 5). Existing prisoners have their cases considered under the new parole system but retain their right to a PED at one-third of their sentence and licence conditions can only be imposed up until the two-thirds point of their sentence (see below).

The unconditional automatic release scheme

11.18   Prisoners serving sentences of less than 12 months must be released after serving one-half of that sentence (s 33(1)(a)). The Act imposes a duty on the Secretary of State to release such prisoners and there is no discretion in the matter. Release is unconditional and is not subject to any licence conditions.

Automatic conditional release scheme

11.19   Prisoners serving less than four years but more than 12 months must be released on licence after serving one-half of their sentence (s 33(1)(b)). Again, there is no discretion in the matter and the Secretary of State is under a duty to authorise release. The details for the implementation of this scheme are contained in Circular Instruction 27/92. As the scheme is automatic, responsibility for administration lies with each individual prison rather than with the Home Office.

11.20   It is the duty of the prison receiving such prisoners from the sentencing court to notify them of their conditional release date (ie the half-way point of their sentence) and to remind them that they will be under supervision on release. The prisoner should also be told of the standard conditions of the automatic release licence and how long the licence will last. This procedure should also be followed whenever a prisoner is transferred to another prison.

11.21   Each prisoner will be allocated to a probation officer on reception to prison. This officer then has responsibility for drawing up a supervision plan and to liaise with any sentence planning at the prison. The Probation Service National Standards require the officer to submit a pre-discharge report to the relevant establishment at least one month before release. This should contain relevant information on the prisoner's home circumstances and may contain recommendations as to any additional licence conditions that are felt to be necessary.

11.22   The licence is produced by the governor of the holding prison and is basically a pro forma. A sample copy is reproduced in Circular Instruction 27/92 at Appendix 2. The licence must be signed and issued by the governor, or an officer duly authorised by the governor. When it is given to the prisoner, the reporting instructions, other requirements of supervision, the length of supervision and the penalties for breach must be explained. The prisoner should then be invited to sign the licence but if s/he refuses, the governor must certify that the requirements have been explained and that the prisoner refused to sign.

11.23   If a prisoner refuses to sign, release must still proceed as the Secretary of State has no discretion to defer release (except in cases where additional days have been awarded, see chapter 7). A refusal to comply with licence conditions, or to co-operate with supervision is a summary offence which can result in a fine (s 38(1)). In addition, the magistrates have the power to suspend the licence for a period of up to six months and to order that the person be returned to prison for the period of suspension of the licence (s 38(2)). If the person does not return to prison on suspension of their licence, they will be deemed to be unlawfully at large (s 38(3)).

The Discretionary Conditional Release Scheme

11.24   The parole system is now entitled the Discretionary Conditional Release Scheme (DCR) and applies only to long-term prisoners serving sentences of four years or more. The Act provides that the Secretary of State may release long-term prisoners after they have served one-half of their sentence, if so recommended by the Parole Board (s 35(1)). Under the old system, parole eligibility commenced at one-third of the sentence and the DCR can therefore be seen to have significantly lengthened the possible time to be served in prison as well as reducing the number of reviews to which a prisoner will be entitled.

11.25 The decision whether to release long-term prisoners rests with the Secretary of State providing the Parole Board have made such a recommendation. However, the Secretary of State has delegated this power to the Board in the case of prisoners serving sentences of less than seven years (CI 26/92, para 4).

11.26 The most important aspect of the new system is the policy decision to have an 'open reporting' process. This provides for prisoners to be given access to a copy of the dossier once it has been prepared. This policy decision was made following considerable debate in the House of Lords, reports from government committees and pressure from the courts (see eg the interlocutory applications in *R v Secretary of State for the Home Department, ex p Benson* (1988) Times, 8 November). Home Office resistance to the concept of open reporting does, however, provide limits to the extent of disclosure. Circular Instruction 26/92 provides that whilst the general principle is for the entire dossier to be disclosed, documents can be withheld for the following reasons:

(i)   in the interests of national security;
(ii) for the prevention of crime or disorder, including information relevant to prison security;
(iii) for the protection of information received in confidence from a third party, or other information which may put a third party at risk;
(iv) if, on medical and/or psychiatric grounds, it is felt necessary to withhold information which could impair the mental and/or physical health of the prisoner.

11.27 There has not been any litigation on failure to disclose information under the DCR at the present time. However, there are detailed guidelines in CI 26/92 as to how the Board should maintain confidentiality for reports which are not to be disclosed (see eg paras 27–29). Consequently, when representations are to be made on behalf of a prisoner, it is always advisable to specifically ask the Parole Board Secretariat to confirm whether there is any undisclosed material.

11.28 The review process for release on parole licence commences some 26 weeks before the prisoners' PED. At this time the prisoner receives notification that the review process will commence and is invited to sign a form consenting to be reviewed. Once the prisoner has indicated his/her consent, requests for the preparation of reports will be sent out.

11.29 The parole dossier must be structured chronologically and should consist of the following reports:

(i)   Summary sheet/index;

(ii) Crown court order for imprisonment and record of conviction including the sentencing judge's comments;
(iii) Court of Appeal papers (if applicable);
(iv) Post-trial police reports;
(v) Previous convictions;
(vi) Pre-sentence/social enquiry reports;
(vii) Pre-sentence psychiatric/medical reports;
(viii) Sentence plan;
(ix) Sentence plan review forms;
(x) Prison parole assessment;
(xi) Prison medical reports;
(xii) Prison psychiatrists'/psychologists' reports;
(xiii) Prison chaplain's report;
(xiv) Home circumstances report;
(xv) Additional information (including job offers, letters of support).

11.30 At all subsequent reviews, the dossier should also include copies of any previous decisions made under the DCR together with the reasons for the decision.

11.31 On receipt of the dossier, the prisoner will be invited to sign a form indicating the documents that have been disclosed and to make written representations in support of the application. If difficult issues of law or fact arise, it is advisable for the prisoner to seek legal advice at this stage and if appropriate, for a legal advisor to draft these representations.

11.32 A prisoner should be interviewed by a member of the Parole Board approximately 11 weeks before his/her PED. There is no right to an oral hearing before the Board and it is this interview with the Board member which replaces consideration of the application by the old LRCs. The interview is designed to be structured around the criteria which are used by the Board when assessing the application (see below). The member's record of interview is subsequently passed to the prisoner for further comment before the papers are finally placed before a panel of the Board.

11.33 The Secretary of State is empowered to give directions to the Board as to the matters it must take into account when considering applications. The two main criteria are described as the need to protect the public from serious harm and the desirability of preventing the commission by them of further offences and of securing rehabilitation (s 6). Under this power, the Secretary of State wrote to the Chair of the Board in 1992 to set out the main criteria. These are available from the Parole Unit at Prison Service Headquarters but they may be summarised as follows:

'The decision should be focused on the risk of further offences being committed when the offender would otherwise be in prison. A balance must be reached between this and whether early release under supervision would aid rehabilitation and lessen the chance of re-offending. The Parole Board must be satisfied that the release plan will help secure rehabilitation and that the offender has demonstrated, through behaviour and attitude in custody that positive efforts have been made to address offending behaviour.'
(Secretary of State's directions for the release and recall of determinate sentence prisoners, 1992, Parole Board Annual Report, p 19)

11.34 There are a number of factors to be considered in each individual's case in order for a decision to be made in accordance with these criteria. The main factors are:

(i)   The prisoner's background, previous criminal record and response to supervision.
(ii) The nature and circumstances of the offence.
(iii) The risk that may be posed to the victim or other persons, including those outside the jurisdiction (a consideration upheld in the case of *R v Parole Board, ex p White* (1994) Times, 30 December, where the court upheld a refusal to release a discretionary life sentence prisoner on completion of his tariff even though the prisoner was subject to a deportation order).
(iv) The likely response of the local community and the victim or the victim's family.
(v)   Statistical indicators as to the likelihood of re-offending.
(vi) Behaviour in custody including offences against discipline, attitude to other inmates and the contribution made to prison life.
(vii) Remorse and insight into offending behaviour including steps taken within available resources to achieve treatment and training objectives (in the case *R v Parole Board, ex p Watson* (24 November 1994, unreported, DC) leave was given to apply for judicial review of a decision not to authorise release for failure to address offending behaviour when the dossier indicated that the applicant had completed all offending behaviour courses available within the prison).
(viii) The realism of release plans including home circumstances reports.

11.35 The interpretation of these criteria will naturally involve the Board making a subjective assessment on the available information. The Board are required to give reasons for any refusal to authorise parole and the normal principles of administrative law will apply when scrutinising such decisions. There has been little reported litigation on decisions made by the Board in respect of determinate sentenced prisoners. This may be due to the fact that prisoners have only become eligible for consideration under the DCR in large numbers since October 1994. Guidance as to the extent of the reasons that must be given for refusal can be obtained from cases relating to life sentence prisoners.

11.36 In the case of *R v Parole Board and the Home Secretary, ex p Evans* (2 November 1994, unreported, DC), Lord Justice Brown commented that:

> 'The Board's duty to give reasons is not in dispute . . . [where] the Board find themselves unable to follow what I have already described as the clear, emphatic and unanimous view of the LRC and those reporting to them, they should explain why, in language sufficiently clear and terms sufficiently full to ensure that the LRC properly understand the basis of the difference of the opinion between them'. (pp 16–17 of the transcript)

11.37 There is no right of appeal against a refusal to grant parole. Prisoners may submit a request/complaint form querying the decision to the Parole

Board Secretariat. In practice, however, this is unlikely to elicit any further reasons. The present policy applied by the Board is only to reconsider cases where there has been a substantial procedural irregularity or if significant new information is made available. These decisions fall outside of the remit of the Prisons' Ombudsman who has no powers to investigate complaints concerning substantive parole refusals.

11.38   When advising on the possibility of judicial review, it is important to closely cross-reference the reports prepared with the criteria for release and the reasons given. Whilst the Board will necessarily be making subjective decisions, the proper balance between the various criteria must be achieved. Applications to the Divisional Court for leave have been approved in various cases and these have subsequently lead to a voluntary reconsideration of the application and release. In the case of *R v Parole Board, ex p Riley* (7 July 1994, unreported, DC), the applicant had been refused release by the Board for failing to address her offending behaviour. She in fact maintained her innocence of complex and technical financial offences but was described as a 'model prisoner' who was allowed regular temporary releases. The leave application was granted on the basis that the Board's decision was irrational, but the case settled before a full hearing. The principle that maintaining innocence is not an automatic barrier to release on licence was upheld in the case of *R v Secretary of State for the Home Department and the Parole Board, ex p Zulfikar* ((1995) Times, 26 July).

Subsequent reviews

11.39   If parole is not recommended at the first review, a prisoner may be entitled to further reviews depending on the length of sentence being served. The minimum parole licence period is one month and therefore, a prisoner will be entitled to a further review if the anniversary of his/her PED is at least one month before their non-parole release date (ie two-thirds of the sentence).

11.40   The Parole Board describe the period of eligibility for parole as a 'parole window'. In order to qualify for a second review, a prisoner will have to be serving a minimum of 66 months' imprisonment.

11.41   The Board do retain the right to order early or special reviews in exceptional circumstances. This will commonly involve ordering a review when there is no longer one scheduled or advancing the date of the next review by six months. The Home Office guidance for when this would be appropriate is contained in Circular Instruction 26/92, paras 59–60. Examples include allowing monitoring of progress on a drugs rehabilitation course or other offence based work. Other examples include discovering procedural irregularities or new factors which substantially change the circumstances. In cases where there has been procedural irregularity it is arguable that, rather than a new review, the prisoner is entitled to immediate reconsideration with supplemental reports if necessary. This will necessarily depend on the nature of the irregularities that have been discovered.

Licence conditions

11.42   When a prisoner is released on licence, in most cases this will remain in force until the three-quarters point of the sentence (s 37(1)). However, the sentencing court does have the power to order that the licence should remain in force until the entire sentence has expired (s 44). This power is reserved for prisoners convicted of sexual offences or in cases where the court feels it is necessary to prevent the commission of further offences or to protect the public from serious harm (see the definitions at s 32(6)).

11.43   The prisoner is obliged to comply with the conditions of the licence (s 37(4)) and these may be varied after consultation with the Board. Provisions are made which enable a set of conditions to be imposed upon a particular class of prisoners if the Board have been consulted about the proposals (s 37(6)).

Young offenders

11.44   The release and supervision arrangements for young offenders, whilst operating under the same general principles, do vary from those for adult prisoners (ss 43 and 65).

11.45   Young offenders who are serving sentences of 12 months or less are to be released after serving one-half of their sentence on a notice of supervision. This is issued by the governor of the releasing prison on behalf of the Home Secretary. The period of supervision is to be three months or until the prisoners' 22nd birthday, whichever is the shorter period. Supervision for this period is obligatory, even when it will extend beyond the length of the sentence.

11.46   Young offenders who are serving sentences of over 12 months are released on the standard automatic conditional release licence. However, supervision must continue for a minimum of three months regardless of the length of the sentences. In cases where the automatic conditional release licence is for a period of less than three months, an additional notice of supervision must be issued. The Criminal Justice Act 1991, s 43(2) makes an important change for young offenders sentenced to periods of imprisonment under the Children and Young Persons Act 1933, s 53(2) in that they are now eligible for parole whereas previously this was not the case. Children and young persons sentenced to Her Majesty's Pleasure or life imprisonment are dealt with under the scheme for adult mandatory lifers (see chapter 10).

RECALL OF DETERMINATE SENTENCE PRISONERS

11.47   Different criteria apply for the recall of prisoners depending upon the length of their sentences.

Short-term prisoners

11.48   The recall of short-term prisoners serving less than four years' imprisonment is governed by the Criminal Justice Act 1991, s 38. This makes it an offence for a short-term prisoner to breach his/her licence conditions. This offence is punishable by a fine. In addition, the magistrates' court may suspend the offender's parole licence for up to six months or the remainder of the licence period, if this is shorter, and order that s/he is recalled to prison.

11.49   The period during which a prisoner is returned to custody is not treated as a fresh sentence, and will not attract any fresh early release entitlement. The prisoner will be serving his/her original sentence and the dates for release will remain the same as they were initially. The recall period runs from the date that the prisoner was convicted for the breach rather than the date upon which it was committed.

11.50   If the prisoner is released again before the licence expiry date then s/he will be subject to further supervision. A new licence with updated reporting conditions will be issued.

11.51   There is no provision emergency recall for short-term prisoners. However, it is possible that where someone is charged with breach of licence conditions that the court may remand them into custody until the case is heard, although this is quite unusual.

Long-term prisoners

11.52   Under the Criminal Justice Act 1991, s 39, prisoners serving sentences of four years or more may be recalled to prison following breach of their licence conditions, or if it is considered (usually by their probation officers) that they may pose a risk.

11.53   In order to recall a long-term prisoner, reference must be made to the Parole Board. Section 39(1) provides that the Parole Board may recommend to the Secretary of State that a prisoner's licence is revoked. However, if it is considered to be in the public interest, a prisoner can be recalled before his case has been considered by the Board (s 39(2)). In these circumstances the case must be referred to the Board as soon as practicable.

11.54   In considering whether to revoke the licence of a long-term prisoner (or uphold the Secretary of State's decision to revoke the licence), the Parole Board should consider:

(i)   whether the offender's continued liberty would present a serious risk to the safety of other persons or the offender is likely to commit further imprisonable offences. In assessing the risk to the community, a small risk of violent offending is to be treated as more serious than a larger risk of non-violent offending;

(ii) the extent to which the offender has complied with the conditions of the licence, or failed to do so or otherwise to have co-operated with the supervising officer;

(iii) whether the offender would be unlikely to comply with the conditions of the licence and submit to supervision if allowed to remain in the community. (Parole Board Annual Report 1994, p 20)

11.55   The Parole Board must take account of the views of the supervising probation officer, and any representations made by the prisoner. Training guidance has been issued to the Board by the Home Secretary, and thus they should also have regard to the following factors:

(i)   the offender's background, including any previous convictions and their pattern and in particular, performance during any previous periods of supervision;

(ii)   the nature and circumstances of the original offence and the offender's present attitude to it;

(iii) how far the causes of offending behaviour have been addressed on release, together with any new areas of concern that have arisen on licence;

(iv)   general behaviour on licence, including response to supervision, compliance with licence requirements, co-operation with the supervising officer and general attitude to authority;

(v)   the proportion of the licence already served and the seriousness of the breach in relation to the amount of licence period successfully completed;

(vi)   the extent and seriousness of any further offences committed while on licence and/or charges which have been laid in connection with such offences;

(vii) the suitability of the offender's current accommodation;

(viii) the offender's relationships with his or her family and people outside the family circle;

(ix)   any contact by the offender with, or concerns expressed by, the victim or victim's family, any adverse local reaction to the offender's release on licence;

(x)   work record – the extent to which jobs have been held down, relationships with colleagues and employer;

(xi)   current medical and psychiatric views, if any;

(xii) any other information, including representations from other people or bodies (eg police, social services) which may have a bearing on whether the offender should be permitted to remain on licence.

11.56   When a prisoner is recalled to prison, the Governor will be advised as to the reasons why, and be asked to convey that information to the prisoner. Prisoners will be given a dossier containing the reasons for their recall and have the right to make written representations (s 39(3)(a)). These will be referred back to the Parole Board for their consideration.

The 'at risk' period

11.57   Prisoners sentenced after commencement of the Criminal Justice Act 1991 are subject to an 'at risk' period which runs until that sentence expires.

This means that if they commit a further offence punishable by imprisonment during that period, they may be returned to prison for the whole or any part of the period between the commission of the offence and the expiry of the original sentence (s 40).

11.58   Thus a magistrates' court can return a prisoner to prison for a maximum of six months, or commit the prisoner to the Crown Court for sentencing (Powers of Criminal Courts Act 1973). The period for which it is ordered that the prisoner is returned to prison may run consecutively or concurrently with any further sentence imposed for the new offence.

COMPASSIONATE RELEASE

11.59   The Criminal Justice Act 1991 created new arrangements to deal with prisoners' compassionate release on licence. Prior to the commencement of the Act, release before the prisoner was granted parole could only be achieved by the exercise of the Royal Prerogative of Mercy. This was generally considered to be unsatisfactory in that the sentence was remitted and once released the prisoner would receive no supervision in the community and could not be recalled to prison if his/her conduct gave cause for concern.

11.60   The Criminal Justice Act 1991, s 36 made provision for the Secretary of State to release a prisoner on compassionate grounds at any point in the sentence if he is satisfied that 'exceptional circumstances' exist. A prisoner so released is subject to licence conditions and may be recalled to prison at any time until the licence expires.

11.61   Early release on compassionate grounds may be applied for by any prisoner serving any length of sentence, provided that they have not yet reached their parole eligibility date/automatic release date. Circular Instruction 36/92 states that prisoners who have reached their parole eligibility date can have their compassionate circumstances considered by the Parole Board as part of their statutory parole review or as part of a 'special parole review'. A special parole review would be applied for in exactly the same way as early release on compassionate grounds for prisoners who were not yet eligible for release on licence.

11.62   Early release on compassionate grounds may be granted in two main cases – the medical condition of a prisoner or if there are tragic family circumstances.

11.63   **Medical condition.**   The types of medical condition which may render a prisoner suitable for early release on compassionate grounds are set out in Circular Instruction 36/92 (paras 12–15):

(i)   Where a prisoner is suffering from a terminal illness and death is likely to occur 'soon' (within 3 months is suggested as a guideline). For the application to be successful it must be considered that there is no prospect of the prisoner committing further offences and that the medical care will be available to the prisoner in the community.

(ii) Where a prisoner will be 'bedridden or severely incapacitated until the end of the sentence and there is no risk of further offences being committed before then'. Examples given of the kinds of illness that would attract such compassionate release are wheelchair bound prisoners, stroke victims, or prisoners who are paralysed.
(iii) Where the prisoner's continued imprisonment would endanger his/her life or seriously shorten their life expectancy.

11.64 Circular Instruction 36/92 goes on to state that if a prisoner's medical condition is self-induced then they would not usually be considered for compassionate release. This provision will apply most commonly to hunger strikers.

11.65 In deciding whether a prisoner's medical condition is one for which they might be released on compassionate grounds, criteria set out in Annex A to Circular Instruction 36/92 are applied. These are:

(i)   the prisoner is suffering from a terminal illness and death is likely to occur soon; or the prisoner is bedridden or similarly incapacitated; *and*
(ii) the risk of further crime is past; *and*
(iii) there are adequate facilities for the prisoner's care and treatment outside prison; *and*
(iv) early release will bring some significant benefit to the prisoner or his/her family; and
(v)   the diagnosis and prognosis; in particular whether there is a specific estimate of life expectancy; and the degree of incapacitation.

11.66 In addition, for both types of compassionate release case the following considerations should also be taken into account:

(i)   whether temporary release under the Prison Rules could significantly reduce the prisoner's and/or family's suffering;
(ii) the length of the sentence still outstanding; the effect on the overall sentence passed by the court if compassionate release is granted; and any remarks which the trial judge made on sentencing which have a bearing on the question of release;
(iii) the wishes of the prisoner and his/her family and the level of benefit which would derive to the prison and/or the family from permanent release.

11.67 An application for early release on the basis of a medical condition is made to the prison itself in the first instance. The managing medical officer at the prison is required to complete forms giving details of the medical condition and including medical reports from consultants or others involved in the care and treatment of the prisoner. The prison probation officer will also be required to report upon the prisoner's home circumstances, and the Governor will report as to whether the prisoner's medical condition was known to the Court at the time that s/he was sentenced.

11.68 Tragic family circumstances. Circular Instruction 36/92 sets out the types of circumstances which may be considered to constitute tragic family circumstances for the purposes of compassionate release (paras 20–25):

(i) Where a prisoner's spouse is seriously ill, or has died, and there is no one to care for their young children. The support available to such a family would be taken into account – in particular how much other family members, friends, or social services are able to assist. The prisoner must be able and willing to care for the children.

(ii) Where a prisoner's spouse is seriously ill, but there are no children compassionate release may still be granted. This will be dependent on the particular illness, life expectancy, and whether any one else is able to care for the spouse.

(iii) Where a prisoner's parents are ill, compassionate release may be considered if the circumstances are 'exceptionally tragic'. This may apply in cases where there is only one parent who is suffering from an incurable illness and there is no one else who is able to care for him/her.

(iv) Compassionate release as a result of the serious illness or death of a child is not normally considered to constitute grounds for compassionate release from prison. However, if it is considered that 'the effect on the other parent combines with other factors to create exceptionally difficult domestic circumstances', the possibility of compassionate release will arise.

11.69 It is not considered that a prisoner's business difficulties would ever give rise to a successful application for compassionate release (para 24). Guidance is given that circumstances not listed above may nevertheless provide grounds for compassionate release. The governor's attention is also drawn to the fact that temporary release on licence may be more appropriate in some cases.

11.70 The criteria for compassionate release due to tragic family circumstances is set out at Annex A of the CI. These provide that for an application to be successful it must be shown that:

(i) the circumstances of the prisoner or the family have changed to the extent that if s/he served the sentence imposed, the hardship suffered would be of exceptional severity greater than the court could have foreseen; *and*

(ii) the risk of further crime is past; *and*

(iii) it can be demonstrated beyond doubt there is a real and urgent need for the prisoner's permanent presence with his/her family; *and*

(iv) early release will bring some significant benefit to the prisoner or his/her family.

11.71 The further grounds listed above (at para **11.66**, (i) and (iii)) will also apply in tragic family circumstances cases. Applications for compassionate release on this basis should be made to the governor of the prison establishment who will report to Prison Service Headquarters on whether the prisoner's domestic circumstances were known to the court when the prisoner was sentenced, the circumstances of the case, the prisoner's custodial behaviour, and an assessment of the risk of re-offending before the sentence is ended. The prison probation officer will also be asked to contribute to the report, and may contact the external probation service to gain further details of the circumstances and supporting evidence, for example medical reports.

11.72   In order for an application for compassionate release to be considered, reports from the prison will be forwarded to the Parole Unit at Prison Service Headquarters who may refer the case to the Parole Board for a recommendation as to the prisoner's release on licence if time allows. The final decision will be taken by ministers.

11.73   Although there are no set time limits for the consideration of cases, guidance is given to the effect that decisions on medical cases should be reached within two weeks of submission to Headquarters, and those on tragic family circumstances within four weeks (para 30). Where an application is refused, the prison may keep the case under review and reactivate it if the situation should deteriorate by submitting further reports to the Parole Board.

11.74   If it is decided that a prisoner is eligible to be released on the basis of their compassionate circumstances, the Parole Unit will send their licence to the prison to be issued. Conditions may be attached to the licence, and may be varied throughout the period that it is in force. The licence will expire at the two-thirds point of their sentence if they were sentenced before 1 October 1992, at the one-half point if they are serving 12 months or less, or at the three-quarters point for all other prisoners, except some sex offenders whose licences will not expire until the 100% point.

11.75   Prisoners released on compassionate grounds may be recalled to prison at any time. However, changes in the circumstances which lead to their release will not constitute grounds for recall. The position is similar to the recall of determinate prisoners who have been released on licence in that the following factors will be grounds for recall to prison:

(i)   where the prisoner's behaviour is posing, or likely to pose, a threat to the safety of the public; *or*
(ii) there has been a breach of conditions on the licence; *or*
(iii) further offences have been committed.

11.76   'Existing prisoners' and those serving sentences of over four years may be recalled by either a magistrates' court, or following the Probation Service's reporting of problems to the Parole Unit. Prisoners serving shorter sentences will be recalled by the magistrates' court if they are in breach of their licence conditions.

11.77   In practice, the Home Secretary appears reluctant to exercise the power to release prisoners under s 36. In the case of *R v Secretary of State for the Home Department, ex p Grice* (10 December 1993, unreported, DC), the prisoner was serving a four year sentence and had developed AIDS before being sent to prison. He was held in an old Victorian prison and his consultant felt that this was unsuitable for someone in his condition. The insanitary conditions were thought to pose a risk that he may develop a potentially fatal infection. Nevertheless, the Home Secretary refused his application for compassionate release on medical grounds, and he was only released following a special early parole review after the Divisional Court granted him leave to apply for judicial review.

DISCHARGE GRANTS

11.78   On discharge from prison, the prisoner is entitled to apply for a discharge grant. The purpose of the grant is to provide prisoners with sufficient money on release to meet immediate needs. The rates are closely linked to social security benefit levels and change each year.

11.79   In order to qualify, the prisoner must be eligible for income support and be travelling to an address within the UK. Those not eligible include prisoners to be deported, civil prisoners, young offenders under the age of 18 (unless exceptional circumstances apply, see below) and unconvicted prisoners released on acquittal or in other circumstances. The grants are payable at standard and higher rates, the higher rate being paid to prisoners who have a need to seek, obtain and pay for accommodation (SO 1I).

11.80   Young offenders aged 16 or 17 may be paid discharge grants where there is a genuine need to seek, obtain and pay for accommodation. This means that where a young offender qualifies for such a grant, it will always be paid at the higher rate. Young offenders aged 14 and 15 do not receive any grant as they are ineligible for statutory social security benefits.

11.81   Travel warrants are given to all prisoners on discharge, save for those who are to be deported. The warrant (or payment of fares) is to their home or a destination in the UK. Prisoners not receiving a discharge grant will be paid a subsistence allowance for the period of their journey or, if necessary, for the full period until a local office of the Department of Social Security can be reached. This will include any intervening night or weekend (SO 1I, para 27).

CHAPTER 12

THE LEARMONT AND WOODCOCK INQUIRIES

12.1 Two major reports into the prison system reported during 1995. The Woodcock Inquiry (Report of the Enquiry into the Escape of Six Prisoners from the Special Security Unit at Whitemoor Prison, Cambridgeshire, on Friday 9 September 1994, Cmnd 2741), was announced on 10 September 1994 when the Home Secretary asked Sir John Woodcock to lead an inquiry into the escape of maximum security prisoners from the special security unit at HMP Whitemoor – a part of the prison system which had previously been considered to be escape proof. The Learmont Inquiry (Review of Prison Service Security in England and Wales and the Escape from Parkhurst Prison on Tuesday 3 January 1995, Cmnd 3020) started life as a review of security throughout the Prison Service and was the Home Secretary's response to the 'dreadful state of affairs' uncovered by the Woodcock Report (Statement to the House of Commons by Michael Howard on 19 December 1994). Less than one month later three life sentence prisoners escaped from Parkhurst prison, and the terms of the Learmont Inquiry were broadened to carrying out an independent investigation into that escape.

12.2 Both reports concluded that the escapes were the end result of the prisons' failures to comply with security policies and procedures. In each case prisoners had been able to manufacture escape equipment undetected in the prisons and had used prison facilities to do so. At both prisons it was thought that illicit articles used in the escapes had been brought in from outside, either by prisoners' visitors or prison staff, and may have gone undetected for considerable periods of time. The possibility that such articles had travelled with the prisoner from previous locations could not be overlooked. The Learmont Inquiry states that Whitemoor and Parkhurst were not alone in their failures to implement the practices outlined in the Prison Service Security Manual but were:

> 'symptomatic of the practices in place in similar establishments throughout the country'. (Learmont Inquiry, para 6.7)

12.3 The Learmont Inquiry made 127 detailed recommendations, many of which duplicated those made by Woodcock. The main recommendations with direct implications for prisoners if they are implemented are as follows.

Searching

12.4
(i) 'A clear written policy on searching procedures should be available to all staff, inmates and visitors and should be monitored and supervised to ensure implementation' (Recommendation 12).
(ii) '"Rub down" searches should be carried out consistently and to a standard specified in the annual security audit, agreed by the area manager' (Recommendation 20).
(iii) 'Cell searches should be undertaken in accordance with the Manual on Security' (Recommendation 21) (see chapter 9 for details).
(iv) 'All prison establishments must implement a searching programme in accordance with the Manual on Security' (Recommendation 92) (see chapter 9 for details).
(v) 'The Prison Service should establish dedicated search teams in all dispersal prisons and at the two new prisons recommended. . . . Such teams should have available to them, on a regular basis, dogs trained to identify firearms, explosives and drugs' (Recommendations 22 and 93).
(vi) '. . . better use must be made of search teams, supported by appropriate equipment and the wider deployment of trained dogs' (Recommendation 94).

Searching of visitors

12.5
(i) 'Sufficient accommodation and equipment should be provided, at the main gate of all prisons holding category A inmates, to enable searching of all staff and visitors to take place at all times. This should be subject to CCTV observation. The main reception area should have direct communication with the visits reception area' (Recommendation 4).
(ii) 'Procedures for searching visitors are laid down in the Security Manual and must be obeyed, to minimise the risk of smuggling. Staff must have the latest equipment and be properly trained and proficient in the use of x-ray and metal detecting machinery, in sufficient numbers to ensure that, at each establishment, all such equipment, in particular at the gatehouse, is operated by qualified staff, who should be fully aware of searching procedures and relevant rules/legislation. Searching procedures should be regularly supervised' (Recommendations 5 and 86) (see chapter 9 for further details of searching procedure).
(iii) 'Visitors to prisons holding category A inmates must be subject to a "rub down" search and x-ray check, in accordance with existing instructions. All hand baggage and loose items (eg coats) should be x-rayed. All baggage and property, except cash for canteens and vending machines, should be left in secure containers at the gatehouse or in a visitors' centre situated outside the prison perimeter' (Recommendation 6) (see chapter 9 for details of existing instructions).

Conduct of visits

12.6
(i) 'Any prisoner or visitor needing to use the toilet facilities during a visit should be searched before and after visits to the toilet. In addition, all toilets should be searched before the end of a visits session and before inmates and visitors are allowed to leave' (Recommendation 13).
(ii) 'Visits rooms should have fixed furniture with a formal and observable layout' (Recommendation 8).
(iii) 'There should be full 360 degree fixed CCTV cover in visits rooms in secure establishments, with video recording facilities' (Recommendation 8).
(iv) 'Inmates on visits should wear some form of distinguishable clothing' (Recommendation 9).
(v) 'Visitors should not make cash transactions in visits rooms except at canteen or vending machines' (Recommendation 10).

Closed Visits

12.7
'In most cases some physical contact should be allowed between inmates and family. Mandatory closed visits are recommended only for exceptional risk category A prisoners. For other than exceptional risk category A prisoners, the option of imposing closed visits should be available in all secure establishments, to be used at the governor's discretion. Governors should make more use of the option, when they have reasonable grounds for suspicion, and Headquarters should support them' (Recommendations 90 and 91).

Family visits

12.8
(i) 'Family visits are not appropriate at dispersal prisons and should be ceased' (Recommendation 15).
(ii) 'In high security prisons, visiting children should be restricted to toys provided in the children's play area. In other prisons, imitation weapons should be banned and other toys brought in by children should be checked' (Recommendation 16).

Prisoners' property

12.9
'A volumetric control of all prisoners' possessions should be introduced forthwith, to reduce dramatically the amount of property in possession/ storage and facilitate effective searching. The volume allowed should be standard to all inmates, whatever their category. Prisoners should be allowed only that amount of property which fits into a maximum of two transit boxes. Prisoners should not be allowed to add to their property, if

it would exceed the allowance, until arrangements are made for excess property to be collected by relatives/friends or stored centrally' (Recommendation 23).

Workshops

12.10
(i) 'Throughout the prison estate, establishments with workshops should set up daily audits of tools and materials. Workshops should be designed to ensure that prisoners can be observed at all times and, subject to health and safety regulations, safety screens should be made of transparent material' (Recommendation 1).
(ii) 'The Prison Service should review the type of work and training available to inmates in dispersal prisons, with emphasis on the central importance of security in all aspects of activity' (Recommendation 3).

Emergencies

12.11
'The Service must keep abreast of work on chemical incapacitants and consider the use of CS gas to quell riotous behaviour. There is a need also for the Service to re-examine the argument for an armed response capability' (Recommendation 101).

Categorisation

12.12
(i) 'Security categorisation should be reviewed and researched to remove dangerous anomalies produced by the current system' (Recommendation 38).
(ii) 'The Prison Service should introduce a new interim categorisation system as soon as possible' (Recommendation 102). (see para 12.16 below)

Privileges and incentives

12.13
(i) 'Cooking facilities on wings should be treated as a privilege and not a right. Access to stores of food must be supervised and regulated' (Recommendation 46).
(ii) 'Early release should be a privilege earned through good behaviour and the Prison Service initiative on this matter should be taken forward urgently' (Recommendation 116).
(iii) 'Private cash should be phased out' (Recommendation 118).
(iv) 'There must be a mandatory minimum entitlement to visits which takes account of the need to retain family links. Additional visits can be used as incentives to good behaviour' (Recommendation 119).
(v) 'Telephone privileges should feature in an incentive scheme' (Recommendation 120).

(vi) 'Television in cells could provide a calming influence and a powerful incentive to good conduct. It could also be used for educational and communication purposes. The right to this privilege should be earned by good behaviour, once the prisoner has earned the right to electricity in the cell' (Recommendation 121).

(vii) 'The Prison Service should explore ways of increasing the availability of home leave and apply firm sanctions to those who abuse the privilege' (Recommendation 122).

Telephones

12.14

'Telephone monitoring should be intelligence driven. Improved facilities need to be in place to monitor foreign language conversations' (Recommendation 43).

Drugs

12.15

'To deal with drug abuse, all prisons must have programmes which inform, educate and help prisoners combat the drug habit. Success on such programmes should be rewarded through the incentive scheme' (Recommendation 85).

The high security estate

12.16

(i) 'Prisoners in new categories 1 and 2 should be housed in a new purpose-built high security prison' (Recommendation 104). (Learmont outlines a new system for categorisation in the main body of the Report. This contains six security categorisations, 1 to 6. Categories 1–3 would be held in dispersal type prison conditions and would be equivalent to category A exceptional risk (1), category A high risk (2) and category A standard risk (3). Category 3 would also include some prisoners who are now category B and held in dispersal conditions. Category 4 would be equivalent to those category B and C prisoners who are currently held in training prisons with cellular accommodation. Those category C prisoners who are now in category C training prisons with non-cellular accommodation would become the new category 5 prisoners. Finally, prisoners in open conditions would be in the lowest security category, 6' (Report of the Learmont Inquiry, para 5.5).

(ii) 'A Control Prison should be established for particularly disruptive prisoners including disruptive prisoners who are mentally ill' (Recommendation 114).

(iii) 'The high security estate should be managed as a whole rather than piecemeal. An operational director should be appointed with the sole task of managing the high security prison, the control prison, and the six dispersal prisons. This director should be a full member of the Prisons Board, have operational experience as the governor of a dispersal prison and have no substantial work other than management of these prisons. The high security, control and dispersal prisons should remain in the public sector' (Recommendation 123).

Other establishments

12.17
(i)   'The Prison Service should provide suitable accommodation for high risk women prisoners and young offenders' (Recommendation 108).
(ii) 'The Prison Service should undertake a review to assess the present open estate and to decide what is required for resettlement units, what should be retained as open accommodation, and what should be upgraded to new security standards' (Recommendation 112).
(iii) 'Women's prisons should be the responsibility of one area manager. All women prisoners should be housed in women's prisons. In the longer term, there should be a thorough review of the female prisoners' estate' (Recommendation 124).

Remand prisoners

12.18
(i)   'In the short term, whenever possible, remand category A prisoners should be held in dispersal prisons but it will be necessary for many of them to be held in other strategically placed prisons with accommodation to category A standard' (Recommendation 97).
(ii) 'The practicality of installing TV links between prisons holding remand prisoners and magistrates' courts should be explored' (Recommendation 98).

12.19   The Prison Service had implemented several of Woodcock's recommendations before Learmont reported (eg the searching procedures outlined in chapter 9, and the system for incentives and earned privileges in chapter 8), but at this stage it is not known how far the Prison Service will go in accepting the findings of the inquiries.

SECTION III

CHAPTER 13

LEGAL AID

INTRODUCTION

13.1   One of the major problems that prisoners have tended to face when seeking legal representation is that lawyers have found it difficult to obtain payment for work undertaken, or have been unaware of what the proper source of legal aid income is for prisoners' cases. The confusion that surrounds this issue has been compounded by the introduction of franchising and the uncertainty that this has produced.

13.2   There is no franchise specifically for prisoners' cases or prison law and the franchise areas into which this has been subsumed may not always afford the best range of representation for prisoners. However, there are benefits that can be found, particularly in respect of the provision of advice and assistance under the Green Form scheme.

13.3   The legal aid scheme makes provision for lawyers to receive payment for acting for prisoners in three ways; for general advice and assistance under the Green Form scheme, for full civil legal aid certificates to be issued and for Advice by Way of Representation (ABWOR) to be granted for discretionary lifer panel hearings and for adjudications carried out by the controllers of contracted out prisons. This chapter assumes that practitioners are familiar with the legal aid scheme and will focus on particular problems that may arise when acting for prisoners.

GREEN FORMS

13.4   The vast majority of work that is undertaken on behalf of prisoners will be carried out under the Green Form scheme. In general, physical representation for prisoners is either not permitted (eg when the Parole Board consider determinate prisoners' and mandatory lifers' cases), or is completely discretionary and very rarely permitted (eg adjudications or internal decision-making 'boards' in the prison itself). The only exception to this general rule is in the case of discretionary life prisoners or adjudications carried out in contracted out prisons.

13.5   By far the majority of cases in which prisoners will seek legal advice will first involve representations being made on their behalf. These representations may be made with the intent of changing an adverse decision, such as recategorisation or temporary release, or may be made with a view to securing a favourable outcome to a decision yet to be made, such as release on parole licence. In either situation, litigation cannot normally be contemplated until initial representations have been made and it is not possible to assess in advance whether there will be grounds to apply for a full civil legal aid certificate and commence litigation. As a consequence, by far the majority of work undertaken for prisoners will only be covered by the Green Form and this may never progress further. Lawyers engaged in this area of work are therefore far more likely to be dependent on this scheme than lawyers involved in any other type of work with the possible exception of employment law.

13.6   The particular problem with prisoners seeking to receive advice has been the manner in which they come to instruct solicitors. As the normal route of booking an appointment and attending the solicitor's office is not possible, prisoners will generally seek to obtain advice either by telephoning a solicitor or writing to him/her. The problem the solicitor and prisoner will then face is how the solicitor will come to be paid for this work. This will be equally true for existing clients who raise new issues relating to their imprisonment as it is for new, possibly unsolicited enquiries.

Non-franchised firms

13.7   The first point to bear in mind is that payment can only be authorised under the Green Form from the time it has been signed. For firms who do not have a franchise, legal aid forms can normally only be signed in the presence of a solicitor or a representative from the solicitor's office (Legal Advice and Assistance Regulations 1989, SI 1989/340, reg 9(3)). There are limited circumstances in which another person can attend on behalf of a client (reg 10), and the notes for guidance specify that these are when a person is ill or lives too far from the office and cannot travel. This could obviously apply to a prisoner who is unable to visit a solicitor.

13.8   There are problems in dealing with new applications for advice and assistance in this manner. Various legal aid area offices have sought to refuse applications for extensions to Green Forms under the discretionary powers conferred by reg 21 of the 1989 Regulations where the firm is not close to the prison on the grounds that a local firm should be instructed. This approach is not always appropriate for prisoners, particularly as they can lawfully be located in any prison in England or Wales and may be subject to many such moves. In those circumstances, it would be reasonable to argue that the concept of a 'local' firm is inappropriate.

13.9   Travelling time and expenses incurred before the Green Form is signed cannot be recovered. In a letter from the Legal Aid Board's legal adviser to the Prisoners' Legal Rights Group in March 1995, the policy of the Board was expressed to be that extensions to cover the time and costs of travel after the Green Form was signed could be met but authority would not be granted before the Green Form had been signed. The solicitor would therefore be left in the faintly ludicrous position of having to ring for an extension from the prison after having completed initial attendance. Retrospective extensions after the work has been incurred will not be granted.

Franchised firms

13.10 Franchised firms are in a different situation as the terms of a franchise can, and usually will, allow for Green Forms to be sent out in the post or to be effective on the basis of a telephone call. Payment will be subject to compliance with any specific provisions in the contract, but in general, the major obstacles are removed for franchised firms.

13.11 The question of which franchise is appropriate for prisoners' cases is open to some debate. The Guidance on the Exercise of Devolved Powers contains reference to which types of work are covered by which franchise (appendix 1). There is no specific mention of prison issues, although Mental Health Act cases were defined as not having a specific franchise category. The Law Society were notified by the Legal Aid Board that the following matters should be included in the crime franchise:

(i) complaints about treatment in prisons;
(ii) parole board issues;
(iii) assaults by prison officers (unless advice was sought as to commencing a civil claim for damages, in which case the personal injury franchise is appropriate);
(iv) advice in relation to panels such as the categorisation of prisoners.

13.12 Whilst it is understandable that this area of work has been subsumed into the criminal franchise, in practice there is often little correlation between criminal matters and prison issues and there is certainly no guarantee that an expert in one field will be expert in the other. If a solicitor has franchises in areas other than crime but does deal with prisoners' cases, it would be advisable for authority to be sought from the area office for them to be included in another franchise category.

CIVIL LEGAL AID CERTIFICATES

Financial assessment

13.13 When prisoners make an application for a civil legal aid certificate, the appropriate form for assessment of their finances is form CLA 4A. Whilst this may seem unusual for people with little or no income, as income support is not available to those serving custodial sentences, a full financial assessment is required. Prisoners should be advised to include details of their prison wages in the section headed 'other relevant information' and not in the section that deals with employment. This is because prison employment is not contractual and prison wages do not, at present, bring applicants above the financial eligibility level. The exceptions will be for those located in resettlement units or prisoners who are employed outside of the prison and receive a wage, and those who are on enhanced earnings schemes within a prison.

13.14 The major problem that will arise with the financial side of the application is the question of whether the finances of a prisoner's partner should also be assessed. The regulations provide that the income and capital of spouses shall be treated as the resources of the applicant, unless they are living apart or the spouse has a contrary interest in the subject matter of the application. Opposite sex couples who live in the same household as if married are also covered by this provision (Civil Legal Aid (Assessment of Resources) Regulations 1989, SI 1989/338, reg 7).

13.15 The Legal Aid Board have widely interpreted this to include couple who *normally* live together as if they are married and this wording appears on the top of the assessment form. Area offices will usually send forms to the spouses and partners of prisoners to declare details of their finances. This can potentially create problems, either if the partner does not comply with the completion of the forms or if they are above the financial limit. It is arguable that in the majority of cases, prisoners' partners should not be included in the financial assessment. Many relationships will not survive the stress of imprisonment and it is not really practical for a long-term prisoner to be classed as 'normally' living with a person outside of prison. Financially, prisoners can only receive a set amount of income each year and their partner will not usually have any direct interest in the outcome of an application. Whilst this argument may be less valid for very short-term prisoners who have a firm intention to return to a matrimonial home at the end of the sentence, refusals to grant legal aid based on the financial situation of a partner may be vulnerable to challenge.

Satisfying the 'benefit' test

13.16 Legal aid certificates can be refused, even where a good case on the merits has been established, if the benefit to the client is not deemed sufficient to justify the costs of the proceedings. This will include cases where the financial claim is small (normally deemed to be under £1,000) or where the costs of the action will exceed the benefit to the client. The standard guidance that is issued for the issue of civil legal aid certificates in such cases is that:

> 'Legal aid should only be granted to pursue a case in which costs are likely to exceed the value of any benefit gained thereby where:
> (a) there is a high prospect of success and the opponent is likely to indemnify the applicant for the legal costs; or
> (b) what is at stake is of such overwhelming importance to the applicant that it overrides the question of costs.' (*Legal Aid Handbook* (1993) Sweet & Maxwell, p 65)

13.17 In prisoners' cases, the benefit of taking proceedings will fall into two categories. In claims for damages (either for personal injury or for other financial loss), the prisoner will have to establish that a claim of potentially more than £1,000 can be made. In personal injury cases, solicitors should have particular regard to any potential psychological damages that would bring the level of damages above that level. If the financial award is likely to be below £1,000, then there will have to be particular circumstances that make the case of sufficient public importance to justify the grant of legal aid.

13.18 In applications for judicial review of administrative decisions, it will have to be shown that there is some benefit to the applicant that is of sufficient importance to override the question of costs. The Legal Aid Board will often use this ground as a reason for refusing initial applications unless this has been specifically addressed in the statement of case. In some applications, the benefit will be obvious. This would commonly include applications to challenge a refusal to release a prisoner on parole licence or a life sentenced prisoner challenging the decision of the Secretary of Sate following a parole review. Nevertheless, it is advisable to spell out that the application relates to the release of a person from prison in such cases to ensure that this test is satisfied.

13.19 In other applications, the benefit may not be immediately obvious to those who are not familiar with prison law and procedure and so it is necessary to explain this in more detail. By and large, the majority of decisions made in respect of prisoners which lead to complaints and applications for judicial review will have a direct impact on either the conditions in which they are held and/or their long-term prospects of progression and release. An award of additional days at an adjudication extends the time that must be served in custody, and a decision to re-categorise a prisoner to a higher security category will result in poorer conditions of detention and decrease the prospects of parole.

13.20 The judicial view of administrative decision-making in respect of prisoners has largely accorded with this view since the judgment in *ex p Doody*. In 1993, Lord Justice Rose commented on the process whereby prisoners are made category A, and compared it to the length of lifers' tariffs. He accepted counsel's arguments that:

> 'In each case reports are made and considered, the decision is based on information about the offence and the prisoners' character, and there is a significant effect on when the prisoner may be released.' (*R v Secretary of State for the Home Department, ex p Duggan*, [1994] 3 All ER 277)

It is difficult to envisage any adverse decisions made in respect of prisoners that will not have similar consequences on conditions of detention and the prospects of release from prison and this point must be made to the Legal Aid Board when submitting applications.

The future?

13.21 The discussion paper on the provision of state funded legal services has concentrated on the concept of contracts being awarded to individual firms and advice agencies to fulfil locally identified need. Financial caps on the budgets available are proposed to limit the costs of providing these services. The provision of advice and representation to prisoners does not fit easily into this equation as it is not possible to identify precisely what the local need is in respect of this area of law. The fact that there is no franchise category to cater specifically for prison law means that firms who bid for such contracts may not be aware of the need that exists from prisoners. Geographical limits on the area which contracts cover could potentially lead to prisoners who are moved around the country being forced to change representative with each move. The nature of imprisonment and the manner in which legal services are delivered to those in custody is unusual and there is no indication that the consultative papers have considered the problems that could arise for this group of people.

CHAPTER 14

PRISONERS' PROPERTY CLAIMS

INTRODUCTION

14.1   Prisoners are entitled to receive compensation when their property is lost in prison so long as they are able to show that the Prison Service are liable for their loss. Applications may be submitted by prisoners themselves through the requests/complaints procedure or through their legal advisers.

14.2   Compensation claims for lost property are initially submitted to the governor of the prison where the property was lost or the area manager, depending on the level of the claim. Instruction to Governors 38/94 gives governors authority to deal with claims up to £3,000, and claims in excess of that sum should be made to the area manager in the first instance. Area managers must seek final authority to settle which is obtained from the Treasury where the value of the property exceeds £20,000.

14.3   It is possible to appeal against decisions made by the governor by submitting an appeal to the area manager, either through the requests/complaints procedure or through a legal representative. If the area manager refuses to authorise compensation, a complaint can be made to the Prisons Ombudsman.

14.4   Applications for compensation should give full details of the lost items, where and when they were purchased, receipts (if possible), and the circumstances of the loss. If no receipts are available, the letters or statements from the persons who purchased the property on behalf of the prisoner should be obtained.

4.5   Prisons keep extensive documentation on prisoners' property and these include records of stored property (property held in boxes in the reception of the prison), in possession property (property which prisoners keep in their cells), and details of boxes of prisoners' property which is in transit between different prisons. In addition, where prisoners are removed from their cells on normal location, officers complete cell clearance sheets (itemised statements of everything removed from the cell). In putting together a property claim it is often helpful to obtain copies of prisoners' property records in order to prove that the items being claimed for were the responsibility of the prison at the time of the loss.

14.6   If claims are successful the money will normally be paid into the prisoner's private cash account at the prison.

ESTABLISHING LIABILITY

14.7   If *stored property* is either lost in reception or in transit then so long as it is clear from the property cards that the prisoner actually owned that property and it was held in the prison then the Prison Service will be liable.

14.8   The Prison Service does not normally accept liability for 'in possession' property (ie property held in the prisoner's cell) on the basis that the inmate may have given it to other prisoners or exchanged it for other items. There are exceptions to this and these are based upon the law of negligence:

(i)   Where the prisoner has been removed from normal location (eg to the segregation block) without prior warning and has therefore been unable to secure their property.
(ii)   Where the prisoner has been removed from normal location because of illness.
(iii) Where the prisoner has been temporarily released.
(iv) Where the prisoner has absconded or escaped.

14.9   In situations (i) and (ii) above in possession property is deemed to be no longer under the inmate's control and thus responsibility reverts back to the Prison Service. Therefore it is important to take instructions from prisoners on whether they have any knowledge of whether the cell was sealed immediately after their removal from normal location (eg via other inmates or if the cell was unsealed on their return to normal location). If the cell was not sealed immediately, was unsealed at any point before it was cleared, or if property shown on the cell clearance sheet was never returned to the prisoner, then the Prison Service would be liable for the loss (*Winson v Home Office* (10 December 1994, unreported) Case Number 9383065 Central London County Court, *Ross v Home Office* (28 July 1994, unreported)).

14.10   In situation (iii) above the Prison Service will argue that the prisoner should have taken reasonable steps to secure his property before temporary release. It is important to obtain instructions as to whether the prisoner was advised by staff to store property in reception during their absence, or if they asked to do so and were refused. If prisoners are temporarily released on a daily basis they should be warned of the increased risk to their property by staff.

14.11   In situation (iv) above the Prison Service will not accept liability for property lost between the time of the abscond/escape and the disappearance being confirmed. When disappearance is confirmed prison staff should take immediate action to secure the in possession property – the cell should be sealed and then cleared without delay. Circular Instruction 48/92 states that the property should be stored until six months after the date of the abscond/escape. At that time the next of kin should be contacted to ask if they wish to claim the property. If after three years the property still has not been claimed

Circular Instruction 48/92 states that it may be disposed of either by competitive tender, or if the items have no value they may be destroyed.

14.12   In all cases a failure to handle a prisoner's property in accordance with the instructions in the Inmate Personal Records System Manual will create a strong presumption in favour of paying compensation (Prisoners' Requests/Complaints Procedure Staff Manual, Annex I, para 2), and it is therefore important to check that the relevant signatures are on property cards, and that there is no evidence that the property has been misrecorded at some stage.

LEGAL ACTION

14.13   In most cases, the amount of the claim will fall below the level for which legal aid is normally granted. The level of compensation that will be offered, whether by the Prison Service or through a court award, is based on the value of the property at the time it was lost and not on the replacement costs of new items. It is possible to argue that the value of a relatively small claim is substantially greater to a prisoner due to the low level of prison wages (eg a claim of £500 is equal to at least six months of prison earnings). However, in most cases legal aid will be refused.

14.14   Due to the fact that legal aid is unlikely to be granted in most cases, complaints to the Prisons Ombudsman are very often the best course of action to pursue before commencing legal proceedings. The Ombudsman's report of the first six months of operation shows that the largest number of complaints received concerned property (18% of the total). In the conclusions to the report the Ombudsman noted that:

> 'Laid down property procedures are often not followed and recording of property, both in possession and in storage, is frequently inaccurate.' (Prisons Ombudsman – Six Month Review, 24 October 1994 – 23 April 1995, para 11.3)

14.15   When a complaint is made to the Ombudsman in cases where legal aid is not available, the primary aim is to secure a favourable recommendation which will be accepted by the Prison Service. In cases where a favourable recommendation is not accepted, the report can form the basis of an application to the county court as it will often contain a clear and impartial account of the loss and where liability should rest. This is, however, a double-edged sword and if the complaint is not upheld it can undermine any potential litigation.

14.16   Where legal aid is not available, prisoners should be advised to commence their own proceedings in the county court local to the prison in which they are located. A summons and explanatory leaflet will be sent to the prisoner on a request to the Chief Clerk. Prisoners should be advised of the following points:

(i)   The proper defendant is the Home Office (not the governor of the prison concerned).

(ii) The address for service is that of the Treasury Solicitor (Queen Anne's Chambers, 28 Broadway, London SW1H 9JS).

(iii) A waiver of court fees may be obtained by making an application to the Lord Chancellor's Office or by completing the county court form 'Application For a Fee Remission' and sending it to the Clerk to the County Court together with the summons.

(iv) The claim is for negligence, and/or conversion, and/or trespass to goods (rather than for 'maladministration' or 'breach of statutory duty' which many prisoners plead).

(v) If attendance at court is necessary, either for the final hearing or interlocutory applications, the normal rules on production at court will apply.

14.17 If the claim is successful (either after correspondence or court proceedings) and the prisoner has signed a Green Form, an application not to enforce the statutory charge will be appropriate in most cases (Legal Advice and Assistance Regulations 1989, reg 33).

CHAPTER 15

PERSONAL INJURY AND ASSAULT CLAIMS

INTRODUCTION

15.1 The substantive law relevant to prisoners' claims for personal injury and assault is discussed in chapter 3. Personal injury claims by prisoners will usually be concerned with three scenarios: assaults by other inmates, assaults by prison officers or claims arising from negligent medical treatment. Lawyers who are familiar with conducting personal injury claims will often be unfamiliar with the bureaucracy of the Prison Service and may face difficulties in obtaining records relevant to the claim. Other aspects of normally routine advice, such as reporting alleged criminal offences to the police and making claims to the Criminal Injuries Compensation Board also need to be considered. This chapter is not designed to provide a detailed examination of how to conduct a personal injury/medical negligence action, but to deal with the particular areas that need to be addressed when advising prisoners in respect of these matters.

REPORTING INCIDENTS TO THE POLICE

15.2 Prisoners may report any incident in which they allege a criminal offence has been committed to the police. There is no restriction on this right simply by virtue of the fact that one is in custody. The practical problem that is faced is how to physically make the report. The police are reluctant to commence an investigation on the basis of information received from a telephone call and will not generally visit prisoners to take a statement without some form of written statement being provided in advance. In cases where a prisoner wishes to make a report, the quickest method of doing this is to make a signed, handwritten statement and for this to be sent to the police station closest to the prison. Most forces have a prisons' liaison officer who will then arrange to attend the prison to take a more formal statement, although in some cases, an investigation can commence simply on the basis of the information in the original statement prepared by the prisoner. Complaints and handwritten statements can also be forwarded by friends or legal representatives.

15.3 In certain circumstances, the governor of a prison may be under a duty to report a matter to the police which could subsequently form the basis of a personal injury claim, such as incidents where an assault is alleged to have been committed by another prisoner. The following guidelines have been issued to governors when deciding whether to report an incident to the police (CI 3/92, appendix A):

(i) serious assaults including allegations of non-consensual buggery or rape, attempted murder and manslaughter and threats to kill where there is a genuine intent;
(ii) assaults that result in serious injury, hostage taking, the use of a weapon that is capable of causing serious injury or persistent sexual violations other than rape and buggery;
(iii) criminal damage or arson unless the damage is negligible and no injury of substantial financial loss has been incurred;
(iv) robbery.

The governor should also report any incidents where the victim of an alleged crime asks for the police to be notified or where there is evidence of racial motivation.

CLAIMS TO THE CRIMINAL INJURIES COMPENSATION BOARD

15.4   Prisoners are able to make claims for compensation to the Criminal Injuries Compensation Board in precisely the same circumstances as any other citizen. It is for this reason that many prisoners are keen to have assaults reported to the police. In practice, claims on behalf of prisoners will rarely be successful. The Board operates within a discretionary framework whereby it is empowered to make ex gratia awards. Paragraph 6(c) of the scheme allows awards to be refused if it is considered inappropriate having taken account of the applicant's character as shown by his/her criminal convictions. As all prisoners, save for remand and civil prisoners will necessarily have criminal convictions, this is a major barrier to making a claim.

15.5   The decision to refuse an award on these grounds is not confined to convictions which have a causal connection with the assault on the inmate. Convictions of all types, not just those of violence can be considered by the Board when reaching a decision on these grounds. The Court of Appeal has upheld the power of the Board to refuse awards on these grounds even where the applicant's conduct, character and past way of life had no bearing on the incident that lead to the injury (*R v Criminal Injuries Compensation Board, ex p Thompstone* [1984] 1 WLR 1234).

15.6   Prisoners with convictions for violence will face great difficulty in mounting a challenge to a refusal on these grounds. The Court of Appeal did state that this power also exists in cases where there are convictions for dishonesty, but the power must be exercised reasonably and each application must be considered on its own merits. Blanket refusals to any persons serving custodial sentences regardless of the nature and extent of their convictions would be susceptible to challenge by way of judicial review.

ACCESS TO MEDICAL RECORDS

15.7   Prison doctors are required to maintain a 'continuous inmate medical record'. This is akin to the notes kept by a GP and will record all entries relevant to a prisoner's medical history whilst in custody. The Access to Health Records Act 1990 allows access to all such records made since 1 November 1991. Prisoners may make an application in writing to see their records and they should be made available within 40 days. Copies can also be obtained although a copying charge is normally made.

15.8   There will also be reference to medical issues in other parts of a prisoner's files, although it is arguable that a prison doctor should also make a note of these on the continuous records. These will include any reception medical examination and views expressed on health and fitness to work, records kept by the prison hospital, if a prisoner has been admitted and any reports of injury to a prisoner. This last document, known as form F213, is required to be completed by the medical officer whenever a prisoner has been injured. This can be of crucial importance to prisoners who wish to commence personal injury actions as contemporaneous proof of the injuries that they allege were suffered and, in cases where limitation dates are close to expiring or where there are difficulties in obtaining an independent report prior to the issue of proceedings, this can be appended to the summons in place of a more detailed medical report to be prepared at a later date. All of these documents form part of the prisoner's health records and disclosure may be sought under the Access to Health Records Act 1990.

15.9   The situation with medical records is generally no different than for people who are imprisoned. Therefore, a refusal to release records, particularly those made before November 1991 would be subject to the same rules of disclosure as in any other personal injury case (ie applications for pre-action discovery etc). It is when making such applications, or initial requests for the release of the records that prisoners and their lawyers should be aware of precisely what documents they are seeking.

DISCLOSURE OF OTHER RECORDS

15.10   Apart from medical records, there is little information that will be freely disclosed prior to the issue of proceedings. There are, however, certain reports and records that a prisoner has a right to see throughout his/her sentence and it can be advisable to obtain these at an early stage to scrutinise them for relevant information. These will include parole dossiers, if the prisoner has been considered for parole. Parole dossiers will contain general reports on behaviour as well as any relevant medical assessments and records of major disciplinary offences, some or all of which may be relevant. All records of adjudications must also be provided to a prisoner or his/her legal representative on request (Discipline Manual, para 9.5). The medical officer is obliged to examine a prisoner before every adjudication to ensure that the person is well enough to attend the hearing and fit enough for any awards that may be awarded. The adjudication records will note that this examination has taken place. Category A prisoners will have had the gist of reports that are prepared each year disclosed to them and lifers will increasingly be given the reports prepared for internal lifer reviews. All of these reports may contain valuable information as to how a prisoner's behaviour has been perceived by staff and whether any specific problems were identified.

15.11   Aside from the documents that are routinely disclosed, a large number of files and forms will be maintained. These documents will normally only be subject to discovery in the normal course of an action in negligence. The most important of these is the prisoner's personal record, a loose-leaf file which accompanies prisoners through their sentence. This contains the following records:

(i)   details of conviction, sentence and release dates;
(ii) a record of each transfer together with applications and governor's observations;
(iii) the medical officer's views on health and work classification;
(iv) the disciplinary record;
(v)   any time spent in segregation and details of transfers in the interests of good order and discipline;
(vi) any special security information, which may include details of escapes and escape attempts, intelligence on visits and correspondence and details of suicide attempts and special medical problems.

15.12   In addition to this general record, the prison is obliged to record all occasions on which force is used against a prisoner, reports of injuries suffered by prisoners to be completed by the medical officer, a register of any non-medical restraints applied to prisoners and the authority for segregation and the reasons why the decision was taken. Decisions to continue periods in segregation, whether taken by the Secretary of State or the Board of Visitors must also be recorded. In addition to the formal records that are required to be kept, each wing will maintain its own set of records, including segregation and hospital wings. Significant events should be noted in these on a daily basis.

INDEPENDENT MEDICAL EXAMINATIONS

15.13   There is no general right for convicted prisoners to be examined by a doctor of their own choice. In situations where there is no litigation in progress, prisoners can request to be seen by a doctor/psychiatrist from outside the prison and this is then at the discretion of the governor. The costs of any such examination must be met by the prisoner, although if a legal aid certificate has been granted, authority can be obtained to cover these costs. There is usually little difficulty in obtaining the consent of the governor in such circumstances – a refusal would be suspicious and would merit being brought to the attention of the court.

15.14   Rule 17(5) of the Prison Rules allows prisoners who are party to any legal proceedings to be afforded reasonable facilities to be examined by a registered medical practitioner selected on his/her behalf. The examination will take place out of the hearing but within the sight of a prison officer. The Secretary of State has also reserved the power to impose directions on this right in particular cases although, at present, none have been issued.

OBTAINING AND PRESERVING EVIDENCE

15.15 Prisoners are at a major disadvantage in preparing negligence claims against the Prison Service in that their ability to prepare and secure evidence is severely impaired. This contrasts sharply with the facilities and resources of the Prison Service who maintain detailed records of all incidents. It is therefore important that prisoners are made aware of what steps they can take to maximise their chances of success.

15.16 In cases where prisoners fear assault by another inmate, they must ensure that these fears are brought to the attention of prison staff and comply with any attempts made by staff to ensure their safety (eg through segregation or transfer). Guidance issued to prison staff lists specific steps that should be taken when one prisoner is thought, or known, to pose a threat to the safety of others. These include reporting the matter to the governor, making appropriate searches where it is thought that a weapon may be used, and to keep a special watch at recognised 'danger points'. These danger points are commonly perceived to be when prisoners are moving to or from work and exercise, in television rooms, at the servery and in any situation involving queuing.

15.17 The importance of ensuring that prisoners make sure their fears in this regard are known and recorded cannot be emphasised enough. If a prisoner feels that they have not been taken seriously or that no formal record has been made of the problem, it is advisable to issue a request/complaint form on the matter to ensure that a formal record is kept. The case law on this area suggests that staff have a duty to balance the need for protection against the need to provide as balanced and open a regime as possible. As a result, in one case where a prisoner was seriously assaulted by another inmate with whom he had previously fought, the claim was unsuccessful as the judge noted that the victim was proficient at defending himself and did not wish to give the appearance of running away from trouble (*Porterfield v Home Office* (1988) Independent, 9 March).

15.18 In all cases, prisoners should keep their own written record wherever possible. When an incident has occurred, it may be some time before a prisoner has access to a solicitor and so by making an immediate record, the events are recorded as contemporaneously as possible. Letters to legal advisers detailing the nature of the complaint can be utilised as such a record. If there are witnesses to an incident, the prisoner should seek to identify them as quickly as possible and ask if they are prepared to make a statement. If they are, then this should be written down immediately rather than to wait for a solicitor to take it. A solicitor can always expand on this statement at a later date. If the complaint relates to a lengthy series of conduct, the prisoner would be advised to keep a diary of all events so that specific times and dates can be given to alleged actions.

15.19   If injuries have been suffered, prisoners should request a copy of the record of those injuries prepared by the medical officer. If s/he feels that the record is not accurate, then a formal request for amendment should be made. It is important that this request is made formally (eg through the requests/complaints procedure) to ensure that the extent of the disagreement is recorded.

15.20   When solicitors receive instructions from prisoners in this situation, then this advice can be given immediately as there is likely to be some delay between the receipt of the complaint and the time when a legal visit can be arranged. Solicitors can themselves shoulder the burden of these duties by raising matters in writing with the governor of the prison in advance of any legal visit.

CHAPTER 16

APPLICATIONS FOR JUDICIAL REVIEW

WHAT DECISIONS ARE REVIEWABLE?

16.1 Judicial review is of crucial importance to prisoners as, aside from investigations by the Prisons Ombudsman, it is the only formal (domestic) method whereby an independent body can exercise control over decisions made in respect of prisoners. The fact of prison life is that each day, many administrative decisions will be made in respect of each prisoner, some of these will be of crucial importance to the individual and others will be more mundane. These decisions can be made by a wide variety of people, from prison officers, to governors, to civil servants acting on behalf of the Secretary of State and the Secretary of State in person.

16.2 The gradual process whereby the Divisional Court has extended its jurisdiction to deal with prisoners' applications has left virtually all decisions made in respect of prisoners amenable to this remedy. Thus, the Divisional Court will entertain applications concerning the categorisation of prisoners, the calculation of their sentences, disciplinary proceedings, the use of quasi-disciplinary powers such as transfers and segregation, medical treatment (eg *R v Secretary of State for the Home Department, ex p Dew* [1987] 1 WLR 881 where a prisoner sought an order for mandamus to require specific medical treatment to be given. The treatment had been provided by the time the case came to be heard and the application was struck out with the prisoner being informed that the proper course of action was then to commence a negligence claim), length of tariff and decisions concerning release. In all cases where a prisoner makes a complaint about the treatment that has been accorded to him/her, if there is no personal injury or financial loss resulting from that treatment, the practitioner should immediately be alerted that judicial review is likely to be the only legal remedy available.

16.3 The use of this remedy is of such importance that all advice given to prisoners, and all action taken on their behalf, should be done with this remedy in mind. It is therefore essential for practitioners to bear in mind the fundamental principles that apply to applications for judicial review and the relief that is available. The technical nature of the remedy is such that many prisoners mistakenly see it as a form of appeal of decisions rather than a process of review. Lord Hailsham emphasised this point clearly when he commented:

'It is important to remember in every case that the purpose of (judicial review) is to ensure that the individual is given fair treatment by the authority to which he has been subjected and that it is no part of that purpose to substitute the opinion of the judiciary or of individual judges for that of the authority constituted by law to decide on the matters in question.' (*Chief Constable of North Wales Police v Evans* [1982] 1 WLR 1155)

16.4   These comments define the area to which the court may direct its powers to cases where an authority has acted without jurisdiction or in excess of its jurisdiction, where there is a failure to follow the rules of natural justice, where there is an error of law on the face of the record or where the decision is unreasonable in the *Wednesbury* sense. The remedies that are available are for the court to quash decisions (certiorari), to prohibit actions or further actions which are unlawful (prohibition), to require the performance of a duty (mandamus) or to make a declaration that an action or decision is unlawful. The court also has powers to grant an injunction and in limited cases to award damages (RSC Order 53 r 1). These remedies do not allow the court to substitute its own decision for that which is being challenged but merely to proscribe unlawful decisions and, if appropriate, to require the body to make a fresh decision in accordance with the law.

16.5   The immediate problem that faces prisoners in such cases is that the majority of administrative decisions made in respect of them have, to a greater or lesser extent, an element of discretion on the part of the decision maker. Given the court's inability to substitute its own opinion for that of the decision maker, it is essential to establish either an error in procedure or law or to obtain evidence to show that the decision was *Wednesbury* unreasonable.

16.6   A further fundamental principle that must be considered is that the court will not normally consider an application for judicial review where there is another avenue of appeal. Although there are circumstances when it may be impractical to pursue all avenues of appeal (*R v Epping and Harlow General Comrs, ex p Goldstraw* [1983] 3 All ER 257), the general principle is that judicial review is a remedy of last resort. Practitioners must therefore be satisfied that they have sought to utilise the formal methods that are in place to appeal or review adverse decisions before making an application to the court.

16.7   The final fundamental principle to bear in mind is that judicial review is a discretionary remedy. Even if a case falls into a category where an application for judicial review lies, the court is not bound to grant it. It is important to consider the purpose of the application and whether, even if there is no practical remedy available, there is a point of law that is important enough to warrant the intervention of the court. For example, if a prisoner is segregated for a period of three days and then is allowed back on to normal location, the court would be unable to provide any tangible relief to that prisoner but may decide to hear an application on the grounds that an important point of law or principle was at issue in terms of how the decision was reached. Conversely, there will be cases where the court will decide that although an unlawful action has taken place, it may not be desirable to grant any relief. An example occurred with an application by a prisoner in connection with compulsory deductions from prisoners' wages for the 'common purpose fund' (a fund designed to provide extra amenities for prisoners). By the time the case came to court, the Prison Service had halted the deductions and the court refused to grant any relief on the basis that the practice had now stopped and that the sums of money were sufficiently small to make it impractical and undesirable for all of the contributions to be traced and restored.

AGAINST WHOM DOES THE APPLICATION LIE?

16.8 Administrative decisions will be made by a sometimes bewildering variety of individuals and departments. However, this vast administration actually derives its authority from a limited number of sources and consequently, applications for judicial review lie against only a small number of people. In effect, these will be the governor of a prison, the Secretary of State for the Home Department and the Parole Board.

The governor

16.9 The majority of decisions made inside a prison are done so on the authority of the governor of that prison. The governor obviously does not personally make each decision, but retains the power to delegate these to a number of other people in the prison. These can range from other governor grades (eg at adjudications or when authorising segregation) to less senior members of staff (eg senior and principal officers will commonly make decisions concerning categorisation or transfers). Whoever formally makes the decision in an individual case, this is ultimately done so on the governor's authority.

16.10 It is possible to identify the powers that a governor will exercise whereby the responsibility for the decision rests with the individual and not higher up the chain of command. These are commonly concerned with the maintenance of security and good order and discipline within the prison and include the following:

(i) Adjudications which must be heard by a governor.
(ii) Decisions to segregate prisoners for the first three days (thereafter, the consent of the Board of Visitors is required and the decision is effectively made by the two bodies in tandem).
(iii) Decisions to transfer prisoners, other than category A prisoners and lifers.
(iv) The security categorisation of prisoners, other than those in category A.
(v) Whether to grant temporary release, except for lifers or in cases where the authority of the area manager is required.
(vi) The proper allowance of visits and correspondence and restrictions placed thereon, such as closed visits.
(vii) In addition, the governor will have responsibility for ensuring that national rules and guidelines for the provision of facilities and the observance of legal rights are observed. An example of when the action

lies against the governor rather than the Secretary of State would be if the governor was not allowing prisoners to receive sealed, privileged legal correspondence contrary to the instructions issued.

16.11   It is possible for all decisions made by prison governors to be 'appealed' to the area manager for that prison, for a complaint to be lodged with the Board of Visitors or for a petition to be presented to the Secretary of State. The question in such cases is whether these options represent established appeal procedures which must be followed before lodging an application to the court. It is safe to say that complaints to the Board of Visitors and petitions cannot properly be considered an established appeals process with the power to overturn the decision of the governor. In *Leech v Deputy Governor of Parkhurst Prison* ([1988] 1 All ER 485), Lord Bridge specifically dismissed the concept that a petition could be an adequate remedy and dismissed the concept of a 'faceless authority in Whitehall' looking at governor's decisions as a proper appeals process.

16.12   This decision was made before the present requests/complaints procedure was introduced. It is arguable that the fact that there is now a formal, established mechanism for reviewing governors' decisions whereby the decision is vulnerable to modification or to be quashed means that an effective internal remedy has been established that must now be followed. There will be an element of discretion depending on the individual facts of each case when deciding whether to pursue this appeal. An example where it may not be appropriate could include where legal correspondence is constantly being interfered with and the governor, whilst accepting the ambit of the relevant rules, is unable to establish a system of ensuring they are complied with. Although an appeal to the area manager would be of little assistance in such cases, as a general rule it would be imprudent not to appeal as the client would run a very serious risk of having the application dismissed.

Decisions of the Secretary of State

16.13   The Prison Service was constituted to have agency status but remains a department of the Home Office. As such, all decisions made by staff at Prison Service Headquarters are done so on behalf of the Home Office and under the authority of the Secretary of State. Consequently, the proper defendant in all such cases is the Secretary of State for the Home Department. The range of decisions that this will encompass will include the majority of decisions concerning category A prisoners and lifers, policy decisions on areas such as temporary release or the provision of facilities and decisions made concerning prisoners in the special units.

16.14   There is no right of appeal against decisions made at this level. It is possible for representations and request/complaint forms to be submitted if a prisoner is unhappy about a decision but the review will be undertaken by the same department, and usually the same person who made the initial decision. On a practical level, it is often worthwhile making written representations to the decision maker partly to seek modification but more importantly, to define the issues which will form the subject of any application to the Divisional Court. There is not, however, any obligation to undertake this course of action and an application for judicial review may be made immediately.

The Parole Board

16.15   The Parole Board was created by statute (Criminal Justice Act 1967) and as such, it is an independent public body whose decisions are amenable to judicial review. Historically, the number of applications made against the Board were fairly few but this can be attributed to the fact that the decision-making process was secretive with neither the material before the Board nor the reasons for their decision being disclosed to the prisoner. This secrecy meant that the material necessary to determine whether a decision was reviewable was simply not available. Since the policy has been changed and all prisoners now have the right of disclosure of all material before the Board and to know of the reasons for decisions, the number of applications for judicial review has increased greatly.

16.16   As with decisions made by the Secretary of State, there is no formal right of appeal against Parole Board decisions. Whilst the Board will consider request/complaint forms and written representations made in respect of their decisions, the general policy is only to reconsider cases whereby new and previously unconsidered information is disclosed. The same matters as are relevant in decisions made on the authority of the Secretary of State should be considered when advising clients as to whether to lodge an appeal. It is important to remember that in the case of determinate prisoners serving sentences of seven years or more, all recommendations for release by the Board will be reviewed on behalf of the Secretary of State. If such a decision is to be challenged, it is important to establish whether the Board recommended release and this was not approved by the minister or whether it was the Parole Board who rejected the application. This should be apparent from the wording of the letter of refusal of parole.

Time limits

16.17   Applications for judicial review must be lodged 'promptly' and in any event within three months from the date when the grounds for the application first arose (RSC Order 53, r 4). It is important to bear in mind that the application is to be a prompt one and that the three month time limit is the final deadline. The court can and will dismiss applications made within the three month limit if it feels that it was not made promptly enough (*R v Independent Television Commission, ex p TV NI Ltd* (1991) Times, 30 December, CA). Given the delays that can often occur before prisoners seek legal advice, it is often essential for immediate action to be taken to ensure that the application is admissible.

16.18   RSC Order 53 refers to the date when the grounds of the action first arose. Problems can arise in cases where representations are made in an attempt to appeal a decision or to have it modified before proceedings are issued, not least because the Prison Service sets itself a six week deadline to reply to such matters. There are three matters to bear in mind if it is thought that the deadline for issuing the application may be exceeded:

(i) If a formal appeal has been lodged, time will start to run from the date that a reply is received to the appeal. Therefore, if a prisoner wishes to challenge an adjudication that took place several weeks ago, an appeal can be lodged with the area manager and if this is unsuccessful, the application should be made as promptly as possible thereafter.

(ii) It is possible to lodge representations to try and secure the modification or substitution of a decision for which there is no right of appeal. It is arguable that the time for judicial review commences from the date of the reply to those representations on the basis that it is the later decision, taken with the benefit of full argument and representations on behalf of the prisoner, that is the subject of court scrutiny.

(iii) Where time limits are an issue, set a definite deadline for a reply and reserve the right to issue proceedings without further notice after that date. This can be particulary important with annual decisions such as parole reviews where a lengthy delay in issuing proceedings in the first place can mean that any judgment of the court would be made redundant by virtue of a new decision being made.

THE OMBUDSMAN AND JUDICIAL REVIEW

16.19 The Ombudsman is unable to accept complaints that are subject to legal proceedings and so it is not possible to pursue both courses of action at the same time. Prisoners are not required to make a complaint to the Ombudsman before making an application for judicial review as the Ombudsman has only an advisory capacity. If a prisoner's complaint is upheld, the Ombudsman can make a recommendation to the Director General of the Prison Service but has no power to make binding directions. Consequently, it is not possible to argue that this presents an effective remedy that must be pursued before making an application to the court.

16.20 Although prisoners cannot be required to complain to the Ombudsman before applying for judicial review, it can be advisable to take this course of action in cases where the initial grounds may not be strong enough or where further information is necessary to strengthen the application. If the Ombudsman finds in favour of the prisoner, a recommendation is issued to the Prison Service. This recommendation will result in a new decision being made in respect of that prisoner. The new decision, if unfavourable and more particularly, if it is contrary to the Ombudsman's report, is more likely to be vulnerable to judicial review. The Ombudsman's report will also often contain a wealth of information that may not otherwise be available. It is important when considering this course of action, however, to advise the client that if the report is unfavourable, it can effectively remove any possibility of subsequently applying to the court.

HOW THE COURTS VIEW PRISONERS' APPLICATIONS

16.21   The history of applications for judicial review brought by prisoners is detailed in chapter 3. Over the past decade, the courts have steadily exerted their authority to consider all aspects of public decision-making and nowhere is this more apparent than in the field of prison law. However, the mere fact that the judiciary have successfully established the concept of the judge looking over the shoulder of all decision makers, there is still something of a dichotomy between the willingness of the courts to look at these areas and their willingness to overturn decisions.

16.22   It is almost possible to divide applications for judicial review brought by prisoners into two categories, those which the courts consider are concerned with fundamental rights and freedoms and those which are more concerned with the day-to-day management of prisoners. The judiciary have shown that they are prepared to become ever more interventionist on matters concerning release from prison and the administration of the mandatory life sentence which has been widely under attack by senior judges. Nowhere is this more apparent than in the comments of Lord Justice Steyn in describing the 'essential unfairness of the mandatory life sentence' and the need for the courts to be 'extra vigilant in the exercise of their powers of judicial review' (*R v Secretary of State for the Home Department, ex p Pegg* (1994) Times, 11 August).

16.23   The contrast between this approach and that of the Court of Appeal in *ex p Ross* (1994) Times, 9 June, concerning a governor's decision to transfer an allegedly disruptive prisoner could not be more apparent. In rejecting an application for leave, Lord Justice Waite held that the need for fairness was discharged by giving general reasons for the transfer of a disruptive prisoner and that the governor was best placed to make that assessment. The court accepted that administrative procedures had to be properly followed and that the right to be given reasons was a valid one, but the approach to the actual substantive issue of the management and control of prisoners was scarcely different from that of Lord Denning in *Becker v Home Office* [1972] 2 QB 407 some 20 years earlier.

CHAPTER 17

THE EUROPEAN CONVENTION ON HUMAN RIGHTS

INTRODUCTION

17.1 The European Convention on Human Rights has a somewhat paradoxical place in prisoners' litigation. On the one hand, applications brought by individual prisoners have lead to some of the more progressive changes to prison law whereas on the other hand, the length of time that it takes for a case to be decided and for the effects of any subsequent changes in the law to be implemented is such that only long-term prisoners will individually benefit from their applications. Nevertheless, in light of the capacity of the Court to force the UK to make legislative and policy changes, it is a remedy that is being increasingly utilised by and on behalf of prisoners. Practitioners should therefore be aware of the key articles to the Convention and as to how to commence applications on behalf of their clients. This chapter does not aim to provide an exhaustive guide to procedure, but simply to underline the main points to bear in mind when making use of this remedy and it is advisable to refer to texts that deal specifically with the Convention when preparing applications. The details of procedure before the European Court of Human Rights are not dealt with as it is the principles and procedure that apply to the first tier, that of the Commission, that are of relevance when making applications on behalf of prisoners.

THE RELEVANT ARTICLES

17.2 The Convention came into force on 3 September 1953 and the UK was the first state to ratify it. Although it has not been formally incorporated into domestic law, the UK has recognised the right of individuals to petition since 1965.

17.3 The aim of the Convention is to protect those rights that are perceived as fundamental in free societies, the context having been set by the Universal Declaration of Human Rights issued by the United Nations in the immediate aftermath of the second world war. Selected articles are reproduced in Appendix 4, and prisoners should pay particular attention to the following:

(i) Article 3 – prohibits the use of torture or inhuman or degrading treatment or punishment.

(ii)   Article 5 (4) – the right of everyone deprived of their liberty to have the lawfulness of that detention decided speedily by a court and release ordered if the detention is not lawful: compensation may be claimed for breaches of this article.

(iii) Article 7 – a prohibition against any criminal penalties being imposed retrospectively.

(iv)   Article 8 – the right to a private and family life and to one's home and correspondence.

(v)   Article 9 – freedom of thought, conscience and religion.

(vi)   Article 10 – freedom of expression and to impart ideas and information.

(vii) Article 12 – the right to marry and found a family.

(viii) Article 1, First Protocol – the right to the peaceful enjoyment of possessions.

(ix)   Article 14 – freedom from discrimination in the enjoyment of any of these rights, although this article can only be invoked in connection with a complaint under one of the other articles.

17.4   Each of these articles must be approached with a degree of caution and the full text examined. This is because the rights discussed are generally not absolute but are expressed in the context of the relevant domestic law that applies. For example, the right to a private and family life (Article 8) is subject to such controls as may be necessary in a democratic society in the interests of public safety. Similarly, Article 4 which prohibits enforced labour does not prevent people who are lawfully detained from being required to undertake ordinary unpaid work as part of the prison regime.

PROCEDURE

17.5   The process by which an individual may make a complaint that his/ her rights under the Convention have been breached is remarkably straightforward compared to domestic court procedures. There is a two-tier mechanism whereby applications are initially made to the Commission, comprising of a representative appointed from each member state. The purpose of the Commission is firstly to decide whether an application is admissible. Admissibility falls into three areas: whether the application has been made within the relevant time limits; whether all domestic remedies have been exhausted; and whether the application is manifestly ill founded.

17.6   In order to lodge the application, the Commission provides a fairly straightforward form to be completed. It is not necessary to actually use this form but the application must contain a minimum amount of detail that includes the name, date and place of birth of the applicant, the nationality of the applicant, the state against whom the complaint is made, the articles that are alleged to have been breached and a brief statement of the facts of the application. In cases where the application needs to be lodged urgently, these details can be very brief and must simply contain the bare minimum to ensure that the application is registered. A fuller memorial, even one which expands the alleged breaches to other articles, can be lodged at a later date. It is not unusual for the Commission to identify breaches themselves that were not particularised in the initial application.

17.7   The Commission conducts its own investigation into the application and will set a procedural timetable in each individual case. The Commission retains the power to extend the time limits if it is considered necessary for the proper preparation of a case. If the application is not struck out at this preliminary stage, then in most cases it will formally communicate the application to the state against who it is lodged and invite written representations. These observations will in turn be communicated to the applicant who has the opportunity to reply. At this point, the Commission will decide whether it requires a hearing to help determine the issues.

17.8   The procedure at this stage is still primarily concerned with the issue of admissibility, however it is normal practice for any oral hearing to also deal with the merits of the application. Oral hearings are markedly different from those in domestic courts. Each party is allotted 30 minutes to address the Commission and this is done in turn. The Commission can decide that witnesses should be asked to give evidence but there is no power to compel their attendance. Following the delivery of speeches, the members of the Commission will set questions to the parties and after a short adjournment will ask for replies to be given.

17.9   Following this hearing, the Commission will reach a decision as to whether the application is admissible. If it is declared inadmissible, that is the end of the matter and there is no right of appeal. If an application is considered to be admissible, a preliminary report on the merits will be drawn up. The Commission has a duty to try and secure a friendly settlement where possible (Article 28) and proposals will be sought from both parties. If no friendly settlement can be reached, then the Commission will formally publish its decision on the merits of the application. At this stage, either the Commission or a member state can refer the matter to the full Court or the Committee of Ministers. As a general rule, cases which raise new points will be referred to the full Court whereas cases concerning established breaches to the Committee of Ministers. There is no right for the individual to require reference of the case to the Court or Committee of Ministers.

17.10   The procedure before the Court is not dissimilar to that before the Commission and can be decided on the basis of either written representations or an oral hearing. There is no formal method of enforcing decisions made by the Court or Committee of Ministers. The Committee of Ministers will usually seek reports from member states as to how they have complied with a decision, but ultimately, the only sanction is to expel the member state from the Council of Europe.

IS THE APPLICANT A VICTIM?

17.11   Article 25 defines who may be considered to be victims. In effect it states that the applicant must have been particularly affected in some way by the breach of the Convention. This is not limited simply to the direct victim, but can include near relatives or third parties who are so prejudiced by the violations that they have a valid personal interest. It is also possible to commence actions to try and prevent a future breach if it can be shown that the applicant belongs to a particular class and that a potential violation already affects their lives (see eg *Norris v Ireland* (1991) 13 EHRR 186, Series A, no 12).

EXHAUSTING DOMESTIC REMEDIES

17.12 It is a general principle that all domestic remedies must be exhausted before the Commission can consider an application (Article 26). This applies only to remedies which can be described as 'effective and sufficient' and so lawyers must pay particular attention to this requirement when advising a client to lodge an application. Remedies that are wholly discretionary are not deemed to be sufficient and as such do not have to be exhausted before an application is lodged. In the prison context, this raises important considerations as to whether internal prison complaints procedures can be considered effective remedies and more fundamentally, whether judicial review needs to be pursued.

17.13 The internal Prison Service complaints procedures do not appear to be sufficiently effective to be considered as remedies within the meaning of the Convention. These do not provide for any proper independent system of investigation and in many cases will not have the ability to offer proper redress for the wrong that has occurred (*Raphie v United Kingdom* (2 December 1993, unreported, No 20035/92). Similarly, complaints to the Prisons Ombudsman cannot be seen as an effective remedy as the powers of the Ombudsman are solely to make recommendations and are not mandatory.

17.14 The most difficult remedy to assess is that of judicial review. It was long argued that as judicial review is a discretionary remedy, it was not sufficient and did not have to be exhausted prior to lodging an application. This point of view is no longer fully sustainable. The Court has defined effective remedies in the following terms:

> 'The only remedies which Article 26 requires to be exhausted are those that relate to the breaches alleged and which are at the same time available and sufficient. The existence of such remedies must be sufficiently certain not only in theory but also in practice, failing which they will lack the requisite accessibility and effectiveness: it falls to the Respondent state to establish the various conditions are satisfied.' (*Navarra v France* Series A/273–B, para 24, (1994) 17 EHRR 594)

17.15 The reality of the present situation is that each application will have to be judged on its own merits in light of what may be obtained by way of judicial review. For example, there are many cases where the Commission have decided on the particular facts of a case that judicial review is not an effective remedy (*Thynne Wilson and Gunnell v United Kingdom* (1990) 13 EHRR 666, Series A, no 190). In cases where it is argued that Article 5(4) has been breached by a failure to provide proper procedures to decide on the lawfulness of detention, judicial control to decide on the exercise of a discretion by the decision-making body would not be sufficient.

17.16   On the other hand, the present attitude of the domestic courts whereby the requirements of the Convention come under more 'anxious scrutiny' can lead to the Commission taking the view that judicial review can promote an effective remedy (see *Vilvarajah v United Kingdom* (1991) 14 EHRR 248 Series A, No 215 and the discussion of the relationship between domestic law and the Convention below). The law in this area is developing at such a bewildering pace that in each individual case, it is necessary to analyse the purpose of a judicial review and the remedy that could be achieved before deciding whether it constitutes an effective remedy.

TIME LIMITS

17.17   Article 26 requires that applications must be lodged within six months of the violation or of the exhaustion of domestic remedies. This time limit is strictly observed. Problems can arise for applicants in complying with this when considering whether domestic remedies have been exhausted. The danger is that a domestic remedy will be pursued unsuccessfully, only for the Commission to decide that the remedy was not effective and the time limit has been exceeded. Alternatively, an application submitted at an early stage can be declared inadmissible on the grounds that domestic remedies have not been exhausted.

17.18   In cases where there is some doubt and the six month time period from the original violation is approaching, it is prudent to lodge an initial application whilst the question of domestic remedies is explored. The Commission are, in many cases, prepared to register an application and then not to proceed with the investigation into admissibility for a set period of time whilst the possibility of a domestic remedy is pursued. In any event, if an application is declared inadmissible on the grounds that domestic remedies have not been exhausted, it can always be resubmitted once this has been done.

LEGAL AID

17.19   The Commission operates a legal aid scheme, but this bears little resemblance to that in operation in this country. The Rules of the Commission allow legal aid to be made available where it is deemed necessary for the proper discharge of their duties and where the applicant is financially eligible. Legal aid is not, therefore, available from the outset and applications can only be submitted from the time that the applicant is asked to make written submissions in reply to the government's observations. There is no method of obtaining payment for the initial application.

17.20   When the application is submitted, the Commission requires proof of the applicant's financial situation. This is done by submitting both the Commission's own legal aid application form and the appropriate English form to the Legal Aid Assessment Department at the Department of Social Security in Preston. They will complete an assessment stating whether the applicant qualifies under the English scheme and this must be forwarded to the Commission with their own form. Legal aid payments are based upon fixed rates for preparing observations and attending any hearing before the Commission and are not assessed according to the time that has been spent on the case. The fixed rates are really no more than nominal although travelling expenses and costs for attending any hearing are paid in full.

APPLICATIONS FROM ENGLISH PRISONERS

17.21 There is no doubt that applications made under the Convention have made a considerable impact on the prison system and the rights of prisoners. These range from the right to marry (*Hamer v United Kingdom* (1982) 4 EHRR 139), disciplinary procedures (*Campbell and Fell v United Kingdom* (1984) 7 EHRR 165, Series A, no 80) and access to the courts (*Silver v United Kingdom* (1983) 5 EHRR 347 Series A, no 61). Major legislative changes have also been adopted in relation to the release of discretionary life sentenced prisoners in the form of the Criminal Justice Act 1991 (*Thynne, Wilson and Gunnell v United Kingdom* (1990) 13 EHRR 666, Series A, no 190).

17.22 There is always a tension between the role of the Commission in protecting the most fundamental of civil rights and the lack of any formal constitution or bill of rights in this country. Consequently, whilst prisoners can be subject to conditions and decisions that many would consider to be prima facie breaches of the Convention, the fact that the Convention allows a measure of discretion to domestic governments in deciding what constraints are necessary in the wider public interest can prevent these breaches from being successfully pursued. The cases where the Commission and the Court have been most willing to find in favour of prisoners have included the right to proper access to lawyers (see eg *Campbell and Fell v United Kingdom* (1984) 7 EHRR 165, Series A, no 80; *Silver v United Kingdom* (1983) 5 EHRR 347 Series A, no 61; *Campbell v United Kingdom* (1992) 15 EHRR 137, Series A No 233–A), basic rights to maintain family contact and the mechanisms by which people's detention is subject to review (*Thynne, Wilson and Gunnell v United Kingdom* (1990) 13 EHRR 666, Series A, no 190). In contrast, applications concerning the day-to-day treatment of prisoners and the general conditions in prisons have been markedly less successful.

17.23 It is a very common complaint from prisoners that general conditions inside of prisons are so poor as to be in breach of Article 3. In recent years, three applications have been considered on this subject, all of which have been unsuccessful. One applicant failed in a complaint about a decision to segregate him in conditions that attracted severe criticism by the Chief Inspector of Prisons and the International Committee for the Prevention of Torture of the conditions that existed. The Commission decided that segregation does not constitute the severe ill treatment necessary to establish a violation and that conditions would have to be particularly severe to succeed (*Delazarus v United Kingdom* 16 February 1993, unreported, No 17525/90). An application by a Scottish prisoner concerning 14 months in a lockdown regime where association had been suspended and exercise was not always available, did not breach Article 3 as there was not complete sensory and social isolation (*Windsor v United Kingdom*, 6 April 1993, unreported No 18942/91). The third case was declared inadmissible for being brought outside of the time limits (*Raphie v United Kingdom*, 2 December 1993, unreported No 20035/92).

17.24 These cases illustrate the sensitivity of such applications and the fact that the Commission will require extremely severe facts to find that particular conditions are in breach of Article 3. Whilst there is still plenty of scope for such applications to be brought, the once held hopes that the Convention could provide a long-term panacea to prison conditions in this country have not materialised.

THE CONVENTION AND DOMESTIC LAW

17.25 The Convention has no formal authority in English courts and does not give rise to any remedies that may be enforced domestically. Many of the member states have incorporated the Convention into domestic law but this has not occurred in this country. The result of this is two-fold: firstly, the UK has a particularly poor record in the Court, often because there is no effective domestic remedy that can be pursued. Secondly, there is a limit to the extent to which the Convention can be relied upon in domestic proceedings.

17.26 The domestic courts are unable to take violations of human rights into account where Parliament has expressly authorised the violation (*Salomon v Customs and Excise Comrs* [1966] 3 All ER 871). In situations where statute is deemed to be in need of interpretation, Lord Denning took the view that whilst the court can have regard for the contents of the Convention, it is obliged to do no more that to take it into account (*R v Secretary of State for the Home Department, ex p Bhajan Singh* [1975] 2 All ER 1081). This view was reaffirmed by Sir Robert Megarry V-C who commented that:

> 'obligations in international law which are not enforceable as part of English law cannot . . . be the subject of declaratory judgments or orders.' (*Uppal v Home Office* (1978) Times, 11 November)

17.27 The House of Lords considered the extent to which ministers are required to have regard for the requirements of the Convention in *R v Secretary of State for the Home Department, ex p Brind* ([1991] 1 AC 696). The House upheld the Court of Appeal's view that a requirement for a minister to conform with the Convention when exercising discretionary powers, is an attempt to incorporate the Convention into domestic law, a decision that could only be made by Parliament.

17.28 The case of *Brind* did establish, however, that in formulating discretionary rules, the requirements of the Convention are a relevant consideration for the Secretary of State. The current debate turns on the extent to which these requirements will be relevant when deciding on matters of public law. Cases concerning asylum seekers have touched upon these issues as they must accord with the highest standards of fairness due to the potential impact on life and limb. When fundamental human rights are at stake, the court requires the Secretary of State to give anxious scrutiny to the Convention (*Bugdaycay v Secretary of State for the Home Department* [1987] AC 514). This is a theme echoed in cases heard by the European Court where the question of whether judicial review is an effective remedy has been aired. In *Vilvarajah v United Kingdom* ((1991) 14 EHRR 248, Series A, no 215), the view that judicial review can be an effective remedy due to need for the Secretary of State to give the 'most anxious scrutiny' to the Convention when deciding on the reasonableness of decisions was accepted.

17.29 It is this interpretation of the role of the Convention that appears to prevail at the present time. In the recent case of *R v Secretary of State for the Home Department, ex p Norney* ((1995) Independent, 28 September) Mr Justice Dyson considered the relevance of the Convention when deciding upon the timing of the referral of discretionary lifers' cases to Panel hearings. He stated that:

> 'I do not consider that *ex p Brind* requires me to ignore the Convention when considering the lawfulness of the exercise of the discretion. I accept that as a general rule, the lawfulness of the exercise of executive discretion is not measured by asking whether it involves an infringement of Convention rights. But where it is clear that the statutory provision which creates the discretion was passed in order to bring the domestic law into line with the Convention, it would in my judgment be perverse to hold that, when considering the lawfulness of the exercise of discretion, the court must ignore the relevant provisions of the Convention. In any event, there is no conflict on this point between the requirements of common law and the Convention.' (transcript, pp 13–14)

17.30 This makes it apparent that whilst the test the courts will apply to ministerial decisions is still one of *Wednesbury* unreasonableness, where fundamental human rights are in issue the minister will need to show a compelling, competing public interest for overriding fundamental human rights. In such cases, the court will continue to subject these decisions to the most anxious scrutiny (see the comments of Lord Justice Simon Brown in the first instance decision of *R v Ministry of Defence, ex p Smith* [1995] 4 All ER 427; affd [1995] NLJR 1689, CA concerning the rights of gays in the military.

PRISON ACT 1952

1952 Chapter 52

An Act to consolidate certain enactments relating to prisons and other institutions for offenders and related matters with corrections and improvements made under the Consolidation of Enactments (Procedure) Act 1949

[1st August 1952]

BE IT ENACTED by the Queen's Most Excellent Majesty, by and with the advice and consent of the Lords Spiritual and Temporal, and Commons, in this present Parliament assembled, and by the authority of the same, as follows:—

Central administration

1 General control over prisons

All powers and jurisdiction in relation to prisons and prisoners which before the commencement of the Prison Act 1877 were exercisable by any other authority shall, subject to the provisions of this Act, be exercisable by the Secretary of State.

Annotations

This section does not extend to Scotland.

3 Officers and servants of [the Secretary of State]

(1) The Secretary of State [may, for the purposes of this Act, appoint such officers and [employ such other persons] as he] may, with the sanction of the Treasury as to number, determine.

(2) There shall be paid out of moneys provided by Parliament to [the officers and servants appointed under this section] such salaries as the Secretary of State may with the consent of the Treasury determine.

Annotations

Section heading: words in square brackets substituted by virtue of SI 1963 No 597, art 3(2), Sch 1.

Sub-s (1): first words in square brackets substituted by SI 1963 No 597, Sch 1, words in square brackets therein substituted by the Criminal Justice and Public Order Act 1994, s 168(2), Sch 10, para 7.

Sub-s (2): words in square brackets substituted by SI 1963 No 597, art 3(2), Sch 1.

This section does not extend to Scotland.

4   General duties of [the Secretary of State]

(1)   [The Secretary of State] shall have the general superintendence of prisons and shall make the contracts and do the other acts necessary for the maintenance of prisons and the maintenance of prisoners.

(2)   [Officers of the Secretary of State duly authorised in that behalf] shall visit all prisons and examine the state of buildings, the conduct of officers, the treatment and conduct of prisoners and all other matters concerning the management of prisons and shall ensure that the provisions of this Act and of any rules made under this Act are duly complied with.

(3)   [The Secretary of State and his officers] may exercise all powers and jurisdiction exercisable at common law, by Act of Parliament, or by charter by visiting justices of a prison.

Annotations

Section heading: words in square brackets substituted by virtue of SI 1963 No 597, art 3(2), Sch 1.

Sub-ss (1)–(3): words in square brackets substituted by SI 1963 No 597, art 3(2), Sch 1.

This section does not extend to Scotland.

5   Annual report of [the Secretary of State]

[(1)   The Secretary of State shall issue an annual report on every prison and shall lay every such report before Parliament.]

(2)   The report shall contain—

(a)   a statement of the accommodation of each prison and the daily average and highest number of prisoners confined therein;

(b)   such particulars of the work done by prisoners in each prison, including the kind and quantities of articles produced and the number of prisoners employed, as may in the opinion of the Secretary of State give the best information to Parliament;

(c)   a statement of the punishments inflicted in each prison and of the offences for which they were inflicted < . . . >

Annotations

Section heading: words in square brackets substituted by virtue of SI 1963 No 597, art 3(2), Sch 1.

Sub-s (1): substituted by SI 1963 No 597, art 3(2), Sch 1.

Sub-s (2): words omitted repealed by the Criminal Justice Act 1967, s 103(2), Sch 7, Part I.

This section does not extend to Scotland.

[5A]   [Appointment and functions of Her Majesty's Chief Inspector of Prisons]

[(1)   Her Majesty may appoint a person to be Chief Inspector of Prisons.

(2)   It shall be the duty of the Chief Inspector to inspect or arrange for the inspection of prisons in England and Wales and to report to the Secretary of State on them.

(3)   The Chief Inspector shall in particular report to the Secretary of State on the treatment of prisoners and conditions in prisons.

(4)   The Secretary of State may refer specific matters connected with prisons in England and Wales and prisoners in them to the Chief Inspector and direct him to report on them.

(5)   The Chief Inspector shall in each year submit to the Secretary of State a report in such form as the Secretary of State may direct, and the Secretary of State shall lay a copy of that report before Parliament.

(6)   The Chief Inspector shall be paid such salary and allowances as the Secretary of State may with the consent of the Treasury determine.]

Annotations

This section was added by the Criminal Justice Act 1982, s 57.

This section does not extend to Scotland.

< . . . > boards of visitors

6   < . . . > boards of visitors

(1)   < . . . >

(2)   The Secretary of State shall appoint for every prison < . . . > a board of visitors of whom not less than two shall be justices of the peace.

(3)   Rules made as aforesaid shall prescribe the functions of < . . . > boards of visitors and shall among other things require members to pay frequent visits to the prison and hear any complaints which may be made by the prisoners and report to the Secretary of State any matter which they consider it expedient to report; and any member of a < . . . > board of visitors may at any time enter the prison and shall have free access to every part of it and to every prisoner.

(4)   < . . . >

Annotations

Words omitted repealed by, or by virtue of, the Courts Act 1971, ss 53 (3), 56(4), Sch 7, Part II, para 4, Sch 11, Part IV.

This section does not extend to Scotland.

Prison officers

7 Prison officers

(1) Every prison shall have a governor, a chaplain and a medical officer and such other officers as may be necessary.

(2) Every prison in which women are received shall have a sufficient number of women officers; < . . . >

(3) A prison which in the opinion of the Secretary of State is large enough to require it may have a deputy governor or an assistant chaplain or both.

(4) The chaplain and any assistant chaplain shall be a clergyman of the Church of England and the medical officer shall be duly registered under the Medical Acts.

(5) < . . . >

Annotations

Sub-s (2): words omitted repealed by the Sex Discriminiation Act 1975, s 18(2).

Sub-s (5): repealed by SI 1963 No 597, art 3(2), Sch 1.

Modified, in relation to contracted out prisons, by the Criminal Justice Act 1991, s 87.

This section does not apply to Scotland.

8 Powers of prison officers

Every prison officer while acting as such shall have all the powers, authority, protection and privileges of a constable.

Annotations

Modified, in relation to contracted out prisons, by the Criminal Justice Act 1991, s 87.

This section does not extend to Scotland.

[8A] [Powers of search by authorised employees]

[(1) An authorised employee at a prison shall have the power to search any prisoner for the purpose of ascertaining whether he has any unauthorised property on his person.

(2) An authorised employee searching a prisoner by virtue of this section—

(a) shall not be entitled to require a prisoner to remove any of his clothing other than an outer coat, jacket, headgear, gloves and footwear;

(b) may use reasonable force where necessary; and

(c) may seize and detain any unauthorised property found on the prisoner in the course of the search.

(3) In this section "authorised employee" means an employee of a description for the time being authorised by the governor to exercise the powers conferred by this section.

(4) The governor of a prison shall take such steps as he considers appropriate to notify to prisoners the descriptions of persons who are for the time being authorised to exercise the powers conferred by this section.

(5) In this section "unauthorised property", in relation to a prisoner, means property which the prisoner is not authorised by prison rules or by the governor to have in his possession or, as the case may be, in his possession in a particular part of the prison.]

Annotations

This section was added by the Criminal Justice and Public Order Act 1994, s 152(1).

Modified, in relation to contracted out prisons, by the Criminal Justice Act 1991, s 87.

This section does not extend to Scotland.

9 Exercise of office of chaplain

(1) A person shall not officiate as chaplain of two prisons unless the prisons are within convenient distance of each other and are together designed to receive not more than one hundred prisoners.

(2) Notice of the nomination of a chaplain or assistant chaplain to a prison shall, within one month after it is made, be given to the bishop of the diocese in which the prison is situate; and the chaplain or assistant chaplain shall not officiate in the prison except under the authority of a licence from the bishop.

Annotations

This section does not extend to Scotland.

10 Appointment of prison ministers

(1) Where in any prison the number of prisoners who belong to a religious denomination other than the Church of England is such as in the opinion of the Secretary of State to require the appointment of a minister of that denomination, the Secretary of State may appoint such a minister to that prison.

(2) The Secretary of State may pay a minister appointed under the preceding subsection such remuneration as he thinks reasonable.

(3) [The Secretary of State] may allow a minister of any denomination other than the Church of England to visit prisoners of his denomination in a prison to which no minister of that denomination has been appointed under this section.

(4)   No prisoner shall be visited against his will by such a minister as is mentioned in the last preceding subsection; but every prisoner not belonging to the Church of England shall be allowed, in accordance with the arrangements in force in the prison in which he is confined, to attend chapel or to be visited by the chaplain.

(5)   The governor of a prison shall on the reception of each prisoner record the religious denomination to which the prisoner declares himself to belong, and shall give to any minister who under this section is appointed to the prison or permitted to visit prisoners therein a list of the prisoners who have declared themselves to belong to his denomination; and the minister shall not be permitted to visit any other prisoners.

Annotations

Sub-s (3): words in square brackets substituted by SI 1963 No 597, art 3(2), Sch 1.

Modified, in relation to contracted out prisons, by the Criminal Justice Act 1991, s 87.

This section does not extend to Scotland.

11 Ejectment of prison officers and their families refusing to quit

(1)   Where any living accommodation is provided for a prison officer or his family by virtue of his office, then, if he ceases to be a prison officer or is suspended from office or dies, he, or, as the case may be, his family, shall quit the accommodation when required to do so by notice of [the Secretary of State].

(2)   Where a prison officer or the family of a prison officer refuses or neglects to quit the accommodation forty-eight hours after the giving of such a notice as aforesaid, any two justices of the peace, on proof made to them of the facts authorising the giving of the notice and of the service of the notice and of the neglect or refusal to comply therewith, may, by warrant under their hands and seals, direct any constable, within a period specified in the warrant, to enter by force, if necessary, into the accommodation and deliver possession of it to [a person acting on behalf of the Secretary of State].

Annotations

Sub-ss (1), (2): words in square brackets substituted by SI 1963 No 597, art 3(2), Sch 1.

Modified, in relation to contracted out prisons, by the Criminal Justice Act 1991, s 87.

This section does not extend to Scotland.

Confinement and treatment of prisoners

12 Place of confinement of prisoners

(1)   A prisoner, whether sentenced to imprisonment or committed to prison

on remand or pending trial or otherwise, may be lawfully confined in any prison.

(2)   Prisoners shall be committed to such prisons as the Secretary of State may from time to time direct; and may by direction of the Secretary of State be removed during the term of their imprisonment from the prison in which they are confined to any other prison.

(3)   A writ, warrant or other legal instrument addressed to the governor of a prison and identifying that prison by its situation or by any other sufficient description shall not be invalidated by reason only that the prison is usually known by a different description.

Annotations

Modified, in relation to contracted out prisons, by the Criminal Justice Act 1991, s 87.

This section does not extend to Scotland.

13 Legal custody of prisoner

(1)   Every prisoner shall be deemed to be in the legal custody of the governor of the prison.

(2)   A prisoner shall be deemed to be in legal custody while he is confined in, or is being taken to or from, any prison and while he is working, or is for any other reason, outside the prison in the custody or under the control of an officer of the prison [and while he is being taken to any place to which he is required or authorised by or under this Act [or the Criminal Justice Act 1982] to be taken, or is kept in custody in pursuance of any such requirement or authorisation].

Annotations

Sub-s (2): first words in square brackets added by the Criminal Justice Act 1961, s 41(1), Sch 4, words in square brackets therein added by the Criminal Justice Act 1982, s 77, Sch 14, para 4.

Modified, in relation to contracted out prisons, by the Criminal Justice Act 1991, s 87.

Modified, in relation to contracted out functions at directly managed prisons, by the Criminal Justice Act 1991, s 88A.

Modified, in relation to contracted out functions at directly managed secure training centres, by the Criminal Justice and Public Order Act 1994, s 11(3).

This section does not extend to Scotland.

14 Cells

(1)   The Secretary of State shall satisfy himself from time to time that in every prison sufficient accommodation is provided for all prisoners.

(2)   No cell shall be used for the confinement of a prisoner unless it is certified by an inspector that its size, lighting, heating, ventilation and fittings are adequate for health and that it allows the prisoner to communicate at any time with a prison officer.

(3)   A certificate given under this section in respect of any cell may limit the period for which a prisoner may be separately confined in the cell and the number of hours a day during which a prisoner may be employed therein.

(4)   The certificate shall identify the cell to which it relates by a number or mark and the cell shall be marked by that number or mark placed in a conspicuous position; and if the number or mark is changed without the consent of an inspector the certificate shall cease to have effect.

(5)   An inspector may withdraw a certificate given under this section in respect of any cell if in his opinion the conditions of the cell are no longer as stated in the certificate.

(6)   In every prison special cells shall be provided for the temporary confinement of refractory or violent prisoners.

Annotations

Modified, in relation to contracted out prisons, by the Criminal Justice Act 1991, s 87.

Modified, in relation to contracted out functions at directly managed prisons, by the Criminal Justice Act 1991, s 88A.

Modification: references to an inspector to be construed as references to an officer (not being an officer of the prison) acting on behalf of the Secretary of State, by virtue of the Prison Commissioners Dissolution Order 1963, SI 1963 No 597, art 3(2), Sch 1.

This section does not extend to Scotland.

16 Photographing and measuring of prisoners

The Secretary of State may make regulations as to the measuring and photographing of prisoners and such regulations may prescribe the time or times at which and the manner and dress in which prisoners shall be measured and photographed and the number of copies of the measurements and photographs of each prisoner which shall be made and the persons to whom they shall be sent.

Annotations

This section does not extend to Scotland.

[16A] [Testing prisoners for drugs]

[(1)   If an authorisation is in force for the prison, any prison officer may, at the prison, in accordance with prison rules, require any prisoner who is confined in the prison to provide a sample of urine for the purpose of ascertaining whether he has any drug in his body.

(2)   If the authorisation so provides, the power conferred by subsection (1) above shall include power to require a prisoner to provide a sample of any other description specified in the authorisation, not being an intimate sample, whether instead of or in addition to a sample of urine.

(3)   In this section—

"authorisation" means an authorisation by the governor;

"drug" means any drug which is a controlled drug for the purposes of the Misuse of Drugs Act 1971;

"intimate sample" has the same meaning as in Part V of the Police and Criminal Evidence Act 1984;

"prison officer" includes a prisoner custody officer within the meaning of Part IV of the Criminal Justice Act 1991; and

"prison rules" means rules under section 47 of this Act.]

Annotations

This section was added by the Criminal Justice and Public Order Act 1994, s 151(1).

Modified, in relation to contracted out prisons, by the Criminal Justice Act 1991, s 87.

This section does not extend to Scotland.

17 Painful tests

The medical officer of a prison shall not apply any painful tests to a prisoner for the purpose of detecting malingering or for any other purpose except with the permission of [the Secretary of State] or the visiting committee or, as the case may be, board of visitors.

Annotations

Words in square brackets substituted by SI 1963 No 597, art 3(2), Sch 1.

This section does not extend to Scotland.

19 Right of justice to visit prison

(1)   A justice of the peace for any county < . . . > may at any time visit any prison in that county < . . . > and any prison in which a prisoner is confined in respect of an offence committed in that county < . . . > , and may examine the condition of the prison and of the prisoners and enter in the visitors' book, to be kept by the governor of the prison, any observations on the condition of the prison or any abuses.

(2)   Nothing in the preceding subsection shall authorise a justice of the peace to communicate with any prisoner except on the subject of his treatment in the prison, or to visit any prisoner under sentence of death.

(3)   The governor of every prison shall bring any entry in the visitors' book to the attention of the visiting committee or the board of visitors at their next visit.

Annotations

Sub-s (1): words omitted repealed by the Local Government Act 1972, s 272(1), Sch 30.

Modified, in relation to contracted out prisons, by the Criminal Justice Act 1991, s 87.

This section does not extend to Scotland.

21 Expenses of conveyance to prison

A prisoner shall not in any case be liable to pay the cost of his conveyance to prison.

Annotations

This section does not extend to Scotland.

22 Removal of prisoners for judicial and other purposes

(1)   Rules made under section forty-seven of this Act may provide in what manner an appellant within the meaning of [Part I of the Criminal Appeal Act 1968], when in custody, is to be taken to, kept in custody at, and brought back from, any place at which he is entitled to be present for the purposes of that Act, or any place to which the Court of Criminal Appeal or any judge thereof may order him to be taken for the purpose of any proceedings of that court.

(2)   The Secretary of State may—

    (a) < . . . >

    (b) if he is satisfied that a person so detained requires [medical investigation or observation or] medical or surgical treatment of any description, direct him to be taken to a hospital or other suitable place for the purpose of the [investigation, observation or] treatment;

and where any person is directed under this subsection to be taken to any place he shall, unless the Secretary of State otherwise directs, be kept in custody while being so taken, while at that place, and while being taken back to the prison in which he is required in accordance with law to be detained.

Annotations

Sub-s (1): words in square brackets substituted by the Criminal Appeal Act 1968, s 52, Sch 5, Part I.

Sub-s (2): para (a) repealed by the Criminal Justice Act 1961, s 41(2), Sch 5; in para (b) words in square brackets added by the Criminal Justice Act 1982, s 77, Sch 14, para 5.

Modification: references to the Court of Criminal Appeal to be construed as a reference to the criminal division of the Court of Appeal, by virtue of the Supreme Court Act 1981, s 151(4), Sch 4, para 3.

This section does not extend to Scotland.

23 Power of constable etc to act outside his jurisdiction

For the purpose of taking a person to or from any prison under the order of any authority competent to give the order a constable or other officer may act outside the area of his jurisdiction and shall notwithstanding that he is so acting have all the powers, authority, protection and privileges of his office.

Annotations

This section does not extend to Scotland.

Length of sentence, release on licence and temporary discharge

24 Calculation of term of sentence

(1) In any sentence of imprisonment the word "month" shall, unless the contrary is expressed, be construed as meaning calendar month.

(2) < . . . >

Annotations

Sub-s (2): repealed by the Criminal Justice Act 1961, s 41(2), Sch 5.

This section does not extend to Scotland.

28 Power of Secretary of State to discharge prisoners temporarily on account of ill health

(1) If the Secretary of State is satisfied that by reason of the condition of a prisoner's health it is undesirable to detain him in prison, but that, such condition of health being due in whole or in part to the prisoner's own conduct in prison, it is desirable that his release should be temporary and conditional only, the Secretary of State may, if he thinks fit, having regard to all the circumstances of the case, by order authorise the temporary discharge of the prisoner for such period and subject to such conditions as may be stated in the order.

(2) Where an order of temporary discharge is made in the case of a prisoner not under sentence, the order shall contain conditions requiring the attendance of the prisoner at any further proceedings on his case at which his presence may be required.

(3) Any prisoner discharged under this section shall comply with any conditions stated in the order of temporary discharge, and shall return to prison at the expiration of the period stated in the order, or of such extended period as may be fixed by any subsequent order of the Secretary of State, and if the prisoner fails so to comply or return, he may be arrested without warrant and taken back to prison.

(4) Where a prisoner under sentence is discharged in pursuance of an order of temporary discharge, the currency of the sentence shall be suspended from the day on which he is discharged from prison under the order to the day on which he is received back into prison, so that the former day shall be reckoned and the latter shall not be reckoned as part of the sentence.

(5) Nothing in this section shall affect the duties of the medical officer of a prison in respect of a prisoner whom the Secretary of State does not think fit to discharge under this section.

Annotations

This section does not extend to Scotland.

Discharged prisoners

[30] [Payments for discharged prisoners]

[The Secretary of State may make such payments to or in respect of persons released or about to be released from prison as he may with the consent of the Treasury determine.]

Annotations

This section was substituted for existing ss 30–32 by the Criminal Justice Act 1967, s 66(3).

This section does not extend to Scotland.

Provision, maintenance and closing of prisons

33 Power to provide prisons, etc

(1)   The Secretary of State may with the approval of the Treasury alter, enlarge or rebuild any prison and build new prisons.

[(2)   The Secretary of State may provide new prisons by declaring to be a prison—

   (a) any building or part of a building built for the purpose or vested in him or under his control; or

   (b) any floating structure or part of such a structure constructed for the purpose or vested in him or under his control.]

(3)   A declaration under this section may with respect to the building or part of a building declared to be a prison make the same provisions as an order under the next following section may make with respect to an existing prison.

(4)   A declaration under this section may at any time be revoked by the Secretary of State.

(5)   A declaration under this section shall not be sufficient to vest the legal estate of any building in the [Secretary of State].

Annotations

Sub-s (2): substituted by the Criminal Justice and Public Order Act 1994, s 100(1).

Sub-s (5): words in square brackets substituted by SI 1963 No 597, art 3(2), Sch 1.

Modification: sub-s (2) modified, in relation to contracted out prisons, by the Criminal Justice and Public Order Act 1994, s 100(2), (3).

This section does not extend to Scotland.

34 Jurisdiction of sheriff, etc

(1) The transfer under the Prison Act 1877 of prisons and of the powers and jurisdiction of prison authorities and of justices in sessions assembled and visiting justices shall not be deemed to have affected the jurisdiction of any sheriff or coroner or, except to the extent of that transfer, of any justice of the peace or other officer.

(2) The Secretary of State may by order direct that, for the purpose of any enactment, rule of law or custom dependent on a prison being the prison of any county or place, any prison situated in that county or in the county in which that place is situated, or any prison provided by him in pursuance of this Act, shall be deemed to be the prison of that county or place.

Annotations

This section does not extend to Scotland.

[35] [Prison property]

[(1) Every prison and all real and personal property belonging to a prison shall be vested in the Secretary of State and may be disposed of in such manner as the Secretary of State, with the consent of the Treasury, may determine.

(2) For the purposes of this section the Secretary of State shall be deemed to be a corporation sole.

(3) Any instrument in connection with the acquisition, management or disposal of any property to which this section applies may be executed on behalf of the Secretary of State by an Under-Secretary of State or any other person authorised by the Secretary of State in that behalf; and any instrument purporting to have been so executed on behalf of the Secretary of State shall be deemed, until the contrary is proved, to have been so executed on his behalf.

(4) The last foregoing subsection shall be without prejudice to the execution of any such instrument as aforesaid, or of any other instrument, on behalf of the Secretary of State in any other manner authorised by law.]

Annotations

This section was substituted by SI 1963 No 597, art 3(2), Sch 1.

See further, in relation to contracted out prisons: the Criminal Justice Act 1991, s 87 and the Criminal Justice and Public Order Act 1994, s 100(2), (4).

This section does not extend to Scotland.

36 Acquisition of land for prisons

(1) [The Secretary of State may purchase by agreement or] compulsorily, any land required for the alteration, enlargement or rebuilding of a prison or for establishing a new prison or for any other purpose connected with the management of a prison (including the provision of accommodation for officers or servants employed in a prison).

[(2) The [Acquisition of Land Act 1981] shall apply to the compulsory purchase of land by the Secretary of State under this section < . . . >]

(3) In relation to the purchase of land by agreement under this section, [the provisions of Part I of the Compulsory Purchase Act 1965 (so far as applicable) other than sections 4 to 8, section 10, and section 31, shall apply].

Annotations

Sub-s (1): words in square brackets substituted by SI 1963 No 597, art 3(2), Sch 1.

Sub-s (2): substituted by SI 1963 No 597, art 3(2), Sch 1; words in square brackets substituted, and words omitted repealed, by the Acquisition of Land Act 1981, s 34, Sch 4, para 1, Sch 6, Part I.

Sub-s (3): words in square brackets substituted by the Compulsory Purchase Act 1965, s 38, Sch 6.

See further: the Criminal Justice Act 1988, s 167.

This section does not extend to Scotland.

37 Closing of prisons

(1) Subject to the next following subsection, the Secretary of State may by order close any prison.

(2) Where a prison is the only prison in the county, the Secretary of State shall not make an order under this section in respect of it except for special reasons, which shall be stated in the order.

(3) In this section the expression "county" means a county at large.

(4) For the purposes of this and the next following section a prison shall not be deemed to be closed by reason only of its appropriation for use as a remand centre, [or young offender institution] [or secure training centre].

Annotations

Sub-s (4): first words in square brackets substituted by virtue of the Criminal Justice Act 1988, s 123, Sch 8, para 1; final words in square brackets added by the Criminal Justice and Public Order Act 1994, s 168(2), Sch 10, para 8.

This section does not extend to Scotland.

Offences

39 Assisting prisoner to escape

Any person who aids any prisoner in escaping or attempting to escape from a prison or who, with intent to facilitate the escape of any prisoner, conveys any thing into a prison or to a prisoner [sends any thing (by post or otherwise) into a prison or to a prisoner] or places any thing anywhere outside a prison with a view to its coming into the possession of a prisoner, shall be guilty of felony and liable to imprisonment for a term not exceeding [ten years].

Annotations

First words in square brackets added and second words in square brackets substituted, by the Prison Security Act 1992, s 2(1), (4).
See further, in relation to felony: the Criminal Law Act 1967, s 12(5)(a).
This section does not extend to Scotland.

40 Unlawful conveyance of spirits or tobacco into prison, etc

Any person who contrary to the regulations of a prison brings or attempts to bring into the prison or to a prisoner any spirituous or fermented liquor or tobacco, or places any such liquor or any tobacco anywhere outside the prison with intent that it shall come into the possession of a prisoner, and any officer who contrary to those regulations allows any such liquor or any tobacco to be sold or used in the prison, shall be liable on summary conviction to imprisonment for a term not exceeding six months or a fine not exceeding [level 3 on the standard scale] or both.

Annotations

Maximum fine increased and converted to a level on the standard scale by the Criminal Justice Act 1982, ss 37, 38, 46.
This section does not extend to Scotland.

41 Unlawful introduction of other articles

Any person who contrary to the regulations of a prison conveys or attempts to convey any letter or any other thing into or out of the prison or to a prisoner or places it anywhere outside the prison with intent that it shall come into the possession of a prisoner shall, where he is not thereby guilty of an offence under either of the two last preceding sections, be liable on summary conviction to a fine not exceeding [level 3 on the standard scale].

Annotations

Maximum fine increased and converted to a level on the standard scale by the Criminal Justice Act 1982, ss 37, 38, 46.
This section does not extend to Scotland.

42 Display of notice of penalties

The Prison Commissioners shall cause to be affixed in a conspicuous place outside every prison a notice of the penalties to which persons committing offences under the three last preceding sections are liable.

Annotations

Functions of the Prison Commissioners transferred to the Secretary of State for the Home Department, by the Prison Commissioners Dissolution Order 1963, SI 1963 No 597.
This section does not extend to Scotland.

Remand centres [and young offender institutions]

43 [Remand centres [and young offender institutions]]

[(1)   The Secretary of State may provide—

(a)   remand centres, that is to say places for the detention of persons not less than fourteen but under 21 years of age who are remanded or committed in custody for trial or sentence [or are ordered to be safely kept in custody on the transfer of proceedings against them for trial];

[(aa) young offender institutions, that is to say places for the detention of offenders sentenced to detention in a young offender institution [or to custody for life];]

(b), (c) < . . . > ; [and]

[(d)   secure training centres, that is to say places in which offenders not less than 12 but under 17 years of age in respect of whom secure training orders have been made under section 1 of the Criminal Justice and Public Order Act 1994 may be detained and given training and education and prepared for their release.]

(2)   The Secretary of State may from time to time direct—

(a)   that a woman aged 21 years or over who is serving a sentence of imprisonment or who has been committed to prison for default shall be detained in a remand centre or a [young offender institution] instead of a prison;

(b)   that a woman aged 21 years or over who is remanded in custody or committed in custody for trial or sentence [or is ordered to be safely kept in custody on the transfer of proceedings against her for trial] shall be detained in a remand centre instead of a prison;

(c)   that a person under 21 but not less than 17 years of age who is remanded in custody or committed in custody for trial or sentence [or ordered to be safely kept in custody on the transfer of proceedings against him for trial] shall be detained in a prison instead of a remand centre or a remand centre instead of a prison, notwithstanding anything in section 27 of the Criminal Justice Act 1948 or section 23(3) of the Children and Young Persons Act 1969.

(3)   Notwithstanding subsection (1) above, any person required to be detained in an institution to which this Act applies may be detained in a remand centre for any temporary purpose [and a person [aged 18 years] or over may be detained in such a centre] for the purpose of providing maintenance and domestic services for that centre.

(4)   Sections 5A, 6(2) and (3), 16, 22, 25 and 36 of this Act shall apply to remand centres [and young offender institutions] and to persons detained in them as they apply to prisons and prisoners.

[(4A) Sections 16, 22 and 36 of this Act shall apply to secure training centres and to persons detained in them as they apply to prisons and prisoners.]

(5)   The other provisions of this Act preceding this section, except sections 28 and 37(2) above, shall apply to [centres of the descriptions specified in subsection (4) above] and to persons detained in them as they apply to prisons and prisoners, but subject to such adaptations and modifications as may be specified in rules made by the Secretary of State.

[(5A) The other provisions of this Act preceding this section, except sections 5, 5A, 6(2) and (3), 12, 14, 19, 25, 28 and 37(2) and (3) above, shall apply to secure training centres and to persons detained in them as they apply to prisons and prisoners, but subject to such adaptations and modifications as may be specified in rules made by the Secretary of State.]

(6)   References in the preceding provisions of this Act to imprisonment shall, so far as those provisions apply to institutions provided under this section, be construed as including references to detention in those institutions.

(7)   Nothing in this section shall be taken to prejudice the operation of section 12 of the Criminal Justice Act 1982.]

Annotations

This section was substituted by the Criminal Justice Act 1982, s 11.

Cross-heading: reference to "young offender institutions" substituted by virtue of the Criminal Justice Act 1988, s 123(6), Sch 8, para 1.

Section heading: reference to "young offender institutions" substituted by virtue of the Criminal Justice Act 1988, s 123(6), Sch 8, para 1.

Sub-s (1): in para (a) words underlined prospectively repealed, and words in square brackets prospectively added, by the Criminal Justice and Public Order Act 1994, ss 44, 168(3), Sch 4, Part II, para 9(2), Sch 11, as from a day to be appointed; para (aa) added by the Criminal Justice Act 1988, s 170, Sch 15, para 11, words in square brackets therein added by the Criminal Justice and Public Order Act 1994, s 18(3); paras (b), (c) repealed by the Criminal Justice Act 1988, s 170, Sch 16; para (d) and word preceding it added by the Criminal Justice and Public Order Act 1994, s 5(2).

Sub-s (2): in para (a) words in square brackets substituted by virtue of the Criminal Justice Act 1988, s 123(6), Sch 8, para 1; in paras (b), (c) words underlined prospectively repealed and words in square brackets prospectively added, by the Criminal Justice and Public Order Act 1994, ss 44, 168(3), Sch 4, Part II, para 9(3), Sch 11, as from a day to be appointed.

Sub-s (3): first words in square brackets substituted by the Criminal Justice Act 1988, s 170(1), Sch 15, para 12, words in square brackets therein substituted by the Criminal Justice Act 1991, s 68, Sch 8, para 2.

Sub-s (4): words in square brackets substituted by virtue of the Criminal Justice Act 1988, s 123(6), Sch 8, para 1.

Sub-ss (4A), (5A): added by the Criminal Justice and Public Order Act 1994, s 5(3), (5).

Sub-s (5): words in square brackets substituted by the Criminal Justice and Public Order Act 1994, s 5(4).

This section does not extend to Scotland.

Rules for the management of prisons and other institutions

47 Rules for the management of prisons, remand centres [and young offender institutions]

(1)   The Secretary of State may make rules for the regulation and management of prisons, remand centres[, young offender institutions or secure training centres] respectively, and for the classification, treatment, employment, discipline and control of persons required to be detained therein.

(2)   Rules made under this section shall make provision for ensuring that a person who is charged with any offence under the rules shall be given a proper opportunity of presenting his case.

(3)   Rules made under this section may provide for the training of particular classes of persons and their allocation for that purpose to any prison or other institution in which they may lawfully be detained.

(4)   Rules made under this section shall provide for the special treatment of the following persons whilst required to be detained in a prison, that is to say—

(a)–(c) < . . . >

(d) any < . . . > person detained in a prison, not being a person serving a sentence or a person imprisoned in default of payment of a sum adjudged to be paid by him on his conviction [or a person committed to custody on his conviction].

[(4A) Rules made under this section shall provide for the inspection of secure training centres and the appointment of independent persons to visit secure training centres and to whom representations may be made by offenders detained in secure training centres.]

(5)   Rules made under this section may provide for the temporary release of persons [detained in a prison, [remand centre][, young offender institution or secure training centre] not being persons committed in custody [ordered to be safely kept in custody on the transfer of proceedings against them] for trial [before the Crown Court] or committed to be sentenced or otherwise dealt with by [the Crown Court] or remanded in custody by any court].

Annotations

Section heading: reference to "young offender institutions" substituted by virtue of the Criminal Justice Act 1988, s 123(6), Sch 8, paras 1, 3(2).

Sub-s (1): words in square brackets substituted by the Criminal Justice and Public Order Act 1994, s 6(2).

Sub-s (4): words omitted repealed and words in square brackets added, by the Criminal Justice Act 1967, ss 66(5), 103(2), Sch 7, Part I.

Sub-s (4A): added by the Criminal Justice and Public Order Act 1994, s 6(3).

Sub-s (5): first words in square brackets substituted by the Criminal Justice Act 1961, s 41(1), (3), Sch 4, first words in square brackets therein substituted by the

Criminal Justice Act 1982, s 77, Sch 14, para 7, second words in square brackets therein substituted by the Criminal Justice and Public Order Act 1994, s 6(4), words underlined therein prospectively repealed and subsequent words in square brackets prospectively substituted by the Criminal Justice and Public Order Act 1994, s 44, Sch 4, Part II, para 10, as from a day to be appointed, fifth and final words in square brackets therein substituted by the Courts Act 1971, s 56(1), Sch 8, Part II, para 33.

This section does not extend to Scotland.

Miscellaneous

49 Persons unlawfully at large

(1)   Any person who, having been sentenced to imprisonment, < . . . > [custody for life or [to detention in a young offender institution]] or ordered to be detained in a < . . . > [or a young offenders institution] [or a secure training centre], or having been committed to a prison or remand centre, is unlawfully at large, may be arrested by a constable without warrant and taken to the place in which he is required in accordance with law to be detained.

(2)   Where any person sentenced to imprisonment, < . . . > or [to detention in a young offender institution], or ordered to be detained in a < . . . > detention centre [young offenders institution or in a secure training centre], is unlawfully at large at any time during the period for which he is liable to be detained in pursuance of the sentence or order, then, unless the Secretary of State otherwise directs, no account shall be taken, in calculating the period for which he is liable to be so detained, of any time during which he is absent from the [place in which he is required in accordance with law to be detained]:

Provided that—

(a) this subsection shall not apply to any period during which any such person as aforesaid is detained in pursuance of the sentence or order or in pursuance of any other sentence of any court [in the United Kingdom] in a prison, [< . . . > , remand centre or [young offender institution]] [remand centre, young offenders institution or secure training centre];

(b), (c) < . . . >

(3)   The provisions of the last preceding subsection shall apply to a person who is detained in custody in default of payment of any sum of money as if he were sentenced to imprisonment.

(4)   For the purposes of this section a person who, after being temporarily released in pursuance of rules made under subsection (5) of section forty-seven of this Act, is at large at any time during the period for which he is liable to be detained in pursuance of his sentence shall be deemed to be unlawfully at large if the period for which he was temporarily released has expired or if an order recalling him has been made by the [Secretary of State] in pursuance of the rules.

Annotations

Sub-s (1): first words omitted repealed by the Criminal Justice Act 1967, s 103(2), Sch 7, Part I; first words in square brackets substituted by the Criminal Justice Act 1982, s 77, Sch 14, para 8, words in square brackets therein substituted by virtue of the Criminal Justice Act 1988, s 123, Sch 8, para 2; second words in square brackets added, by the Criminal Justice Act 1982, s 77, Sch 14, para 8; final words omitted repealed by virtue of the Criminal Justice Act 1988, s 123, Sch 8, paras 1, 2; final words in square brackets prospectively added by the Criminal Justice and Public Order Act 1994, s 168(2), Sch 10, para 9(2), as from a day to be appointed.

Sub-s (2): first words omitted repealed in part by the Criminal Justice Act 1967, s 103(2), Sch 7, Part I, remainder repealed by virtue of the Criminal Justice Act 1988, s 123, Sch 8, para 2; second words omitted repealed by the Children and Young Persons Act 1969, s 72(4), Sch 6; first and second words in square brackets substituted by virtue of the Criminal Justice Act 1988, s 123, Sch 8, paras 1, 2; words underlined prospectively repealed and subsequent words in square brackets prospectively substituted by the Criminal Justice and Public Order Act 1994, s 168(2), Sch 10, para 9(3), (4), as from a day to be appointed; fourth words in square brackets substituted, and para (b) repealed, by the Criminal Justice Act 1982, ss 77, 78, Sch 14, para 8, Sch 16; fifth words in square brackets added and para (c) repealed, by the Criminal Justice Act 1961, ss 30(4), 41, Schs 4, 5; sixth words in square brackets substituted by the Criminal Justice Act 1982, s 77, Sch 14, para 8, words omitted therein repealed and words in square brackets therein substituted, by virtue of the Criminal Justice Act 1988, s 123, Sch 8, para 1.

Sub-s (4): words in square brackets substituted by SI 1963 No 597, art 3(2), Sch 1.

This section does not extend to Scotland.

Supplemental

51 Payment of expenses out of moneys provided by Parliament

All expenses incurred in the maintenance of prisons and in the maintenance of prisoners and all other expenses of the Secretary of State < . . . > incurred under this Act shall be defrayed out of moneys provided by Parliament.

Annotations

Words omitted repealed by SI 1963 No 597, art 3(2), Sch 1.

This section does not extend to Scotland.

52 Exercise of power to make orders, rules and regulations

(1)   Any power of the Secretary of State to make rules or regulations under this Act and the power of the Secretary of State to make an order under section thirty-four or section thirty-seven of this Act shall be exercisable by statutory instrument.

(2)   Any statutory instrument containing regulations made under section sixteen or an order made under section thirty-seven of this Act, < . . . > shall be laid before Parliament.

(3)   The power of the Secretary of State to make an order under section six or section thirty-four of this Act shall include power to revoke or vary such an order.

Annotations

Sub-s (2): words omitted repealed by the Criminal Justice Act 1967, ss 66(4), 103(2), Sch 7, Part I.

This section does not extend to Scotland.

53 Interpretation

(1) In this Act the following expressions have the following meanings:—

"Attendance centre" means a centre provided by the Secretary of State under [section 16 of the Criminal Justice Act 1982];

"Prison" does not include a naval, military or air force prison;

< . . . >

(2) For the purposes of this Act the maintenance of a prisoner shall include all necessary expenses incurred in respect of the prisoner for food, clothing, custody and removal from one place to another, from the period of his committal to prison until his death or discharge from prison.

(3) References in this Act to the Church of England shall be construed as including references to the Church in Wales.

(4) References in this Act to any enactment shall be construed as references to that enactment as amended by any other enactment.

Annotations

Sub-s (1): words in square brackets substituted by the Criminal Justice Act 1982, s 77, Sch 14, para 9; words omitted repealed by the Children and Young Persons Act 1969, s 72(4), Sch 6.

This section does not extend to Scotland.

54 Consequential amendments, repeals and savings

(1), (2)   < . . . >

(3) Nothing in this repeal shall affect any rule, order, regulation or declaration made, direction or certificate given or thing done under any enactment repealed by this Act and every such rule, order, regulation, direction, certificate or thing shall, if in force at the commencement of this Act, continue in force and be deemed to have been made, given or done under the corresponding provision of this Act.

(4) Any document referring to any Act or enactment repealed by this Act shall be construed as referring to this Act or to the corresponding enactment in this Act.

(5) The mention of particular matters in this section shall not be taken to affect the general application to this Act of section thirty-eight of the Interpretation Act 1889 (which relates to the effect of repeals).

Annotations

Sub-s (1): repealed by the Statute Law (Repeals) Act 1993.

Sub-s (2): repealed by the Statute Laws (Repeals) Act 1974.

This section does not extend to Scotland.

55 Short title, commencement and extent

(1)   This Act may be cited as the Prison Act 1952.

(2)   This Act shall come into operation on the first day of October, nineteen hundred and fifty-two.

(3)   < . . . >

(4)   Except as provided in < . . . > [the Criminal Justice Act 1961], this Act shall not extend to Scotland.

(5)   This Act shall not extend to Northern Ireland.

Annotations

Sub-s (3): repealed by the Statute Law (Repeals) Act 1993.

Sub-s (4): words omitted repealed by the Statute Law (Repeals) Act 1993; words in square brackets substituted by the Criminal Justice Act 1961, s 41, Sch 4.

PRISON RULES 1964

SI 1964/388

Made 11th March 1964

PART I
PRISONERS

General

1 Purpose of prison training and treatment

The purpose of the training and treatment of convicted prisoners shall be to encourage and assist them to lead a good and useful life.

2 Maintenance of order and discipline

(1) Order and discipline shall be maintained with firmness, but with no more restriction than is required for safe custody and well ordered community life.

(2) In the control of prisoners, officers shall seek to influence them through their own example and leadership, and to enlist their willing co-operation.

(3) At all times the treatment of prisoners shall be such as to encourage their self-respect and a sense of personal responsibility, but a prisoner shall not be employed in any disciplinary capacity.

3 Classification of prisoners

(1) Prisoners shall be classified, in accordance with any directions of the Secretary of State, having regard to their age, temperament and record and with a view to maintaining good order, and facilitating training and, in the case of convicted prisoners, of furthering the purpose of their training and treatment as provided by Rule 1 of these Rules.

[(2) Unconvicted prisoners:

    (a) shall be kept out of contact with convicted prisoners as far as the governor considers this can reasonably be done, unless and to the extent that they have consented to share residential accommodation or participate in any activity with convicted prisoners; and

    (b) shall under no circumstances be required to share a cell with a convicted prisoner.]

(3)   Nothing in this Rule shall require a prisoner to be deprived unduly of the society of other persons.

Annotations

Para (2): substituted by SI 1995 No 983, r 2, Schedule, para 1.

[4] [Privileges]

[(1)   There shall be established at every prison systems of privileges approved by the Secretary of State and appropriate to the classes of prisoners there, which shall include arrangements under which money earned by prisoners in prison may be spent by them within the prison.

(2)   Systems of privileges approved under paragraph (1) may include arrangements under which prisoners may be allowed time outside the cells and in association with one another, in excess of the minimum time which, subject to the other provisions of these Rules apart from this rule, is otherwise allowed to prisoners at the prison for this purpose.

(3)   Systems of privileges approved under paragraph (1) may include arrangements under which privileges may be granted to prisoners only in so far as they have met, and for so long as they continue to meet, specified standards in their behaviour and their performance in work or other activities.

(4)   Systems of privileges which include arrangements of the kind referred to in paragraph (3) shall include procedures to be followed in determining whether or not any of the privileges concerned shall be granted, or shall continue to be granted, to a prisoner; such procedures shall include a requirement that the prisoner be given reasons for any decision adverse to him together with a statement of the means by which he may appeal against it.

(5)   Nothing in this rule shall be taken to confer on a prisoner any entitlement to any privilege or to affect any provision in these Rules other than this rule as a result of which any privilege may be forfeited or otherwise lost or a prisoner deprived of association with other prisoners.]

Annotations

This rule was substituted by SI 1995 No 1598, r 2, Schedule, para 1.

[6] [Temporary release]

[(1)   The Secretary of State may, in accordance with the other provisions of this rule, release temporarily a prisoner to whom this rule applies.

(2)   A prisoner may be released under this rule for any period or periods and subject to any conditions.

(3)   A prisoner may only be released under this rule:

(a) on compassionate grounds or for the purpose of receiving medical treatment;

(b) to engage in employment or voluntary work;

(c) to receive instruction or training which cannot reasonably be provided in the prison;

(d) to enable him to participate in any proceedings before any court, tribunal or inquiry;

(e) to enable him to consult with his legal adviser in circumstances where it is not reasonably practicable for the consultation to take place in the prison;

(f)   to assist any police officer in any enquiries;

(g) to facilitate the prisoner's transfer between prisons;

(h) to assist him in maintaining family ties or in his transition from prison life to freedom; or

(i)   to enable him to make a visit in the locality of the prison, [as a privilege under rule 4 of these Rules].

(4)   A prisoner shall not be released under this rule unless the Secretary of State is satisfied that there would not be an unacceptable risk of his committing offences whilst released or otherwise of his failing to comply with any condition upon which he is released.

(5)   The Secretary of State shall not release under this rule a prisoner serving a sentence of imprisonment if, having regard to:

(a) the period or proportion of his sentence which the prisoner has served; and

(b) the frequency with which the prisoner has been granted temporary release under this rule,

the Secretary of State is of the opinion that the release of the prisoner would be likely to undermine public confidence in the administration of justice.

(6)   If a prisoner has been temporarily released under this rule during the relevant period and has been sentenced to imprisonment for a criminal offence committed whilst at large following that release, he shall not be released under this rule unless his release, having regard to the circumstances of his conviction, would not, in the opinion of the Secretary of State, be likely to undermine public confidence in the administration of justice; and for this purpose "the relevant period":

(a) in the case of a prisoner serving a determinate sentence of imprisonment, is, if the prisoner has previously been released on licence under Part II of the Criminal Justice Act 1991 during that sentence, the period since the date of his last recall or return to prison in respect of that sentence or, where the prisoner has not been so released, the period he has served in respect of that sentence;

(b) in the case of a prisoner serving an indeterminate sentence of imprisonment, is, if the prisoner has previously been released on licence under Part II of the Criminal Justice Act 1991, the period since the date of his last recall to prison in respect of that sentence or, where the prisoner has not been so released, the period he has served in respect of that sentence, or

(c) in the case of a prisoner detained in prison for any other reason, is the period for which the prisoner has been detained for that reason,

save that where a prisoner falls within two or more of sub-paragraphs (a) to (c) above, the "relevant period", in the case of that prisoner, shall be determined by whichever of the applicable sub-paragraphs that produces the longer period.

(7) A prisoner released under this rule may be recalled to prison at any time whether the conditions of his release have been broken or not.

(8) This rule applies to prisoners other than persons committed in custody for trial or to be sentenced or otherwise dealt with before or by the Crown Court or remanded in custody by any court.

(9) For the purposes of any reference in this rule to a prisoner's sentence, consecutive terms and terms which are wholly or partly concurrent shall be treated as a single term; in addition in this rule:

(a) any reference to a sentence of imprisonment shall be construed as including any sentence to detention or custody; and

(b) any reference to release on licence under Part II of the Criminal Justice Act 1991 includes any release on licence under any earlier legislation providing for early release on licence.]

Annotations

This rule was substituted by SI 1995 No 983, r 2, Schedule, para 2.

Para (3): in sub-para (i) words in square brackets substituted by SI 1995 No 1598, r 2, Schedule , para 2.

See further, for provision as to the interpretation of references herein to rule 6: the Prison (Amendment) Rules 1995, SI 1995 No 983, r 3(2).

7 Information to prisoners

[(1) Every prisoner shall be provided, as soon as possible after his reception into prison, and in any case within 24 hours, with information in writing about those provisions of these Rules and other matters which it is necessary that he should know, including earnings and privileges, and the proper method of making requests and complaints < . . . > .

(2) In the case of a prisoner aged less than 18, or a prisoner aged 18 or over who cannot read or appears to have difficulty in understanding

the information so provided, the governor, or an officer deputed by him, shall so explain it to him that he can understand his rights and obligations.

(3)   A copy of these Rules shall be made available to any prisoner who requests it.]

Annotations

This rule was substituted by SI 1983 No 568, r 3, Schedule, Pt I.

Para (1): words omitted revoked by SI 1990 No 1762, r 2(a).

[8] [Requests and Complaints]

[(1)   A request or complaint to the governor or Board of Visitors relating to a prisoner's imprisonment shall be made orally or in writing by that prisoner.

(2)   On every day the governor shall hear any requests and complaints that are made to him under paragraph (1) above.

(3)   A written request or complaint under paragraph (1) above may be made in confidence.]

Annotations

This rule was substituted by SI 1990 No 1762, r 2(b).

9 Women prisoners

(1)   Women prisoners shall be kept entirely separate from male prisoners.

(2)   < . . . >

(3)   The Secretary of State may, subject to any conditions he thinks fit, permit a woman prisoner to have her baby with her in prison, and everything necessary for the baby's maintenance and care may be provided there.

Annotations

Para (2): revoked by SI 1976 No 503, r 2.

Religion

10 Religious denomination

[A prisoner shall be treated as being of the religious denomination stated in the record made in pursuance of section 10(5) of the Prison Act 1952 but the governor may, in a proper case and after due enquiry, direct that record to be amended.]

Annotations

This rule was substituted by SI 1974 No 713, r 2.

11 Special duties of chaplains and prison ministers

(1)   The chaplain or prison minister of a prison shall—

    (a) interview every prisoner of his denomination individually soon after the prisoner's reception into that prison and shortly before his release; and

    (b) if no further arrangements are made, read the burial service at the funeral of any prisoner of his denomination who dies in that prison.

(2)   The chaplain shall visit daily all prisoners belonging to the Church of England who are sick, under restraint or undergoing cellular confinement; and a prison minister shall do the same, as far as he reasonably can, for prisoners of his own denomination.

(3)   If the prisoner is willing, the chaplain shall visit any prisoner not of the Church of England who is sick, under restraint or undergoing cellular confinement, and is not regularly visited by a minister of his own denomination.

12 Regular visits by ministers of religion

(1)   The chaplain shall visit regularly the prisoners belonging to the Church of England.

(2)   A prison minister shall visit the prisoners of his denomination as regularly as he reasonably can.

(3)   Where a prisoner belongs to a denomination for which no prison minister has been appointed, the governor shall do what he reasonably can, if so requested by the prisoner, to arrange for him to be visited regularly by a minister of that denomination.

13 Religious services

(1)   The chaplain shall conduct Divine Service for prisoners belonging to the Church of England at least once every Sunday, Christmas Day and Good Friday, and such celebrations of Holy Communion and weekday services as may be arranged.

(2)   Prison ministers shall conduct Divine Service for prisoners of their denominations at such times as may be arranged.

14 Substitute for chaplain or prison ministers

(1)   A person approved by the Secretary of State may act for the chaplain in his absence.

(2)   A prison minister may, with the leave of the Secretary of State, appoint a substitute to act for him in his absence.

15 Sunday work

Arrangements shall be made so as not to require prisoners of the Christian religion to do any unnecessary work on Sunday, Christmas Day or Good

Friday, or prisoners of other religions on their recognised days of religious observance.

16 Religious books

There shall, so far as reasonably practicable, be available for the personal use of every prisoner such religious books recognised by his denomination as are approved by the Secretary of State for use in prisons.

Medical attention, etc

17 Medical attendance

(1)   The medical officer of a prison shall have the care of the health, mental and physical, of the prisoners in that prison.

(2)   Every request by a prisoner to see the medical officer shall be recorded by the officer to whom it is made and promptly passed on to the medical officer.

(3)   The medical officer may call another medical practitioner into consultation at his discretion, and shall do so if time permits before performing any serious operation.

(4)   If an unconvicted prisoner desires the attendance of a registered medical practitioner or dentist, and will pay any expense incurred, the governor shall, if he is satisfied that there are reasonable grounds for the request and unless the Secretary of State otherwise directs, allow him to be visited and treated by that practitioner or dentist in consultation with the medical officer.

[(5)   Subject to any directions given in the particular case by the Secretary of State, a registered medical practitioner selected by or on behalf of a prisoner who is a party to any legal proceedings shall be afforded reasonable facilities for examining him in connection with the proceedings, and may do so out of hearing but in the sight of an officer.]

Annotations

Para (5): added by SI 1993 No 3075, r 2, Schedule, para 1.

18 Special illnesses and conditions

(1)   The medical officer shall report to the governor on the case of any prisoner whose health is likely to be injuriously affected by continued imprisonment or any conditions of imprisonment. The governor shall send the report to the Secretary of State without delay, together with his own recommendations.

(2)   The medical officer shall pay special attention to any prisoner whose mental condition appears to require it, and make any special arrangements which appear necessary for his supervision or care.

(3)   The medical officer shall inform the governor if he suspects any prisoner of having suicidal intentions, and the prisoner shall be placed under special observation.

Medical attention, etc

19 Notification of illness or death

(1)   If a prisoner dies, becomes seriously ill, sustains any severe injury or is removed to hospital on account of mental disorder, the governor shall, if he knows his or her address, at once inform the prisoner's spouse or next of kin, and also any person who the prisoner may reasonably have asked should be informed.

(2)   If a prisoner dies, the governor shall give notice immediately to the coroner having jurisdiction, to the < . . . > board of visitors and to the Secretary of State.

Annotations

Para (2): words omitted revoked by SI 1971 No 2019, r 4.

Physical welfare and work

20 Clothing

[(1)   An unconvicted prisoner may wear clothing of his own if and in so far as it is suitable, tidy and clean, and shall be permitted to arrange for the supply to him from outside prison of sufficient clean clothing:

Provided that, subject to the provisions of rule 38(3) of these Rules:

(a)   he may be required, if and for so long as there are reasonable grounds to believe that there is a serious risk of his attempting to escape, to wear items of clothing which are distinctive by virtue of being specially marked or coloured or both; and

(b)   he may be required, if and for so long as the Secretary of State is of the opinion that he would, if he escaped, be highly dangerous to the public or the police or the security of the State, to wear clothing provided under this rule.

(1A)   Subject to paragraph (1) above, the provisions of this rule shall apply to an unconvicted prisoner as to a convicted prisoner.]

(2)   A convicted prisoner shall be provided with clothing adequate for warmth and health in accordance with a scale approved by the Secretary of State.

(3)   The clothing provided under this Rule shall include suitable protective clothing for use at work, where this is needed.

(4)   Subject to the provisions of Rule 38(3) of these Rules, a convicted

prisoner shall wear clothing provided under this Rule and no other, except on the directions of the Secretary of State [or as a privilege under rule 4 of these Rules].

(5)   A prisoner may be provided, where necessary, with suitable and adequate clothing on his release.

Annotations

Paras (1), (1A): substituted for para (1) as originally enacted, by SI 1995 No 1598, r 2, Schedule, para 3.

Para (4): words in square brackets added by SI 1995 No 1598, r 2, Schedule, para 3(b).

21 Food

(1)   < . . . >

(2)   Subject to any directions of the Secretary of State, no < . . . > prisoner shall be allowed, except as authorised by the medical officer, to have any food other than that ordinarily provided.

(3)   No < . . . > prisoner shall be given less food than is ordinarily provided, except < . . . > upon the written recommendation of the medical officer.

(4)   The food provided shall be wholesome, nutritious, well prepared and served, reasonably varied and sufficient in quantity.

(5)   The medical officer shall regularly inspect the food both before and after it is cooked, and shall report any deficiency or defect to the governor.

(6)   In this Rule "food" includes drink.

Annotations

Para (1): revoked by SI 1988 No 89, r 2(a).

Para (2): word omitted revoked by SI 1988 No 89, r 2(a).

Para (3): first word omitted revoked by SI 1988 No 89, r 2(a); second words omitted revoked by SI 1976 No 503, r 3.

22 Alcohol and tobacco

(1)   No prisoner shall be allowed to have any intoxicating liquor except under a written order of the medical officer specifying the quantity and the name of the prisoner < . . . > .

(2)   No prisoner shall be allowed to smoke or to have any tobacco except as a privilege under Rule 4 of these Rules and in accordance with any orders of the governor.

Annotations

Para (1): words omitted revoked by SI 1988 No 89, r 2(b).

23 Sleeping accommodation

(1)   No room or cell shall be used as sleeping accommodation for a prisoner

unless it has been certified in the manner required by section 14 of the Prison Act 1952 in the case of a cell used for the confinement of a prisoner.

(2) A certificate given under that section or this Rule shall specify the maximum number of prisoners who may sleep or be confined at one time in the room or cell to which it relates, and the number so specified shall not be exceeded without the leave of the Secretary of State.

24 Beds and bedding

Each prisoner shall be provided with a separate bed and with separate bedding adequate for warmth and health.

25 Special accommodation

The governor or < . . .. > board of visitors may, on application by an unconvicted prisoner, permit him on payment of a sum fixed by the Secretary of State—

(a) to occupy a room or cell specially fitted for such prisoners and provided with suitable bedding and other articles in addition to, or different from, those ordinarily provided, and to have at his own expense the use of private furniture and utensils approved by the governor; and

(b) to be relieved of the duty of cleaning his room or cell and similar duties.

Annotations

Words omitted revoked by SI 1971 No 2019, r 4.

26 Hygiene

(1) Every prisoner shall be provided with toilet articles necessary for his health and cleanliness, which shall be replaced as necessary.

(2) Every prisoner shall be required to wash at proper times, have a hot bath on reception and thereafter at least once a week and, in the case of a man not excused or excepted by the governor or medical officer, to shave or be shaved daily, and to have his hair cut as may be necessary for neatness:

Provided that an unconvicted prisoner [or a convicted prisoner who has not yet been sentenced] shall not be required to have his hair cut or any beard or moustache usually worn by him shaved off except where the medical officer directs this to be done for the sake of health or cleanliness.

(3) A woman prisoner's hair shall not be cut without her consent except where the medical officer certifies in writing that this is necessary for the sake of health or cleanliness.

Annotations

Para (2): words in square brackets added by SI 1971 No 2019, r 2.

27 Daily exercise

(1)   A prisoner not engaged in outdoor work, or detained in an open prison, shall be given exercise in the open air for not less than one hour in all, each day, if weather permits:

Provided that exercise consisting of physical training may be given indoors instead of in the open air.

(2)   The Secretary of State may in special circumstances authorise the reduction of the period aforesaid to half an hour a day.

(3)   The medical officer shall decide upon the fitness of every prisoner for exercise and physical training, and may excuse a prisoner from, or modify, any activity on medical grounds.

28 Work

(1)   A convicted prisoner shall be required to do useful work for not more than ten hours a day, and arrangements shall be made to allow prisoners to work, where possible, outside the cells and in association with one another.

(2)   The medical officer may excuse a prisoner from work on medical grounds, and no prisoner shall be set to do work which is not of a class for which he has been passed by the medical officer as being fit.

(3)   No prisoner shall be set to do work of a kind not authorised by the Secretary of State.

(4)   No prisoner shall work in the service of another prisoner or an officer, or for the private benefit of any person, without the authority of the Secretary of State.

(5)   An unconvicted prisoner shall be permitted, if he wishes, to work as if he were a convicted prisoner.

(6)   Prisoners may be paid for their work at rates approved by the Secretary of State, either generally or in relation to particular cases.

Education and social welfare

29 Education

(1)   Every prisoner able to profit from the educational facilities provided at a prison shall be encouraged to do so.

(2)   Programmes of evening educational classes shall be arranged at every prison and, subject to any directions of the Secretary of State, reasonable facilities shall be afforded to prisoners who wish to do so to improve

their education by correspondence courses or private study, or to practise handicrafts, in their spare time.

(3) Special attention shall be paid to the education of illiterate prisoners, and if necessary they shall be taught within the hours normally allotted to work.

30 Library books

A library shall be provided in every prison and, subject to any directions of the Secretary of State, every prisoner shall be allowed to have library books and to exchange them.

31 Outside contracts

(1) Special attention shall be paid to the maintenance of such relations between a prisoner and his family as are desirable in the best interests of both.

(2) A prisoner shall be encouraged and assisted to establish and maintain such relations with persons and agencies outside prison as may, in the opinion of the governor, best promote the interests of his family and his own social rehabilitation.

32 After-care

From the beginning of a prisoner's sentence, consideration shall be given, in consultation with the appropriate after-care organisation, to the prisoner's future and the assistance to be given him on and after his release.

Letters and visits

33 Letters and visits generally

(1) The Secretary of State may, with a view to securing discipline and good order or the prevention of crime or in the interests of any persons, impose restrictions, either generally or in a particular case, upon the communications to be permitted between a prisoner and other persons.

(2) Except as provided by statute or these Rules, a prisoner shall not be permitted to communicate with any outside person, or that person with him, without the leave of the Secretary of State [or as a privilege under rule 4 of these Rules].

(3) Except as provided by these Rules, every letter or communication to or from a prisoner [may] be read or examined by the governor or an officer deputed by him, and the governor may, at his discretion, stop any letter or communication on the ground that its contents are objectionable or that it is of inordinate length.

(4) Every visit to a prisoner shall take place within the sight of an officer, unless the Secretary of State otherwise directs.

(5)   Except as provided by these Rules, every visit to a prisoner shall take place within the hearing of an officer, unless the Secretary of State otherwise directs.

(6)   The Secretary of State may give directions, generally or in relation to any visit or class of visits, concerning the days and times when prisoners may be visited.

Annotations

Para (2): words in square brackets added by SI 1995 No 1598, r 2, Schedule, para 4.
Para (3): word in square brackets substituted by SI 1974 No 713, r 3.

34 Personal letters and visits

(1)   An unconvicted prisoner may send and receive as many letters and may receive as many visits as he wishes within such limits and subject to such conditions as the Secretary of State may direct, either generally or in a particular case.

(2)   A convicted prisoner shall be entitled—

    (a)   to send and to receive a letter on his reception into a prison and thereafter once a week; and

    (b)   to receive a visit [twice in every period of four weeks, but only once in every such period if the Secretary of State so directs].

(3)   The governor may allow a prisoner an additional letter or visit [as a privilege under rule 4 of these Rules or] where necessary for his welfare or that of his family.

(4)   The governor may allow a prisoner entitled to a visit to send and to receive a letter instead.

(5)   The governor may defer the right of a prisoner to a visit until the expiration of any period of cellular confinement.

(6)   The < . . . > board of visitors may allow a prisoner an additional letter or visit in special circumstances, and may direct that a visit may extend beyond the normal duration.

(7)   The Secretary of State may allow additional letters and visits in relation to any prisoner or class of prisoners.

(8)   A prisoner shall not be entitled under this Rule to [receive a visit from] any person other than a relative or friend, except with the leave of the Secretary of State.

(9)   Any letter or visit under the succeeding provisions of these Rules shall not be counted as a letter or visit for the purposes of this Rule.

Annotations

Para (2): words in square brackets substituted by SI 1992 No 514, r 2(1), Schedule, para 1; words omitted revoked by SI 1974 No 713, r 4.
Para (3): words in square brackets added by SI 1995 No 1598, r 2, Schedule, para 5.

Para (6): words omitted revoked by SI 1971 No 2019, r 4.

Para (8): words in square brackets substituted by SI 1983 No 568, r 4.

35 Police interviews

A police officer may, on production of an order issued by or on behalf of a chief officer of police, interview any prisoner willing to see him.

36 Securing release

A person detained in prison in default of finding a surety, or of payment of a sum of money, may communicate with, and be visited at any reasonable time on a weekday by, any relative or friend to arrange for a surety or payment in order to secure his release from prison.

37 Legal advisers

(1) The legal adviser of a prisoner in any legal proceedings, civil or criminal, to which the prisoner is a party shall be afforded reasonable facilities for interviewing him in connection with those proceedings, and may do so out of hearing but in the sight of an officer.

[(2) A prisoner's legal adviser may, subject to any directions given by the Secretary of State, interview the prisoner in connection with any other legal business out of hearing but in the sight of an officer.]

Annotations

Para (2): substituted by SI 1989 No 330, r 2(a).

[37A] [Correspondence with legal advisers and courts]

[(1) A prisoner may correspond with his legal adviser and any court and such correspondence may only be opened, read or stopped by the governor in accordance with the provisions of this rule.

(2) Correspondence to which this rule applies may be opened if the governor has reasonable cause to believe that it contains an illicit enclosure and any such enclosure shall be dealt with in accordance with the other provisions of these Rules.

(3) Correspondence to which this rule applies may be opened, read and stopped if the governor has reasonable cause to believe its contents endanger prison security or the safety of others or are otherwise of a criminal nature.

(4) A prisoner shall be given the opportunity to be present when any correspondence to which this rule applies is opened and shall be informed if it or any enclosure is to be read or stopped.

(5) A prisoner shall on request be provided with any writing materials necessary for the purposes of paragraph (1) of this rule.

(6) In this rule, "court" includes the European Commission of Human Rights, the European Court of Human Rights and the European Court

of Justice; and "illicit enclosure" includes any article possession of which has not been authorised in accordance with the other provisions of these Rules and any correspondence to or from a person other than the prisoner concerned, his legal adviser or a court.]

Annotations

This rule was added by SI 1972 No 1860, r 3.

This rule was substituted by SI 1993 No 3075, r 2, Schedule, para 2.

Removal, record and property

38 Custody outside prison

(1) A person being taken to or from a prison in custody shall be exposed as little as possible to public observation, and proper care shall be taken to protect him from curiosity and insult.

(2) A prisoner required to be taken in custody anywhere outside a prison shall be kept in the custody of an officer appointed < . . . > or a police officer.

[(3) A prisoner required to be taken in custody to any court shall, when he appears before the court, wear his own clothing or ordinary civilian clothing provided by the governor.]

Annotations

Para (2): words omitted revoked by SI 1992 No 514, r 2(1), Schedule, para 2.

Para (3): substituted by SI 1995 No 1598, r 2, Schedule, para 6.

39 Search

(1) Every prisoner shall be searched when taken into custody by an officer, on his reception into a prison and subsequently as the governor thinks necessary.

(2) A prisoner shall be searched in as seemly a manner as is consistent with discovering anything concealed.

(3) No prisoner shall be stripped and searched in the sight of another prisoner [or in the sight or presence of an officer not of the same sex].

(4) < . . . >

Annotations

Para (3): words in square brackets added by SI 1988 No 1421, r 2(b).

Para (4): revoked by SI 1992 No 2080, r 2, Schedule, para 1.

40 Record and photograph

(1) A personal record of each prisoner shall be prepared and maintained in such manner as the Secretary of State may direct.

(2)   Every prisoner may be photographed on reception and subsequently, but no copy of the photograph shall be given to any person not authorised to receive it.

41 Prisoners' property

(1)   Subject to any directions of the Secretary of State, an unconvicted prisoner may have supplied to him at his expense and retain for his own use books, newspapers, writing materials and other means of occupation, except any that appear objectionable to the < . . . > board of visitors or, pending consideration by them, to the governor.

(2)   Anything, other than cash, which a prisoner has at a prison and which he is not allowed to retain for his own use shall be taken into the governor's custody. An inventory of a prisoner's property shall be kept, and he shall be required to sign it, after having a proper opportunity to see that it is correct.

(3)   Any cash which a prisoner has at a prison shall be paid into an account under the control of the governor and the prisoner shall be credited with the amount in the books of the prison.

[(3A) Any article belonging to a prisoner which remains unclaimed for a period of more than 3 years after he leaves prison, or dies, may be sold or otherwise disposed of; and the net proceeds of any sale shall be paid to the National Association for the Care and Resettlement of Offenders, for its general purposes.]

(4)   The governor may confiscate any unauthorised article found in the possession of a prisoner after his reception into prison, or concealed or deposited anywhere within a prison.

Annotations

Para (1): words omitted revoked by SI 1971 No 2019, r 4.
Para (3A): added by SI 1976 No 503, r 5.

42 Money and articles received by post

(1)   Any money or other article (other than a letter or other communication) sent to a convicted prisoner through the post office shall be dealt with in accordance with the provisions of this Rule, and the prisoner shall be informed of the manner in which it is dealt with.

(2)   Any cash shall, at the discretion of the governor, be—

(a) dealt with in accordance with Rule 41(3) of these Rules; or

(b) returned to the sender; or

(c) in a case where the sender's name and address are not known, paid [to the National Association for the Care and Resettlement of Offenders, for its general purposes:]

Provided that in relation to a prisoner committed to prison in default of payment of any sum of money, the prisoner shall be informed of the receipt of the cash and, unless he objects to its being so applied, it shall be applied in or towards the satisfaction of the amount due from him.

(3)   Any security for money shall, at the discretion of the governor, be—

(a)   delivered to the prisoner or placed with his property at the prison; or

(b)   returned to the sender; or

(c)   encashed and the cash dealt with in accordance with paragraph (2) of this Rule.

(4)   Any other article to which this Rule applies shall, at the discretion of the governor, be—

(a)   delivered to the prisoner or placed with his property at the prison; or

(b)   returned to the sender; or

(c)   in a case where the sender's name and address are not known or the article is of such a nature that it would be unreasonable to return it, sold or otherwise disposed of, and the net proceeds of any sale applied in accordance with paragraph (2) of this Rule.

Annotations

Para (2): words in square brackets substituted by SI 1976 No 503, r 5.

Special control and restraint

43 Removal from association

(1)   Where it appears desirable, for the maintenance of good order or discipline or in his own interests, that a prisoner should not associate with other prisoners, either generally or for particular purposes, the governor may arrange for the prisoner's removal from association accordingly.

(2)   A prisoner shall not be removed under this Rule for a period of more than [3 days] without the authority of a member of the < . . . > board of visitors, or of the Secretary of State. An authority given under this paragraph shall be for a period not exceeding one month, but may be renewed from month to month [except that, in the case of a person aged less than 21 years who is detained in prison < . . . > , such an authority shall be for a period not exceeding 14 days, but may be renewed from time to time for a like period].

(3)   The governor may arrange at his discretion for such a prisoner as aforesaid to resume association with other prisoners, and shall do so if in any case the medical officer so advises on medical grounds.

Annotations

Para (2): first words in square brackets substituted and second words omitted revoked by SI 1989 No 2141, r 2(a); first words omitted revoked by SI 1971 No 2019, r 4; second words in square brackets substituted by SI 1988 No 1421, r 2(c).

44 Use of force

(1)   An officer in dealing with a prisoner shall not use force unnecessarily and, when the application of force to a prisoner is necessary, no more force than is necessary shall be used.

(2)   No officer shall act deliberately in a manner calculated to provoke a prisoner.

45 Temporary Confinement

The governor may order a refractory or violent prisoner to be confined temporarily in a special cell, but a prisoner shall not be so confined as a punishment, or after he has ceased to be refractory or violent.

46 Restraints

(1)   The governor may order a prisoner to be put under restraint where this is necessary to prevent the prisoner from injuring himself or others, damaging property or creating a disturbance.

(2)   Notice of such an order shall be given without delay to a member of the < . . . > board of visitors, and to the medical officer.

(3)   On receipt of the notice the medical officer shall inform the governor whether he concurs in the order. The governor shall give effect to any recommendation which the medical officer may make.

(4)   A prisoner shall not be kept under restraint longer than necessary, nor shall he be so kept for longer than 24 hours without a direction in writing given by a member of the < . . . > board of visitors or by an officer of the Secretary of State (not being an officer of a prison). Such a direction shall state the grounds for the restraint and the time during which it may continue.

(5)   Particulars of every case of restraint under the foregoing provisions of this Rule shall be forthwith recorded.

(6)   Except as provided by this Rule no prisoner shall be put under restraint otherwise than for the safe custody removal, or on medical grounds by direction of the medical officer. No prisoner shall be put under restraint as a punishment.

(7)   Any means of restraint shall be of a pattern authorised by the Secretary of State, and shall be used in such manner and under such conditions as the Secretary of State may direct.

Annotations

Paras (2), (4): words omitted revoked by SI 1971 No 2019, r 4.

[46A] [Compulsory Testing for Controlled Drugs]

[(1)   This rule applies where an officer, acting under the powers conferred by section 16A of the Prison Act 1952 (power to test prisoners for drugs), requires a prisoner to provide a sample for the purpose of ascertaining whether he has any controlled drug in his body.

(2) In this rule "sample" means a sample of urine or any other description of sample specified in the authorisation by the governor for the purposes of section 16A.

(3) When requiring a prisoner to provide a sample, an officer shall, so far as is reasonably practicable, inform the prisoner:

(a) that he is being required to provide a sample in accordance with section 16A of the Prison Act 1952; and

(b) that a refusal to provide a sample may lead to disciplinary proceedings being brought against him.

(4) An officer shall require a prisoner to provide a fresh sample, free from any adulteration.

(5) An officer requiring a sample shall make such arrangements and give the prisoner such instructions for its provision as may be reasonably necessary in order to prevent or detect its adulteration or falsification.

(6) A prisoner who is required to provide a sample may be kept apart from other prisoners for a period not exceeding one hour to enable arrangements to be made for the provision of the sample.

(7) A prisoner who is unable to provide a sample of urine when required to do so may be kept apart from other prisoners until he has provided the required sample, save that a prisoner may not be kept apart under this paragraph for a period of more than 5 hours.

(8) A prisoner required to provide a sample of urine shall be afforded such degree of privacy for the purposes of providing the sample as may be compatible with the need to prevent or detect any adulteration or falsification of the sample; in particular a prisoner shall not be required to provide such a sample in the sight of a person of the opposite sex.]

Annotations

This rule was added by SI 1994 No 3195, r 2, Schedule, para 1.

Offences against discipline

[47] [Offences against discipline]

[A prisoner is guilty of an offence against discipline if he—

(1) commits any assault;

(2) detains any person against his will;

[(3) denies access to any part of the prison to any officer or any person (other than a prisoner) who is at the prison for the purpose of working there;]

(4) fights with any person;

(5) intentionally endangers the health or personal safety of others or, by his conduct, is reckless whether such health or personal safety is endangered;

[(6) intentionally obstructs an officer in the execution of his duty, or any person (other than a prisoner) who is at the prison for the purpose of working there, in the performance of his work;]

(7) escapes or absconds from prison or from legal custody;

(8) fails—

    (a) < . . . >

    (b) to comply with any condition upon which he is [temporarily released under rule 6 of these Rules];

[(8A)   administers a controlled drug to himself or fails to prevent the administration of a controlled drug to him by another person (but subject to rule 47A below);]

(9) has in his possession—

    (a) any unauthorised article, or

    (b) a greater quantity of any article than he is authorised to have;

(10) sells or delivers to any person any unauthorised article;

(11) sells or, without permission, delivers to any person any article which he is allowed to have only for his own use;

(12) takes improperly any article belonging to another person or to a prison;

(13) intentionally or recklessly sets fire to any part of a prison or any other property, whether or not his own;

(14) destroys or damages any part of a prison or any other property, other than his own;

(15) absents himself from any place where he is required to be or is present at any place where he is not authorised to be;

[(16)is disrespectful to any officer, or any person (other than a prisoner) who is at the prison for the purpose of working there, or any person visiting a prison;]

(17) uses threatening, abusive or insulting words or behaviour;

(18) intentionally fails to work properly or, being required to work, refuses to do so;

(19) disobeys any lawful order;

(20) disobeys or fails to comply with any rule or regulation applying to him;

(21) in any way offends against good order and discipline;

(22)

    (a) attempts to commit,

    (b) incites another prisoner to commit, or

    (c) assists another prisoner to commit or to attempt to commit,

any of the foregoing offences.]

Annotations

This rule was substituted by SI 1989 No 330, r 2(b).

Paras (3), (6), (16): substituted by SI 1994 No 3195, r 2, Schedule, paras 2, 3, 5.

Para (8): sub-para (a) revoked, and in sub-para (b) words in square brackets substituted, by SI 1992 No 514, r 2(1), Schedule, paras 3, 4.

Para (8A): added by SI 1994 No 3195, r 2, Schedule, para 4.

See further, in relation to the interpretation of references in para (8) above to rule 6: the Prison (Amendment) Rules 1995, SI 1995 No 983, r 3(2).

47A

[It shall be a defence for a prisoner charged with an offence under rule 47(8A) to show that:

    (a) the controlled drug had been, prior to its administration, lawfully in his possession for his use or was administered to him in the course of a lawful supply of the drug to him by another person;

    (b) the controlled drug was administered by or to him in circumstances in which he did not know and had no reason to suspect that such a drug was being administered; or

    (c) the controlled drug was administered by or to him under duress or to him without his consent in circumstances where it was not reasonable for him to have resisted.]

Annotations

This rule was added by SI 1994 No 3195, r 2, Schedule, para 6.

[48] [Disciplinary charges]

[(1) Where a prisoner is to be charged with an offence against discipline, the charge shall be laid as soon as possible and, save in exceptional circumstances, within 48 hours of the discovery of the offence.

(2) < . . . >

(3) Every charge shall be inquired into < . . . > by the governor.

(4) Every charge shall be first inquired into not later, save in exceptional circumstances, than the next day, not being a Sunday or public holiday, after it is laid.]

[(5) A prisoner who is to be charged with an offence against discipline may be kept apart from other prisoners pending the governor's first inquiry.]

Annotations

This rule was substituted by SI 1989 No 330, r 2(b).

Para (2): revoked by SI 1992 No 514, r 2(1), Schedule, para 5.

Para (3): words omitted revoked by SI 1992 No 514, r 2(1), Schedule, para 6.

Para (5): added by SI 1992 No 514, r 2(1), Schedule, para 7.

[49] [Rights of prisoner charged]

[(1)   Where a prisoner is charged with an offence against discipline, he shall be informed of the charge as soon as possible and, in any case, before the time when it is inquired into by the governor.

(2)   At any inquiry into a charge against a prisoner he shall be given a full opportunity of hearing what is alleged against him and of presenting his own case.]

Annotations

This rule was substituted by SI 1989 No 330, r 2(b).

Offences against discipline

[50] [Governor's punishments]

[(1)   If he finds a prisoner guilty of an offence against discipline the governor may, subject to rule 52 of these Rules, impose one or more of the following punishments:

(a)   caution;

(b)   forfeiture for a period not exceeding 28 days [42 days] of any of the privileges under rule 4 of these Rules;

(c)   exclusion from associated work for a period not exceeding 14 days [21 days];

(d)   [stoppage of or deduction from earnings for a period not exceeding 56 days [84 days] of an amount not exceeding 28 days' earnings [42 days' earnings]];

(e)   cellular confinement for a period not exceeding [14 days];

(f)   [in the case of a short-term or long-term prisoner, an award of additional days not exceeding 28 days [42 days];]

(g)   in the case of a prisoner otherwise entitled to them, forfeiture for any period of the right, under rule 41(1) of these Rules, to have the articles there mentioned;

(h)   < . . . >

(2)   If a prisoner is found guilty of more than one charge arising out of an incident, punishments under this rule may be ordered to run consecutively [but, [in the case of an award of additional days, the total period added] shall not exceed 28 days [42 days]].]

Annotations

This rule was substituted by SI 1989 No 330, r 2.

Para (1): in sub-paras (b), (c) words underlined revoked with savings and subsequent words in square brackets substituted with savings by SI 1995 No 983, r 2, Schedule, para 3(a)(i), (ii), for savings see r 4 thereof; sub-para (d) substituted by SI 1992 No 514, r 2(1), Schedule, para 8, words underlined revoked with savings and subsequent words in square brackets substituted with savings by SI 1995 No 983, r 2, Schedule, para 3(a)(iii), for savings see r 4 thereof; in sub-para (e) words in square brackets substituted by SI 1993 No 3075, r 2, Schedule, para 3; sub-para (f) substituted by SI 1992 No 2080, r 2, Schedule, para 3(a), words underlined revoked with savings and subsequent words in square brackets substituted with savings by SI 1995 No 983, r 2, Schedule, para 3(a)(iv); sub-para (h) revoked by SI 1995 No 1598, r 2, Schedule, para 7.

Para (2): first words in square brackets added by SI 1989 No 2141, r 2(b), first words in square brackets therein substituted by SI 1992 No 2080, r 2, Schedule, para 3(b), words underlined revoked with savings and subsequent words in square brackets substituted with savings by SI 1995 No 983, r 2, Schedule, para 3(b), for savings see r 4 thereof.

[51]   [Forfeiture of remission to be treated as an award of additional days]

[(1)   In this rule, "existing prisoner" and "existing licensee" have the meanings assigned to them by paragraph 8(1) of Schedule 12 to the Criminal Justice Act 1991.

(2)   In relation to any existing prisoner or existing licensee who has forfeited any remission of his sentence, the provisions of Part II of the Criminal Justice Act 1991 shall apply as if he had been awarded such number of additional days as equals the number of days of remission which he has forfeited.]

Annotations

Original rule 51 was revoked by SI 1992 No 514, r 2(1), Schedule; new rule added by SI 1992 No 2080, r 2, Schedule, para 4.

Offences against discipline

[52]   [Offences committed by young persons]

[(1)   In the case of an offence against discipline committed by an inmate who was under the age of 21 when the offence was committed (other than an offender in relation to whom the Secretary of State has given a direction under section 13(1) of the Criminal Justice Act 1982 that he shall be treated as if he had been sentenced to imprisonment)—

    (a)   rule 50 of these Rules shall have effect, but—

        (i)   the maximum period of forfeiture of privileges under rule 4 of these Rules shall be 14 days [21 days]; and

        [(ii) the maximum period of stoppage of or deduction from earnings shall be 28 days [42 days] and the maximum amount shall be 14 days [21 days].]

[(iii) the maximum period of cellular confinement shall be 7 days.]

(b)   < . . . >

(2)   In the case of an inmate who has been sentenced to a term of youth custody or detention in a young offender institution, and by virtue of a direction of the Secretary of State under section 13 of the Criminal Justice Act 1982, is treated as if he had been sentenced to imprisonment for that term, any punishment imposed on him for an offence against discipline before the said direction was given shall, if it has not been exhausted or remitted, continue to have effect as if made pursuant to rule 50 < . . . > of these Rules < . . . >

(3)   In the case of an inmate detained in a prison who, by virtue of paragraph 12 of Schedule 8 to the Criminal Justice Act 1988, on 1st October 1988 fell to be treated for all purposes of detention, release and supervision as if his sentence had been a sentence of detention in a young offender institution, any award for an offence against discipline made in respect of him before that date under rule 50, 51 or 52 of the Prison Rules 1964, which were then in force, or treated by virtue of rule 5(4A) as having been imposed under those Rules, shall, if it has not been exhausted or remitted, continue to have effect as if it were a punishment imposed pursuant to rule 50 < . . . > of these Rules < . . . > .]

Annotations

This rule was substituted by SI 1989 No 330, r 2(b).

Para (1): in sub-para (a), in para (i) words underlined revoked with savings and subsequent words in square brackets substituted with savings by SI 1995 No 983, r 2, Schedule, para 4(a), for savings see r 4 thereof, para (ii) substituted by SI 1993 No 3075, r 2, Schedule, para 4, words underlined revoked with savings and subsequent words in square brackets substituted with savings by SI 1995 No 983, r 2, Schedule, para 4(b), for savings see r 4 thereof, para (iii) added by SI 1993 No 3075, r 2, Schedule, para 5; sub-para (b) revoked by SI 1992 No 514, r 2(1), Schedule, para 10.

Paras (2), (3): words omitted revoked by SI 1992 No 514, r 2(1), Schedule, paras 11, 12.

[53] [Particular punishments]

[(1)   < . . . >

(2)   No punishment of cellular confinement shall be imposed unless the medical officer has certified that the prisoner is in a fit state of health to be so dealt with.]

Annotations

This rule was substituted by SI 1989 No 330, r 2(b).

Para (1): revoked by SI 1992 No 514, r 2(1), Schedule, para 13.

[54] [Prospective award of additional days]

[(1)   Subject to paragraph (2), where an offence against discipline is committed by a prisoner who is detained only on remand, additional days may be awarded notwithstanding that the prisoner has not (or had not at the time of the offence) been sentenced.

(2)　An award of additional days under paragraph (1) shall have effect only if the prisoner in question subsequently becomes a short-term or long-term prisoner whose sentence is reduced, under section 67 of the Criminal Justice Act 1967, by a period which includes the time when the offence against discipline was committed.]

Annotations

This rule was substituted by SI 1992 No 2080, r 2, Schedule, para 5.

[55] [Suspended Punishments]

[(1)　Subject to any directions given by the Secretary of State, the power to impose a disciplinary punishment (other than a caution) shall include power to direct that the punishment is not to take effect unless, during a period specified in the direction (not being more than six months from the date of the direction) the prisoner commits another offence against discipline and a direction is given under paragraph (2) below.

(2)　Where a prisoner commits an offence against discipline during the period specified in a direction given under paragraph (1) above the person < . . . > dealing with that offence may—

(a)　direct that the suspended punishment shall take effect,

(b)　reduce the period or amount of the suspended punishment and direct that it shall take effect as so reduced,

(c)　vary the original direction by substituting for the period specified a period expiring not later than six months from the date of variation, or

(d)　give no direction with respect to the suspended punishment.]

Annotations

This rule was substituted by SI 1989 No 330, r 2(b).
Para (2): words omitted revoked by SI 1992 No 514, r 2(1), Schedule, para 14.

[56] [Remission and mitigation of punishments and quashing of findings of guilt]

[(1)　The Secretary of State may quash any finding of guilt and may remit any punishment or mitigate it either by reducing it or by substituting another award which is, in his opinion, less severe.

(2)　Subject to any directions given by the Secretary of State, the governor may remit or mitigate any punishment imposed by a governor, [or the Board of Visitors].]

Annotations

This rule was substituted by SI 1989 No 330, r 2(b).
Para (2): words in square brackets substituted by SI 1992 No 514, r 2(1), Schedule, para 15.

269

Other particular classes

63 Prisoners committed for contempt, etc

(1)   A prisoner committed or attached for contempt of court, or for failing to do or abstain from doing anything required to be done or left undone, shall have the same privileges as an unconvicted prisoner under [Rule] 34(1) of these Rules.

(2)   Such prisoners shall be treated as a separate class for the purposes of Rule 3 of these Rules but, notwithstanding anything in that Rule, such prisoners may be permitted to associate with any other class of prisoners if they are willing to do so.

(3)   < . . . >

Annotations

Para (1): word in square brackets substituted by SI 1987 No 2176, r 2(d).
Para (3): revoked by SI 1992 No 2080, r 2, Schedule, para 6.

Prisoners under sentence of death

72 Application of foregoing Rules

The foregoing provisions of these Rules shall apply in relation to a prisoner under sentence of death only in so far as they are compatible with that sentence and with Rules 73 to 76 of these Rules.

73 Search

A prisoner under sentence of death shall be searched with special care and every article shall be taken from him which it might be dangerous or inexpedient to leave in his possession.

74 Confinement

(1)   A prisoner under sentence of death shall be confined in a separate cell and shall be kept apart from all other prisoners.

(2)   He shall be kept by day and night in the constant charge of two officers.

(3)   He shall not be required to work, but shall, if he wishes, be given work to do in his cell.

(4)   Subject to the provisions of Rule 75 of these Rules, no person other than a member of the [board of visitors] or an officer shall have access to a prisoner under sentence of death without the leave of the Secretary of State.

Annotations

Para (4): words in square brackets substituted by SI 1971 No 2019, r 4.

75 Visits

(1) Every visit to a prisoner under sentence of death, other than a visit by the chaplain or a prison minister, shall take place in the sight and hearing of an officer.

(2) Such a prisoner may be visited by any relation, friend or legal adviser whom he wishes to see, and who is authorised to visit him by an order in writing of a member of the [board of visitors] or the Secretary of State.

(3) The chaplain shall have free access to every such prisoner belonging to the Church of England, and to every other such prisoner who wishes to see him.

(4) Where such a prisoner belongs to a denomination other than the Church of England, a minister of that denomination shall have free access to him.

Annotations

Para (2): words in square brackets substituted by SI 1971 No 2019, r 4.

76 Correspondence

A prisoner under sentence of death shall be given all necessary facilities to enable him to correspond with his legal advisers, relatives and friends.

PART II

OFFICERS OF PRISONS

77 General duty of officers

(1) It shall be the duty of every officer to conform to these Rules and the rules and regulations of the prison, to assist and support the governor in their maintenance and to obey his lawful instructions.

(2) An officer shall inform the governor promptly of any abuse or impropriety which comes to his knowledge.

78 Gratuities forbidden

No officer shall receive any unauthorised fee, gratuity or other consideration in connection with his office.

79 Search of officers

An officer shall submit himself to be searched in the prison if the governor so directs.

80 Transactions with prisoners

(1) No officer shall take part in any business or pecuniary transaction

with or on behalf of a prisoner without the leave of the Secretary of State.

(2)   No officer shall without authority bring in or take out, or attempt to bring in or take out, or knowingly allow to be brought in or taken out, to or for a prisoner, or deposit in any place with intent that it shall come into the possession of a prisoner, any article whatsoever.

81 Contact with former prisoners, etc

No officer shall, without the knowledge of the governor, communicate with any person whom he knows to be a former prisoner or a relative or friend of a prisoner or former prisoner.

82 Communications to the press, etc

(1)   No officer shall make, directly or indirectly, any unauthorised communication to a representative of the press or any other person concerning matters which have become known to him in the course of his duty.

(2)   No officer shall, without authority, publish any matter or make any public pronouncement relating to the administration of any institution to which the Prison Act 1952 applies or to any of its inmates.

83 Quarters

An officer shall occupy any quarters which may be assigned to him.

84 Code of discipline

The Secretary of State may approve a code of discipline to have effect in relation to officers, or such classes of officers as it may specify, setting out the offences against discipline, the awards which may be made in respect of them and the procedure for dealing with charges.

PART III

PERSONS HAVING ACCESS TO A PRISON

85 Prohibited articles

No person shall, without authority, convey into or throw into or deposit in a prison, or convey or throw out of a prison, or convey to a prisoner, or deposit in any place with intent that it shall come into the possession of a prisoner, any money, clothing, food, drink, tobacco, letter, paper, book, tool or other article whatever. Anything so conveyed, thrown or deposited may be confiscated by the governor.

86 Control of persons and vehicles

(1)   Any person or vehicle entering or leaving a prison may be stopped, examined and searched.

(2) The governor may direct the removal from a prison of any person who does not leave on being required to do so.

87 Viewing of prisons

(1) No outside person shall be permitted to view a prison unless authorised by statute or the Secretary of State.

(2) No person viewing a prison shall be permitted to take a photograph, make a sketch or communicate with a prisoner unless authorised by statute or the Secretary of State.

PART **IV**

BOARDS OF VISITORS

88 Disqualification for membership

Any person interested in any contract for the supply of goods or services to a prison shall not be a member of the < . . . > board of visitors for that prison.

Annotations

Words omitted revoked by SI 1971 No 2019, r 4.

92 Board of visitors

(1) A member of the board of visitors for a prison appointed by the Secretary of State under section 6(2) of the Prison Act 1952 shall [subject to paragraph (1A) below] hold office for three years, or such less period as the Secretary of State may appoint.

[(1A) The Secretary of State may terminate the appointment of a member if he is satisfied that—

   (a) he has failed satisfactorily to perform his duties,

   (b) he is by reason of physical or mental illness, or for any other reason, incapable of carrying out his duties, or

   (c) he has been convicted of such a criminal offence, or his conduct has been such, that it is not in the Secretary of State's opinion fitting that he should remain a member.]

(2) When a board is first constituted, the Secretary of State shall appoint one of its members to be chairman for a period not exceeding twelve months.

[(3) Subject to paragraph (2) above, at their first meeting in any year of office the Board shall appoint one of their members to be chairman and one to be vice-chairman for that year and thereafter shall fill any casual vacancy in either office promptly.

(4) The vice-chairman's term of office shall come to an end when, for whatever reason, that of the chairman comes to an end.]

Annotations

Para (1): words in square brackets added by SI 1989 No 330, r 2(c).

Para (1A): added by SI 1989 No 330, r 2(c).

Paras (3), (4): substituted by SI 1989 No 330, r 2(c).

93 Proceedings of boards

(1)   The < . . . > board of visitors for a prison shall meet at the prison once a month or, if they resolve for reasons specified in the resolution that less frequent meetings are sufficient, not fewer than eight times in twelve months.

(2)   The < . . . > board may fix a quorum of not fewer than three members for proceedings < . . . >.

(3)   The < . . . > board shall keep minutes of their proceedings.

(4)   The proceedings of the < . . . > board shall not be invalidated by any vacancy in the membership or any defect in the appointment of a member.

Annotations

Paras (1), (3), (4): words omitted revoked by SI 1971 No 2019, r 4.

Para (2): first words omitted revoked by SI 1971 No 2019, r 4; second words omitted revoked by SI 1992 No 514, r 2(1), Schedule, para 16.

94 General duties of boards

(1)   The < . . . > board of visitors for a prison shall satisfy themselves as to the state of the prison premises, the administration of the prison and the treatment of the prisoners.

(2)   The < . . . > board shall inquire into and report upon any matter into which the Secretary of State asks them to inquire.

(3)   The < . . . > board shall direct the attention of the governor to any matter which calls for his attention, and shall report to the Secretary of State any matter which they consider it expedient to report.

(4)   The < . . . > board shall inform the Secretary of State immediately of any abuse which comes to their knowledge < . . . >.

(5)   Before exercising any power under these Rules < . . . > the < . . . > board and any member of the < . . . > board shall consult the governor in relation to any matter which may affect discipline.

Annotations

Paras (1)–(3): words omitted revoked by SI 1971 No 2019, r 4.

Para 4: first words omitted revoked by SI 1971 No 2019, r 4; second words omitted revoked by SI 1989 No 330, r 2(d).

Para (5): first and final words omitted revoked by SI 1971 No 2019, r 4; second words omitted revoked by SI 1992 No 514, r 2(1), Schedule, para 17.

95 Particular duties

(1)   The < . . . > board of visitors for a prison and any member of the < . . . > board shall hear any complaint or request which a prisoner wishes to make to them or him.

(2)   The < . . . > board shall arrange for the food of the prisoners to be inspected by a member of the board at frequent intervals.

(3)   The < . . . > board shall inquire into any report made to them, whether or not by a member of the < . . . > board, that a prisoner's health, mental or physical, is likely to be injuriously affected by any conditions of his imprisonment.

Annotations

Paras (1)–(3): words omitted revoked by SI 1971 No 2019, r 4.

96 Members visiting prisons

(1)   The members of the < . . . > board of visitors for a prison shall visit the prison frequently, and the < . . . > board shall arrange a rota whereby at least one of its members visits the prison < . . . > between meetings of the board.

(2)   A member of the < . . . > board shall have access at any time to every part of the prison and to every prisoner, and he may interview any prisoner out of the sight and hearing of officers.

(3)   A member of the < . . . > board shall have access to the records of the prison.

Annotations

Paras (1)–(3): words omitted revoked by SI 1971 No 2019, r 4.

97 Annual report

The < . . . > board of visitors for a prison shall make an annual report to the Secretary of State at the end of each year concerning the state of the prison and its administration, including in it any advice and suggestions they consider appropriate.

Annotations

Words omitted revoked by SI 1971 No 2019, r 4.

Part V
Supplemental

98 Delegation by governor

The governor of a prison may, with the leave of the Secretary of State, delegate any of his powers and duties under these Rules to another officer of that prison.

[98A] [Contracted out prisons]

[(1)   Where the Secretary of State has entered into a contract for the running of a prison under section 84 of the Criminal Justice Act 1991 ("the 1991 Act") these rules [shall have effect in relation to that prison] with the following modifications—

   (a) references to an officer in the Rules shall include references to a prisoner custody officer certified as such under section 89(1) of the 1991 Act;

   (b) references to a governor in the Rules shall include references to a director approved by the Secretary of State for the purposes of section 85(1)(a) of the 1991 Act except—

      (i) in rule 43, 45, 46, 48, 49, 50, 56 and 98 where references to a governor shall include references to a controller appointed by the Secretary of State under section 85(1)(b) of the 1991 Act, and

      (ii) in rules 77(1), 81 and 94 where references to a governor shall include references to the director and the controller;

   (c) Rule 84 shall not apply [in relation to a prisoner custody officer certified as such under section 89(1) of the 1991 Act and performing custodial duties].

(2)   Where a director exercises the powers set out in section 85(3)(b) of the 1991 Act (removal from association, temporary confinement and restraints) in cases of urgency, he shall notify the controller of that fact forthwith.]

Annotations

This rule was added by SI 1992 No 514, r 2(1), Schedule, para 18.

Para (1): first words in square brackets substituted, and in sub-para (c) words in square brackets added, by SI 1994 No 3195, r 2, Schedule, para 7.

[98B] [Contracted out parts of prison]

[Where the Secretary of State has entered into a contract for the running of part of a prison under section 84(1) of the Criminal Justice Act 1991, that part and the remaining part shall each be treated for the purposes of Parts I to III and Part V of these Rules as if they were separate prisons.]

Annotations

This rule was added by SI 1994 No 3195, r 2, Schedule, para 8.

[98C] [Contracted out functions at directly managed prisons]

[(1)   Where the Secretary of State has entered into a contract under section 88A(1) of the Criminal Justice Act 1991 ("the 1991 Act") for any functions at a directly managed prison to be performed by prisoner custody officers who are authorised to perform custodial duties under section 89(1) of the 1991 Act, references to an officer in these Rules shall, subject to paragraph (2) below, include references to a prisoner custody officer who is so authorised and who is performing contracted out functions for the purposes of, or for purposes connected with, the prison.

(2) Paragraph (1) shall not apply to references to an officer in rule 84.

(3) In this rule, "directly managed prison" has the meaning assigned to it by section 88A(5) of the 1991 Act.]

Annotations

This rule was added by SI 1994 No 3195, r 2, Schedule, para 8.

99 Interpretation

(1) In these Rules, where the context so admits, the expression—

    < . . . >

["controlled drug" means any drug which is a controlled drug for the purposes of the Misuse of Drugs Act 1971;]

"convicted prisoner" means, subject to the provisions of [Rule 63] of these Rules, a prisoner who has been convicted or found guilty of an offence or committed or attached for contempt of court or for failing to do or abstain from doing anything required to be done or left undone, and the expression "unconvicted prisoner" shall be construed accordingly;

"governor" includes an officer for the time being in charge of a prison;

"legal adviser" means, in relation to a prisoner, his counsel or solicitor, and includes a clerk acting on behalf of his solicitor;

    < . . . >

"officer" means an officer of a prison [and, for the purposes of rule 38(2) of these Rules, includes a prisoner custody officer who is authorised to perform escort functions in accordance with section 89 of the Criminal Justice Act 1991;]

"prison minister" means, in relation to a prison, a minister appointed to that prison under section 10 of the Prison Act 1952.

["short-term prisoner" and "long-term prisoner" have the meanings assigned to them by section 33(5) of the Criminal Justice Act 1991, as extended by sections 43(1) and 45(1) of that Act.]

(2) In these Rules a reference to

[(a) an award of additional days means additional days awarded under these Rules by virtue of section 42 of the Criminal Justice Act 1991; and

(b)] the Church of England includes a reference to the Church in Wales.

(3) The Interpretation Act 1889 shall apply for the interpretation of these Rules as it applies for the interpretation of an Act of Parliament.

Annotations

Para (1): first definition omitted revoked, and in definition "convicted prisoner" words in square brackets substituted, by SI 1972 No 1860, r 4; definition "controlled drug" added by SI 1994 No 3195, r 2, Schedule, para 9; second definition omitted revoked by SI 1971 No 2019, r 4; definitions "short-term prisoner" and "long-term prisoner" added by SI 1992 No 2080, r 2, Schedule, para 7; in definition "officer" words in square brackets added by SI 1993 No 516, r 2.

Para (2): words in square brackets added by SI 1992 No 2080, r 2, Schedule, para 7.

Modified by the Solicitors' Incorporated Practices Order 1991, SI 1991 No 2684, arts 4, 5, Sch 2.

100 Revocations and savings

(1)   The Rules specified in the Schedule to these Rules are hereby revoked.

(2)   For the purposes of these Rules any appointment, approval, authority, certificate, condition, direction or restriction made, given or imposed under any provision of any of the Rules revoked by this Rule shall be treated as having been made, given or imposed under the corresponding provision of these Rules.

101 Citation and commencement

These Rules may be cited as the Prison Rules 1964 and shall come into operation on the fourteenth day after the day on which they are made.

YOUNG OFFENDER INSTITUTION RULES 1988

SI 1988/1422

Made 5th August 1988

PART I

PRELIMINARY

1 Citation and commencement

These Rules may be cited as the Young Offender Institution Rules 1988 and shall come into force on 1st October 1988.

2 Interpretation

(1)   In these Rules, where the context so admits, the expression:—

"compulsory school age" has the same meaning as in the Education Act 1944;

["controlled drug" means any drug which is a controlled drug for the purposes of the Misuse of Drugs Act 1971;]

"governor" includes an officer for the time being in charge of a young offender institution;

"inmate" means a person detained in a young offender institution;

"legal adviser" means, in relation to an inmate, his counsel or solicitor, and includes a clerk acting on behalf of his solicitor;

"minister appointed to a young offender institution" means a minister so appointed under section 10 of the Prison Act 1952;

"officer" means an officer of a young offender institution.

["short-term prisoner" and "long-term prisoner" have the meanings assigned to them by section 33(5) of the Criminal Justice Act 1991, as extended by sections 43(1) and 45(1) of that Act.]

(2)   In these Rules a reference to the Church of England includes a reference to:

[(a) an award of additional days means additional days awarded under these Rules by virtue of section 42 of the Criminal Justice Act 1991; and

(b)] the Church in Wales.

(3)   The Rules set out in the Schedule to this Order are hereby revoked.

Annotations

Para (1): definition "controlled drug" added by SI 1994 No 3194, r 2, Schedule, para 1; definitions "short-term prisoner" and "long-term prisoner" added by SI 1992 No 2081, r 2, Schedule, para 1(a).

Para (2): words in square brackets added by SI 1992 No 2081, r 2, Schedule, para 1(b).

PART II

INMATES

General

3 Aims and general principles of young offender institutions

(1)   The aim of a young offender institution shall be to help offenders to prepare for their return to the outside community.

(2)   The aim mentioned in paragraph (1) above shall be achieved, in particular, by—

(a)   providing a programme of activities, including education, training and work designed to assist offenders to acquire or develop personal responsibility, self-discipline, physical fitness, interests and skills and to obtain suitable employment after release;

(b)   fostering links between the offender and the outside community;

(c)   co-operating with the services responsible for the offender's supervision after release.

4 Classification of inmates

Inmates may be classified, in accordance with any directions of the Secretary of State, taking into account their ages, characters and circumstances.

Release

[6] [Temporary release]

[(1)   The Secretary of State may, in accordance with the other provisions of this rule, release temporarily an inmate to whom this rule applies.

(2)   An inmate may be released under this rule for any period or periods and subject to any conditions.

(3) An inmate may only be released under this rule:

    (a) on compassionate grounds or for the purpose of receiving medical treatment;

    (b) to engage in employment or voluntary work;

    (c) to receive instruction or training which cannot reasonably be provided in the young offender institution;

    (d) to enable him to participate in any proceedings before any court, tribunal or inquiry;

    (e) to enable him to consult with his legal adviser in circumstances where it is not reasonably practicable for the consultation to take place in the young offender institution;

    (f) to assist any police officer in any enquiries;

    (g) to facilitate the inmate's transfer between the young offender institution and another penal establishment;

    (h) to assist him in maintaining family ties or in his transition from life in the young offender institution to freedom; or

    (i) to enable him to make a visit in the locality of the young offender institution, [as a privilege under rule 4 of these Rules].

(4) An inmate shall not be released under this rule unless the Secretary of State is satisfied that there would not be an unacceptable risk of his committing offences whilst released or otherwise of his failing to comply with any condition upon which he is released.

(5) The Secretary of State shall not release under this rule an inmate if, having regard to:

    (a) the period or proportion of his sentence which the inmate has served; and

    (b) the frequency with which the inmate has been granted temporary release under this rule,

the Secretary of State is of the opinion that the release of the inmate would be likely to undermine public confidence in the administration of justice.

(6) If an inmate has been temporarily released under this rule during the relevant period and has been sentenced to any period of detention, custody or imprisonment for a criminal offence committed whilst at large following that release, he shall not be released under this rule unless his release, having regard to the circumstances of his conviction, would not, in the opinion of the Secretary of State, be likely to undermine public confidence in the administration of justice; and for this purpose "the relevant period":

    (a) in the case of an inmate serving a determinate sentence of imprisonment, detention or custody, is, if the inmate has previously been released on licence under Part II of the Criminal Justice Act 1991 during that sentence, the period since the date of his last recall or return to a penal establishment in respect of that sentence or, where the inmate has not been so released, the period he has served in respect of that sentence; or

(b) in the case of an inmate serving an indeterminate sentence of imprisonment, detention or custody, is, if the inmate has previously been released on licence under Part II of the Criminal Justice Act 1991, the period since the date of his last recall to a penal establishment in respect of that sentence or, where the inmate has not been so released, the period he has served in respect of that sentence,

save that where an inmate falls within both of sub-paragraphs (a) and (b) above, the "relevant period", in the case of that inmate, shall be determined by whichever of the applicable sub-paragraphs that produces the longer period.

(7)   An inmate released under this rule may be recalled at any time whether the conditions of his release have been broken or not.

(8)   This rule applies to inmates other than persons committed in custody for trial or to be sentenced or otherwise dealt with before or by the Crown Court or remanded in custody by any court.

(9)   For the purposes of any reference in this rule to an inmate's sentence, consecutive terms and terms which are wholly or partly concurrent shall be treated as a single term and any reference in this rule to release on licence under Part II of the Criminal Justice Act 1991 includes any release on licence under any earlier legislation providing for early release on licence.]

Annotations

This rule was substituted by SI 1995 No 984, r 2, Schedule, para 1.

Para (3): in sub-para (i) words in square brackets substituted by SI 1995 No 1599, r 2, Schedule, para 1.

See further, for provision as to the interpretation of references herein to rule 6: the Young Offender Institution (Amendment) Rules 1995, SI 1995 No 984, r 3(2).

Conditions

[7] [Privileges]

[(1)   There shall be established at every young offender institution systems of privileges approved by the Secretary of State and appropriate to the classes of inmates thereof and their ages, characters and circumstances, which shall include arrangements under which money earned by inmates may be spent by them within the young offender institution.

(2)   Systems of privileges approved under paragraph (1) may include arrangements under which inmates may be allowed time outside the cells and in association with one another, in excess of the minimum time which, subject to the other provisions of these Rules apart from

this rule, is otherwise allowed to inmates at the young offender institution for this purpose.

(3)   Systems of privileges approved under paragraph (1) may include arrangements under which privileges may be granted to inmates only in so far as they have met, and for so long as they continue to meet, specified standards in their behaviour and their performance in work or other activities.

(4)   Systems of privileges which include arrangements of the kind referred to in paragraph (3) shall include procedures to be followed in determining whether or not any of the privileges concerned shall be granted, or shall continue to be granted, to an inmate; such procedures shall include a requirement that the inmate be given reasons for any decision adverse to him together with a statement of the means by which he may appeal against it.

(5)   Nothing in this rule shall be taken to confer on an inmate any entitlement to any privilege or to affect any provision in these Rules other than this rule as a result of which any privilege may be forfeited or otherwise lost or an inmate deprived of association with other inmates.]

Annotations

This rule was substituted by SI 1995 No 1599, r 2, Schedule, para 2.

8   Information to inmates

(1)   Every inmate shall be provided, as soon as possible after his reception into the young offender institution, and in any case within 24 hours, with information in writing about those provisions of these Rules and other matters which it is necessary that he should know, including earnings and privileges, and the proper method of making requests and complaints < . . . > .

(2)   In the case of an inmate aged less than 18, or an inmate aged 18 or over who cannot read or appears to have difficulty in understanding the information so provided, the governor, or an officer deputed by him, shall so explain it to him that he can understand his rights and obligations.

(3)   A copy of these Rules shall be made available to any inmate who requests it.

Annotations

Para (1): words omitted revoked by SI 1990 No 1763, r 2(a).

[9]   [Requests and Complaints]

[(1)   A request or complaint to the governor or Board of Visitors relating to an inmate's detention shall be made orally or in writing by that inmate.

(2)   On every day the governor shall hear any oral requests and complaints that are made to him under paragraph (1) above.

(3)   A written request or complaint under paragraph (1) above may be made in confidence.]

Annotations

Substituted by SI 1990 No 1763, r 2(b).

10 Letters and visits generally

(1)   The Secretary of State may, with a view to securing discipline and good order or the prevention of crime or in the interests of any persons, impose restrictions, either generally or in a particular case, upon the communications to be permitted between an inmate and other persons.

(2)   Except as provided by statute or these Rules, an inmate shall not be permitted to communicate with any outside person, or that person with him, without the leave of the Secretary of State [or as a privilege under rule 7 of these Rules].

(3)   Except as provided by these Rules, every letter or communication to or from an inmate may be read or examined by the governor or an officer deputed by him, and the governor may, at his discretion, stop any communication on the ground that its contents are objectionable or that it is of inordinate length.

(4)   Subject to the provisions of these Rules, the governor may give such directions as he thinks fit for the supervision of visits to inmates, either generally or in a particular case.

Annotations

Para (2): words in square brackets added by SI 1995 No 1599, r 2, Schedule, para 3.

11 Personal letters and visits

(1)   An inmate shall be entitled—

  (a) to send and to receive a letter on his reception into a young offender institution and thereafter once a week; and

  (b) to receive a visit [twice in every period of four weeks, but only once in every such period if the Secretary of State so directs].

(2)   The governor may allow an inmate an additional letter or visit [as a privilege under rule 7 of these Rules or] when necessary for his welfare or that of his family.

(3)   The governor may allow an inmate entitled to a visit to send and to receive a letter instead.

(4)   The governor may defer the right of an inmate to a visit until the expiration of any period of confinement to a cell or room.

(5)   The board of visitors may allow an inmate an additional letter or visit in special circumstances, and may direct that a visit may extend beyond the normal duration.

(6)   The Secretary of State may allow additional letters and visits in relation to any inmate or class of inmates.

(7)   An inmate shall not be entitled under this rule to receive a visit from any person other than a relative or friend, except with the leave of the Secretary of State.

(8)   Any letter or visit under the succeeding provisions of these Rules shall not be counted as a letter or visit for the purposes of this rule.

Annotations

Para (1): words in square brackets substituted by SI 1992 No 513, r 2(1), Schedule, para 1.
Para (2): words in square brackets added by SI 1995 No 1599, r 2, Schedule, para 4.

12 Police interviews

A police officer may, on production of an order issued by or on behalf of a chief officer of police, interview any inmate willing to see him.

13 Legal advisers

(1)   The legal adviser of an inmate in any legal proceedings, civil or criminal, to which the inmate is a party shall be afforded reasonable facilities for interviewing him in connection with those proceedings, and may do so out of hearing of an officer.

(2)   An inmate's legal adviser may, with the leave of the Secretary of State, interview the inmate in connection with any other legal business.

[14] [Correspondence with legal advisers and courts]

[(1)   An inmate may correspond with his legal adviser and any court and such correspondence may only be opened, read or stopped by the governor in accordance with the provisions of this rule.

(2)   Correspondence to which this rule applies may be opened if the governor has reasonable cause to believe that it contains an illicit enclosure and any such enclosure shall be dealt with in accordance with the other provisions of these Rules.

(3)   Correspondence to which this rule applies may be opened, read and stopped if the governor has reasonable cause to believe its contents endanger prison or young offender institution security or the safety of others or are otherwise of a criminal nature.

(4)   An inmate shall be given the opportunity to be present when any correspondence to which this rule applies is opened and shall be informed if it or any enclosure is to be read or stopped.

(5)   An inmate shall on request be provided with any writing materials necessary for the purposes of paragraph (1) of this rule.

(6)   In this rule, "court" includes the European Commission of Human Rights, the European Court of Human Rights and the European Court

of Justice; and "illicit enclosure" includes any article possession of which has not been authorised in accordance with the other provisions of these Rules and any correspondence to or from a person other than the inmate concerned, his legal adviser or a court.]

Annotations

Substituted by SI 1993 No 3076, r 2, Schedule, para 1.

15 Securing release of defaulters

An inmate detained in a young offender institution in default of payment of a fine or any other sum of money may communicate with, and be visited at any reasonable time on a weekday by, any relative or friend to arrange for payment in order to secure his release.

16 Clothing

(1) An inmate shall be provided with clothing adequate for warmth and health in accordance with a scale approved by the Secretary of State.

(2) The clothing provided under this rule shall include suitable protective clothing for use at work, where this is needed.

(3) Subject to the provisions of rule 42(3) of these Rules, an inmate shall wear clothing provided under this rule and no other, except on the directions of the Secretary of State [or as a privilege under rule 7 of these Rules].

(4) An inmate shall where necessary be provided with suitable and adequate clothing on his release.

Annotations

Para (3): words in square brackets added by SI 1995 No 1599, r 2, Schedule, para 5.

17 Food

(1) Subject to any directions of the Secretary of State, no inmate shall be allowed, except as authorised by the medical officer, to have any food other than that ordinarily provided.

(2) The food provided shall be wholesome, nutritious, well prepared and served, reasonably varied and sufficient in quantity.

(3) The medical officer shall regularly inspect the food both before and after it is cooked, and shall report any deficiency or defect to the governor.

(4) In this rule, "food" includes drink.

18 Alcohol and tobacco

(1) No inmate shall be allowed to have any intoxicating liquor except under a written order of the medical officer specifying the quantity and the name of the inmate.

[(2)   No inmate shall be allowed to smoke or to have any tobacco except in accordance with any directions of the Secretary of State.]

Annotations

Para (2): substituted by SI 1992 No 2081, r 2, Schedule, para 3.

19 Sleeping accommodation

(1)   No room or cell shall be used as sleeping accommodation for an inmate unless it has been certified by an officer of the Secretary of State (not being an officer of a young offender institution) that its size, lighting, heating, ventilation and fittings are adequate for health, and that it allows the inmate to communicate at any time with an officer.

(2)   A certificate given under this rule shall specify the maximum number of inmates who may sleep in the room or cell at one time, and the number so specified shall not be exceeded without the leave of the Secretary of State.

20 Beds and bedding

Each inmate shall be provided with a separate bed and with separate bedding adequate for warmth and health.

21 Hygiene

(1)   Every inmate shall be provided with toilet articles necessary for his health and cleanliness, which shall be replaced as necessary.

(2)   Every inmate shall be required to wash at proper times, have a hot bath or shower on reception and thereafter at least once a week.

(3)   Subject to any directions of the Secretary of State, a male inmate may be required by the governor to shave or be shaved and to have his hair cut as may be necessary for neatness or, as directed by the medical officer, for health and cleanliness.

(4)   A female inmates' hair shall not be cut without her consent except where the medical officer directs that it is necessary for health or cleanliness.

22 Female inmates

The Secretary of State may, subject to any conditions he thinks fit, permit a female inmate to have her baby with her in a young offender institution, and everything necessary for the baby's maintenance and care may be provided there.

23 Library books

A library shall be provided in every young offender institution and, subject to any directions of the Secretary of State, every inmate shall be allowed to have library books and to exchange them.

Medical attention

24 Medical attendance

(1) The medical officer of a young offender institution shall have the care of the health, mental and physical, of the inmates of that institution.

(2) Every request by an inmate to see the medical officer shall be recorded by the officer to whom it is made and promptly passed on to the medical officer.

(3) The medical officer may call another medical practitioner into consultation at his discretion, and shall do so if time permits before performing any serious operation.

[(4) Subject to any directions given in the particular case by the Secretary of State, a registered medical practitioner selected by or on behalf of an inmate who is a party to any legal proceedings shall be afforded reasonable facilities for examining him in connection with the proceedings, and may do so out of hearing but in the sight of an officer.]

Annotations

Para 4: added by SI 1993 No 3076, r 2, Schedule, para 2.

25 Special illnesses and conditions

(1) The medical officer shall report to the governor on the case of any inmate whose health is likely to be injuriously affected by continued detention or any conditions of detention. The governor shall send the report to the Secretary of State without delay, together with his own recommendations.

(2) The medical officer shall pay special attention to any inmate whose mental condition appears to require it, and make any special arrangements which appear necessary for his supervision or care.

(3) The medical officer shall inform the governor if he suspects any inmate of having suicidal intentions, and the inmate shall be placed under special observation.

Mecical attention

26 Notification of illness or death

(1) If an inmate dies, becomes seriously ill, sustains any severe injury or is removed to hospital on account of mental disorder, the governor shall, if he knows his or her address, at once inform the inmate's spouse or next of kin, and also any person who the inmate may reasonably have asked should be informed.

(2) If an inmate dies, the governor shall give notice immediately to the coroner having jurisdiction, to the board of visitors and to the Secretary of State.

Religion

27 Religious denomination

An inmate shall be treated as being of the religious denomination stated in the record made in pursuance of section 10(5) of the Prison Act 1952, but the governor may, in a proper case after due inquiry, direct that record to be amended.

28 Special duties of chaplains and appointed ministers

(1)   The chaplain or a minister appointed to a young offender institution shall—

    (a) interview every inmate of his denomination individually as soon as he reasonably can after the inmate's reception into that institution and shortly before his release; and

    (b) if no other arrangements are made, read the burial service at the funeral of any inmate of his denomination who dies in that institution.

(2)   The chaplain shall visit daily all inmates belonging to the Church of England who are sick, under restraint or confined to a room or cell; and a minister appointed to a young offender institution shall do the same, as far as he reasonably can, for inmates of his own denomination.

(3)   If the inmate is willing, the chaplain shall visit any inmate not of the Church of England who is sick, under restraint or confined to a room or cell, and is not regularly visited by a minister of his own denomination.

29 Regular visits by ministers of religion, etc

(1)   The chaplain shall visit regularly the inmates belonging to the Church of England.

(2)   A minister appointed to a young offender institution shall visit the inmates of his denomination as regularly as he reasonably can.

(3)   The governor shall, if so requested by an inmate belonging to a denomination for which no minister has been appointed to a young offender institution do what he reasonably can to arrange for that inmate to be visited regularly by a minister of that denomination.

(4)   Every request by an inmate to see the chaplain or a minister appointed to a young offender institution shall be promptly passed on to the chaplain or minister.

30 Religious services

(1)   The chaplain shall conduct Divine Service for inmates belonging to the Church of England at least once every Sunday, Christmas Day and Good Friday, and such celebrations of Holy Communion and weekday services as may be arranged.

(2)   A minister appointed to a young offender institution shall conduct Divine Service for inmates of his denomination at such times as may be arranged.

31 Substitute for chaplain or appointed minister

(1)   A person approved by the Secretary of State may act for the chaplain in his absence.

(2)   A minister appointed to a young offender institution may, with the leave of the Secretary of State, appoint a substitute to act for him in his absence.

32 Sunday work

Arrangements shall be made so as not to require inmates to do any unnecessary work on Sunday, Christmas Day or Good Friday nor inmates of religions other than the Christian religion to do any unnecessary work on their recognised days of religious observance (as an alternative, but not in addition, to those days).

33 Religious books

There shall, so far as reasonably practicable, be available for the personal use of every inmate such religious books recognised by his denomination as are approved by the Secretary of State for use in young offender institutions.

Occupation and links with the community

34 Regime activities

(1)   An inmate shall be occupied in education, training courses, work and physical education provided in accordance with rule 3 of these Rules.

(2)   In all such activities regard shall be paid to individual assessment and personal development.

(3)   The medical officer may excuse an inmate from work or any other activity on medical grounds; and no inmate shall be set to participate in work or any other activity of a kind for which he is considered by the medical officer to be unfit.

(4)   An inmate may be required to participate in regime activities for no more than 8 hours a day.

(5)   Inmates may be paid for their work or participation in other activities at rates approved by the Secretary of State, either generally or in relation to particular cases.

Occupation and links with the community

35 Education

(1)   Provision shall be made at a young offender institution for the education of inmates by means of programmes of class teaching or private study within the normal working week and, so far as practicable, programmes of evening and weekend educational classes or private study. The educational activities shall, so far as practicable, be such as will foster personal responsibility and an inmate's interests and skills and help him to prepare for his return to the community.

(2)   In the case of an inmate aged less than 17, arrangements shall be made for his participation in education or training courses for at least 15 hours a week within the normal working week.

(3)   In the case of an inmate aged 17 or over who is illiterate or backward, arrangements shall be made for education appropriate to his needs, if necessary within the normal working week.

(4)   In the case of a female inmate aged 21 or over who is serving a sentence of imprisonment or who has been committed to prison for default and who is detained in a young offender institution instead of a prison, reasonable facilities shall be afforded if she wishes to improve her education, by class teaching or private study.

36 Training courses

(1)   Provision shall be made at a young offender institution for the training of inmates by means of training courses, in acccordance with directions of the Secretary of State.

(2)   Training courses shall be such as will foster personal responsibility and an inmate's interests and skills and improve his prospects of finding suitable employment after release.

(3)   Training courses shall, so far as practicable, be such as to enable inmates to acquire suitable qualifications.

37 Work

(1)   Work shall, so far as practicable, be such as will foster personal responsibility and an inmate's interests and skills and help him to prepare for his return to the community.

(2)   No inmate shall be set to do work of a kind not authorised by the Secretary of State.

38 Physical education

(1)   Provision shall be made at a young offender institution for the physical education of inmates within the normal working week, as well as evening and weekend physical recreation. The physical education

activities shall be such as will foster personal responsibility and an inmate's interests and skills and encourage him to make good use of his leisure on release.

(2) Arrangements shall be made for each inmate, other than one to whom paragraph (4) of this rule applies, to participate in physical education for at least two hours a week on average or, in the case of inmates detained in such institutions or parts of institutions as the Secretary of State may direct, for at least 1 hour each weekday on average, but outside the hours allotted to education under rule 35(2) in the case of an inmate of compulsory school age.

(3) In the case of an inmate with a need for remedial physical activity, appropriate facilities shall be provided.

(4) A female inmate aged 21 years or over who is serving a sentence of imprisonment or who has been committed to prison for default and who is detained in a young offender institution instead of a prison shall, if not engaged in outdoor work or detained in an open institution, be given the opportunity of exercise in the open air for not less than one hour in all, each day, if weather permits; but the Secretary of State may in special circumstances authorise the reduction of the period aforesaid to half an hour a day:

Provided that exercise consisting of physical education may be given indoors instead of in the open air.

39 Outside contacts

(1) The governor shall encourage links between the young offender institution and the community by taking steps to establish and maintain relations with suitable persons and agencies outside the institution.

(2) The governor shall ensure that special attention is paid to the maintenance of such relations between an inmate and his family as seem desirable in the best interests of both.

(3) Subject to any directions of the Secretary of State, an inmate shall be encouraged, as far as practicable, to participate in activities outside the young offender institution which will be of benefit to the community or of benefit to the inmate in helping him to prepare for his return to the community.

40 After-care

(1) From the beginning of his sentence, consideration shall be given, in consultation with the appropriate supervising service, to an inmate's future and the help to be given to him in preparation for and after his return to the community.

(2) Every inmate who is liable to supervision after release shall be given a careful explanation of his liability and the requirements to which he will be subject while under supervision.

Discipline and control

41 Maintenance of order and discipline

(1) Order and discipline shall be maintained, but with no more restriction than is required in the interests of security and well-ordered community life.

(2) In the control of inmates, officers shall seek to influence them through their own example and leadership, and to enlist their willing co-operation.

Discipline and control

42 Custody outside a young offender institution

(1) A person being taken to or from a young offender institution in custody shall be exposed as little as possible to public observation and proper care shall be taken to protect him from curiosity and insult.

(2) An inmate required to be taken in custody anywhere outside a young offender institution shall be kept in the custody of an officer appointed under section 3 of the Prison Act 1952 or of a police officer.

[(3) An inmate required to be taken in custody to any court shall, when he appears before the court, wear his own clothing or ordinary civilian clothing provided by the governor.]

Annotations

Para (3): substituted by SI 1995 No 1599, r 2, Schedule, para 6.

Discipline and control

43 Search

(1) Every inmate shall be searched when taken into custody by an officer, on his reception into a young offender institution and subsequently as the governor thinks necessary.

(2) An inmate shall be searched in as seemly a manner as is consistent with discovering anything concealed.

(3) No inmate shall be stripped and searched in the sight of another inmate or in the sight or presence of an officer not of the same sex.

(4) < . . . >

Annotations

Para 4: revoked by SI 1992 No 2081, r 2, Schedule, para 4.

44 Record and photograph

(1)   A personal record of each inmate shall be prepared and maintained in such manner as the Secretary of State may direct, but no part of the record shall be disclosed to any person not authorised to receive it.

(2)   Every inmate may be photographed on reception and subsequently, but no copy of the photograph shall be given to any person not authorised to receive it.

45 Inmates' property

(1)   Anything, other than cash, which an inmate has at a young offender institution and which he is not allowed to retain for his own use shall be taken into the governor's custody.

(2)   Any cash which an inmate has at a young offender institution shall be paid into an account under the control of the governor and the inmate shall be credited with the amount in the books of the institution.

(3)   Any article belonging to an inmate which remains unclaimed for a period of more than 3 years after he is released, or dies, may be sold or otherwise disposed of; and the net proceeds of any sale shall be paid to the National Association for the Care and Resettlement of Offenders, for its general purposes.

(4)   The governor may confiscate any unauthorised article found in the possession of an inmate after his reception into a young offender institution, or concealed or deposited within a young offender institution.

46 Removal from association

(1)   Where it appears desirable, for the maintenance of good order or discipline or in his own interests, that an inmate should not associate with other inmates, either generally or for particular purposes, the governor may arrange for the inmate's removal from association accordingly.

(2)   An inmate shall not be removed under this rule for a period of more than [3 days] without the authority of a member of the board of visitors or of the Secretary of State. An authority given under this paragraph shall in the case of a female inmate aged 21 years or over, be for a period not exceeding one month and, in the case of any other inmate, be for a period not exceeding 14 days, but may be renewed from time to time for a like period.

(3)   The governor may arrange at his discretion for such an inmate as aforesaid to resume association with other inmates, and shall do so if in any case the medical officer so advises on medical grounds.

Annotations

Para (2): words in square brackets substituted by SI 1989 No 2142, r 2(a).

47 Use of force

(1)   An officer in dealing with an inmate shall not use force unnecessarily and, when the application of force to an inmate is necessary, no more force than is necessary shall be used.

(2)   No officer shall act deliberately in a manner calculated to provoke an inmate.

48 Temporary confinement

(1)   The governor may order an inmate who is refractory or violent to be confined temporarily in a special cell or room, but an inmate shall not be so confined as a punishment, or after he has ceased to be refractory or violent.

(2)   A cell or room shall not be used for the purpose of this rule unless it has been certified by an officer of the Secretary of State (not being an officer of a young offender institution) that it is suitable for the purpose, that its size, lighting, heating, ventilation and fittings are adequate for health, and that it allows the inmate to communicate at any time with an officer.

(3)   In relation to any young offender institution, section 14(6) of the Prison Act 1952 shall have effect so as to enable the provision of special rooms instead of special cells for the temporary confinement of refractory or violent inmates.

49 Restraints

(1)   The governor may order an inmate, other than an inmate aged less than 17, to be put under restraint where this is necessary to prevent the inmate from injuring himself or others, damaging property or creating a disturbance.

(2)   Notice of such an order shall be given without delay to a member of the board of visitors and to the medical officer.

(3)   On receipt of the notice the medical officer shall inform the governor whether he concurs in the order. The governor shall give effect to any recommendation which the medical officer may make.

(4)   An inmate shall not be kept under restraint longer than necessary, nor shall he be so kept for longer than 24 hours without a direction in writing given by a member of the board of visitors or by an officer of the Secretary of State (not being an officer of a young offender institution). Such a direction shall state the grounds for the restraint and the time during which it may continue.

(5)   Particulars of every case of restraint under the foregoing provisions of this rule shall be forthwith recorded.

(6)   Except as provided by this rule no inmate shall be put under restraint otherwise than for safe custody during removal, or on medical grounds

by direction of the medical officer. No inmate shall be put under restraint as a punishment.

(7)   Any means of restraint shall be of a pattern authorised by the Secretary of State, and shall be used in such manner and under such conditions as the Secretary of State may direct.

[49A] [Compulsory Testing for Controlled Drugs]

[(1)   This rule applies where an officer, acting under the powers conferred by section 16A of the Prison Act 1952 (power to test inmates for drugs), requires an inmate to provide a sample for the purpose of ascertaining whether he has any controlled drug in his body.

(2)   In this rule "sample" means a sample of urine or any other description of sample specified in the authorisation by the governor for the purposes of section 16A.

(3)   When requiring an inmate to provide a sample, an officer shall, so far as is reasonably practicable, inform the inmate:

   (a) that he is being required to provide a sample in accordance with section 16A of the Prison Act 1952; and

   (b) that a refusal to provide a sample may lead to disciplinary proceedings being brought against him.

(4)   An officer shall require an inmate to provide a fresh sample, free from any adulteration.

(5)   An officer requiring a sample shall make such arrangements and give the inmate such instructions for its provision as may be reasonably necessary in order to prevent or detect its adulteration or falsification.

(6)   An inmate who is required to provide a sample may be kept apart from other inmates for a period not exceeding one hour to enable arrangements to be made for the provision of the sample.

(7)   An inmate who is unable to provide a sample of urine when required to do so may be kept apart from other inmates until he has provided the required sample, save that an inmate may not be kept apart under this paragraph for a period of more than 5 hours.

(8)   An inmate required to provide a sample of urine shall be afforded such degree of privacy for the purposes of providing the sample as may be compatible with the need to prevent or detect any adulteration or falsification of the sample; in particular an inmate shall not be required to provide such a sample in the sight of a person of the opposite sex.]

Annotations

This rule was added by SI 1994 No 3194, r 2, Schedule, para 2.

50 Offences against discipline

[An inmate is guilty of an offence against discipline if he—

(1) commits any assault;

(2) detains any person against his will;

[(3) denies access to any part of the young offender institution to any officer or any person (other than an inmate) who is at the young offender institution for the purpose of working there;]

(4) fights with any person;

(5) internationally endangers the health or personal safety of others or, by his conduct, is reckless whether such health or personal safety is endangered;

[(6) intentionally obstructs an officer in the execution of his duty, or any person (other than an inmate) who is at the young offender institution for the purpose of working there, in the performance of his work;]

(7) escapes or absconds from a young offender institution or from legal custody;

(8) fails—

    (a) < . . . >

    (b) to comply with any condition upon which he was [temporarily released under rule 6 of these rules];

[(8A) administers a controlled drug to himself or fails to prevent the administration of a controlled drug to him by another person (but subject to rule 50A below);]

(9) has in his possession—

    (a) any unauthorised article, or

    (b) a greater quantity of any article than he is authorised to have;

(10) sells or delivers to any person any unauthorised article;

(11) sells or, without permission, delivers to any person any article which he is allowed to have only for his own use;

(12) takes improperly any article belonging to another person or to a young offender institution;

(13) intentionally or recklessly sets fire to any part of a young offender institution or any other property, whether or not his own;

(14) destroys or damages any part of a young offender institution or any other property other than his own;

(15) absents himself from any place where he is required to be or is present at any place where he is not authorised to be;

[(16) is disrespectful to any officer, or any person (other than an inmate) who is at the young offender institution for the purpose of working there, or any person visiting a young offender institution;]

(17) uses threatening, abusive or insulting words or behaviour;

(18) intentionally fails to work properly or, being required to work, refuses to do so;

(19) disobeys any lawful order;

(20) disobeys or fails to comply with any rule or regulation applying to him;

(21) in any way offends against good order and discipline;

(22)

    (a) attempts to commit,

    (b) incites another inmate to commit, or

    (c) assists another inmate to commit or to attempt to commit any of the foregoing offences.]

Annotations

This rule was substituted by SI 1989 No 331, r 2(a).

Paras (3), (6), (16): substituted by SI 1994 No 3194, r 2, Schedule, paras 3, 4, 6.

Para (8): sub-para (a) revoked, and words in square brackets in sub-para (b) substituted, by SI 1992 No 513, r 2(1), Schedule, paras 2, 3.

Para (8A): added by SI 1994 No 3194, r 2, Schedule, para 5.

See further, in relation to the interpretation of references in para (8) above to rule 6: the Young Offender Institution (Amendment) Rules 1995, SI 1995 No 984, r 3(2).

50A

[It shall be a defence for an inmate charged with an offence under rule 50(8A) to show that—

    (a) the controlled drug had been, prior to its administration, lawfully in his possession for his use or was administered to him in the course of a lawful supply of the drug to him by another person;

    (b) the controlled drug was administered by or to him in circumstances in which he did not know and had no reason to suspect that such a drug was being administered; or

    (c) the controlled drug was administered by or to him under duress or to him without his consent in circumstances where it was not reasonable for him to have resisted.]

Annotations

This rule was added by SI 1994 No 3194, r 2, Schedule, para 7.

51 Disciplinary charges

[(1) Where an inmate is to be charged with an offence against discipline, the charge shall be laid as soon as possible and, save in exceptional circumstances, within 48 hours of the discovery of the offence.

(2)   < . . . >

(3)   Every charge shall be inquired into < . . . > by the governor.

(4)   Every charge shall be first inquired into not later, save in exceptional circumstances, than the next day, not being a Sunday or public holiday, after it is laid.]

[(5)   An inmate who is to be charged with an offence against discipline may be kept apart from other inmates pending the governor's first inquiry.]

Annotations

Substituted by SI 1989 No 331, r 2(a).

Para (2): revoked by SI 1992 No 513, r 2(1), Schedule, para 4.

Para (3): words omitted revoked by SI 1992 No 513, r 2(1), Schedule, para 5.

Para (5): added by SI 1992 No 513, r 2(1), Schedule, para 6.

52 Rights of inmates charged

[(1)   Where an inmate is charged with an offence against discipline, he shall be informed of the charge as soon as possible and, in any case, before the time when it is inquired into by the governor.

(2)   At any inquiry into a charge against an inmate he shall be given a full opportunity of hearing what is alleged against him and of presenting his own case.]

Annotations

Substituted by SI 1989 No 331, r 2(a).

[53] [Governor's punishments]

[(1)   If he finds an inmate guilty of an offence against discipline the governor may, subject to rule 60 of these Rules, impose one or more of the following punishments:

(a) caution;

(b) forfeiture for a period not exceeding [21 days] of any of the privileges under rule 7 of these Rules;

(c) removal for a period not exceeding [21 days] from any particular activity or activities of the young offender institution, other than education, training courses, work and physical education in accordance with rules 34, 35, 36, 37 and 38 of these Rules;

(d) extra work outside the normal working week for a period not exceeding [21 days] and for not more than 2 hours on any day;

(e) [stoppage of or deduction from earnings for a period not exceeding [42 days] of an amount not exceeding [21 days' earnings];]

(f) confinement to a cell or room for a period not exceeding [7 days];

(g) removal from his wing or living unit for a period not exceeding [21 days];

(h) [in the case of an inmate who is a short-term or long-term prisoner, an award of additional days not exceeding [42 days].]

(2) If an inmate is found guilty of more than one charge arising out of an incident punishments under this rule may be ordered to run consecutively[, but, [in the case of an award of additional days, the total period added] shall not exceed [42 days]].]

Annotations

This rule was substituted by SI 1989 No 331, r 2(a).

Para (1): in sub-paras (b)–(d), (g) words in square brackets substituted by SI 1995 No 984, r 2, Schedule, para 2(a)(i)–(iii), (v); sub-para (e) substituted by SI 1992 No 513, r 2(1), Schedule, para 7, words in square brackets substituted by SI 1995 No 984, r 2, Schedule, para 2(a)(iv); in sub-para (f) words in square brackets substituted by SI 1993 No 3076, r 2, Schedule, para 3; sub-para (h) substituted by SI 1992 No 2081, r 2, Schedule, para 5, words in square brackets substituted by SI 1995 No 984, r 2, Schedule, para 2(a)(vi).

Para (2): first words in square brackets added by SI 1989 No 2142, r 2(b), first words in square brackets therein substituted by SI 1992 No 2081, r 2, Schedule, para 5, second words in square brackets therein substituted by SI 1995 No 984, r 2, Schedule, para 2(b).

56 Confinement to a cell or room

[(1) No punishment of confinement to a cell or room shall be imposed unless the medical officer has certified that the inmate is in a fit state of health to be so dealt with.

(2) No cell or room shall be used as a detention cell or room for the purpose of a punishment of confinement to a cell or room unless it has been certified by an officer of the Secretary of State (not being an officer of a young offender institution) that it is suitable for the purpose; that its size, lighting, heating, ventilation and fittings are adequate for health; and that it allows the inmate to communicate at any time with an officer.]

Annotations

Substituted by SI 1989 No 331, r 2(a).

57 Removal from wing or living unit

[Following the imposition of a punishment of removal from his wing or living unit, an inmate shall be accommodated in a separate part of the young offender institution under such restrictions of earnings and activities as the Secretary of State may direct.]

Annotations

Substituted by SI 1989 No 331, r 2(a).

[58] [Suspended punishments]

[(1) Subject to any directions of the Secretary of State, the power to impose a disciplinary punishment (other than a caution) shall include a power to direct that the punishment is not to take effect unless, during a period specified in the direction (not being more than 6 months from the date of the direction), the inmate commits another offence against discipline and a direction is given under paragraph (2) below.

(2)   Where an inmate commits an offence against discipline during the period specified in a direction given under paragraph (1) above, the person < . . . > dealing with that offence may—

(a) direct that the suspended punishment shall take effect; or

(b) reduce the period or amount of the suspended punishment and direct that it shall take effect as so reduced; or

(c) vary the original direction by substituting for the period specified therein a period expiring not later than 6 months from the date of variation; or

(d) give no direction with respect to the suspended punishment.]

Annotations

Substituted by SI 1989 No 331, r 2(a).

Para (2): words omitted revoked by SI 1992 No 513, r 2(1), Schedule, para 10.

[59] [Remission and mitigation of punishments and quashing of findings of guilt]

[(1)   The Secretary of State may quash any finding of guilt and may remit a disciplinary punishment or mitigate it either by reducing it or by substituting a punishment which is, in his opinion, less severe.

(2)   Subject to any directions of the Secretary of State, the governor may remit or mitigate any punishment imposed by a governor [or the board of visitors].]

Annotations

Substituted by SI 1989 No 331, r 2(a).

Para (2): words in square brackets substituted by SI 1992 No 513, r 2(1), Schedule, para 11.

[60] [Adult female inmates: disciplinary punishments]

[(1)   In the case of a female inmate aged 21 years or over who is serving a sentence of imprisonment or who has been committed to prison for default—

(i) rule 53 of these Rules shall not apply, but the governor may, if he finds the inmate guilty of an offence against discipline, impose one or more of the following punishments:

(a) caution;

(b) forfeiture for a period not exceeding [42 days] of any of the privileges under rule 7 of these Rules;

(c) removal for a period not exceeding [21 days] from any

particular activity or activities of the young offender institution, other than education, training courses, work and physical education in accordance with rules 34, 35, 36, 37 and 38 of these Rules;

(d) extra work outside the normal working week for a period not exceeding [21 days] and for not more than 2 hours on any day;

(e) [stoppage of or deduction from earnings for a period not exceeding [84 days] of an amount not exceeding [42 days' earnings];]

(f) confinement to a cell or room for a period not exceeding [14 days];

(g) [in the case of an inmate who is a short-term or long-term prisoner, an award of additional days not exceeding [42 days];]

(ii) < . . . >

(2)   < . . . >

(3)   If an inmate is found guilty of more than one charge arising out of an incident, punishments under this rule may be ordered to run consecutively, but [in the case of an award of additional days, the total period added] shall not exceed [42 days].]

Annotations

This rule was substituted by SI 1989 No 331, r 2(a).

Para (1): in sub-paras (i)(b)–(d) words in square brackets substituted by SI 1995 No 984, r 2, Schedule, para 3(a)(i)–(iii); sub-para (i)(e) substituted by SI 1992 No 513, r 2(1), Schedule, para 12, words in square brackets substituted by SI 1995 No 984, r 2, Schedule, para 3(a)(iv); in sub-para (i)(f) words in square brackets substituted by SI 1993 No 3076, r 2, Schedule, para 4; sub-para (i)(g) substituted by SI 1992 No 2081, r 2, Schedule, para 6, words in square brackets substituted by SI 1995 No 984, r 2, Schedule, para 3(a)(v); sub-para (ii) revoked by SI 1992 No 513, r 2(1), Schedule, para 13.

Para (2): revoked by SI 1992 No 513, r 2(1), Schedule, para 13.

Para (3): first words in square brackets substituted by SI 1992 No 2081, r 2, Schedule, para 6; second words in square brackets substituted by SI 1995 No 984, r 2, Schedule, para 3(b).

60A Forfeiture of remission to be treated as an award of additional days

[(1) In this rule, "existing prisoner" and "existing licensee" have the meanings assigned to them by paragraph 8(1) of Schedule 12 to the Criminal Justice Act 1991.

(2) In relation to any existing prisoner or existing licensee who has forfeited any remission of his sentence, the provisions of Part II of the Criminal Justice Act 1991 shall apply as if he had been awarded such number of additional days as equals the number of days of remission which he has forfeited.]

Annotations

Added by SI 1992 No 2081, r 2, Schedule, para 7.

PART III
OFFICERS OF YOUNG OFFENDER INSTITUTIONS

61 General duty of officers

(1)   It shall be the duty of every officer to conform to these Rules and the rules and regulations of the young offender institution, to assist and support the governor in their maintenance and to obey his lawful instructions.

(2)   An officer shall inform the governor promptly of any abuse or impropriety which comes to his knowledge.

62 Gratuities forbidden

No officer shall receive any unauthorised fee, gratuity or other consideration in connection with his office.

63 Search of officers

An officer shall submit himself to be searched in a young offender institution if the governor so directs.

64 Transactions with inmates

(1)   No officer shall take part in any business or pecuniary transaction with or on behalf of an inmate without the leave of the Secretary of State.

(2)   No officer shall, without authority, bring in or take out, or attempt to bring in or take out, or knowingly allow to be brought in or taken out, to or for an inmate, or deposit in any place with intent that it shall come into the possession of an inmate, any article whatsoever.

65 Contact with former inmates, etc

No officer shall, without the knowledge of the governor, communicate with any person who he knows to be a former inmate or a relative or friend of an inmate or former inmate.

66 Communications to the press, etc

(1)   No officer shall make, directly or indirectly, any unauthorised communication to a representative of the press or any other person concerning matters which have become known to him in the course of his duty.

(2)   No officer shall, without authority, publish any matter or make any public pronouncement relating to the administration of any institution to which the Prison Act 1952 applies or to any of its inmates.

67 Quarters

An officer shall occupy any quarters which may be assigned to him.

68 Code of discipline

The Secretary of State may approve a code of discipline to have effect in relation to officers, or such classes of officers as it may specify, setting out the offences against discipline, the awards which may be made in respect of them and the procedure for dealing with charges.

PART IV
PERSONS HAVING ACCESS TO A YOUNG OFFENDER INSTITUTION

69 Prohibited articles

No person shall, without authority, convey into or throw into or deposit in a young offender institution, or convey to an inmate, or deposit in any place with intent that it shall come into the possession of an inmate, any article whatsoever. Anything so conveyed, thrown or deposited may be confiscated by the governor.

70 Control of persons and vehicles

(1)   Any person or vehicle entering or leaving a young offender institution may be stopped, examined and searched.

(2)   The governor may direct the removal from a young offender institution of any person who does not leave on being required to do so.

71 Viewing of young offender institutions

(1)   No outside person shall be permitted to view a young offender institution unless authorised by statute or the Secretary of State.

(2)   No person viewing a young offender institution shall be permitted to take a photograph, make a sketch or communicate with an inmate unless authorised by statute or the Secretary of State.

PART V
BOARDS OF VISITORS

72 Disqualification for membership

Any person interested in any contract for the supply of goods or services to a young offender institution shall not be a member of the board of visitors for that institution.

73 Appointment

(1)   A member of the board of visitors for a young offender institution appointed by the Secretary of State under section 6(2) of the Prison Act 1952 [subject to paragraph (1A) below], shall hold office for 3 years or such less period as the Secretary of State may appoint.

[(1A) The Secretary of State may terminate the appointment of a member if satisfied that—

(a)   he has failed satisfactorily to perform his duties,

(b)   he is by reason of physical or mental illness, or for any other reason, incapable of carrying out his duties, or

(c)   he has been convicted of such a criminal offence, or his conduct has been such, that it is not in the Secretary of State's opinion fitting that he should remain a member.]

(2)   When a board is first constituted, the Secretary of State shall appoint one of its members to be chairman for a period not exceeding twelve months.

[(3)   Subject to paragraph (2) above, at their first meeting in any year of office the Board shall appoint one of their members to be chairman and one to be vice-chairman for that year and thereafter shall fill any casual vacancy in either office promptly.

(4)   The vice-chairman's term of office shall come to an end when, for whatever reason, that of the chairman comes to an end.]

Annotations

Para (1): words in square brackets added by SI 1989 No 331, r 2(b).

Paras (1A), (3), (4): substituted by SI 1989 No 331, r 2(b).

74 Proceedings of boards

(1)   The board of visitors for a young offender institution shall meet at the institution at least once a month.

(2)   The board may fix a quorum of not fewer than 3 members for proceedings < . . . > .

(3)   The board shall keep minutes of their proceedings.

(4)   The proceedings of the board shall not be invalidated by any vacancy in the membership or any defect in the appointment of a member.

Annotations

Para (2): words omitted revoked by SI 1992 No 513, r 2(1), Schedule, para 15.

75 General duties of boards

(1)   The board of visitors for a young offender institution shall satisfy themselves as to the state of the premises, the administration of the institution and the treatment of the inmates.

(2)   The board shall inquire into and report upon any matter into which the Secretary of State asks them to inquire.

(3)   The board shall direct the attention of the governor to any matter which calls for his attention, and shall report to the Secretary of State any matters which they consider it expedient to report.

(4)   The board shall inform the Secretary of State immediately of any abuse which comes to their knowledge < ... > .

(5)   Before exercising any power under these Rules < . . . > the board and any member of the board shall consult the governor in relation to any matter which may affect discipline.

Annotations

Para (4): words omitted revoked by SI 1989 No 331, r 2(c).

Para (5): words omitted revoked by SI 1992 No 513, r 2(1), Schedule, para 16.

76 Particular duties

(1)   The board of visitors for a young offender institution and any member of the board shall hear any complaint or request which an inmate wishes to make to them or him.

(2)   The board shall arrange for the food of the inmates to be inspected by a member of the board at frequent intervals.

(3)   The board shall inquire into any report made to them, whether or not by a member of the board, that an inmate's health, mental or physical, is likely to be injuriously affected by any conditions of his detention.

77 Members visiting young offender institutions

(1)   The members of the board of visitors for a young offender institution shall visit the institution frequently, and the board shall arrange a rota for the purpose.

(2)   A member of the board shall have access at any time to every part of the institution and to every inmate, and he may interview any inmate out of the sight and hearing of officers.

(3)   A member of the board shall have access to the records of the young offender institution.

78 Annual report

The board of visitors for a young offender institution shall make an annual report to the Secretary of State at the end of each year concerning the state of the institution and its administration, including in it any advice and suggestions they consider appropriate.

Part **VI**

Supplemental

79 Delegation by governor

The governor of a young offender institution may, with the leave of the Secretary of State, delegate any of his powers and duties under these Rules to another officer of that institution.

80 Transitional

In the case of an inmate who, by virtue of paragraph 12 of Schedule 8 to the Criminal Justice Act 1988, falls to be treated for all purposes of detention, release and supervision as if he had been sentenced to detention in a young offender institution or who, under paragraph 13 of the said Schedule 8, is detained in such an institution, any award for an offence against discipline made in respect of him under rule 53 or 54 of the Detention Centre Rules 1983 or rule 53 or 54 of the Youth Custody Centre Rules 1983 shall, if it has not been exhausted or remitted, continue to have effect as if it had been made under rule 53 or 54, respectively, of those Rules.

SCHEDULE

Instruments Revoked

Rule 2(3)

< . . . >

Annotations

This Schedule revokes SI 1983 No 569, SI 1983 No 570, SI 1987 No 1255, SI 1987 No 1257.

EUROPEAN CONVENTION FOR THE PROTECTION OF HUMAN RIGHTS AND FUNDAMENTAL FREEDOMS

Article 1

The High Contracting Parties shall secure to everyone within their jurisdiction the rights and freedoms defined in section 1 of this Convention.

Section 1

Article 2

1. Everyone's right to life shall be protected by law. No one shall be deprived of his life intentionally save in the execution of a sentence of a court following his conviction for a crime for which this penalty is provided by law.
2. Deprivation of life shall not be regarded as inflicted in contravention of this Article when it results from the use of force which is no more than absolutely necessary:
   a. in defence of any person from unlawful violence;
   b. in order to effect a lawful arrest or to prevent the escape of a person lawfully detained;
   c. in action lawfully taken for the purpose of quelling a riot or insurrection.

Article 3

No one shall be subjected to torture or to inhuman or degrading treatment or punishment.

Article 4

1. No one shall be held in slavery or servitude.
2. No one shall be required to perform forced or compulsory labour.
3. For the purpose of this Article the term 'forced or compulsory labour' shall not include:
   a. any work required to be done in the ordinary course of detention imposed according to the provisions of Article 5 of this Convention or during conditional release from such detention;
   b. any service of a military character or, in case of conscientious objectors in countries where they are recognised, service exacted instead of compulsory military service;

    c.   any service exacted in case of an emergency or calamity threatening the life or well-being of the community;

    d.   any work or service which forms part of normal civic obligations.

Article 5

1.   Everyone has the right to liberty and security of person. No one shall be deprived of his liberty save in the following cases and in accordance with a procedure prescribed by law:

    a.   the lawful detention of a person after conviction by a competent court;

    b.   the lawful arrest or detention of a person for non-compliance with the lawful order of a court or in order to secure the fulfilment of any obligation prescribed by law;

    c.   the lawful arrest or detention of a person effected for the purpose of bringing him before the competent legal authority on reasonable suspicion of having committed an offence or when it is reasonably considered necessary to prevent his committing any offence or fleeing after having done so;

    d.   the detention of a minor by lawful order for the purpose of educational supervision or his lawful detention for the purpose of bringing him before the competent legal authority;

    e.   the lawful detention of persons for the prevention of the spreading of infectious diseases, of persons of unsound mind, alcoholics or drug addicts or vagrants;

    f.   the lawful arrest or detention of a person to prevent his effecting an unauthorised entry into the country or of a person against whom action is being taken with a view to deportation or extradition.

2.   Everyone who is arrested shall be informed promptly, in a language which he understands, of the reasons for his arrest and of any charge against him.

3.   Everyone arrested or detained in accordance with the provisions of paragraph 1. c. of this Article shall be brought promptly before a judge or other officer authorised by law to exercise judicial power and shall be entitled to trial within a reasonable time or to release pending trial. Release may be conditioned by guarantees to appear for trial.

4.   Everyone who is deprived of his liberty by arrest or detention shall be entitled to take proceedings by which the lawfulness of his detention shall be decided speedily by a court and his release ordered if the detention is not lawful.

5.   Everyone who has been the victim of arrest or detention in contravention of the provisions of this Article shall have an enforceable right to compensation.

Article 6

1.   In the determination of his civil rights and obligations or of any criminal charge against him, everyone is entitled to a fair and public hearing within a reasonable time by an independent and impartial tribunal established by law. Judgment shall be pronounced publicly but the press and public may be excluded from all or part of the trial in the interest of morals, public order or national security in a democratic society, where

the interests of juveniles or the protection of the private life of the parties
so require, or to the extent strictly necessary in the opinion of the court
in special circumstances where publicity would prejudice the interests of
justice.

2. Everyone charged with a criminal offence shall be presumed innocent
   until proved guilty according to law.
3. Everyone charged with a criminal offence has the following minimum
   rights:
   a. to be informed promptly, in a language which he understands and in
      detail, of the nature and cause of the accusation against him;
   b. to have adequate time and facilities for the preparation of his defence;
   c. to defend himself in person or through legal assistance of his own
      choosing or, if he has not sufficient means to pay for legal assistance,
      to be given it free when the interests of justice so require;
   d. to examine or have examined witnesses against him and to obtain
      the attendance and examination of witnesses on his behalf under the
      same conditions as witnesses against him;
   e. to have the free assistance of an interpreter if he cannot understand
      or speak the language used in court.

Article 7

1. No one shall be held guilty of any criminal offence on account of any
   act or omission which did not constitute a criminal offence under national
   or international law at the time when it was committed. Nor shall a
   heavier penalty be imposed than the one that was applicable at the time
   the criminal offence was committed.
2. This Article shall not prejudice the trial and punishment of any person
   for any act or omission which, at the time when it was committed, was
   criminal according to the general principles of law recognised by civilised
   nations.

Article 8

1. Everyone has the right to respect for his private and family life, his
   home and his correspondence.
2. There shall be no interference by a public authority with the exercise of
   this right except such as is in accordance with the law and is necessary
   in a democratic society in the interests of national security, public safety
   or the economic well-being of the country, for the prevention of disorder
   or crime, for the protection of health or morals, or for the protection of
   the rights and freedoms of others.

Article 9

1. Everyone has the right to freedom of thought, conscience and religion;
   this right includes freedom to change his religion or belief and freedom,
   either alone or in community with others and in public or in private, to
   manifest his religion or belief, in worship, teaching, practice and
   observance.
2. Freedom to manifest one's religion or beliefs shall be subject only to
   such limitations as are prescribed by law and are necessary in a

democratic society in the interests of public safety, for the protection of public order, health or morals, or for the protection of the rights and freedoms of others.

Article 10

1. Everyone has the right to freedom of expression. This right shall include freedom to hold opinions and to receive and impart information and ideas without interference by public authority and regardless of frontiers. This Article shall not prevent States from requiring the licensing of broadcasting, television or cinema enterprises.
2. The exercise of these freedoms, since it carries with it duties and responsibilities, may be subject to such formalities, conditions, restrictions or penalties as are prescribed by law and are necessary in a democratic society, in the interests of national security, territorial integrity or public safety, for the prevention of disorder or crime, for the protection of health or morals, for the protection of the reputation or rights of others, for preventing the disclosure of information received in confidence, or for maintaining the authority and impartiality of the judiciary.

Article 11

1. Everyone has the right to freedom of peaceful assembly and to freedom of association with others, including the right to form and join trade unions for the protection of his interests.
2. No restrictions shall be placed on the exercise of these rights other than such as are prescribed by law and are necessary in a democratic society in the interests of national security or public safety, for the prevention of disorder or crime, for the protection of health or morals or for the protection of the rights and freedoms of others. This Article shall not prevent the imposition of lawful restrictions on the exercise of these rights by members of the armed forces, of the police or of the administration of the State.

Article 12

Men and women of marriageable age have the right to marry and to found a family, according to the national laws governing the exercise of this right.

Article 13

Everyone whose rights and freedoms as set forth in this Convention are violated shall have an effective remedy before a national authority notwithstanding that the violation has been committed by persons acting in an official capacity.

Article 14

The enjoyment of the rights and freedoms set forth in this Convention shall be secured without discrimination on any ground such as sex, race, colour, language, religion, political or other opinion, national or social origin, association with a national minority, property, birth or other status.

First Protocol to the Convention for the Protection of Human Rights and Fundamental Freedoms

Article 1

Every natural or legal person is entitled to the peaceful enjoyment of his possessions. No one shall be deprived of his possessions except in the public interest and subject to the conditions provided for by law and by the general principles of international law.

The preceding provisions shall not, however, in any way impair the right of a State to enforce such laws as it deems necessary to control the use of property in accordance with the general interest or to secure the payment of taxes or other contributions or penalties.

Article 2

No person shall be denied the right to education. In the exercise of any functions which it assumes in relation to education and to teaching, the State shall respect the right of parents to ensure such education and teaching in conformity with their own religious and philosophical convictions.

INDEX

Page numbers in *italic* type refer to page numbers in the appendices.

315